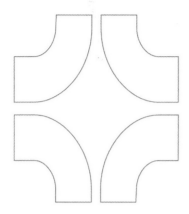

PROGRAMMING WITH MICROSOFT® VISUAL BASIC® 2005

Third Edition

Diane Zak

THOMSON

COURSE TECHNOLOGY ™

THOMSON

™

COURSE TECHNOLOGY

Programming with Microsoft® Visual Basic® 2005, Third Edition

by Diane Zak

Managing Editor:
Tricia Coia

Production Editor:
Melissa Panagos

Manufacturing Coordinator:
Julio Esperas

Marketing Manager:
Guy Baskaran

Art Director:
Beth Paquin

Editorial Assistant:
Erin Kennedy

Compositor:
Integra

Disclaimer
Course Technology reserves the right to revise this publication and make changes from time to time in its content without notice.

ISBN-13: 978-1-4188-3674-0
ISBN-10: 1-4188-3674-5

PREFACE

Programming with Microsoft Visual Basic 2005, Third Edition uses Visual Basic 2005, an object-oriented language, to teach programming concepts. This book is designed for a beginning programming course. However, it assumes students have learned basic Windows skills and file management from one of Course Technology's other books that cover the Microsoft Windows operating system.

ORGANIZATION AND COVERAGE

Programming with Microsoft Visual Basic 2005, Third Edition contains an Overview and twelve chapters that present hands-on instruction; it also contains three appendices. A thirteenth chapter, which covers ASP.NET 2.0, can be obtained electronically from the Course Technology Web site (**www.course.com**), by navigating to the page for this book. Also available electronically are additional appendices covering printing, collections, and other topics not included in the text.

In the chapters, students with no previous programming experience learn how to plan and create their own interactive Windows applications. GUI design skills and OOP concepts are emphasized throughout the book. By the end of the book, students will have learned how to use TOE charts, pseudocode, and flowcharts to plan an application. They also will learn how to work with controls and write Visual Basic statements such as If...Then...Else, Select Case, Do...Loop, For...Next, and For Each...Next. Students also will learn how to create and manipulate variables, constants, strings, sequential access files, structures, classes, and arrays. In Chapter 12, they will learn how to use ADO.NET 2.0 to connect an application to a Microsoft SQL Server database. (A Microsoft Access version of Chapter 12 can be obtained electronically from **www.course.com**, by navigating to the page for this book.)

APPROACH

Programming with Microsoft Visual Basic 2005, Third Edition teaches programming concepts using a task-driven rather than a command-driven approach. By working through the chapters, which are each motivated by a realistic case, students learn how to develop applications they are likely to encounter in the workplace. This is much more effective than memorizing a list of commands out of context. The book motivates students by demonstrating why they need to learn the concepts and skills covered in each chapter.

FEATURES

Programming with Microsoft Visual Basic 2005, Third Edition is an exceptional textbook because it also includes the following features:

» **Read This Before You Begin** This section is consistent with Course Technology's unequaled commitment to helping instructors introduce technology into the classroom. Technical considerations and assumptions about hardware, software, and default settings are listed in one place to help instructors save time and eliminate unnecessary aggravation.

» **Option Statements** All programs include the `Option Explicit On` and `Option Strict On` statements.

NEW!
» **Naming Conventions** Variable, class, and object names follow industry-accepted standards. Control names now begin with the lowercase letter "x" so that the names are listed together when using the IntelliSense feature in the Code Editor window.

NEW!
» **Visual Studio 2005 Methods** The book focuses on Visual Studio 2005 methods rather than on Visual Basic functions. This is because the Visual Studio methods can be used in any .NET language, whereas the Visual Basic functions can be used only in Visual Basic. Exceptions to this are the Val and Format functions, which are introduced in Chapter 2. These functions are covered in the book simply because it is likely that students will encounter them in existing Visual Basic programs. However, in Chapter 3, the student is taught to use the TryParse method and the Convert class methods rather than the Val function. Also in Chapter 3, the Format function is replaced with the ToString method.

» **Figures** Figures that introduce new statements, functions, or methods contain both the syntax and examples of using the syntax. Including the syntax in the figures makes the examples more meaningful.

» **Chapter Cases** Each chapter begins with a programming-related problem that students could reasonably expect to encounter in business, followed by a demonstration of an application that could be used to solve the problem. Showing the students the completed application before they learn how to create it is motivational and instructionally sound. By allowing the students to see the type of application they will be able to create after completing the chapter, the students will be more motivated to learn because they can see how the programming concepts they are about to learn can be used and, therefore, why the concepts are important.

» **Lessons** Each chapter is divided into three lessons—A, B, and C. Lesson A introduces the programming concepts that will be used in the completed application. In Lessons B and C, the student creates the application required to solve the problem specified in the Chapter Case.

» **Lesson A** Lesson A contains programming concepts, which are illustrated with code examples and sample applications. The user interface for each sample application is provided to the student. Also provided is the code needed to complete the application, as well as tutorial-style steps that guide the student on running and testing the application. Each sample application allows the student to observe how the current concept can be used before the next concept is introduced.

NEW!

» **Chapter 12** Chapter 12 teaches how to use ADO.NET 2.0 to access the information contained in a Microsoft SQL Server database. A Microsoft Access version of Chapter 12 can be obtained electronically from the Course Technology Web site (**www.course.com**), by navigating to the page for this book.

NEW!

» **Appendices A, B, and C** *Programming with Microsoft Visual Basic 2005, Third Edition* contains three new appendices.

NEW!

> » Appendix A summarizes the GUI design tips taught in the chapters, making it easier for the student to follow the guidelines when designing an application's interface.
>
> » Appendix B lists the Visual Basic type conversion functions.
>
> » Appendix C shows how to create a SQL Server database.

» **HELP?** These notes anticipate the problems students are likely to encounter and help them resolve the problems on their own. This feature facilitates independent learning and frees the instructor to focus on substantive conceptual issues rather than on common procedural errors.

» **TIP** These notes provide additional information about a procedure, such as an alternative method of performing the procedure. They also relate the OOP terminology learned in the Overview to applications created in Visual Basic 2005.

» **GUI DESIGN TIPS** These contain guidelines and recommendations for designing applications that follow Windows standards. Appendix A provides a summary of the GUI design guidelines covered in the chapters.

» **SUMMARY** Following each lesson is a summary, which recaps the programming concepts, commands, and objects covered in the lesson.

» **QUESTIONS and EXERCISES** Each lesson concludes with meaningful, conceptual questions that test students' understanding of what they learned in the lesson. The questions are followed by exercises, which provide students with additional practice of the skills and concepts they learned in the lesson.

» **DISCOVERY EXERCISES** The Windows environment allows students to learn by exploring and discovering what they can do. The Discovery Exercises encourage students to challenge and independently develop their own programming skills while exploring the capabilities of Visual Basic 2005.

» DEBUGGING EXERCISES One of the most important programming skills a student can learn is the ability to find and fix problems in an existing application. The Debugging Exercises provide an opportunity for students to detect and correct errors in an existing application.

TEACHING TOOLS

The following supplemental materials are available when this book is used in a classroom setting. All of the teaching tools available with this book are provided to the instructor on a single CD-ROM. Most are also available (password protected) at the Course Technology Web site—**www.course.com**.

Electronic Instructor's Manual The Instructor's Manual that accompanies this textbook includes additional instructional material to assist in class preparation, including items such as Sample Syllabi, Chapter Outlines, Technical Notes, Lecture Notes, Quick Quizzes, Teaching Tips, Discussion Topics, and Key Terms.

ExamView® This textbook is accompanied by ExamView, a powerful testing software package that allows instructors to create and administer printed, computer (LAN-based), and Internet exams. ExamView includes hundreds of questions that correspond to the topics covered in this text, enabling students to generate detailed study guides that include page references for further review. The computer-based and Internet testing components allow students to take exams at their computers, and also save the instructor time by grading each exam automatically.

PowerPoint Presentations This book offers Microsoft PowerPoint slides for each chapter. These are included as a teaching aid for classroom presentation, to make available to students on the network for chapter review, or to be printed for classroom distribution. Instructors can add their own slides for additional topics they introduce to the class.

Data Files Data Files to accompany this text contain all of the data necessary for steps within the chapters and the end-of-lesson Exercises. Both students and instructors should have access to these, so they are not password protected.

Solution Files Solutions to end-of-lesson Questions and Exercises are also provided. The solutions are password protected.

Thomson Course Technology is proud to present online test banks in WebCT and Blackboard to provide the most complete and dynamic learning experience possible. Instructors are encouraged to make the most of the course, both online and offline. For more information on how to access the online test bank, contact your local Thomson Course Technology sales representative.

ACKNOWLEDGMENTS

Writing a book is a team effort rather than an individual one. I would like to take this opportunity to thank my team, especially Tricia Coia (Senior Product Manager), Melissa Panagos (Production Editor), and the Quality Assurance testers who carefully test each chapter. Thank you for your support, enthusiasm, patience, and hard work. I could not have completed this project without you. Last, but certainly not least, I want to thank the following reviewers for their invaluable ideas and comments: Jim Ball, Indiana State University; Cliff Brozo, Monroe College; Dave Courtaway, DeVry University (Pomona); Neil Dunlop, Vista Community College; Bill Sypawka, Pitt Community College.

Diane Zak

CONTENTS

CONTENTS

CONTENTS

CHAPTER 7

CONTENTS

CONTENTS

READ THIS BEFORE YOU BEGIN

TO THE USER

DATA FILES

To complete the steps and exercises, you will need the data files created for this book. Your instructor will provide the data files to you. You also can obtain the files electronically from the Course Technology Web site (**www.course.com**), by navigating to the page for this book.

Each chapter in this book has its own set of data files, which are stored in a separate folder within the VB2005 folder. For example, the files for Chapter 1 are stored in the VB2005\Chap01 folder. Similarly, the files for Chapter 2 are stored in the VB2005\Chap02 folder. Throughout this book, you will be instructed to open files from or save files to these folders.

You can use a computer in your school lab or your own computer to complete the steps and exercises in this book.

USING YOUR OWN COMPUTER

To use your own computer to complete the material in this book, you will need the following:

» **A PentiumII-class processor, 600 MHz or higher, personal computer running Microsoft Windows.** This book was written and Quality Assurance tested using Microsoft Windows XP.

» **Microsoft Visual Studio 2005 Standard Edition or Professional Edition or Team System Edition, or Microsoft Visual Basic 2005 Express Edition installed on your computer.** This book was written using Microsoft Visual Studio 2005 Professional Edition and Quality Assurance tested using Microsoft Visual Basic 2005 Express Edition. If your book came with a copy of the software (Microsoft Visual Studio 2005 or Microsoft Visual Basic 2005 Express Edition), then you may install that on your computer and use it to complete the material.

» **If you are using either the Standard Edition of Visual Studio or the Express Edition of Visual Basic, you will not be able to complete Appendix C unless Microsoft SQL Server 2005 Express Edition or Microsoft SQL Server 2005 is installed on your computer.** At the time of this writing, you can download a free copy of Microsoft SQL Server 2005 Express Edition from *http://msdn.microsoft.com/vstudio/express/sql/download/*. Also at the time of this writing, you can request a free 180-day trial version of Microsoft SQL Server 2005 on DVD from *http://msdn.microsoft.com/sql*.

» **If you are using the Express Edition of Visual Basic, you won't be able to complete Chapter 13 (the ASP.NET 2.0 chapter that is available online) unless Visual Web Developer 2005 Express Edition is installed on your computer.** At the time of this writing, you can download a copy of Visual Web Developer 2005 Express Edition from *http://msdn.microsoft.com/vstudio/express/vwd/download.*

» **Data files** You will not be able to complete the material in this book using your own computer unless you have the data files. You can get the data files from your instructor, or you can obtain them electronically from the Course Technology Web site (**www.course.com**), and then navigating to the page for this book.

FIGURES

The figures in this book reflect how your screen will look if you are using Visual Studio 2005 and a Microsoft Windows XP system. However, when the screen in Visual Basic 2005 Express Edition differs greatly from the screen in Visual Studio 2005, both screens are shown in the book. Be aware that your screen may appear slightly different in some instances if you are using another version of Microsoft Windows.

VISIT OUR WORLD WIDE WEB SITE

Additional materials designed especially for you might be available for your course on the World Wide Web. Go to **www.course.com**. Periodically search this site for more details.

TO THE INSTRUCTOR

To complete the material in this book, your users must use a set of data files. These files are included on the Instructor's Resource CD. They also may be obtained electronically through the Course Technology Web site at **www.course.com**. Follow the instructions in the Help file to copy the data files to your server or standalone computer. You can view the Help file using a text editor such as WordPad or Notepad. Once the files are copied, you should instruct your users how to copy the files to their own computers or workstations.

The material in this book was written using Microsoft Visual Studio 2005 Professional Edition and Quality Assurance tested using Microsoft Visual Basic 2005 Express Edition on a Microsoft Windows XP system.

COURSE TECHNOLOGY DATA FILES

You are granted a license to copy the data files to any computer or computer network used by individuals who have purchased this book.

OVERVIEW
OBJECTIVES

THIS OVERVIEW CONTAINS BASIC DEFINITIONS
AND BACKGROUND INFORMATION, INCLUDING:

» A brief history of programming languages

» An explanation of the role of the .NET Framework class
library and CLR

» An introduction to the terminology used in object-oriented
programming languages

» A Visual Basic 2005 demonstration

» Information on using the chapters effectively

AN OVERVIEW OF PROGRAMMING

A HISTORY AND A DEMONSTRATION OF VISUAL BASIC 2005

PROGRAMMERS

Although computers appear to be amazingly intelligent machines, they cannot yet think on their own. Computers still rely on human beings to give them directions. The directions are called **programs**, and the people who write the programs are called **programmers**. Programmers make it possible for us to communicate with our personal computers; without them, we wouldn't be able to use the computer to write a letter or play a game.

Typical tasks performed by a computer programmer include analyzing a problem statement or project specification, planning an appropriate solution, and converting the solution to a language that the computer can follow. Generally speaking, programmers are either applications programmers or systems programmers. **Applications programmers** write and maintain programs that handle a specific task, such as calculating a company's payroll. They also may customize off-the-shelf programs to match a company's unique requirements. **Systems programmers**, on the other hand, write and maintain programs that help the computer carry out its basic operating functions. Examples of such programs include operating systems, device drivers, and utilities.

According to the 2004-05 Edition of the *Occupational Outlook Handbook* (OOH), published by the U.S. Department of Labor's Bureau of Labor Statistics, "When hiring programmers, employers look for people with the necessary programming skills who can think logically and pay close attention to detail. The job calls for patience, persistence, and the ability to work on exacting analytical work, especially under pressure. Ingenuity, creativity, and imagination also are particularly important when programmers design solutions and test their work for potential failures. The ability to work with abstract concepts and to do technical analysis is especially important for systems programmers, because they work with the software that controls the computer's operation. Because programmers are expected to work in teams and interact directly with users, employers want programmers who are able to communicate with nontechnical personnel."

The Bureau of Labor Statistics predicts that employment of programmers will grow 10-20% between 2002 and 2012. "Jobs for both systems and applications programmers should be most plentiful in data processing service firms, software houses, and computer consulting businesses." The OOH also reports that "according to Robert Half International, a firm providing specialized staffing services, average annual starting salaries in 2003 ranged from $51,500 to $80,500 for applications development programmers/analysts, and from $55,000 to $87,750 for software developers. Average starting salaries for mainframe systems programmers ranged from $53,250 to $68,750 in 2003."

A BRIEF HISTORY OF PROGRAMMING LANGUAGES

Just as human beings communicate with each other through the use of languages such as English, Spanish, Hindi, and Chinese, programmers use a variety of special languages, called **programming languages**, to communicate with the computer. Some popular programming languages are Visual Basic, Visual C#, C++, Visual C++, Java, Perl (Practical Extraction and Report Language), C, and COBOL (Common Business Oriented Language). In the next sections, you follow the progression of programming languages from machine languages to assembly languages, and then to high-level languages.

MACHINE LANGUAGES

Within a computer, all data is represented by microscopic electronic switches that can be either off or on. The off switch is designated by a 0, and the on switch is designated by a 1. Because computers can understand only these on and off switches, the first programmers had to write the program instructions using nothing but combinations of 0s and 1s; for example, a program might contain the instruction `00101 10001 10000`. Instructions written in 0s and 1s are called **machine language** or **machine code**. The machine languages (each type of machine has its own language) represent the only way to communicate directly with the computer. As you can imagine, programming in machine language is very tedious and error-prone and requires highly trained programmers.

ASSEMBLY LANGUAGES

Slightly more advanced programming languages are called **assembly languages**. The assembly languages simplify the programmer's job by allowing the programmer to use mnemonics in place of the 0s and 1s in the program. Mnemonics are memory aids—in this case, alphabetic abbreviations for instructions. For example, most assembly languages use the mnemonic ADD to represent an add operation and the mnemonic MUL to represent a multiply operation. An example of an instruction written in an assembly language is `ADD bx, ax`.

Programs written in an assembly language require an **assembler**, which also is a program, to convert the assembly instructions into machine code—the 0s and 1s the computer can understand. Although it is much easier to write programs in assembly language than in machine language, programming in assembly language is tedious and requires highly trained programmers.

HIGH-LEVEL LANGUAGES

High-level languages represent the next major development in programming languages. High-level languages are a vast improvement over machine and assembly languages, because they allow the programmer to use instructions that more closely resemble the English language. An example of an instruction written in a high-level language is `grossPay = hours * rate`.

Programs written in a high-level language require either an interpreter or a compiler to convert the English-like instructions into the 0s and 1s the computer can understand. Like assemblers, both interpreters and compilers are separate programs. An **interpreter** translates the high-level instructions into machine code, line by line, as the program is running, whereas (in most cases) a **compiler** translates the entire program into machine code before running the program.

Like their predecessors, the first high-level languages were used to create procedure-oriented programs. When writing a **procedure-oriented program**, the programmer concentrates on the major tasks that the program needs to perform. A payroll program, for example, typically performs several major tasks, such as inputting the employee data, calculating the gross pay, calculating the taxes, calculating the net pay, and outputting a paycheck. The programmer must instruct the computer every step of the way, from the start of the task to its completion. In a procedure-oriented program, the programmer determines and controls the order in which the computer processes the instructions. In other words, the programmer must determine not only the proper instructions to give the computer, but the correct sequence of those instructions as well. Examples of high-level languages used to create procedure-oriented programs include COBOL, BASIC (Beginner's All-Purpose Symbolic Instruction Code), and C.

Recently, more advanced high-level languages have emerged; these languages are used to create object-oriented programs. Different from a procedure-oriented program, which focuses on the individual tasks the program must perform, an **object-oriented program** requires the programmer to focus on the objects that the program can use to accomplish its goal. The objects can take many different forms. For example, programs written for the Windows environment typically use objects such as check boxes, list boxes, and buttons. A payroll program, on the other hand, might utilize objects found in the real world, such as a time card object, an employee object, and a check object. Because each object is viewed as an independent unit, an object can be used in more than one program, usually with little or no modification. A check object used in a payroll program, for example, also can be used in a sales revenue program (which receives checks from customers) and an accounts payable program (which issues checks to creditors). The ability to use an object for more than one purpose saves programming time and money—an advantage that contributes to the popularity of object-oriented programming. Examples of high-level languages used to create object-oriented programs include Visual Basic, Java, C++, Visual C++, and Visual C#.

In this book, you learn how to create object-oriented programs using the Visual Basic 2005 language. Visual Basic 2005 is available as a stand-alone product (called Visual Basic 2005 Express Edition) or as part of Visual Studio 2005.

»TIP

Most objects in an object-oriented program have one or more tasks to perform. The tasks are programmed using the same techniques used in procedure-oriented programming.

VISUAL STUDIO 2005

Visual Studio 2005 is Microsoft's newest integrated development environment. An **integrated development environment (IDE)** is an environment that contains all of the tools and features you need to create, run, and test your programs. For example, an IDE contains an editor for entering your program instructions, and a compiler for running and testing the program.

Included in Visual Studio 2005 are the Visual Basic 2005, Visual C++ 2005, Visual C# 2005, and Visual J# 2005 programming languages. You can use the languages available in Visual Studio 2005 to create Windows-based or Web-based programs, referred to as **applications**. A **Windows-based application** has a Windows user interface and runs on a desktop computer. A **user interface** is what you see and interact with when using an application. Examples of Windows-based applications include graphics programs, data-entry systems, and games.

A **Web-based application**, on the other hand, has a Web user interface and runs on a server. You access a Web-based application using your computer's browser. Examples of Web-based applications include e-commerce applications available on the Internet and employee handbook applications accessible on a company's intranet.

The programming languages in Visual Studio 2005, as well as many other programming languages, run in the **Microsoft .NET Framework 2.0**, which is a platform on which you create the applications. As a result, the programming languages are often referred to as **.NET languages**, and applications created using the .NET languages are commonly called **.NET applications.**

The driving force behind the .NET Framework is Microsoft's goal of connecting information, people, systems, and devices. To accomplish that goal, the Framework provides support for standard networking protocols and specifications (such as TCP/IP, SOAP, XML, and HTTP), as well as support for different platforms (such as Windows XP, Windows CE, and Unix).

The .NET Framework also provides for easier development of applications. One way it does so is by supporting a variety of programming languages. This support allows programmers to use their preferred .NET language when developing applications. An application can even be written in more than one .NET language.

Ease of development can also be attributed to a component of the .NET Framework, called the **.NET Framework class library**. Every .NET language has access to the class library, which contains an extensive set of classes that can be used in .NET applications. Using a class from the class library in an application is beneficial for two reasons: First, it saves you from having to create the class on your own. Second, it provides consistency among applications, making code easier to understand and reuse.

In addition to the class library, the .NET Framework also contains a component called the Common Language Runtime.

>> TIP

You also can create console applications in Visual Studio 2005. A console application runs in a Command Prompt window, which has a text user interface rather than a graphical one.

>> TIP

.NET is pronounced "dot net". A list of .NET languages can be found at *www.dotnetpowered.com/languages.aspx.*

THE COMMON LANGUAGE RUNTIME

Each .NET language has its own compiler, and each language-specific compiler performs the same task, which is to translate .NET program instructions into a language that the **Common Language Runtime (CLR)** can understand. The language is called **Microsoft Intermediate Language (MSIL)** or, more simply, **Intermediate Language (IL)**. The CLR is responsible for managing the execution of the IL instructions. It does this by providing a **just-in-time (JIT)** compiler that converts the IL into native machine code that can be executed by the computer. Figure 1 illustrates the role of the CLR.

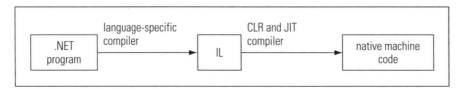

Figure 1: Illustration of the CLR's role

The CLR allows compiled IL to be reused in any application written in any .NET language. This is because the CLR does not make a distinction between the IL created by one language-specific compiler and the IL created by a different language-specific compiler. To the CLR, all IL is the same, regardless of the original language used to create it.

OOP TERMINOLOGY

Although you may have either heard or read that object-oriented programs are difficult to write, do not be intimidated. Admittedly, creating object-oriented programs does take some practice. However, you already are familiar with many of the concepts upon which object-oriented programming is based. Much of the anxiety of object-oriented programming stems from the terminology used when discussing it. Many of the terms are unfamiliar, because they typically are not used in everyday conversations. This section will help to familiarize you with the terms used in discussions about object-oriented programming. Do not be concerned if you do not understand everything right away; you will see further explanations and examples of these terms throughout this book.

When discussing object-oriented programs, you will hear programmers use the terms OOP (pronounced like *loop*) and OOD (pronounced like *mood*). **OOP** is an acronym for object-oriented programming and simply means that you are using an object-oriented language to create a program that contains one or more objects. OOD, on the other hand, is an acronym for object-oriented design. Like top-down design, which is used to plan procedure-oriented programs, **OOD** also is a design methodology, but it is used to plan object-oriented programs. Unlike top-down design, which breaks up a problem into one or more tasks, OOD divides a problem into one or more objects.

An **object** is anything that can be seen, touched, or used; in other words, an object is nearly any *thing*. As mentioned earlier, the objects used in an object-oriented program can take on many different forms. The menus, check boxes, and buttons included in most Windows programs are objects. An object also can represent something encountered in real life—such as a wristwatch, a car, a credit card receipt, and an employee.

Every object has attributes and behaviors. The **attributes**, also called **properties**, are the characteristics that describe the object. When you tell someone that your wristwatch is a Farentino Model 35A, you are describing the watch (an object) in terms of some of its attributes—in this case, its maker and model number. A watch also has many other attributes, such as a crown, dial, hour hand, minute hand, and movement.

An object's **behaviors** include methods and events. **Methods** are the operations (actions) that the object is capable of performing. A watch, for example, can keep track of the time. Some watches also can keep track of the date. **Events** are the actions to which the object can respond. For example, some watches illuminate their dials when a button on the watch is pushed.

You also will hear the term "class" in OOP discussions. A **class** is a pattern or blueprint used to create an object. Every object used in an object-oriented program comes from a class. A class contains—or, in OOP terms, it **encapsulates**—all of the attributes and behaviors that describe the object the class creates. The blueprint for the Farentino Model 35A watch, for example, encapsulates all of the watch's attributes and behaviors. Objects created from a class are referred to as **instances** of the class, and are said to be "instantiated" from the class. All Farentino Model 35A watches are instances of the Farentino Model 35A class.

"Abstraction" is another term used in OOP discussions. **Abstraction** refers to the hiding of the internal details of an object from the user. Hiding the internal details helps prevent the user from making inadvertent changes to the object. The internal mechanism of a watch, for example, is enclosed (hidden) in a case to protect the mechanism from damage. Attributes and behaviors that are not **hidden** are said to be **exposed** to the user. Exposed on a Farentino Model 35A watch are the crown used to set the hour and minute hands, and the button used to illuminate the dial. The idea behind abstraction is to expose to the user only those attributes and behaviors that are necessary to use the object, and to hide everything else.

Another OOP term, **inheritance**, refers to the fact that you can create one class from another class. The new class, called the **derived class**, inherits the attributes and behaviors of the original class, called the **base class**. For example, the Farentino Company might create a blueprint of the Model 35B watch from the blueprint of the Model 35A watch. The Model 35B blueprint (the derived class) will inherit all of the attributes and behaviors of the Model 35A blueprint (the base class), but it then can be modified to include an additional feature, such as an alarm.

Finally, you also will hear the term "polymorphism" in OOP discussions. **Polymorphism** is the object-oriented feature that allows the same instruction to be carried out differently depending on the object. For example, you open a door, but you also open an envelope, a jar, and your eyes. Similarly, you can set the time, date, and alarm on a Farentino watch. Although the meaning of the verbs "open" and "set" are different in each case, you can understand each instruction because the combination of the verb and the object makes the instruction clear. Figure 2 uses the wristwatch example to illustrate most of the OOP terms discussed in this section.

》》TIP

You can use the acronym APIE (Abstraction, Polymorphism, Inheritance, and Encapsulation) to remember some of the OOP terms.

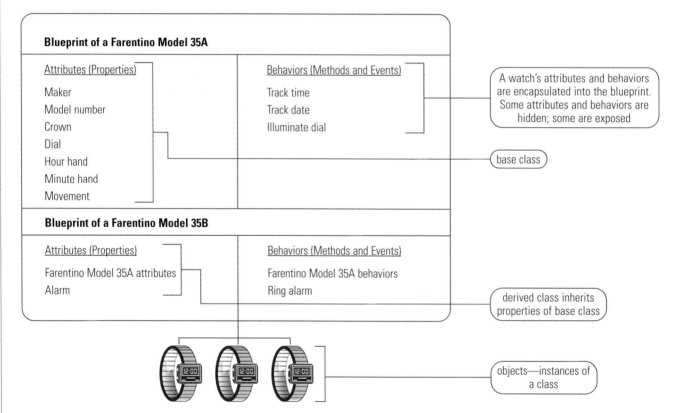

Figure 2: Illustration of OOP terms

In the next section, you run a Visual Basic 2005 application that gives you a quick look at some of the objects you learn how to create in the following chapters.

A VISUAL BASIC 2005 DEMONSTRATION

The Visual Basic 2005 application you are about to run shows you only some of the objects you learn how to create in the chapters. For now, it is not important for you to understand how these objects were created or why the objects perform the way they do. Those questions will be answered in the chapters.

To run the Visual Basic 2005 application:

1 Click the **Start** button on the Windows taskbar, and then click **Run** on the Start menu to open the Run dialog box. Click the **Browse** button in the Run dialog box. The Browse dialog box opens.

2 Locate and then open the VB2005\Overview folder on your computer's hard disk. Click **MonthPay** (MonthPay.exe) in the list of filenames, and then click the **Open** button. The Browse dialog box closes and the Run dialog box appears again. Click the **OK** button. After a few moments, the Monthly Payment Calculator application shown in Figure 3 appears on the screen.

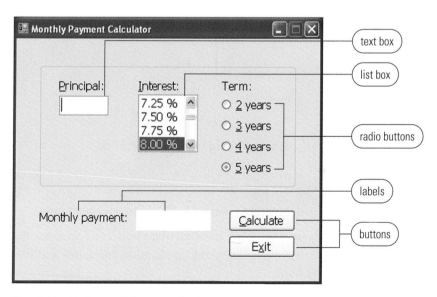

Figure 3: Monthly Payment Calculator application

Figure 3 identifies some of the different objects appearing in the application's interface. Notice that the interface contains a text box, a list box, buttons, radio buttons, and labels. You can use this application to calculate the monthly payment for a car loan. For example, determine the monthly payment for a $20,000 loan at 7.5% interest for five years.

To compute a monthly car payment:

1 Type **20000** in the Principal text box, and then click **7.50 %** in the Interest list box. The radio button corresponding to the five-year term is already selected, so you just need to click the **Calculate** button to compute the monthly payment. The Monthly Payment Calculator application indicates that your monthly payment would be $400.76, as shown in Figure 4.

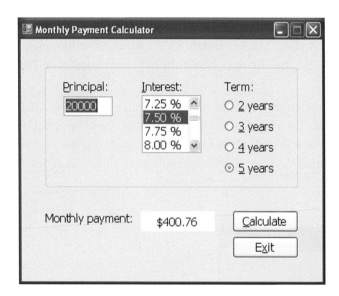

Figure 4: Computed monthly payment

Now determine what your monthly payment would be if you borrowed $10,000 at 7% interest for four years.

2 Type **10000** in the Principal text box.

3 Scroll up the Interest list box until the 7.00 % rate is visible, and then click **7.00 %**.

4 Click the **4 years** radio button, and then click the **Calculate** button to compute the monthly payment. The Monthly Payment Calculator application computes and displays the monthly payment of $239.46.

5 Click the **Exit** button to close the Monthly Payment Calculator application.

USING THE CHAPTERS EFFECTIVELY

The chapters in this book will help you learn how to write programs using Microsoft Visual Basic 2005. The chapters are designed to be used at your computer. Begin by reading the text that explains the concepts. Then when you come to the numbered steps, follow the steps on your computer. Read each step carefully and completely before you try it.

As you work, compare your screen with the figures to verify your results. Don't worry if your screen display differs slightly from the figures. The important parts of the screen display are labeled in each figure. Just be sure you have these parts on your screen. (The figures in this book reflect how your screen will look if you are using a Microsoft Windows XP system. Your screen may appear slightly different in some instances if you are using another version of Microsoft Windows.)

Do not worry about making mistakes; that's part of the learning process. HELP notes identify common problems and explain how to get back on track. You should complete the steps in the HELP notes only if you are having the problem described. TIP notes provide additional information about a procedure—for example, an alternative method of performing the procedure.

Each chapter is divided into three lessons. You might want to take a break between lessons. Following each lesson is a Summary section that lists the important elements of the lesson. After the Summary section are questions and exercises designed to review and reinforce that lesson's concepts. You should complete all of the end-of-lesson questions and exercises before going on to the next lesson. It takes a great deal of practice to acquire the skills needed to create good programs, and future chapters assume that you have mastered the information found in the previous chapters. Some of the end-of-lesson exercises are Discovery exercises, which allow you to both "discover" the solutions to problems on your own and experiment with material that is not covered in the chapter.

In each chapter you will find one or more Debugging exercises. In programming, the term **debugging** refers to the process of finding and fixing any errors in a program. Debugging exercises provide debugging tips and allow you to practice debugging applications.

Throughout the book you will find GUI (Graphical User Interface) design tips. These tips contain guidelines and recommendations for designing applications. You should follow these guidelines and recommendations so that your applications follow the Windows standard.

This book is designed for a beginning programming course; however, it assumes students have learned basic Windows skills and file management from one of Course Technology's other books that covers the Microsoft Windows operating system.

QUESTIONS

1. The set of directions given to a computer is called _____.

   a. computerese   b. commands

   c. instructions   d. a program

2. Instructions written in 0s and 1s are called _____.

   a. assembly language   b. computerese

   c. machine code   d. mnemonics

3. _____ languages allow the programmer to use alphabetic abbreviations for instructions.

   a. Assembly   b. High-level

   c. Machine   d. Object

4. _____ languages allow the programmer to use instructions that more closely resemble the English language.

   a. Assembly   b. High-level

   c. Machine   d. Object

5. The .NET Framework 2.0 contains _____.

   a. a class library

   b. the CLR

   c. support for different programming languages and different platforms

   d. All of the above.

6. The _____ translates intermediate language into machine code.

   a. CLR   b. JIT compiler

   c. MSIL   d. None of the above.

7. A(n) _____ is a pattern or blueprint.

   a. attribute   b. behavior

   c. class   d. instance

8. Which of the following is *not* an attribute that can be used to describe a human being?

   a. brown eyes   b. female

   c. red hair   d. talk

9. The object that you create from a class is called a(n) _____.

   a. abstraction   b. attribute

   c. instance   d. subclass

10. In the context of OOP, the combining of an object's attributes and behaviors into one package is called _____.

    a. abstraction   b. encapsulation

    c. inheritance   d. polymorphism

11. In the context of OOP, the hiding of the internal details of an object from the user is called _____.

    a. abstraction   b. encapsulation

    c. inheritance   d. polymorphism

12. _____ is the OOP feature that allows the same instruction to be carried out differently depending on the object.

    a. Abstraction   b. Encapsulation

    c. Inheritance   d. Polymorphism

13. Alcon Toys manufactures several versions of a basic doll. Assume that the basic doll is called Model A and the versions are called Models B, C, and D. In the context of OOP, the Model A doll is called the _____ class; the other dolls are called the _____ class.

    a. base, derived   b. derived, base

    c. exposed, hidden   d. inherited, derived

14. In the context of OOP, _____ refers to the fact that you can create one class from another class.

    a. abstraction   b. encapsulation

    c. exposition   d. inheritance

15. Use Figure 5 to answer the following questions:

Dog class	
Head	Eat
Body	Run
Legs	Play
Heart	Walk
Lungs	Bark

Figure 5

    a. What are the attributes (data or properties) associated with a dog class?

    b. What are the behaviors associated with a dog class?

    c. How many instances (objects) of the dog class are shown in Figure 5?

1

AN INTRODUCTION TO VISUAL BASIC 2005

CREATING A COPYRIGHT SCREEN

Interlocking Software Company, a small firm specializing in custom programs, hires you as a programmer trainee. In that capacity, you learn to create applications using Visual Basic 2005, Microsoft's newest version of the Visual Basic programming language.

On your second day of work, Chris Statton, the senior programmer at Interlocking Software, assigns you your first task: create a copyright screen. The copyright screen will serve as a splash screen for each custom application created by Interlocking Software. A **splash screen** is the first image that appears when an application is started. It is used to introduce the application and to hold the user's attention while the application is being read into the computer's memory. The copyright screen you create will identify the application's author and copyright year and include the Interlocking Software Company logo. Although this first task is small, creating the copyright screen will give you an opportunity to learn the fundamentals of Visual Basic 2005 without having to worry about the design issues and programming concepts necessary for larger applications.

PREVIEWING THE COPYRIGHT SCREEN

Before you start the first lesson in this chapter, you will preview a completed copyright screen. The copyright screen is stored in the VB2005\Chap01\Copyright.exe file on your computer's hard disk. (Computer lab configurations vary. Ask your instructor or technical support person for the location of the files for this book.)

To preview a completed copyright screen:

1 Click the **Start** button on the Windows taskbar, and then click **Run** on the Start menu. When the Run dialog box opens, click the **Browse** button. The Browse dialog box opens. Locate and then open the **VB2005\Chap01** folder.

2 Click the **Copyright** (Copyright.exe) filename to select it. (Depending on how Windows is set up on your computer, you may see the .exe extension on the filename. If you do, click the Copyright.exe filename.) Click the **Open** button. The Browse dialog box closes and the Run dialog box appears again.

3 Click the **OK** button in the Run dialog box. The copyright screen appears. The author's name and the copyright year appear on the copyright screen, as shown in Figure 1-1. After eight seconds have elapsed, the copyright screen closes.

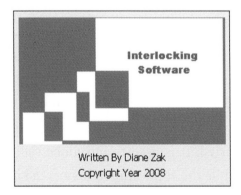

Figure 1-1: Copyright screen

In this chapter, you learn how to create your own copyright screen.

Chapter 1 is designed to help you get comfortable with the Visual Studio 2005 integrated development environment (IDE). You also learn about the Visual Basic 2005 language. Remember that each chapter contains three lessons. You should complete a lesson in full and do the end-of-lesson questions and exercises before moving on to the next lesson.

LESSON A
OBJECTIVES

AFTER STUDYING LESSON A, YOU SHOULD
BE ABLE TO:

» Start and customize Visual Studio 2005 or Visual Basic
2005 Express Edition

» Create a Visual Basic 2005 Windows-based application

» Manage the windows in the IDE

» Set the properties of an object

» Restore a property to its default setting

» Save a solution

» Close a solution

» Open an existing solution

CREATING A WINDOWS-BASED APPLICATION IN VISUAL BASIC 2005

STARTING VISUAL STUDIO 2005 OR VISUAL BASIC 2005 EXPRESS EDITION

In this chapter, you use Visual Basic 2005 to create a copyright screen. As you learned in the Overview, Visual Basic 2005 is available as a stand-alone product (called Visual Basic 2005 Express Edition) or as part of Visual Studio 2005. Before you can use Visual Basic 2005 to create an application, you first must start either Visual Studio 2005 or the Express Edition of Visual Basic.

To start Visual Studio 2005 or Visual Basic 2005 Express Edition:

1 Click the **Start** button on the Windows taskbar to open the Start menu, then point to **All Programs**.

2 *If you are using Visual Studio 2005*, point to **Microsoft Visual Studio 2005**, and then click **Microsoft Visual Studio 2005**. The Microsoft Visual Studio 2005 copyright screen appears momentarily, and then the Microsoft Visual Studio window opens.

   If you are using Visual Basic 2005 Express Edition, click **Microsoft Visual Basic 2005 Express Edition**. The Microsoft Visual Basic 2005 Express Edition copyright screen appears momentarily, and then the Microsoft Visual Basic 2005 Express Edition window opens.

3 Click **Window** on the menu bar, then click **Reset Window Layout**. A message box appears and asks whether you are sure you want to restore the default window layout for the environment. Click the **Yes** button.

When you start the Professional Edition of Microsoft Visual Studio 2005, your screen will appear similar to the screen shown in Figure 1-2. When you start the Express Edition of Visual Basic 2005, on the other hand, your screen will appear similar to the screen shown in Figure 1-3. In either case, your Recent Projects list might include the names of projects or solutions with which you have recently worked.

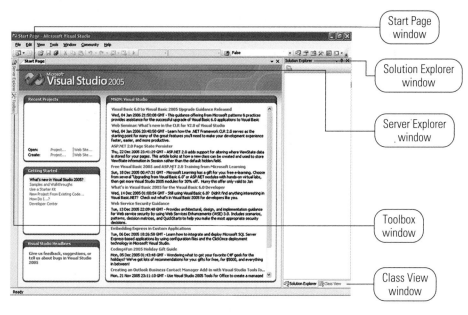

Figure 1-2: Microsoft Visual Studio 2005 startup screen

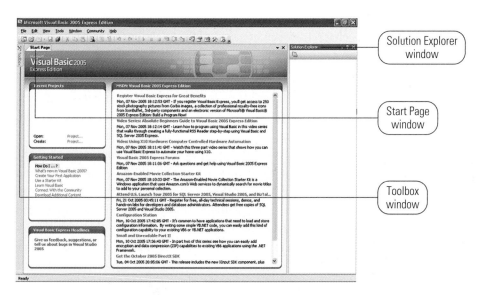

Figure 1-3: Microsoft Visual Basic 2005 Express Edition startup screen

As Figure 1-2 indicates, the Visual Studio 2005 startup screen contains five windows: Start Page, Server Explorer, Toolbox, Solution Explorer, and Class View. The Visual Basic 2005 Express Edition startup screen, however, contains only the Start Page, Toolbox, and Solution Explorer windows, as indicated in Figure 1-3. Figure 1-4 briefly describes the purpose of each window. You will learn more about the Solution Explorer window later in this lesson, and about the Toolbox window in Lesson B.

Window	Purpose
Class View	display the classes, methods, and properties included in a solution
Server Explorer	display data connections and servers
Solution Explorer	display the names of projects and files included in a solution
Start Page	create and open projects, access information on how to get started using Visual Studio 2005, access news and technical articles regarding .NET
Toolbox	display items that you can use when creating a project

Figure 1-4: Purpose of the windows included in the IDE

CREATING THE COPYRIGHT SCREEN APPLICATION

Recall that your task in this chapter is to create a simple application: a copyright screen. The copyright screen will be a Windows-based application, which means it will have a Windows user interface and run on a desktop computer.

Applications created in Visual Basic 2005 are composed of solutions, projects, and files. A **solution** is a container that stores the projects and files for an entire application. A **project** also is a container, but it stores files associated with only a specific piece of the solution. Although the idea of solutions, projects, and files may sound confusing, the concept of placing things in containers is nothing new to you. Think of a solution as being similar to a drawer in a filing cabinet. A project then is similar to a file folder that you store in the drawer, and a file is similar to a document that you store in the file folder. You can place many file folders in a filing cabinet drawer, just as you can place many projects in a solution. You also can store many documents in a file folder, similar to the way you can store many files in a project. Figure 1-5 illustrates this analogy.

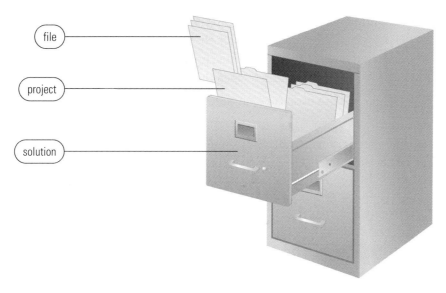

file

project

solution

Figure 1-5: Illustration of a solution, project, and file

To create a Visual Basic 2005 Windows-based application:

1 Click **Tools** on the menu bar, then click **Options** to open the Options dialog box. Click **Projects and Solutions**. If necessary, select the **Save new projects when created** and **Always show solution** check boxes, and deselect the **Show Output window when build starts** check box. Click the **OK** button to close the Options dialog box.

2 *If you are using Visual Studio 2005*, click **File** on the menu bar, point to **New**, and then click **Project**. The New Project dialog box opens. If necessary, expand the Visual Basic node in the Project types list, then click Windows.

If you are using Visual Basic 2005 Express Edition, click **File** on the menu bar, then click **New Project**. The New Project dialog box opens.

3 If necessary, click **Windows Application** in the Visual Studio installed templates section of the Templates list.

A **template** is a pattern that the computer uses to create solutions and projects. Each template listed in the Templates list includes a set of standard folders and files appropriate for the solution or project. The folders and files are automatically created on your computer's hard disk (or on the device designated by your instructor or technical support person) when you click the OK button in the New Project dialog box.

4 Change the name entered in the Name text box to **Copyright Project**.

» TIP
You also can use the Start Page to open the New Project dialog box. To do so, click Project . . ., which appears next to Create in the Recent Projects list.

5 Click the **Browse** button, which appears next to the Location text box. The Project Location dialog box opens. Locate and then click the **VB2005\Chap01** folder on your computer's hard disk (or on the device designated by your instructor or technical support person), then click the **Open** button to open the folder.

6 If necessary, select the **Create directory for solution** check box in the New Project dialog box.

7 Change the name entered in the Solution Name text box to **Copyright Solution**. Figure 1-6 shows the completed New Project dialog box if you are using Visual Studio 2005. Figure 1-7 shows the completed New Project dialog box if you are using Visual Basic 2005 Express Edition.

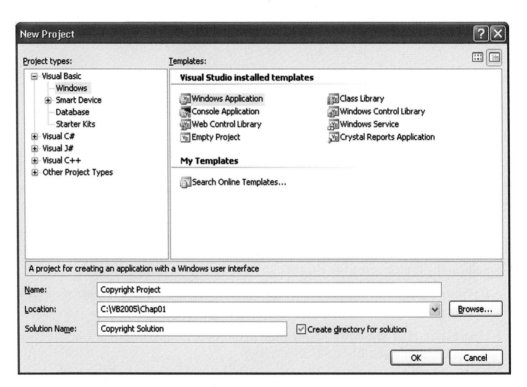

Figure 1-6: Completed New Project dialog box in Visual Studio 2005

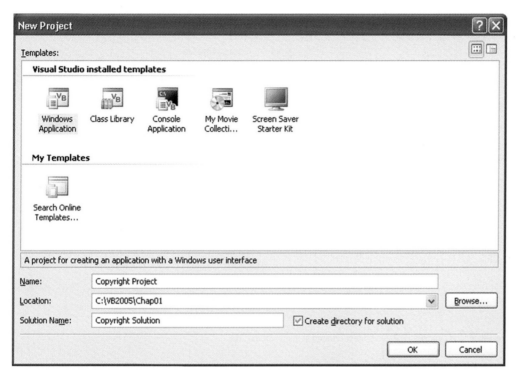

Figure 1-7: Completed New Project dialog box in Visual Basic 2005 Express Edition

8 Click the **OK** button to close the New Project dialog box.

When you click the OK button in the New Project dialog box, the computer creates a solution and adds a Visual Basic project to the solution. It also records the names of the solution and project, as well as other information pertaining to the project, in the Solution Explorer window. See Figure 1-8 (Visual Studio 2005) or Figure 1-9 (Visual Basic 2005 Express Edition).

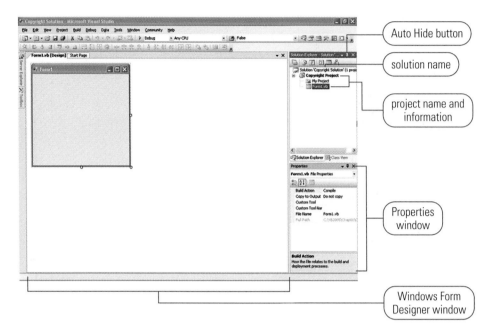

Figure 1-8: Solution and Visual Basic project created in Visual Studio 2005

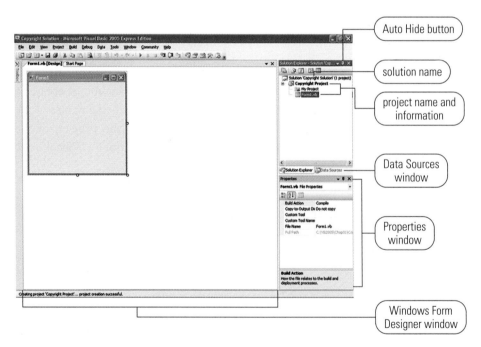

Figure 1-9: Solution and Visual Basic project created in Visual Basic 2005 Express Edition

>> **HELP?** If your screen does not look similar to either Figure 1-8 or Figure 1-9, click Window on the menu bar, then click Reset Window Layout, and then click the Yes button.

>> **HELP?** You might need to widen the Solution Explorer window to view its contents. To do so, position your mouse pointer ⌖ on the window's left border until ⌖ becomes ⬌ , then drag the border to the left.

Important Note: Subsequent figures in this book will reflect how your screen will appear if you are using Visual Studio 2005. The only exception to this is when the screen in Visual Basic 2005 Express Edition differs greatly from the screen in Visual Studio 2005; in those cases, you will be shown both screens.

Notice that, in addition to the windows discussed earlier, two new windows appear in the development environment: the Windows Form Designer window and the Properties window. In Visual Basic 2005 Express Edition, a third new window, called the Data Sources window, also appears. Having so many windows open at the same time can be confusing, especially when you are first learning the IDE. In most cases, you will find it easier to work in the IDE if you either close or auto-hide the windows you are not currently using. In the next section, you learn how to manage the windows in the IDE.

MANAGING THE WINDOWS IN THE IDE

The easiest way to close an open window in the IDE is to click the Close button on the window's title bar. In most cases, the View menu provides an appropriate option for opening a closed window. To open the Toolbox window, for instance, you click View on the menu bar, and then click Toolbox on the menu. Similarly, you click View, point to Other Windows, and then click Start Page to open the Start Page window.

You can use the Auto Hide button (shown earlier in Figures 1-8 and 1-9) on a window's title bar to auto-hide a window. When you auto-hide a window and then move the mouse pointer away from the window, the window is minimized and appears as a tab on the edge of the IDE. In addition, the vertical pushpin on the Auto Hide button is replaced by a horizontal pushpin, which indicates that the window is auto-hidden. The Server Explorer window shown in Figure 1-8 and the Toolbox windows shown in Figures 1-8 and 1-9 are examples of auto-hidden windows.

To temporarily display a window that has been auto-hidden, you simply place your mouse pointer on the window's tab; doing so slides the window into view. You can permanently display an auto-hidden window by clicking the Auto Hide button on the window's title bar. When you do so, the horizontal pushpin on the button is replaced by a vertical pushpin, which indicates that the window is not auto-hidden.

In the next set of steps, you will close the windows that you will not need to create the copyright screen. You also will practice auto-hiding and displaying the Solution Explorer window.

To close some of the windows in the IDE, and then auto-hide and display the Solution Explorer window:

1 *If you are using Visual Studio 2005*, place your mouse pointer on the **Server Explorer** tab. (The Server Explorer tab is usually located on the left edge of the IDE.) When the Server Explorer window slides into view, which may take several moments, click the **Close** button on its title bar.

Now you will close the Start Page window, as well as either the Class View window or the Data Sources window.

2 Click the **Start Page** tab to make the Start Page window the active window, then click the **Close** button on its title bar.

3 *If you are using Visual Studio 2005*, click the **Class View** tab to make the Class View window the active window, then click the **Close** button on its title bar.

If you are using Visual Basic 2005 Express Edition, click the **Data Sources** tab to make the Data Sources window the active window, then click the **Close** button on its title bar.

Next, you will auto-hide the Solution Explorer window.

4 Click the **Auto Hide** button (the vertical pushpin) on the Solution Explorer window's title bar, then move the mouse pointer away from the window. The Solution Explorer window is minimized and appears as a tab on the right edge of the IDE.

> **▶▶HELP?** If the Solution Explorer window remains on the screen when you move your mouse pointer away from the window, click another window's title bar.

Now you will temporarily display the Solution Explorer window.

5 Place your mouse pointer on the **Solution Explorer** tab. The Solution Explorer window slides into view. Notice that a horizontal pushpin now appears on the Auto Hide button.

6 Move your mouse pointer away from the Solution Explorer window. The window is minimized and appears as a tab again.

Next, you will use the Auto Hide button to permanently display the Solution Explorer window on the screen.

7 Place your mouse pointer on the **Solution Explorer** tab. When the Solution Explorer window slides into view, click the **Auto Hide** button (the horizontal pushpin) on its title bar. Notice that a vertical pushpin replaces the horizontal pushpin on the button.

8 Move your mouse pointer away from the Solution Explorer window. The window remains displayed on the screen. Figure 1-10 shows the current status of the windows in the development environment. *If you are using Visual Basic 2005 Express Edition, your title bar will contain Microsoft Visual Basic 2005 Express Edition rather than Microsoft Visual Studio.*

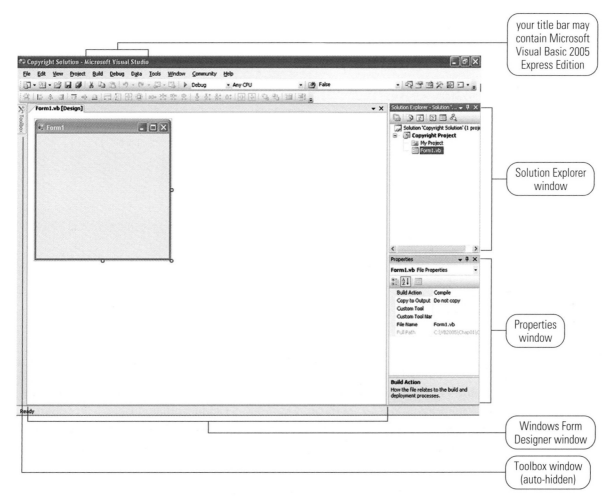

Figure 1-10: Current status of the windows in the development environment

Notice that only four (rather than seven) windows are open: the Toolbox window (which is auto-hidden), the Windows Form Designer window, the Solution Explorer window, and the Properties window.

In the next several sections, you will take a closer look at the Windows Form Designer, Solution Explorer, and Properties windows. (Recall that the Toolbox window is covered in Lesson B.)

THE WINDOWS FORM DESIGNER WINDOW

Figure 1-11 shows the **Windows Form Designer window**, where you create (or design) the graphical user interface, referred to as a **GUI**, for your project. Recall that a user interface is what you see and interact with when using an application.

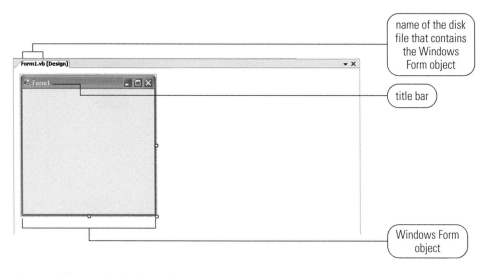

name of the disk file that contains the Windows Form object

title bar

Windows Form object

Figure 1-11: Windows Form Designer window

Only a Windows Form object appears in the designer window shown in Figure 1-11. A **Windows Form object**, or **form**, is the foundation for the user interface in a Windows-based application. You create the user interface by adding other objects, such as buttons and text boxes, to the form. Notice that a title bar appears at the top of the form. The title bar contains a default caption—in this case, Form1—as well as Minimize, Maximize, and Close buttons.

At the top of the designer window is a tab labeled Form1.vb [Design]. [Design] identifies the window as the designer window. Form1.vb is the name of the file (on your computer's hard disk or on another device) that contains the Visual Basic instructions associated with the Windows Form object.

As you learned in the Overview, all objects in an object-oriented program come from—or, in OOP terms, are instances of—a class. The Windows Form object, for example, is an instance of the Windows Form class. The form object is automatically instantiated for you when you create a Windows-based application.

THE SOLUTION EXPLORER WINDOW

The **Solution Explorer window** displays a list of the projects contained in the current solution, and the items contained in each project. Figure 1-12 shows the Solution Explorer window for the Copyright Solution.

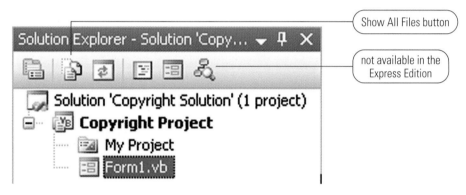

Figure 1-12: Solution Explorer window

As shown in Figure 1-12, the Copyright Solution contains one project named Copyright Project. Within the Copyright Project is a My Project folder and a file named Form1.vb. The .vb on the filename indicates that the file is a "Visual Basic" source file. A **source file** is a file that contains program instructions, called **code**. The Form1.vb file contains the code associated with the Windows Form object, or form, displayed in the Windows Form Designer window. You can use the Code Editor window, which you learn about in Lesson C, to view the contents of the Form1.vb file.

The Form1.vb source file is referred to as a **form file**, because it contains the code associated with a Windows Form object. The code associated with the first Windows Form object included in a project is automatically stored in a form file named Form1.vb. The code associated with the second Windows Form object in the same project is stored in a form file named Form2.vb, and so on. Because a project can contain many Windows Form objects and, therefore, many form files, it is a good practice to give each form file a more meaningful name. Doing this will help you keep track of the various form files in the project. You can use the Properties window to change the filename.

> **» TIP**
>
> The Copyright Project contains items in addition to the ones shown in Figure 1-12. To display the additional items, which typically are kept hidden, click the Show All Files button located below the title bar in the Solution Explorer window. To hide the items, click the Show All Files button again.

THE PROPERTIES WINDOW

As is everything in an object-oriented language, a file is an object. Each object has a set of attributes that determine its appearance and behavior. The attributes, called **properties**, are listed in the **Properties window**. In the context of OOP, the Properties window exposes the object's properties to the programmer.

When an object is created, a default value is assigned to each of its properties. The Properties window shown in Figure 1-13, for example, lists the default values assigned to the properties of the Form1.vb file contained in the Copyright Project. (You do not need to widen your Properties window to match Figure 1-13.)

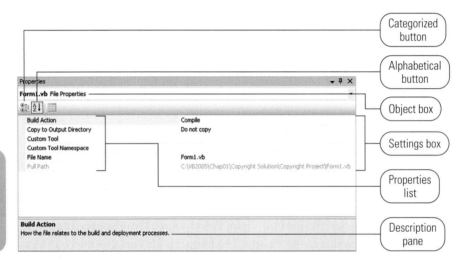

Figure 1-13: Properties window showing the properties of the Form1.vb file object

As indicated in Figure 1-13, the Properties window includes an Object box and a Properties list. The Object box is located immediately below the Properties window's title bar. The **Object box** contains the name of the selected object; in this case, it contains Form1.vb, which is the name of the form file object. When an object is selected, its properties appear in the Properties window.

The **Properties list** has two columns. The left column displays the names of the properties associated with the selected object. You can use the Alphabetical or Categorized buttons, which are located below the Object box, to display the property names either alphabetically or by category. Most times, it's easier to work with the Properties window when the property names are listed in alphabetical order.

The right column in the Properties list is called the **Settings box** and displays the current value, or setting, of each of the properties. For example, the current value of the Build Action property shown in Figure 1-13 is Compile. Notice that a brief description of the selected property appears in the Description pane located at the bottom of the Properties window.

Depending on the property, you can change the default value by selecting the property in the Properties list, and then either typing a new value in the Settings box or selecting a predefined value from a list or dialog box. For example, to change the value of the File Name property, you click File Name in the Properties list and then type the new filename in the Settings box. However, to change the value of the Build Action property, you click Build Action in the Properties list, then click the list arrow button in the Settings box, and then click one of the predefined settings from a drop-down list.

In the next set of steps, you will use the Properties window to change the name of the form file object from Form1.vb to Copyright Form.vb.

To change the name of the form file object:

1 Verify that Form1.vb File Properties appears in the Object box in the Properties window.

> **»HELP?** If Form1.vb File Properties does not appear in the Object box, click Form1.vb in the Solution Explorer window.

> **»HELP?** If the properties are not listed in alphabetical order, click the Alphabetical button in the Properties window. Most times, it's easier to work with the Properties window when the property names are listed in alphabetical order.

2 Click **File Name** in the Properties list. The Description pane indicates that the File Name property is used to set the name of the file or folder.

> **»HELP?** If the Description pane is not displayed in the Properties window, right-click anywhere on the Properties window (except on the title bar), and then click Description on the context menu.

3 Type **Copyright Form.vb** and press **Enter**. (Be sure to include the .vb extension on the filename; otherwise, the computer will not recognize the file as a source file.) Copyright Form.vb appears in the Solution Explorer and Properties windows and on the designer window's tab, as shown in Figure 1-14.

> **»TIP**
> You also can change the File Name property by right-clicking Form1.vb in the Solution Explorer window, and then clicking Rename on the context menu.

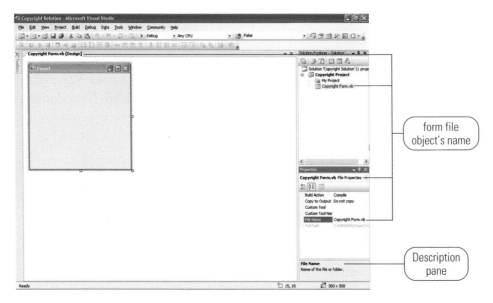

Figure 1-14: Form file object's name displayed in the designer, Solution Explorer, and Properties windows

Notice that you do not have to erase the old value in the Settings box before entering the new value. You need simply to select the appropriate property and then type the new value; as you type the new value, it replaces the old value.

Next, you will view the properties of the Windows Form object.

PROPERTIES OF THE WINDOWS FORM OBJECT

Like the form file object, the Windows Form object also has a set of properties. The properties will appear in the Properties window when you select the Windows Form object in the designer window.

To view the properties of the Windows Form object:

1 Click the **Windows Form** object in the designer window. The properties of the Windows Form object appear in the Properties window.

2 Click the **Auto Hide** button on the Solution Explorer window's title bar, then move the mouse pointer away from the window. Auto-hiding the Solution Explorer window allows you to view more of the Properties window.

The names of the properties can be listed either alphabetically or by category.

3 If the properties are listed alphabetically, click the **Categorized** button to view the category display, then click the **Alphabetical** button. If the properties in your Properties window are listed by category, click the **Alphabetical** button. The Properties window in Figure 1-15 shows a partial listing of the properties of a Windows Form object. The vertical scroll bar on the Properties window indicates that there are more properties to view.

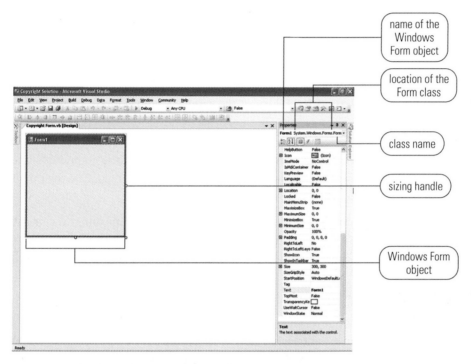

Figure 1-15: Windows Form object properties listed alphabetically in the Properties window

The sizing handles that appear on the form indicate that the form is selected. You can use the sizing handles to change the size of the form.

Notice that Form1 System.Windows.Forms.Form appears in the Object box in Figure 1-15. Form1 is the name of the Windows Form object. The name is automatically assigned to the form when the form is created—or, in OOP terms, instantiated. In System.Windows.Forms.Form, Form is the name of the class used to instantiate the Windows Form object. The forms in a project inherit the attributes and behaviors of the Form class. System.Windows.Forms, on the other hand, is the namespace that contains the Form class definition. A **class definition** is a block of code that specifies (or defines) the attributes and behaviors of an object. All class definitions in Visual Basic 2005 are contained in namespaces, which you can picture as blocks of memory cells inside the

»TIP
Recall that every object used in an object-oriented program is instantiated from a class.

computer. Each **namespace** contains the code that defines a group of related classes. The System.Windows.Forms namespace, for instance, contains the definition of the Windows Form class. It also contains the class definitions for objects you add to a form, such as buttons and text boxes.

The period that separates each word in System.Windows.Forms.Form is called the **dot member access operator**. Similar to the backslash (\) in a folder path, the dot member access operator indicates a hierarchy, but of namespaces rather than folders. In other words, the backslash in the path C:\VB2005\Chap01\Copyright Solution\Copyright Project\Copyright Form.vb indicates that the Copyright Form.vb file is contained in (or is a member of) the Copyright Project folder, which is a member of the Copyright Solution folder, which is a member of the Chap01 folder, which is a member of the VB2005 folder, which is a member of the C: drive. Likewise, the name System.Windows.Forms.Form indicates that the Form class is a member of the Forms namespace, which is a member of the Windows namespace, which is a member of the System namespace. The dot member access operator allows the computer to locate the Form class in the computer's internal memory, similar to the way the backslash (\) allows the computer to locate the Copyright Form.vb file on your computer's hard disk.

As you did with the form file object, you should assign a more meaningful name to the Windows Form object; doing this will help you keep track of the various forms in a project. Keep in mind that the names of the forms within the same project must be unique.

THE NAME PROPERTY

Unlike a file object, a Windows Form object has a Name property rather than a File Name property. You use the name entered in an object's **Name property** to refer to the object in code. The name must begin with a letter and it can contain only letters, numbers, and the underscore character. You cannot use punctuation characters or spaces in the name.

For many years, most Visual Basic programmers used Hungarian notation when naming objects, and many programmers still follow this practice. **Hungarian notation** is a naming convention that uses the first three (or more) characters in the name to represent the object's type (form, button, and so on), and the remaining characters to represent the object's purpose. For example, using Hungarian notation, you might assign the name frmCopyright to the current form. The "frm" identifies the object as a form, and "Copyright" reminds you of the form's purpose. Hungarian notation names are entered using **camel case**, which means that you lowercase the characters that represent the object's type and then uppercase the first letter of each word in the name. Camel case refers to the fact that the uppercase letters, which are taller than the lowercase letters, appear as "humps" in the name.

▶▶ TIP
Visit *www.irritatedVowel.com/Programming/Standards.aspx* for an interesting article on why Hungarian notation has fallen out of favor with many programmers.

Recently, a different naming convention for forms has emerged, and this is the naming convention used in this book. In this naming convention, the name begins with the form's purpose, followed by the form's class (Form). In addition, form names are entered using Pascal case rather than camel case. Using **Pascal case**, you capitalize the first letter in the form's name, as well as the first letter of each subsequent word in the name. Following this naming convention, you would assign the name CopyrightForm to the current form.

To change the name of the Windows Form object:

1 Drag the scroll box in the Properties window to the top of the vertical scroll bar. As you scroll, notice the various properties associated with a form.

2 Click (**Name**) in the Properties list, then type **CopyrightForm** and press **Enter**. Notice that the designer window's tab now includes an asterisk (*) after [Design]. The asterisk indicates that the form has been changed since the last time it was saved to the form file. You learn how to save changes made to the form file later in this lesson.

Next, you will set the Text property of the Windows Form object.

THE TEXT PROPERTY

Programmers who create applications for the Windows environment need to be aware of the conventions used in Windows applications. One such convention is that the name of the application (for example, Microsoft Visual Studio or Microsoft Word) usually appears in the application window's title bar. Because the Windows Form object in the designer window will become your application's window when the application is started, its title bar should display an appropriate name.

A form's **Text property** controls the caption that appears in the form's title bar. The content of the Text property also appears on the application's button on the taskbar while the application is running. The default caption, Form1, is automatically assigned to the Text property of the first form in a project. A better, more descriptive caption would be "Interlocking Software Company"—the name of the company responsible for the copyright screen application.

To set the Text property of the Windows Form object:

1 Scroll down the Properties window until you see the Text property in the Properties list, then click **Text** in the Properties list.

2 Type **Interlocking Software Company** and press **Enter**. The new text appears in the Settings box to the right of the Text property, and also appears in the form's title bar.

A form's Name and Text properties always should be changed to more meaningful values. At times, you also may want to change a form's StartPosition property.

>> TIP
Your company (or instructor) may have a different naming convention you are expected to use. Your company's (or instructor's) naming convention supersedes the one used in this book.

>> TIP
Pascal is a programming language that was created by Niklaus Wirth in the late 1960s. It was named in honor of the seventeenth-century French mathematician Blaise Pascal, and is used to develop scientific applications.

>> TIP
You also can scroll the Properties window using the up and down arrow keys on your keyboard, as well as the Home, End, Page Down, and Page Up keys; however, you first must make the Properties window the active window.

>> TIP
The programmer uses the Name property when coding an application. The user reads the Text property while an application is running.

THE STARTPOSITION PROPERTY

You use the **StartPosition property** to determine where the form is positioned when the application is started and the form first appears on the screen. A form that represents a splash screen, for example, always should appear in the middle of the screen.

To center a form on the screen when the application is started:

1 Click **StartPosition** in the Properties list. The list arrow button in the Settings box indicates that the StartPosition property has predefined settings. When you click the list arrow button, a list appears containing the valid settings for the StartPosition property. You then select the setting you want from the list.

2 Click the **list arrow** button in the Settings box, then click **CenterScreen** in the list.

Next you will set the Size property of the Windows Form object.

THE SIZE PROPERTY

As you can with any Windows object, you can size a form by selecting it and then dragging the sizing handles that appear around it. You also can set its **Size property**.

To set the Size property of the form:

1 Click **Size** in the Properties list. Notice that the Size property contains two numbers separated by a comma and a space. The first number represents the width of the form, measured in pixels. The second number represents the height, also measured in pixels.

A **pixel**, which is short for "picture element," is one spot in a grid of thousands of such spots that form an image produced on the screen by a computer or printed on a page by a printer. You can click the plus box that appears next to the Size property to verify that the first number listed in the property represents the width and the second number represents the height.

2 Click the **plus box** that appears next to the Size property. The Width and Height properties appear below the Size property in the Properties window.

Assume you want to change the Width property to 370 pixels and change the Height property to 315 pixels. You can do so by entering 370 in the Width property's Settings box and entering 315 in the Height property's Settings box; or, you can simply enter 370, 315 in the Size property's Settings box.

3 Type **370, 315** in the Size property's Settings box and press **Enter**. Figure 1-16 shows the current status of the copyright screen application.

»TIP

For some properties, such as the BackColor property, a color palette rather than a list appears when you click the list arrow button in the Settings box.

»TIP

You also can size an object (such as a form) by selecting it and then pressing and holding down the Shift key as you press the up, down, right, or left key on your keyboard.

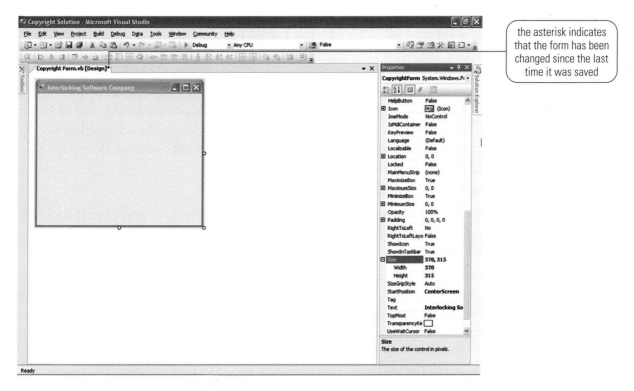

Figure 1-16: Current status of the copyright screen application

Before you learn how to save the form file, you will practice setting and then restoring the value of a property.

SETTING AND RESTORING THE VALUE OF A PROPERTY

In the next set of steps, you set and then restore the value of the form's **BackColor property**, which specifies the background color of the form.

To set and then restore the value of the form's BackColor property:

1 Click **BackColor** in the Properties list, then click the **list arrow** button in the Settings box. Click the **Custom** tab, then click a **red square**. The background color of the form changes to red.

You can restore the BackColor property to its default setting by right-clicking the property and then clicking Reset on the context menu.

2 Right-click **BackColor** in the Properties list, then click **Reset** on the context menu. The background color of the form returns to its default setting.

SAVING A SOLUTION

It is a good practice to save the current solution every 10 or 15 minutes so that you will not lose a lot of your work if the computer loses power. One way to save the solution is to click File on the menu bar, and then click Save All. You also can click the Save All button on the Standard toolbar. When you save the solution, the computer saves any changes made to the files included in the solution. Saving the solution also removes the asterisk that appears on the designer window.

To save the current solution:

1 Click **File** on the menu bar, and then click **Save All**. Notice that an asterisk no longer appears on the designer window. This indicates that all changes made to the form have been saved.

You also can use the Save button on the Standard toolbar to save the solution, but you first must select the solution's name in the Solution Explorer window, because the Save button saves only the changes made to the selected item. For example, if the form file is selected, then the Save button saves only the changes made to the form file. Similarly, if the project name is selected, then only changes made to the files included in the project will be saved. The tooltip box that appears when you rest your mouse pointer on the Save button indicates which files will be saved. In this case, the tooltip box will say Save Copyright Form.vb if the form file's name is selected in the Solution Explorer window, Save Copyright Project if the project name is selected, and Save Copyright Solution.sln if the solution name is selected.

Next, you will learn how to close the current solution, and how to open an existing solution. Both of these skills will help you complete the end-of-lesson exercises.

CLOSING THE CURRENT SOLUTION

You close a solution using the Close Solution option on the File menu. Notice that you use the Close Solution option rather than the Close option. The Close option on the File menu does not close the solution; instead, it closes the designer window in the IDE.

When you close a solution, all projects and files contained in the solution also are closed. If unsaved changes were made to the solution, project, or form, a dialog box opens and prompts you to save the appropriate files. The dialog box contains Yes, No, and Cancel buttons. You click the Yes button to save the files before the solution is closed. You click the No button to close the solution without saving the files. You click the Cancel button to leave the solution open.

To close the Copyright Solution:

1 Click **File** on the menu bar, and then click **Close Solution**.

2 Temporarily display the Solution Explorer window to verify that the entire Copyright Solution is closed.

OPENING AN EXISTING SOLUTION

You can use the File menu to open an existing solution. If a solution is already open in the IDE, it is closed before another solution is opened. In other words, only one solution can be open in the IDE at any one time.

To open the Copyright Solution:

1 *If you are using Visual Studio 2005*, click **File** on the menu bar, then point to **Open**, and then click **Project/Solution**. The Open Project dialog box opens.

   If you are using Visual Basic 2005 Express Edition, click **File** on the menu bar, then click **Open Project**. The Open Project dialog box opens.

2 Locate and then open the **VB2005\Chap01\Copyright Solution** folder on your computer's hard disk (or on the device designated by your instructor or technical support person).

3 Click **Copyright Solution** (Copyright Solution.sln) in the list of filenames, then click the **Open** button. (The ".sln" on the filename stands for "solution.")

4 If the Windows Form Designer window is not open, click **Copyright Form.vb** in the Solution Explorer window, then click **View** on the menu bar, and then click **Designer**.

5 Temporarily display the Solution Explorer window to verify that the solution is open.

Lastly, you learn how to exit Visual Studio 2005 or Visual Basic 2005 Express Edition. You will complete the copyright screen in the remaining two lessons.

EXITING VISUAL STUDIO 2005 OR VISUAL BASIC 2005 EXPRESS EDITION

As in most Windows applications, you exit an application using either the Close button on the application window's title bar, or the Exit option on the File menu.

To exit Visual Studio 2005 or Visual Basic 2005 Express Edition:

1 Click **File** on the menu bar, and then click **Exit**.

You have completed Lesson A. You can either take a break or complete the end-of-lesson questions and exercises before moving on to the next lesson.

SUMMARY

TO START VISUAL STUDIO 2005 OR VISUAL BASIC 2005 EXPRESS EDITION:

» *If you are using Visual Studio 2005*, click the Start button on the taskbar. Point to All Programs, then point to Microsoft Visual Studio 2005, and then click Microsoft Visual Studio 2005.

» *If you are using Visual Basic 2005 Express Edition*, click the Start button on the taskbar. Point to All Programs, then click Microsoft Visual Basic 2005 Express Edition.

TO CREATE A VISUAL BASIC 2005 WINDOWS-BASED APPLICATION:

» Start either Visual Studio 2005 or Visual Basic 2005 Express Edition.

» Click Tools on the menu bar, then click Options, and then click Projects and Solutions. If necessary, select the Save new projects when created and Always show solution check boxes, and deselect the Show Output window when build starts check box. Click the OK button to close the Options dialog box.

» *If you are using Visual Studio 2005*, click File on the menu bar, point to New, then click Project. If necessary, expand the Visual Basic node in the Project types list, then click Windows. *If you are using Visual Basic 2005 Express Edition*, click File on the menu bar, and then click New Project.

» If necessary, click Windows Application in the Visual Studio installed templates section of the Templates list.

» Enter an appropriate name and location in the Name and Location text boxes, respectively.

» If necessary, select the Create directory for solution check box.

» Enter an appropriate name in the Solution Name text box.

» Click the OK button to close the New Project dialog box.

TO RESET THE WINDOW LAYOUT IN THE IDE:

» Click Window on the menu bar, then click Reset Window Layout, and then click the Yes button.

TO CLOSE A WINDOW IN THE IDE:

» Click the window's Close button.

TO OPEN A CLOSED WINDOW IN THE IDE:

» Use the appropriate option on the View menu.

TO AUTO-HIDE A WINDOW IN THE IDE:

» Click the Auto Hide (vertical pushpin) button on the window's title bar.

TO TEMPORARILY DISPLAY AN AUTO-HIDDEN WINDOW IN THE IDE:

» Place your mouse pointer on the window's tab.

TO PERMANENTLY DISPLAY AN AUTO-HIDDEN WINDOW IN THE IDE:

» Click the Auto Hide (horizontal pushpin) button on the window's title bar.

TO SET THE VALUE OF A PROPERTY:

» Select the object whose property you want to set, then select the appropriate property in the Properties list. Type the new property value in the selected property's Settings box, or choose the value from the list, color palette, or dialog box.

TO GIVE A MORE MEANINGFUL NAME TO AN OBJECT:

» Set the object's Name property.

TO CONTROL THE TEXT APPEARING IN THE FORM'S TITLE BAR, AND ON THE APPLICATION'S BUTTON ON THE TASKBAR WHEN THE APPLICATION IS RUNNING:

» Set the form's Text property.

TO CONTROL THE STARTING LOCATION OF THE FORM:

» Set the form's StartPosition property.

TO SIZE A FORM:

» Drag the form's sizing handles. You also can set the form's Size, Height, and Width properties in the Properties window. In addition, you can select the form and then press and hold down the Shift key as you press the up, down, left, or right key on your keyboard.

TO CHANGE THE BACKGROUND COLOR OF A FORM:

» Set the form's BackColor property.

TO RESTORE A PROPERTY TO ITS DEFAULT SETTING:

» Right-click the property in the Properties list, and then click Reset.

TO SAVE A SOLUTION:

» Click File on the menu bar, and then click Save All. You also can click the Save All button 📰 on the Standard toolbar.

TO OPEN AN EXISTING SOLUTION:

» *If you are using Visual Studio 2005*, click File on the menu bar, point to Open, and then click Project/Solution. *If you are using Visual Basic 2005 Express Edition*, click File on the menu bar, and then click Open Project.

» Locate and then click the solution filename, which is contained in the application's solution folder, and then click the Open button. (The solution filename has an .sln filename extension.)

» If the Windows Form Designer window is not open, click the form file's name in the Solution Explorer window, then click View on the menu bar, and then click Designer.

TO EXIT VISUAL STUDIO 2005 OR VISUAL BASIC 2005 EXPRESS EDITION:

» Click the Close button on the Visual Studio 2005 or Visual Basic 2005 Express Edition title bar. You also can click File on the menu bar, and then click Exit.

QUESTIONS

1. You use the _____ window to set the characteristics that control an object's appearance and behavior.

   a. Characteristics   b. Object

   c. Properties   d. Windows Form Designer

2. The _____ window lists the projects and files included in a solution.

   a. Object   b. Project

   c. Properties   d. Solution Explorer

3. Solution files in Visual Basic 2005 have a(n) _____ extension on their filenames.

   a. .prg   b. .sln

   c. .src   d. .vb

4. Which of the following statements are true?

   a. You can auto-hide a window by clicking the Auto-Hide (vertical pushpin) button on its title bar.

   b. An auto-hidden window appears as a tab on the edge of the IDE.

   c. You temporarily display an auto-hidden window by placing your mouse pointer on its tab.

   d. All of the above.

5. The _____ property controls the text displayed in a form's title bar.

   a. Caption   b. Text

   c. Title   d. TitleBar

6. You give an object a more meaningful name by setting the object's _____ property.

   a. Application   b. Caption

   c. Name   d. Text

7. The _____ property determines the position of a form when the application is started and the form first appears on the screen.

   a. InitialLocation   b. Location

   c. StartLocation   d. StartPosition

8. Explain the difference between a form's Text property and its Name property.

9. Explain the difference between a form file object and a Windows Form object.

10. What does the dot member access operator indicate in the text System.Windows.Forms.Label?

EXERCISES

1. In this exercise, you change the properties of a form contained in an existing Visual Basic 2005 Windows-based application.

   a. If necessary, start Visual Studio 2005 or Visual Basic 2005 Express Edition and permanently display the Solution Explorer window.

   b. *If you are using Visual Studio 2005*, click File on the menu bar, then point to Open, and then click Project/Solution. *If you are using Visual Basic 2005 Express Edition*, click File on the menu bar, and then click Open Project.

   c. Open the Charities Solution (Charities Solution.sln) file, which is contained in the VB2005\Chap01\Charities Solution folder. If necessary, click the form file's name in the Solution Explorer window, then use the View menu to open the designer window.

   d. Change the following properties of the Windows Form object:

Name:	MainForm
BackColor:	Select a light blue square on the Custom tab
Size:	300, 350
StartPosition:	CenterScreen
Text:	Charities Unlimited

   e. Click File on the menu bar, and then click Save All to save the solution.

   f. Click File on the menu bar, and then click Close Solution to close the solution.

2. In this exercise, you create a Visual Basic 2005 Windows-based application.

   a. If necessary, start Visual Studio 2005 or Visual Basic 2005 Express Edition and permanently display the Solution Explorer window.

   b. Create a Visual Basic Windows-based application. Name the solution Photo Solution, and name the project Photo Project. Save the application in the VB2005\Chap01 folder.

   c. Assign the filename Main Form.vb to the form file object.

   d. Assign the name MainForm to the Windows Form object.

   e. The form's title bar should say Photos Incorporated. Set the appropriate property.

   f. The form should be centered on the screen when it first appears. Set the appropriate property.

   g. Change the background color of the form to light blue.

   h. Save and then close the solution.

3. In this exercise, you create a Visual Basic 2005 Windows-based application.

   a. If necessary, start Visual Studio 2005 or Visual Basic 2005 Express Edition and permanently display the Solution Explorer window.

   b. Create a Visual Basic Windows-based application. Name the solution Yorktown Solution, and name the project Yorktown Project. Save the solution in the VB2005\Chap01 folder.

   c. Assign the filename Main Form.vb to the form file object.

   d. Assign the name MainForm to the Windows Form object.

   e. The form's title bar should say Yorktown Shopping Center. Set the appropriate property.

   f. The form should be centered on the screen when it first appears. Set the appropriate property.

   g. Save and then close the solution.

DISCOVERY EXERCISE
4. In this exercise, you learn about the ControlBox, MaximizeBox, and MinimizeBox properties of a Windows Form object.

   a. If necessary, start Visual Studio 2005 or Visual Basic 2005 Express Edition and permanently display the Solution Explorer window.

   b. Open the Greenwood Solution (Greenwood Solution.sln) file, which is contained in the VB2005\Chap01\Greenwood Solution folder. If necessary, click the form file's name in the Solution Explorer window, then use the View menu to open the designer window.

   c. Use the Properties window to view the properties of the form.

   d. Click the ControlBox property. What is the purpose of this property? (Refer to the Description pane in the Properties window.)

   e. Set the ControlBox property to False. How does this setting affect the form?

   f. Set the ControlBox property to True.

   g. Click the MaximizeBox property. What is the purpose of this property?

   h. Set the MaximizeBox property to False. How does this setting affect the form?

   i. Set the MaximizeBox property to True.

   j. Click the MinimizeBox property. What is the purpose of this property?

   k. Set the MinimizeBox property to False. How does this setting affect the form?

   l. Set the MinimizeBox property to True.

   m. Close the solution without saving it.

DISCOVERY EXERCISE

5. In this exercise, you use the Description pane in the Properties window to research two properties of a form.

   a. If necessary, start Visual Studio 2005 or Visual Basic 2005 Express Edition and permanently display the Solution Explorer window.

   b. Open the Greenwood Solution (Greenwood Solution.sln) file, which is contained in the VB2005\Chap01\Greenwood Solution folder. If necessary, click the form file's name in the Solution Explorer window, then use the View menu to open the designer window.

   c. Use the Properties window to view the properties of the form.

   d. What property determines whether an icon is displayed in the form's title bar?

   e. What property determines whether the value stored in the form's Text property appears on the Windows taskbar when the application is running?

   f. Close the solution without saving it.

LESSON B
OBJECTIVES

AFTER STUDYING LESSON B, YOU SHOULD
BE ABLE TO:

» Add a control to a form

» Set the properties of a label, picture box, and button control

» Select multiple controls

» Center controls on the form

» Open the Project Designer window

» Start and end an application

» Enter code in the Code Editor window

» Terminate an application using the Me.Close method

WORKING WITH CONTROLS

THE TOOLBOX WINDOW

In Lesson A, you learned about the Windows Form Designer, Solution Explorer, and Properties windows. In this lesson, you will learn about the Toolbox window. First, however, you will open the Copyright Solution you created in Lesson A.

To open the Copyright Solution and display the Toolbox window:

1 If necessary, start Visual Studio 2005 or Visual Basic 2005 Express Edition.

You will not need the Start Page window, so you can close it.

2 Close the Start Page window.

3 *If you are using Visual Studio 2005*, click **File** on the menu bar, then point to **Open**, and then click **Project/Solution**.

   If you are using Visual Basic 2005 Express Edition, click **File** on the menu bar, and then click **Open Project**.

4 Locate and then open the **VB2005\Chap01\Copyright Solution** folder. Click **Copyright Solution** (Copyright Solution.sln) in the list of filenames, and then click the **Open** button. If necessary, open the designer window.

5 If necessary, permanently display the Properties window and auto-hide the Solution Explorer window.

6 Permanently display the Toolbox window.

7 Rest your mouse pointer on the word ListBox in the Toolbox window, as shown in Figure 1-17.

The **Toolbox window**, or **toolbox**, contains the tools you use when creating your application. The contents of the toolbox vary depending on the designer in use. The toolbox shown in Figure 1-17 appears when you are using the Windows Form Designer. Notice that both an icon and a name identify each tool in the toolbox. When you rest your mouse pointer on either the tool's name or its icon, the tool's purpose appears in a box, as shown in Figure 1-17.

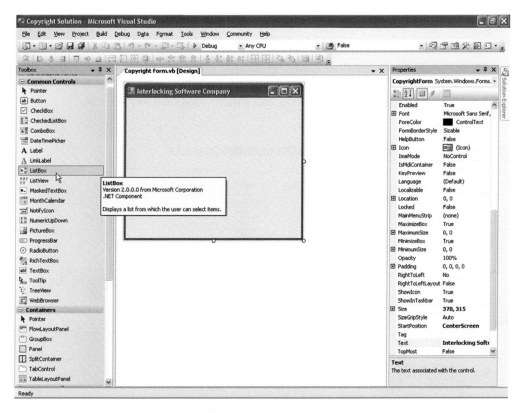

Figure 1-17: Box describing the purpose of the ListBox tool

In the context of OOP, each tool in the toolbox represents a class, which is a pattern from which one or more objects are instantiated. The object's attributes (properties) and behaviors (methods and events) are encapsulated (combined) in the tool. The tools allow you to instantiate objects such as text boxes, list boxes, and radio buttons. The objects, called **controls**, will appear on the form.

The first tool you will learn about is the Label tool.

USING THE LABEL TOOL

You use the **Label tool** to instantiate a label control. The purpose of a **label control** is to display text that the user is not allowed to edit while the application is running. In this application, for example, you do not want the user to change the author name and copyright year on the copyright screen. Therefore, you will display the information using two label controls: one for the name of the application's author and the other for the copyright year.

To use the Label tool to create two label controls:

1 Click the **Label** tool in the toolbox, but do not release the mouse button. Hold down the mouse button as you drag the mouse pointer to the lower-left corner of the form. As you drag the mouse pointer, you will see a solid box, as well as an outline of a rectangle and a plus box, following the mouse pointer, as shown in Figure 1-18.

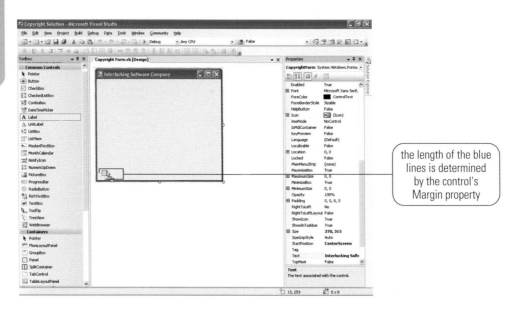

the length of the blue lines is determined by the control's Margin property

Figure 1-18: Label tool being dragged to the form

Notice that a blue line appears between the form's left border and the control's left border, and between the form's bottom border and the control's bottom border. The blue lines are called margin lines, because their size is determined by the contents of the control's Margin property. The purpose of the margin lines is to assist you in spacing the controls properly on the form.

2 Release the mouse button. A label control appears on the form, as shown in Figure 1-19.

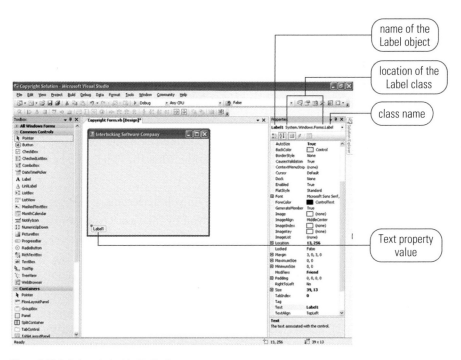

Figure 1-19: Label control added to the form

»HELP? If the wrong control appears on the form, press Delete to remove the control, then repeat Steps 1 and 2.

Notice that Label1 System.Windows.Forms.Label appears in the Object box in the Properties window. (You may need to widen the Properties window to view the entire contents of the Object box.) Label1 is the default name assigned to the label control. System.Windows.Forms.Label indicates that the control is an instance of the Label class, which is defined in the System.Windows.Forms namespace.

Recall from Lesson A that a default value is assigned to each of an object's properties when the object is created. Label1, for example, is the default value assigned to the Text and Name properties of the first label control added to a form. The value of the Text property appears inside the label control, as indicated in Figure 1-19. (You can verify that the Name property also contains Label1 by scrolling to the top of the Properties window.)

3 Click the **Label** tool in the toolbox, and then drag the tool to the form, positioning it above the existing label control. (Do not worry about the exact location.) Release the mouse button. Notice that Label2 is assigned to the Text property of the second label control added to a form. Label2 also is assigned to the control's Name property.

Some programmers assign meaningful names to all of the controls in an interface, while others do so only for controls that are either coded or referred to in code; in subsequent chapters in this book, you follow the latter convention. In the copyright screen application, however, you will assign a meaningful name to each control in the interface.

As you learned in Lesson A, for many years most Visual Basic programmers used Hungarian notation when naming objects, and many programmers still follow this practice. Using Hungarian notation, a programmer might assign the name lblAuthor to the label control that displays the author's name. The "lbl" identifies the object as a label control, and "Author" indicates the control's purpose.

Recently, several different naming conventions for controls have emerged. One of the naming conventions uses the control's purpose followed by its class. Using this naming convention, a programmer might assign the name authorLabel to the label control that displays the author's name. Notice that the name is entered using camel case, which means that you lowercase the first word in the control's name and then uppercase the first letter of each subsequent word in the name. Other naming conventions for controls suggest using a common prefix on each name, such as the letters *ui* (for "user interface"), the letters *ux* (for "user experience"), or simply the letter *x* (which doesn't stand for anything in particular, but is one fewer character to type in each name). Using a common prefix ensures that the control names are listed together when using the IntelliSense feature in the Code Editor window, which you view later in this lesson. In this book, you will begin all control names with the letter *x*. For example, you will assign the name xAuthorLabel to the label control that displays the author's name, and you will assign the name xYearLabel to the label control that displays the copyright year.

To assign a more meaningful name to the label controls:

1 Click the **Label1** control on the form. This selects the control and displays its properties in the Properties window.

2 Scroll to the top of the Properties list, and then click **(Name)**.

3 Type **xAuthorLabel** in the Settings box and press **Enter**.

4 Click the **Label2** control on the form. Click **(Name)** in the Properties list, then type **xYearLabel** and press **Enter**.

Next, you will set the Text property for both label controls.

SETTING THE TEXT PROPERTY

As you learned earlier, a label control's Text property determines the value that appears inside the control. In this application, you want the words "Written by" and your name to appear in the xAuthorLabel control, and the words "Copyright Year" and the year 2008 to appear in the xYearLabel control. Therefore, you will need to set the Text property of both controls.

To set the Text property of the two label controls:

1 Currently, the xYearLabel control is selected on the form. Scroll down the Properties window until you locate the control's Text property. Click **Text** in the Properties list, then type **Copyright Year 2008** and press **Enter**. The new text appears in the Text property's Settings box and in the xYearLabel control.

Notice that the designer automatically sizes the xYearLabel control to fit its current contents; this is because the default setting of a Label control's **AutoSize property** is True. (You can verify that fact by viewing the AutoSize property in the Properties window.)

2 Click the **xAuthorLabel** control on the form, then click **Text** in the Properties list. Type **Written By** and press the **spacebar**, then type your name and press **Enter**. The xAuthorLabel control stretches automatically to fit the contents of its Text property.

Now you will specify the placement of the two label controls on the form.

SETTING THE LOCATION PROPERTY

You can move a control to a different location on the form by placing your mouse pointer ⬉ on the control until ⬉ becomes ✛ , and then dragging the control to the desired location. You also can set the control's **Location property**, because the property specifies the position of the upper-left corner of the control.

To set the Location property of the two label controls:

1 Click the **xYearLabel** control to select it.

2 Click **Location** in the Properties list, then click the **plus box** next to the property's name. Two additional properties, X and Y, appear below the Location property in the Properties list.

The **X property** specifies the number of pixels from the left border of the form to the left border of the control. The **Y property** specifies the number of pixels between the top border of the form and the top border of the control. In other words, the X property refers to the control's horizontal location on the form, whereas the Y property refers to its vertical location. You will change the X value to 175, and change the Y value to 250.

3 Type **175, 250** in the **Location** property and press **Enter**. The xYearLabel control moves to its new location.

4 Click the **minus box** next to the Location property's name.

Now you will select the xAuthorLabel control and then set its Location property. In addition to selecting a control by clicking it on the form, you also can select a control by clicking its entry (name and class) in the Object box in the Properties window. You will try this next.

> **»TIP**
>
> You also can move a control by selecting it and then pressing and holding down the Control (Ctrl) key as you press the up, down, left, or right key on your keyboard.

5 Click the **list arrow** button in the Properties window's Object box, and then click **xAuthorLabel System.Windows.Forms.Label** in the list. Set the control's **Location** property to **175, 225**. The xAuthorLabel control moves to its new location.

6 Click **File** on the menu bar, and then click **Save All** to save the solution.

Now you will set the Font property of the two label controls. As you will see in the next section, you can set the Font property for both controls at the same time.

CHANGING THE PROPERTY FOR MORE THAN ONE CONTROL AT A TIME

You can use an object's **Font property** to change the type, style, and size of the font used to display the text in an object. A **font** is the general shape of the characters in the text. Tahoma, Courier, and Microsoft Sans Serif are examples of font types. Font styles include regular, bold, and italic. The numbers 8.25, 10, and 18 are examples of font sizes, which typically are measured in points, with one **point** equaling $\frac{1}{72}$ of an inch.

One reason for changing a font is to bring attention to a specific part of the screen. In the copyright screen, for example, you can make the text in the two label controls more noticeable by increasing the size of the font used to display the text. You can change the font size for both controls at the same time by clicking one control and then pressing and holding down the Control key as you click the other control on the form. You can use the Control+click method to select as many controls as you want. To cancel the selection of one of the selected controls, press and hold down the Control key as you click the control. To cancel the selection of all of the selected controls, release the Control key, then click the form or an unselected control on the form.

You also can select a group of controls on the form by placing the mouse pointer slightly above and to the left of the first control you want to select, then pressing the left mouse button and dragging. A dotted rectangle appears as you drag. When all of the controls you want to select are within (or at least touched by) the dotted rectangle, release the mouse button. All of the controls surrounded or touched by the dotted rectangle will be selected.

To select both label controls, and then set their Font property:

1 Verify that the xAuthorLabel control is selected.

2 Press and hold down the **Ctrl** (or Control) key as you click the **xYearLabel** control, then release the Ctrl key. Both controls are selected, as shown in Figure 1-20.

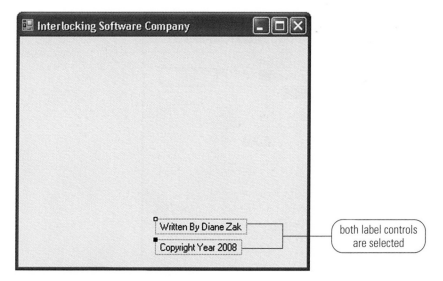

Figure 1-20: Label controls selected on the form

3 Click **Font** in the Properties list, then click the . . . (ellipsis) button in the Settings box. The Font dialog box opens.

Typically, the default font is the regular style of the Microsoft Sans Serif font, and the default font size is approximately 8 points, or $\frac{1}{9}$ of an inch. (Recall that one point is $\frac{1}{72}$ of an inch.) For applications that will run on computer systems running Windows 2000 or Windows XP, it is recommended that you use the Tahoma font because it offers improved readability and globalization support. You will change the font type to Tahoma, and increase the font size to 12 points ($\frac{1}{6}$ of an inch).

4 Scroll the Font list box and click **Tahoma**, then click **12** in the Size list box. Figure 1-21 shows the completed Font dialog box.

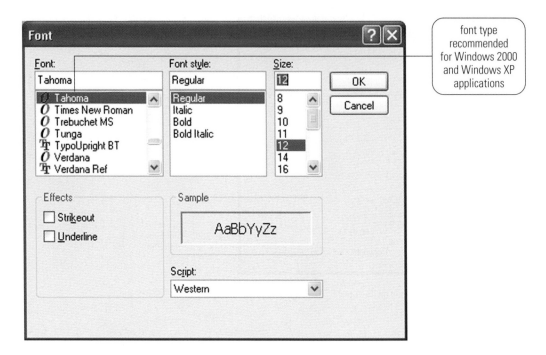

Figure 1-21: Completed Font dialog box

5 Click the **OK** button. The Font dialog box closes, and the text in the two label controls appears in the new font and font size. Depending on the number of characters in your name, the xAuthorLabel control might extend beyond the right border of the form. You will fix that problem in the next section.

Next, you will learn how to use the Format menu to adjust the size and alignment of the controls on the form.

USING THE FORMAT MENU

The Format menu provides options that allow you to manipulate the controls in the user interface. The Align option, for example, allows you to align two or more controls by their left, right, top, or bottom borders. You can use the Make Same Size option to make two or more controls the same width and/or height. However, before you can use the Format menu to change the alignment or size of two or more controls, you first must select the controls. The first control you select should always be the one whose size or location you want to match. For example, to align the left border of the Label1 and Label2 controls on a form with the left border of the Label3 control on the same form, you first select the Label3 control, and then select the Label1 and Label2 controls. However, to align the left border of the Label2 and Label3 controls with the left border of the Label1 control, you must select the Label1 control before selecting the Label2 and Label 3 controls. (You will practice with the Align and Make Same Size options in Discovery Exercise 4 at the end of this lesson.)

The Format menu also has a Center in Form option that centers one or more controls either horizontally or vertically on the form. In the next set of steps, you will use the Center in Form option to center the two label controls on the form.

To center the xAuthorLabel and xYearLabel controls horizontally on the form:

1 Click the **Copyright Form.vb [Design]*** tab to make the designer window the active window. The two label controls should still be selected.

2 Click **Format** on the menu bar. Point to **Center in Form**, then click **Horizontally**. The designer centers the two label controls horizontally on the form.

3 Click the **form** to deselect the label controls.

4 Click **File** on the menu bar, and then click **Save All** to save the solution.

Next, you will use the PictureBox tool to add a picture box control to the form.

USING THE PICTUREBOX TOOL

According to the application you previewed at the beginning of the chapter, you need to include the Interlocking Software Company logo on your copyright screen. You can do so by displaying the logo in a **picture box control**, which you instantiate using the **PictureBox tool**.

To add a picture box control to the form:

1 Click the **PictureBox** tool in the toolbox, then drag the mouse pointer to the form. (You do not need to worry about the exact location.) Release the mouse button. See Figure 1-22. The picture box control's properties appear in the Properties list, and PictureBox1 System.Windows.Forms.PictureBox appears in the Object box. PictureBox1 is the default name assigned to the first picture box control added to a form. System.Windows.Forms.PictureBox indicates that the control is an instance of the PictureBox class, which is defined in the System.Windows.Forms namespace.

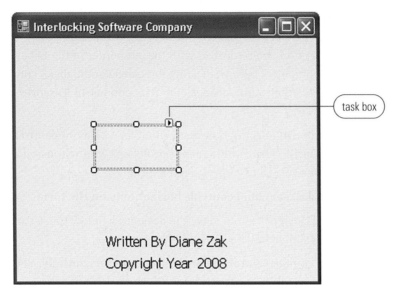

Figure 1-22: Picture box control added to the form

Notice that a box containing a triangle appears on the picture box control in Figure 1-22. The box is referred to as the task box because, when you click it, it displays a list of the tasks commonly performed when using the control. Each task in the list is associated with one or more properties. You can set the properties using the task list or the Properties window.

2 Click the **task box** on the PictureBox1 control. A list of tasks associated with a picture box appears, as shown in Figure 1-23.

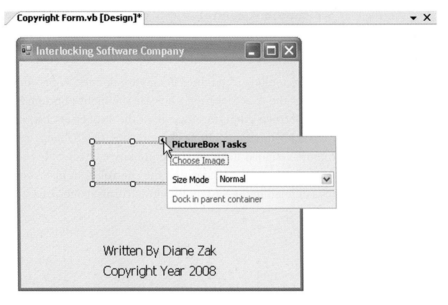

Figure 1-23: Task list for a picture box control

3 Click **Choose Image**. The Select Resource dialog box opens.

4 Verify that the Project resource file radio button is selected in the dialog box.

5 Click the **Import** button. The Open dialog box opens.

The Interlocking Software Company logo is stored in the Logo (Logo.bmp) file, which is contained in the VB2005\Chap01 folder.

6 Open the VB2005\Chap01 folder, then click **Logo** (Logo.bmp) in the list of filenames. Click the **Open** button. The completed Select Resource dialog box is shown in Figure 1-24.

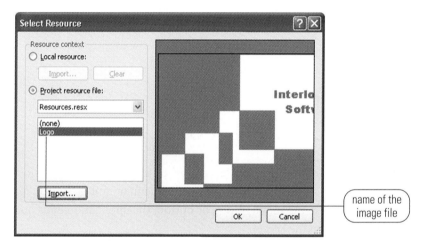

Figure 1-24: Completed Select Resource dialog box

7 Click the **OK** button. A small portion of the image appears in the picture box control on the form, and Copyright_Project.My.Resources.Resources.Logo appears in the control's Image property in the Properties window.

8 Click the **Size Mode** list arrow, and then click **AutoSize** in the list. The designer stretches the picture box control to fit its contents, and AutoSize appears in the SizeMode property in the Properties window.

9 Click the **picture box** control to close the task list.

10 Use the Properties window to set the picture box control's **(Name)** property to **xLogoPictureBox** and its **Location** property to **8, 10**.

11 Click the **form's title bar** to deselect the picture box control. Figure 1-25 shows the Interlocking Software Company logo displayed in the picture box control.

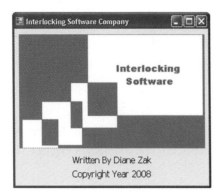

Figure 1-25: Logo displayed in the picture box control

The last tool you learn about in this lesson is the Button tool.

USING THE BUTTON TOOL

Every Windows application should give the user a way to exit the program. Most Windows applications provide either an Exit option on a File menu or an Exit button for this purpose. When the user clicks the menu option or button, the application ends and the user interface is removed from the screen.

Recall that the copyright screen will serve as a splash screen for each custom application created by Interlocking Software. Splash screens typically do not contain an Exit button; rather, they use a Timer control to automatically remove the splash screen after a set period of time. You learn how to include a Timer control in a splash screen in Lesson C. In this lesson, the copyright screen will provide an Exit button.

In Windows applications, a **button control** is used to perform an immediate action when clicked. The OK and Cancel buttons are examples of button controls found in most Windows applications. You instantiate a button using the **Button tool** in the toolbox.

To add a button control to the form:

1 Click the **Button** tool in the toolbox, then drag the tool to the form. Release the mouse button, then position the button control to the immediate right of the label controls. (You do not need to worry about the exact location.) Notice that Button1 System.Windows.Forms.Button appears in the Object box in the Properties window. Button1 is the default name assigned to the first button control added to a form. System.Windows.Forms.Button tells you that the control is an instance of the Button class, which is defined in the System.Windows.Forms namespace.

First, you will assign a more meaningful name to the button control. You then will change the button control's location and font.

2 Set the button control's **(Name)** property to **xExitButton**. Set its **Location** property to **270, 237**. Then set its **Font** property to **Tahoma, 12 pt**.

The button control's Text property determines the caption that appears on the button. Because the button will be used to exit the application, you will change the Text property from Button1 to Exit.

3 Set the button control's **Text** property to **Exit**, then set its **Size** property to **75, 26**. Figure 1-26 shows the button control added to the form.

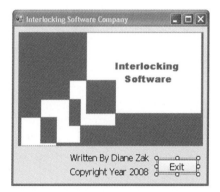

Figure 1-26: Button control added to the form

You will not need the Toolbox and Properties windows, so you can auto-hide them.

4 Auto-hide the Toolbox and Properties windows.

5 Click **File** on the menu bar, and then click **Save All** to save the solution.

Now that the user interface is complete, you can start the copyright screen application to see how it will appear to the user.

STARTING AND ENDING AN APPLICATION

Before you start an application for the first time, you should open the Project Designer window and verify the name of the **startup form**, which is the form that the computer automatically displays each time the application is started. You can open the Project

Designer window by right-clicking My Project in the Solution Explorer window, and then clicking Open on the context menu. Or, you can click Project on the menu bar, and then click *<project name>* Properties on the menu.

To verify the name of the startup form:

1 Right-click **My Project** in the Solution Explorer window, and then click **Open**. The Copyright Project Designer window opens. If necessary, click the Application tab to display the Application pane, which is shown in Figure 1-27.

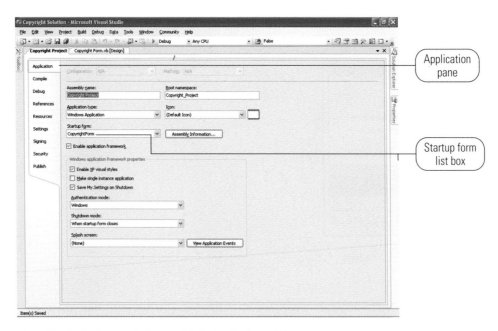

Figure 1-27: Application pane in the Copyright Project Designer window

2 If CopyrightForm does not appear in the Startup form list box, click the **Startup form** list arrow, and then click **CopyrightForm** in the list.

You can start an application by clicking Debug on the menu bar, and then clicking Start Debugging; or, more simply, you can press the F5 key on your keyboard. When you start a Visual Basic application, the computer automatically creates a file that can be run outside of the IDE; for example, it can be run from the Run dialog box in Windows. The file, referred to as an **executable file**, has the same name as the project, but with an .exe file-name extension. For example, the name of the executable file for the Copyright Project is Copyright Project.exe. The computer stores the executable file in the project's

»TIP

In most cases, you give the user only the executable file, because it does not allow him or her to modify the application's code. To allow someone to modify the code, you need to provide the entire solution.

bin\Debug folder. In this case, for example, the Copyright Project.exe file will be stored in the VB2005\Copyright Solution\Copyright Project\bin\Debug folder. You can use the Project Designer window to change the name of the executable file.

To change the name of the executable file, then save the solution and start and end the application:

1   The Copyright Project Designer window should still be open. Change the filename in the Assembly name text box to **Copyright**, as shown in Figure 1-28.

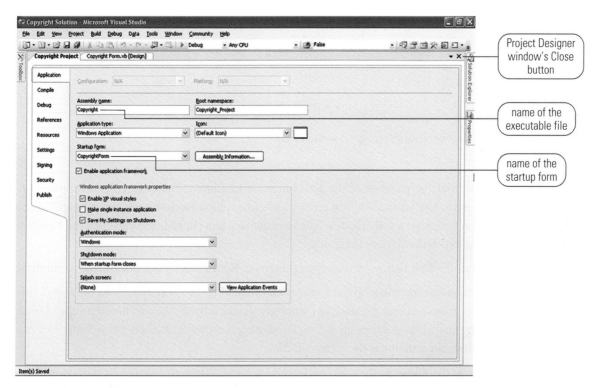

Figure 1-28: Completed Copyright Project Designer window

2   Click the **Save All** button 📇 to save the solution.

3   Close the Copyright Project Designer window by clicking its **Close** button.

4   Click **Debug** on the menu bar, and then click **Start Debugging** to start the application. See Figure 1-29. (Do not be concerned about any windows that appear at the bottom of the screen.)

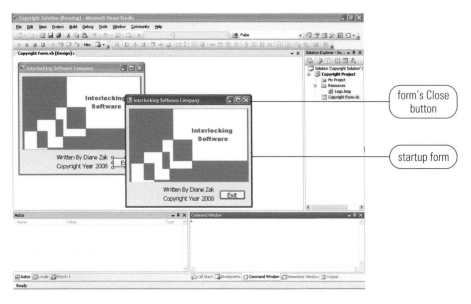

Figure 1-29: Result of starting the copyright screen application

Recall that the purpose of the Exit button is to allow the user to end the application. Currently, the button will not work as intended, because you have not yet entered the instructions that tell the button how to respond when clicked. You can click the Exit button to verify that it does not work.

5 Click the **Exit** button on the copyright screen. Notice that it does not end the application.

At this point, you can stop the application by clicking the Close button on the form's title bar. You also can click the designer window to make it the active window, then click Debug on the menu bar, and then click Stop Debugging; another option is to press Shift+F5 when the designer window is the active window.

6 Click the **Close** button on the form's title bar. When the application ends, you are returned to the IDE.

In the next section, you will learn how to instruct the Exit button to stop the copyright screen application when the button is clicked.

WRITING VISUAL BASIC 2005 CODE

Think about the Windows environment for a moment. Did you ever wonder why the OK and Cancel buttons respond the way they do when you click them, or how the Exit option on the File menu knows to close the application? The answer to these questions is very simple: a programmer gave the menu option and buttons explicit instructions on how to respond to the actions of the user. Those actions—such as clicking, double-clicking, and scrolling—are called **events**. The set of Visual Basic instructions, or code, that tells an object how to respond to an event is called an **event procedure**.

At this point, the Exit button in the copyright screen does not know what it is supposed to do. You tell the button what to do by writing an event procedure for it. You enter the event procedure in the Code Editor window, which is a window you have not yet seen. You can use various methods to open the Code Editor window. For example, you can right-click anywhere on the form (except the form's title bar), and then click View Code on the context menu. You also can click View on the menu bar, and then click Code; or you can press the F7 key on your keyboard. (To use the View menu or the F7 key, the designer window should be the active window.) In addition, you can click the form or a control on the form, then click the Events button in the Properties window, and then double-click the desired event.

To open the Code Editor window:

1   Right-click the **form**, and then click **View Code** on the context menu. The Code Editor window opens in the IDE, as shown in Figure 1-30. Notice that the Code Editor window already contains some Visual Basic instructions, called code.

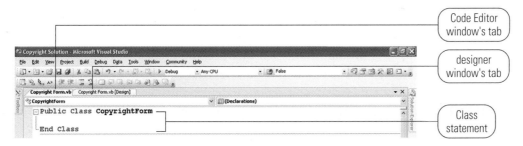

Figure 1-30: Code Editor window opened in the IDE

As Figure 1-30 indicates, the Code Editor window contains the Visual Basic Class statement, which is used to create a class. In this case, the Class statement begins with the `Public Class CopyrightForm` instruction and ends with the `End Class` instruction. Within the Class statement you enter the code to tell the form and its objects how to react to the user's actions.

If the Code Editor window contains many lines of code, you might want to hide the sections of code that you are not presently working with or that you do not want to print. You hide, or collapse, a section (or region) of code by clicking the minus box that appears next to it. To unhide, or expand, the code, you click the plus box that appears next to the code. In the next set of steps, you will try collapsing and expanding a region of code.

To collapse and expand a region of code in the Code Editor window:

1 Click the **minus box** that appears next to the `Public Class CopyrightForm` instruction in the Code Editor window. Clicking the minus box collapses the Class statement, as shown in Figure 1-31.

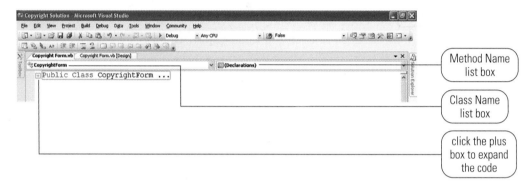

Figure 1-31: Code collapsed in the Code Editor window

2 Click the **plus box** that appears next to the code in the Code Editor window. Clicking the plus box expands the code.

As Figure 1-31 indicates, the Code Editor window contains a Class Name list box and a Method Name list box. The **Class Name list box** lists the names of the objects included in the user interface. The **Method Name list box** lists the events to which the selected object is capable of responding. Recall from the Overview that, in OOP, events are considered behaviors because they represent actions to which the object can respond. (Recall that methods, which are actions that an object can perform, are considered behaviors also.) The Code Editor window exposes an object's behaviors to the programmer.

You use the Class Name and Method Name list boxes to select the object and event, respectively, that you want to code. In this case, for example, you want the Exit button to end the application when the button is clicked. Therefore, you will select xExitButton in the Class Name list box and select Click in the Method Name list box.

To select the xExitButton object's Click event:

1 Click the **Class Name** list arrow, then click **xExitButton** in the list.

2 Click the **Method Name** list arrow, then click **Click** in the list. See Figure 1-32. (Do not be concerned if you cannot view all of the xExitButton control's code. The font used to display the text in the Code Editor window shown in Figure 1-32 was changed to 12-point Microsoft Sans Serif so that you could view all of the code in the figure. It is not necessary for you to change the font.)

»TIP

To change the font used to display text in the Code Editor window, click Tools on the menu bar, and then click Options. Expand the Environment node in the Options dialog box, then click Fonts and Colors. Select Text Editor from the Show settings for list box.

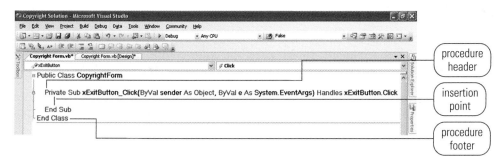

Figure 1-32: xExitButton's Click event procedure shown in the Code Editor window

Notice that, when you select an object and event, additional code automatically appears in the Code Editor window. The additional code is called a **code template**. The Code Editor provides the code template to help you follow the rules of the Visual Basic language. The rules of a programming language are called the language's **syntax**. The first line in the code template is called the **procedure header**, and the last line is called the **procedure footer**.

The procedure header begins with the two keywords `Private Sub`. A **keyword** is a word that has a special meaning in a programming language. The `Private` keyword indicates that the procedure can be used only within the class in which it is defined; in this case, it can be used only within the CopyrightForm class. The `Sub` keyword is an abbreviation of the term **sub procedure**, which, in programming terminology, refers to a block of code that performs a specific task. Following the `Sub` keyword is the name of the object (`xExitButton`), an underscore (`_`), the name of the event (`Click`), and parentheses containing `ByVal sender as Object, ByVal e As System.EventArgs`. The items within the parentheses are called parameters and represent information that is passed to the procedure when it is invoked. For now, you do not need to worry about the parameters; you learn more about parameters later in this book.

Following the items in parentheses in the procedure header is `Handles xExitButton.Click`. This part of the procedure header indicates that the procedure handles (or is associated with) the xExitButton's Click event. In other words, the procedure will be processed when the xExitButton is clicked. As you learn later in this book, you can associate the same procedure with more than one event. To do so, you list each event, separated by commas, in the `Handles` section of the procedure header.

The code template ends with the procedure footer, which contains the keywords `End Sub`. You enter your Visual Basic instructions between the `Private Sub` and `End Sub` lines. In this case, the instructions you enter will tell the xExitButton how to respond to the Click event.

Notice that the keywords in the code appear in a different color from the rest of the code. The Code Editor window displays keywords in a different color to help you quickly identify these elements. In this case, the color coding helps you easily locate the procedure header and footer.

The insertion point located in the xExitButton's Click event procedure indicates where you enter your code for the procedure. The Code Editor automatically indents the line between the procedure header and footer, as shown earlier in Figure 1-32. Indenting the lines within a procedure makes the instructions easier to read and is a common programming practice.

When the user clicks the Exit button on the copyright screen, it indicates that he or she wants to end the application. If an application contains only one form, you stop the application by entering the Me.Close method in a procedure within the form.

THE ME.CLOSE METHOD

You use the **Me.Close method** to instruct the computer to close the current form, which you refer to using the keyword Me. A **method** is a predefined Visual Basic procedure that you can call (or invoke) when needed. You call the Me.Close method by entering the instruction Me.Close() in a procedure in the Code Editor window. In this case, the Me.Close method should be entered in the Exit button's Click event procedure, because you want the method processed when the user clicks the button.

Notice the empty set of parentheses after the method's name in the Me.Close() instruction. The parentheses are required when calling any of the Visual Basic methods; however, depending on the method, the parentheses may or may not be empty.

You can type the Me.Close() instruction on your own; or you can use the IntelliSense feature that is built into the Code Editor. In the next set of steps, you will use the IntelliSense feature.

To code the xExitButton's Click event procedure, then save and start the application:

1 Type **me.** (but don't press Enter). When you type the period, the Code Editor's IntelliSense feature displays a list of properties, methods, and so on from which you can select. If necessary, click the **All** tab. See Figure 1-33. The All tab on the list displays all of the items, whereas the Common tab displays only the most commonly used items.

»TIP

If the current form is the main form in the application, closing it terminates the application.

»TIP

If you forget to enter the parentheses after a method's name, the Code Editor will enter them for you when you move the insertion point to another line in the Code Editor window.

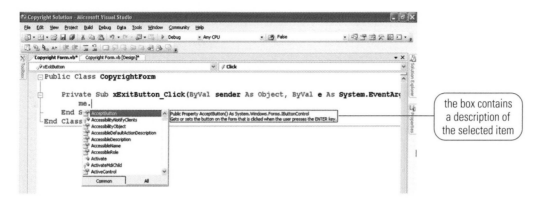

Figure 1-33: The IntelliSense feature displays a list of choices

»HELP? If the list of choices does not appear, the IntelliSense feature on your computer may have been turned off. To turn it on, click Tools on the menu bar, and then click Options to open the Options dialog box. If you are using Visual Basic 2005 Express Edition, select the Show all settings check box. Expand the Text Editor node, and then click Basic. Select the Auto list members check box, then click the OK button to close the Options dialog box.

2 Click the **Common** tab.

3 Type **cl** (but don't press Enter). The IntelliSense feature highlights the Close method in the list, as shown in Figure 1-34.

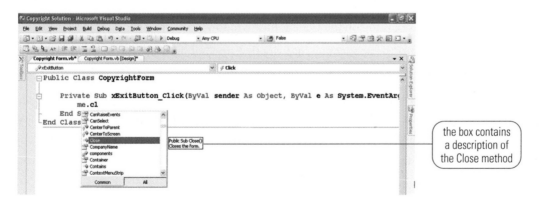

Figure 1-34: The Close method highlighted in the list

4 Press the **Enter** key on your keyboard to select the Close method. The Code Editor enters the Me.Close() instruction in the procedure, as shown in Figure 1-35.

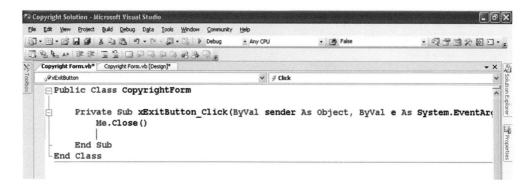

Figure 1-35: Me.Close() instruction entered in the procedure

When the copyright application is running and the user clicks the Exit button, the computer processes the instructions shown in the xExitButton_Click procedure one after another in the order in which they appear in the procedure. In programming, this is referred to as **sequential processing** or as the **sequence structure**. (You learn about two other programming structures [selection and repetition] in future chapters.)

Notice the asterisk (*) that appears on the designer and Code Editor tabs in Figure 1-35. The asterisk indicates that a change was made to the solution since the last time it was saved.

5 Click the **Save All** button to save the solution.

You are finished with the Code Editor window, so you will close it.

6 Click the **Close** button on the Code Editor window's title bar.

Now you will start the application to verify that the Exit button ends the application.

7 Click **Debug** on the menu bar, and then click **Start Debugging**. The copyright screen appears.

8 Click the **Exit** button to end the application. The application ends and you are returned to the designer window.

9 Click **File** on the menu bar, and then click **Close Solution**.

You have completed Lesson B. You can either take a break or complete the end-of-lesson questions and exercises before moving on to the next lesson.

SUMMARY

TO ADD A CONTROL TO A FORM:

» Click a tool in the toolbox, but do not release the mouse button. Hold down the mouse button as you drag the tool to the form, then release the mouse button.

» You also can add a control to a form by clicking a tool in the toolbox and then clicking the form. In addition, you can click a tool in the toolbox, then place the mouse pointer on the form, and then press the left mouse button and drag the mouse pointer until the control is the desired size.

TO DISPLAY TEXT THAT THE USER CANNOT EDIT WHILE THE APPLICATION IS RUNNING:

» Use the Label tool to instantiate a label control, then set the label control's Text property.

TO MOVE A CONTROL TO A DIFFERENT LOCATION ON THE FORM:

» Drag the control to the desired location. You also can set the control's Location, X, and Y properties. In addition, you can select the control and then press and hold down the Control key as you press the up, down, right, or left key on your keyboard.

TO CONTROL THE TYPE, STYLE, AND SIZE OF THE FONT USED TO DISPLAY TEXT IN A CONTROL:

» Set the control's Font property.

TO SELECT MULTIPLE CONTROLS:

» Click the first control you want to select, then Ctrl + click each of the other controls you want to select.

» You also can select a group of controls on the form by placing the mouse pointer slightly above and to the left of the first control you want to select, then pressing the left mouse button and dragging. A dotted rectangle appears as you drag. When all of the controls you want to select are within (or at least touched by) the dotted rectangle, release the mouse button. All of the controls surrounded or touched by the dotted rectangle will be selected.

TO CANCEL THE SELECTION OF ONE OR MORE CONTROLS:

» You cancel the selection of one of the selected controls by pressing and holding down the Control key as you click the control.

» You cancel the selection of all of the selected controls by releasing the Control key and then clicking the form or an unselected control on the form.

TO CENTER ONE OR MORE CONTROLS ON THE FORM:

» Select the controls you want to center. Click Format on the menu bar, point to Center in Form, and then click either Horizontally or Vertically.

TO ALIGN THE BORDERS OF TWO OR MORE CONTROLS ON THE FORM:

» Select the controls you want to align. The first control selected is the reference control (refer to Lesson B's Discovery Exercise 4). Click Format on the menu bar, then point to Align, and then click the appropriate option.

TO MAKE TWO OR MORE CONTROLS ON THE FORM THE SAME SIZE:

» Select the controls you want to size. The first control selected is the reference control (refer to Lesson B's Discovery Exercise 4). Click Format on the menu bar, then point to Make Same Size, and then click the appropriate option.

TO DISPLAY A GRAPHIC IN A CONTROL IN THE USER INTERFACE:

» Use the PictureBox tool to instantiate a picture box control, then use the task box or Properties window to set the control's Image and SizeMode properties.

TO DISPLAY A STANDARD BUTTON THAT PERFORMS AN ACTION WHEN CLICKED:

» Use the Button tool to instantiate a button control.

TO CHANGE THE NAMES OF THE STARTUP FORM AND/OR EXECUTABLE FILE:

» Use the Application pane in the Project Designer window. You can open the Project Designer window by right-clicking My Project in the Solution Explorer window, and then clicking Open on the context menu. Or, you can click Project on the menu bar, and then click <project name> Properties on the menu.

TO START AND STOP AN APPLICATION:

» You can start an application by clicking Debug on the menu bar, and then clicking Start Debugging. You also can press the F5 key on your keyboard.

» You can stop an application by clicking the form's Close button. You also can first make the designer window the active window, and then click Debug on the menu bar and then click Stop Debugging. You also can press Shift+F5 when the designer window is the active window.

TO OPEN THE CODE EDITOR WINDOW:

» Right-click the form, and then click View Code on the context menu. You also can click View on the menu bar, and then click Code; or you can press the F7 key on your keyboard.

(To use the View menu or the F7 key, the designer window should be the active window.) You also can open the Code Editor window by clicking the form or a control on the form, then clicking the Events button in the Properties window, and then double-clicking the desired event. In addition, you can double-click the form or a control on the form to open the Code Editor window and display the object's default event procedure.

TO DISPLAY AN OBJECT'S EVENT PROCEDURE IN THE CODE EDITOR WINDOW:

» Open the Code Editor window. Use the Class Name list box to select the desired object, and then use the Method Name list box to select the desired event.

TO CLOSE THE CURRENT FORM WHILE AN APPLICATION IS RUNNING:

» Enter the `Me.Close()` instruction in an event procedure.

QUESTIONS

1. The purpose of the _____ control is to display text that the user is not allowed to edit while the application is running.

   a. Button   b. DisplayBox

   c. Label   d. PictureBox

2. The caption displayed on a button control is stored in the control's _____ property.

   a. Caption   b. Label

   c. Name   d. Text

3. The Font property allows you to change the _____ of the font used to display text in an object.

   a. type   b. style

   c. size   d. All of the above.

4. The Format menu contains options that allow you to _____.

   a. align two or more controls

   b. center one or more controls horizontally within the form

   c. make two or more controls the same size

   d. All of the above.

5. The Button class is defined in the _____ namespace.

a. System.Windows.Forms

b. System.Windows.Forms.Button

c. Windows.Button

d. Windows.Forms

6. Which of the following statements is false?

a. You can start an application by clicking Debug on the menu bar, and then clicking Start Debugging.

b. The executable file that Visual Basic automatically creates when you start an application has the same name as the solution, but with an .exe extension.

c. You can use the Project Designer window to change the name of an application's executable file.

d. You can use the Project Designer window to select the startup form.

7. You can use the _____ method to terminate a running application.

a. Me.Close

b. Me.Done

c. Me.Finish

d. Me.Stop

8. Define the term "syntax."

9. Explain the purpose of the Class Name and Method Name list boxes in the Code Editor window.

10. Define the term "keyword."

EXERCISES

1. In this exercise, you add controls to a form. You also change some of the properties of the form and its controls.

a. If necessary, start Visual Studio 2005 or Visual Basic 2005 Express Edition.

b. Open the Mechanics Solution (Mechanics Solution.sln) file, which is contained in the VB2005\Chap01\Mechanics Solution folder. If necessary, use the View menu to open the designer window.

    c. Assign the filename Main Form.vb to the form file object.

    d. Assign the name MainForm to the form.

    e. The form's title bar should say IMA. Set the appropriate property.

    f. The form should be centered on the screen when it first appears. Set the appropriate property.

    g. Add a label control to the form. The label control should display the text "International Mechanics Association" (without the quotation marks). Set the appropriate property.

    h. Display the label control's text in italics using the Tahoma font. Change the size of the text to 12 points.

    i. The label control should be located 16 pixels from the top of the form.

    j. Center the label control horizontally on the form.

    k. Add a button control to the form. Change the button control's name to xExitButton.

    l. The button control should display the text "Exit" (without the quotation marks). Set the appropriate property.

    m. Display the button control's text using the Tahoma font. Change the size of the text to 12 points.

    n. The button control should be located 200 pixels from the left border of the form, and 240 pixels from the top of the form.

    o. Open the Code Editor window. Enter the `Me.Close()` instruction in the xExitButton's Click event procedure.

    p. Display the Mechanics Project Designer window. Verify that the name of the start-up form is MainForm. Also use the Assembly name box to change the executable file's name to IMA.

    q. Save the solution. Start the application, then use the Exit button to stop the application.

    r. Close the solution.

2. In this exercise, you create the user interface shown in Figure 1-36.

    a. If necessary, start Visual Studio 2005 or Visual Basic 2005 Express Edition.

    b. Create the user interface shown in Figure 1-36. You can use any font type, style, and size for the label controls. Name the solution Costello Solution, and name the project Costello Project. Save the application in the VB2005\Chap01 folder.

Figure 1-36

    c. Name the form file Main Form.vb.

    d. The MainForm should be centered on the screen when the application is started.

    e. Code the Exit button so that it closes the application when it is clicked.

    f. Open the Project Designer window. Verify that the name of the startup form is MainForm. Change the executable file's name to Costello Motors.

    g. Save the solution. Start the application, then use the Exit button to stop the application.

    h. Close the solution.

3. In this exercise, you create the user interface shown in Figure 1-37.

    a. If necessary, start Visual Studio 2005 or Visual Basic 2005 Express Edition.

    b. Create the user interface shown in Figure 1-37. You can use any font type, style, and size for the label control and Exit button. Name the solution Tabatha Solution, and name the project Tabatha Project. Save the application in the VB2005\Chap01 folder.

Figure 1-37

c. Name the form file Main Form.vb. Name the Exit button xExitButton. Center the form on the screen when the application is started.

d. Code the Exit button so that it terminates the application when it is clicked.

e. Verify that the name of the startup form is MainForm. Change the executable file's name to Tabatha.

f. Save the solution. Start the application, then use the Exit button to stop the application.

g. Close the solution.

DISCOVERY EXERCISE

4. In this exercise, you learn about the Format menu's Align and Make Same Size options.

a. If necessary, start Visual Studio 2005 or Visual Basic 2005 Express Edition.

b. Open the Jerrods Solution (Jerrods Solution.sln) file, which is contained in the VB2005\Chap01\Jerrods Solution folder. If necessary, use the View menu to open the designer window.

c. Click one of the button controls on the form, then press and hold down the Ctrl (or Control) key as you click the remaining two button controls.

Notice that the sizing handles on the first button that you selected are white, while the sizing handles on the other two buttons are black. The Align and Make Same Size options on the Format menu use the control with the white sizing handles as the reference control when aligning and sizing the selected controls. First, practice with the Align option by aligning the three buttons by their left borders.

d. Click Format, point to Align, and then click Lefts. The left borders of the last two buttons you selected are aligned with the left border of the first button you selected.

The Make Same Size option makes the selected objects the same height, width, or both. Here again, the first object you select determines the size.

e. Click the form to deselect the three buttons. Click Button2, then Ctrl+click Button3, and then Ctrl+click Button1. Click Format, point to Make Same Size, and then click Both. The height and width of the last two controls you selected now match the height and width of the first control you selected.

f. Click the form to deselect the buttons.

g. Save and then close the solution.

LESSON C
OBJECTIVES

AFTER STUDYING LESSON C, YOU SHOULD
BE ABLE TO:

» Set the properties of a timer control

» Delete a control from the form

» Delete code from the Code Editor window

» Code the timer control's Tick event procedure

» Remove and/or disable a form's Minimize, Maximize,
and Close buttons

» Prevent the user from sizing a form

» Print the project's code

COMPLETING THE COPYRIGHT SCREEN

USING THE TIMER TOOL

Recall that the copyright screen will serve as a splash screen for each custom application created by Interlocking Software. Splash screens typically do not contain an Exit button; instead, they use a timer control to automatically remove the splash screen after a set period of time. You instantiate a timer control using the **Timer tool** in the toolbox. In this lesson, you remove the Exit button from the copyright screen and replace it with a timer control. First, you will open the Copyright Solution from Lesson B.

To open the Copyright Solution:

1 If necessary, start Visual Studio 2005 or Visual Basic 2005 Express Edition and close the Start Page window.

2 *If you are using Visual Studio 2005*, click **File** on the menu bar, then point to **Open**, and then click **Project/Solution** to open the Open Project dialog box.

   If you are using Visual Basic 2005 Express Edition, click **File** on the menu bar, and then click **Open Project**.

3 Open the **Copyright Solution** (Copyright Solution.sln) file, which is contained in the VB2005\Chap01\Copyright Solution folder. If necessary, open the designer window.

4 If necessary, permanently display the Toolbox and Properties windows, and auto-hide the Solution Explorer window.

The Timer tool is located in the Components section of the toolbox, and it is used to instantiate timer controls. The purpose of a **timer control** is to process code at one or more regular intervals. The length of each interval is specified in milliseconds and entered in the timer's **Interval property**. A **millisecond** is $\frac{1}{1000}$ of a second; in other words, there are 1000 milliseconds in a second.

A timer's **Enabled property**, which can be set to either the Boolean value True or the Boolean value False, indicates the timer's state. When its Enabled property is set to True, the timer is running; when it is set to False, the timer is stopped. If the timer is running, its **Tick event** occurs each time an interval has elapsed. Therefore, you enter the code you want processed in the timer's Tick event procedure. If the timer is stopped, on the other hand, the Tick event does not occur and the code entered in the Tick event procedure is not processed.

»TIP

The Boolean values (True and False) are named after the English mathematician George Boole.

When you instantiate a timer control, the control does not appear on the form in the designer window. Instead, it is placed in the component tray, which is a special area in the IDE. The **component tray** stores all controls that do not appear in the user interface when an application is running. In other words, the user will not see the timer when the splash screen appears on the screen.

To add a timer control to the copyright screen, and then change its properties:

1 If necessary, expand the Components node in the toolbox. Click the **Timer** tool in the Components section of the toolbox, and then drag the tool to the form. (Do not worry about the exact location.) When you release the mouse button, a timer control appears in the component tray, as shown in Figure 1-38.

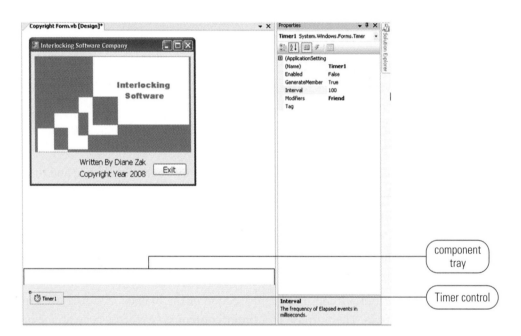

Figure 1-38: Timer control placed in the component tray

2 Set the timer control's **(Name)** property to **xExitTimer**, and set its **Enabled** property to **True**.

You will have the timer control end the application after eight seconds, which are 8000 milliseconds.

3 Set the timer control's **Interval** property to **8000**.

4 Auto-hide the Toolbox and Properties windows.

Now that you have a timer control on the form, you no longer need the Exit button, so you can delete it and its associated code. You then will enter the Me.Close method in the timer control's Tick event procedure.

To delete the xExitButton and its code, and then code the xExitTimer:

1 Click the **Exit** button to select it, then press **Delete** to delete the control from the form.

Deleting a control from the form does not delete the control's code, which remains in the Code Editor window.

2 Open the Code Editor window by right-clicking the **form**, and then clicking **View Code**. Select the entire Click event procedure for the xExitButton, as shown in Figure 1-39. (Do not be concerned if you cannot view all of the xExitButton's code. The font used to display the text in the Code Editor window shown in Figure 1-39 was changed to 12-point Microsoft Sans Serif so that you could view all of the code in the figure. It is not necessary for you to change the font.)

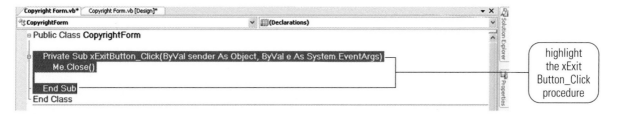

Figure 1-39: The xExitButton's Click event procedure selected in the Code Editor window

3 Press **Delete** to delete the selected code from the Code Editor window.

Now you will enter the Me.Close method in the xExitTimer's Tick event procedure.

4 Click the **Class Name** list arrow, and then click **xExitTimer** in the list. Click the **Method Name** list arrow, and then click **Tick** in the list. The xExitTimer's Tick event procedure appears in the Code Editor window.

5 Type **me.close( )** and press **Enter**. See Figure 1-40. (Recall that the font used to display the text shown in the Code Editor was changed to 12-point Microsoft Sans Serif.)

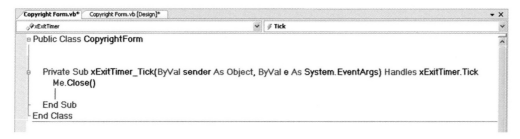

Figure 1-40: Code entered in the xExitTimer's Tick event procedure

Now you will save the solution and then start the application.

6 Click the **Save All** button 🖫 to save the solution, and then press the **F5** key on your keyboard to start the application. The CopyrightForm appears on the screen.

7 Place your mouse pointer ⬚ on the right border of the form until ⬚ becomes ↔, then drag the form's border to the left. Notice that you can size the form while the application is running. As a general rule, the user typically is not allowed to change the size of a splash screen. You can prevent the user from sizing the form by changing the form's FormBorderStyle property, which you will do in the next set of steps.

When eight seconds have elapsed, the application ends and the copyright screen is removed from view.

8 Click the **Copyright Form.vb [Design]** tab to make the designer window the active window.

Next, you will learn about the FormBorderStyle property of a form.

SETTING THE FORMBORDERSTYLE PROPERTY

A form's **FormBorderStyle property** determines the border style of the form. Figure 1-41 lists the valid settings for the FormBorderStyle property and provides a brief description of the border provided by each setting.

FormBorderStyle setting	Description of the border
Fixed3D	fixed, three-dimensional
FixedDialog	fixed, thick dialog style
FixedSingle	fixed, thin line
FixedToolWindow	fixed, tool window style
None	no border
Sizable	sizable, normal style (default setting)
SizableToolWindow	sizable, tool window style

Figure 1-41: FormBorderStyle settings

For most applications, you will leave the FormBorderStyle setting at its default value, Sizable. When the FormBorderStyle property is set to Sizable, the user can drag the form's borders to change the form's size while the application is running. In applications where you want to prevent the user from sizing the form, you can set the FormBorderStyle property to None or to any of the fixed settings shown in Figure 1-41; splash screens, for example, typically use either the None setting or the FixedSingle setting. When the FormBorderStyle property is set to None, no border is drawn around the form. Setting the FormBorderStyle property to FixedSingle, on the other hand, draws a fixed, thin line around the form. You will set the copyright screen's FormBorderStyle property to FixedSingle.

To change the FormBorderStyle property, then save and start the application:

1 Click the **form's title bar** to select the form.

2 Set the **FormBorderStyle** property to **FixedSingle**.

3 Save the solution, then start the application.

4 Try to size the form by dragging one of its borders. You will notice that you cannot size the form using its border.

5 After eight seconds have elapsed, the application ends. Press the **F5** key to start the application again. Notice that the copyright screen's title bar contains a Minimize button, a Maximize button, and a Close button; as a general rule, most splash screens do not contain these elements. You will learn how to remove the elements, as well as the title bar itself, in the next section. Here again, the application ends after eight seconds have elapsed.

Next, you learn about a form's MinimizeBox, MaximizeBox, and ControlBox properties.

THE MINIMIZEBOX, MAXIMIZEBOX, AND CONTROLBOX PROPERTIES

You can use a form's **MinimizeBox property** to disable the Minimize button that appears on the form's title bar. Similarly, you can use the **MaximizeBox property** to disable the Maximize button. You experiment with both properties in the next set of steps.

To experiment with the MinimizeBox and MaximizeBox properties:

1 If necessary, click the **form's title bar** to select the form.

First, you will disable the Minimize button.

2 Set the form's **MinimizeBox** property to **False**. Notice that the Minimize button appears dimmed (grayed-out) on the title bar. This indicates that the button is not available for use.

Now you will enable the Minimize button and disable the Maximize button.

3 Set the **MinimizeBox** property to **True**, then set the **MaximizeBox** property to **False**. Now only the Maximize button appears dimmed (grayed-out) on the title bar.

Now observe what happens if both the MinimizeBox and MaximizeBox properties are set to False.

4 Set the **MinimizeBox** property to **False**. (The MaximizeBox property is already set to False.) Notice that when both properties are set to False, the buttons are not disabled; instead, they are removed from the title bar.

Now return the buttons to their original state.

5 Set the **MinimizeBox** and **MaximizeBox** properties to **True**.

Unlike most applications, splash screens typically do not contain a title bar. You can remove the title bar by setting the form's **ControlBox property** to False, and then removing the text from its Text property. You will try this next.

To remove the title bar from the copyright screen:

1 Set the form's **ControlBox** property to **False**. Notice that setting this property to False removes the title bar elements (icon and buttons) from the form; however, it does not remove the title bar itself. To remove the title bar, you must delete the contents of the form's Text property.

2 Delete the contents of the form's Text property.

> **»HELP?** You can delete the contents of the Text property by clicking Text in the Properties list, then pressing the Backspace key, and then pressing Enter. Or you can select the text in the Text property, then press the Delete key, and then press Enter.

3 Save the solution, then start the application. The copyright screen appears without a title bar, as shown in Figure 1-42. The application ends after eight seconds have elapsed.

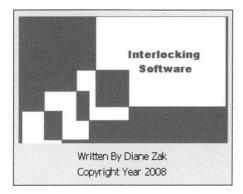

Figure 1-42: Completed copyright screen

Before ending this lesson, you will learn how to print the application.

PRINTING YOUR CODE

You always should print a copy of your application's code, because the printout will help you understand and maintain the application in the future. To print the code, the Code Editor window must be the active (current) window.

To print the copyright screen's code:

1 Click the **Copyright Form.vb** tab to make the Code Editor window the active window.

2 Click **File** on the menu bar, and then click **Print**. The Print dialog box opens. See Figure 1-43.

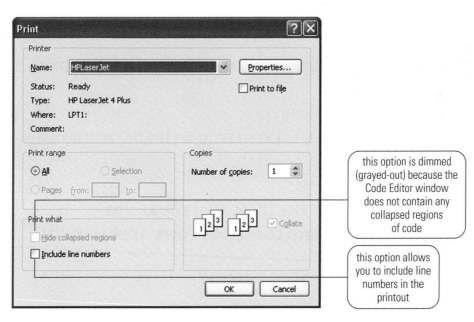

this option is dimmed (grayed-out) because the Code Editor window does not contain any collapsed regions of code

this option allows you to include line numbers in the printout

Figure 1-43: Print dialog box

Notice that you can include line numbers in the printout. You also can choose to hide the collapsed regions of code. Currently, the Hide collapsed regions check box is grayed-out; this is because the Code Editor window does not contain any collapsed regions of code.

3 If your computer is connected to a printer, click the **OK** button to begin printing; otherwise, click the **Cancel** button. If you clicked the OK button, your printer prints the code.

4 Close the Code Editor window by clicking the **Close** button on its title bar.

5 Click **File** on the menu bar, and then click **Close Solution** to close the solution.

6 Click **File** on the menu bar, and then click **Exit** to exit Visual Studio 2005 or Visual Basic 2005 Express Edition.

You have completed Lesson C and Chapter 1. You can either take a break or complete the end-of lesson questions and exercises.

SUMMARY

TO PROCESS CODE AT SPECIFIED INTERVALS OF TIME:
» Use the Timer tool to instantiate a timer control. Set the timer's Interval property to the number of milliseconds for each interval. Set the timer's Enabled property to True to turn the timer on. Enter the code in the timer's Tick event procedure.

TO DELETE A CONTROL:
» Select the control you want to delete, then press Delete. If the control contains code, open the Code Editor window and delete the code contained in the control's event procedures.

TO ENABLE/DISABLE THE MINIMIZE BUTTON ON THE FORM'S TITLE BAR:
» Set the form's MinimizeBox property.

TO ENABLE/DISABLE THE MAXIMIZE BUTTON ON THE FORM'S TITLE BAR:
» Set the form's MaximizeBox property.

TO CONTROL WHETHER THE ICON, AS WELL AS THE MINIMIZE, MAXIMIZE, AND CLOSE BUTTONS, APPEAR IN THE FORM'S TITLE BAR:
» Set the form's ControlBox property.

TO CONTROL THE BORDER STYLE OF THE FORM:

» Set the form's FormBorderStyle property.

TO PRINT THE VISUAL BASIC CODE:

» Open the Code Editor window. Collapse any code that you do not want to print. Click File on the menu bar, and then click Print. If you don't want to print the collapsed code, select the Hide collapsed regions check box. If you want to print line numbers, select the Include line numbers check box. Click the OK button in the Print dialog box.

QUESTIONS

1. You can use a _____ control to process code at regular time intervals.

   a. clock   b. stopwatch

   c. timer   d. watch

2. The _____ property determines whether an object can respond to an event.

   a. Enabled   b. Event

   c. PermitResponse   d. Respond

3. The code in a timer control's _____ event procedure is processed after each time interval has elapsed.

   a. Interval   b. Tick

   c. Timed   d. Timer

4. Ten seconds equals _____ milliseconds.

   a. 100   b. 1000

   c. 10,000   d. 100,000

5. Which of the following is false?

   a. When you add a timer control to a form, the control appears in the component tray.

   b. The user can see a timer control while the application is running.

   c. You can delete a control from the form by clicking it and then pressing Delete.

   d. The number entered in a timer control's Interval property represents the number of milliseconds for each interval.

6. To disable the Minimize button on a form's title bar, set the form's _____ property to False.

   a. ButtonMinimize   b. Minimize

   c. MinimizeBox   d. MinimizeButton

7. The _____ property determines whether the user can drag a form's borders while the application is running.

   a. BorderStyle   b. Drag

   c. FormBorder   d. FormBorderStyle

8. You can remove the Minimize, Maximize, and Close buttons from a form's title bar by setting the form's _____ property to False.

   a. ControlBox   b. ControlButton

   c. TitleBar   d. TitleBarElements

9. Explain how you print a project's code.

10. Explain how you delete a control that contains code.

EXERCISES

1. In this exercise, you modify an existing form by replacing its button control with a timer control.

   a. If necessary, start Visual Studio 2005 or Visual Basic 2005 Express Edition.

   b. Open the Jefferson Solution (Jefferson Solution.sln) file, which is contained in the VB2005\Chap01\Jefferson Solution folder. If necessary, open the designer window.

   c. Delete the Exit button from the form, then delete the xExitButton's code from the Code Editor window.

   d. Return to the designer window. Add a timer control to the form. Change the timer control's name to xExitTimer.

   e. Set the timer control's Enabled property to True.

   f. The timer control should end the application after 10 seconds have elapsed. Set the appropriate property. Then, enter the `Me.Close()` instruction in the appropriate event procedure in the Code Editor window.

g. Save the solution, then start the application. After 10 seconds have elapsed, the application ends.

h. Remove the elements (icon and buttons) from the form's title bar.

i. Delete the text that appears in the form's title bar.

j. Set the form's FormBorderStyle property to FixedSingle.

k. Save the solution, then start the application. After 10 seconds, the application should end.

l. Close the solution.

2. In this exercise, you design your own user interface.

a. If necessary, start Visual Studio 2005 or Visual Basic 2005 Express Edition.

b. Create your own splash screen. Name the solution Splash Solution, and name the project Splash Project. Save the application in the VB2005\Chap01 folder.

c. Save the solution, then start the application.

d. When the application ends, close the solution.

DISCOVERY EXERCISE

3. In this exercise, you learn how to enter an assignment statement in an event procedure.

a. If necessary, start Visual Studio 2005 or Visual Basic 2005 Express Edition.

b. Create a Visual Basic Windows-based application. Name the solution OnOff Solution, and name the project OnOff Project. Save the application in the VB2005\Chap01 folder.

c. Assign the filename Main Form.vb to the form file object.

d. Assign the name MainForm to the form.

e. Add a picture box control and three buttons to the form. (The location and size of the controls are not important.) Name the controls xIconPictureBox, xOnButton, xOffButton, and xExitButton.

f. Include any graphic in the picture box control.

g. The captions for the three buttons should be On, Off, and Exit. Change the appropriate property for each button.

h. The Exit button should end the application when clicked. Enter the appropriate code in the Code Editor window.

i. Display the xOffButton's Click event procedure in the Code Editor window. In the procedure, enter the instruction `Me.xIconPictureBox.Visible = False`. This instruction is called an assignment statement, because it assigns a value to a container. In this case, the container is the Visible property of the xIconPictureBox control. When you click the xOffButton, the `Me.xIconPictureBox.Visible = False` instruction will hide the picture box from view.

j. Display the xOnButton's Click event procedure in the Code Editor window. In the procedure, enter an instruction that will display the picture box.

k. Save the solution, then start the application. Use the Off button to hide the picture box, then use the On button to display the picture box. Finally, use the Exit button to end the application.

l. Close the solution.

DISCOVERY EXERCISE

4. In this exercise, you learn how to display a graphic on the face of a button control. (This exercise assumes that you have completed Discovery Exercise 3.)

a. Use Windows to make a copy of the OnOff Solution folder, which is contained in the VB2005\Chap01 folder. Rename the folder Modified OnOff Solution.

b. If necessary, start Visual Studio 2005 or Visual Basic 2005 Express Edition.

c. Open the OnOff Solution (OnOff Solution.sln) file contained in the VB2005\Chap01\Modified OnOff Solution folder. Open the designer window.

You use a button's Image property to specify the graphic you want displayed on the face of the button. You use a button's ImageAlign property to specify the graphic's alignment on the button.

d. Click the On button. Set the Image property to any graphic file.

e. Set the On button's ImageAlign property to TopLeft. (*Hint*: When you click the ImageAlign property's list arrow, nine buttons will appear in the list. Select the button in the top left corner.)

f. Set the Image and ImageAlign properties of the Off and Exit buttons. (Use any graphics for the Image properties.)

g. Save the solution, then start the application. Test each button, and then close the solution.

DISCOVERY EXERCISE

5. In this exercise, you learn how to display a tooltip.

   a. If necessary, start Visual Studio 2005 or Visual Basic 2005 Express Edition.

   b. Open the Tooltip Solution (Tooltip Solution.sln) file, which is contained in the VB2005\Chap01\Tooltip Solution folder. If necessary, open the designer window.

   c. Click the ToolTip tool in the toolbox, then drag the tool to the form. Notice that a tooltip control appears in the component tray rather than on the form.

   d. Click the xExitButton to select it. Set the button's ToolTip on ToolTip1 property to "Ends the application." (without the quotation marks).

   e. Save the solution, then start the application. Hover your mouse pointer over the Exit button. The tooltip "Ends the application." appears in a tooltip box.

   f. Click the Exit button to end the application.

   g. Close the solution.

DEBUGGING EXERCISE

6. In this exercise, you debug an existing application.

   a. If necessary, start Visual Studio 2005 or Visual Basic 2005 Express Edition.

   b. Open the Debug Solution (Debug Solution.sln) file, which is contained in the VB2005\Chap01\Debug Solution folder. If necessary, open the designer window.

   c. Start the application. Click the Exit button. Notice that the Exit button does not end the application.

   d. Click the Close button on the form's title bar to end the application.

   e. Locate and then correct the error.

   f. Save the solution, then start the application. Click the Exit button, which should end the application.

   g. Close the solution.

2

DESIGNING APPLICATIONS

CREATING AN ORDER SCREEN

During your second week at Interlocking Software, you and Chris Statton, the senior programmer, meet with the sales manager of Skate-Away Sales. The sales manager, Jacques Cousard, tells you that his company sells skateboards by phone. The skateboards are priced at $100 each and are available in two colors—yellow and blue. The company employs 20 salespeople to answer the phones. The salespeople record each order on a form that contains the customer's name, address, and the number of blue and yellow skateboards ordered. The salespeople then calculate the total number of skateboards ordered and the total price of the skateboards, including a 5% sales tax.

Mr. Cousard feels that having the salespeople manually perform the necessary calculations is much too time-consuming and prone to errors. He wants Interlocking to create a computerized application that will solve the problems of the current order-taking system.

SOLVING THE PROBLEM USING A PROCEDURE-ORIENTED APPROACH

As you learned in the Overview, the first high-level languages were used to create procedure-oriented programs. When writing a procedure-oriented program, the programmer concentrates on the major tasks that the program needs to perform. The programmer must instruct the computer every step of the way, from the start of each task to its completion. The procedure-oriented approach to problem solving requires a programmer to think in a step-by-step, top-to-bottom fashion. Planning tools such as flowcharts and pseudocode make this approach easier. A **flowchart** uses standardized symbols to show the steps needed to solve a problem, whereas **pseudocode** uses English phrases to describe the required steps. Some programmers prefer to use flowcharts, while others prefer pseudocode. You learn more about pseudocode and flowcharts in Lesson C of this chapter, because these planning tools also are useful in object-oriented programming.

First, you will take a look at a procedure-oriented approach to solving Skate-Away's problem. Figure 2-1 shows the solution written in pseudocode.

---

1. get customer name, street address, city, state, ZIP code, number of blue skateboards ordered, number of yellow skateboards ordered

2. calculate total skateboards ordered = number of blue skateboards ordered + number of yellow skateboards ordered

3. calculate total price = total skateboards ordered * $100 * 105%

4. print customer name, street address, city, state, ZIP code, number of blue skateboards ordered, number of yellow skateboards ordered, total skateboards ordered, total price

5. end

Figure 2-1: Pseudocode for the procedure-oriented solution

Notice that the pseudocode indicates the sequence of steps the computer must take to process an order. Using the pseudocode as a guide, the programmer then translates the solution into a language that the computer can understand. Figure 2-2 shows the pseudocode translated into Microsoft's QuickBASIC language. QuickBASIC is a predecessor of the Visual Basic programming language and is used to create procedure-oriented programs.

```
Ans$ = "Y"
While Ans$ = "Y" or Ans$ = "y"
    Input "Enter the customer's name", Names$
    Input "Enter the street address:", Address$
    Input "Enter the city:", City$
    Input "Enter the state:", State$
    Input "Enter the zip code:", Zip$
    Input "Enter the number of blue skateboards:", Blue
    Input "Enter the number of yellow skateboards:", Yellow
    Totboards = Blue + Yellow
    Totprice = Totboards * 100 * 1.05
    Print "Customer name:", Names$
    Print "Address:", Address$
    Print "City:", City$
    Print "State:", State$
    Print "Zip:", Zip$
    Print "Blue skateboards:", Blue
    Print "Yellow skateboards:", Yellow
    Print "Total skateboards:", Totboards
    Print "Total price: $", Totprice
    Input "Do you want to enter another order? Enter Y if you do, or
    N if you don't.", Ans$
Wend

End
```

Figure 2-2: Procedure-oriented program written in QuickBASIC

In the next set of steps, you will practice entering an order using this procedure-oriented program.

To use the procedure-oriented program to enter an order:

1 Use the Run command on the Windows Start menu to run the **Procedure (Procedure.exe)** file, which is contained in the VB2005\Chap02 folder. A prompt requesting the customer's name appears on the screen.

Sport Warehouse wants to place an order for 10 blue skateboards and 20 yellow skateboards.

2 Type **Sport Warehouse** and press **Enter**. A prompt requesting the street address appears on the screen.

3 Type **123 Main** and press **Enter**, then type **Glendale** for the city and press **Enter**, then type **IL** for the state and press **Enter**, and then type **60134** for the ZIP code and press **Enter**. The program now prompts you to enter the number of blue skateboards ordered.

4 Type **10** as the number of blue skateboards ordered, then press **Enter**. A prompt requesting the number of yellow skateboards ordered appears next.

5 Type **20** as the number of yellow skateboards ordered, then press **Enter**. The program computes and displays the total skateboards ordered (30) and the total price of the order ($3,150.00). (Recall that skateboards are $100 each and there is a 5% sales tax.) See Figure 2-3.

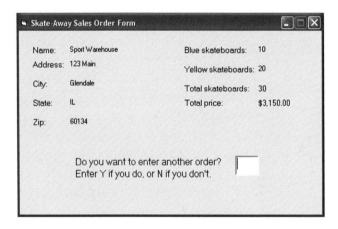

Figure 2-3: Results of the procedure-oriented program

Notice that the screen also contains a prompt that asks whether you want to enter another order.

6 Type **n** and press **Enter** to end the program.

Although Skate-Away Sales could use the procedure-oriented program to record its phone orders, the program has one very important limitation that is inherent in all procedure-oriented programs: the user has little (if any) control over the processing of the program. For example, recall that you could not control the sequence in which the order information was entered. What if the customer wants to order the yellow skateboards before the blue skateboards? Also recall that you could not change the information once you entered it. What if the customer changes his or her mind about the number of blue skateboards to order? And, finally, recall that you had no control over when the program calculated the total order and the total price. What if the customer wants to know the total price of the blue skateboards before placing the yellow skateboard order?

SOLVING THE PROBLEM USING AN OBJECT-ORIENTED (OO) APPROACH

In object-oriented languages, the emphasis of a program is on the **objects** included in the user interface (such as buttons or list boxes) and the **events** that occur on those objects (such as clicking or double-clicking). Unlike the procedure-oriented approach to problem solving, the object-oriented (OO) approach does not view the solution as a step-by-step, top-to-bottom process. Instead, the OO programmer's goal is to give the user as much control over the program as possible.

When using the OO approach to problem solving, the programmer begins by identifying the tasks the application needs to perform. Then the programmer decides on the appropriate objects to which the tasks will be assigned and on any events necessary to trigger the objects to perform their assigned task(s). For example, the copyright screen you created in Chapter 1 had to provide a way to end the application. Recall that you assigned the task to the Exit button in Lesson B, and to the timer control in Lesson C. The event that triggered the Exit button to perform its assigned task was the Click event. The event that triggered the timer to perform its assigned task was the Tick event. In this book, you will use a **TOE (Task, Object, Event) chart** to assist you in planning your object-oriented programs.

Before you learn how to plan an OO application, you will run an OO application written in Visual Basic 2005 and designed to solve Skate-Away's problem.

To run the OO application:

1 Use the Run command on the Start menu to run the **OO (OO.exe)** file, which is contained in the VB2005\Chap02 folder. The order screen shown in Figure 2-4 appears.

In addition to the picture box, label, and button controls (all of which you learned about in Chapter 1), the order screen contains seven text boxes. You use a **text box** to provide areas in the form where the user can enter information. Notice that the computer displays an insertion point in the first text box shown in Figure 2-4. The label control to the left of the text box identifies the information the user should enter. In this case, the user should enter the customer's name.

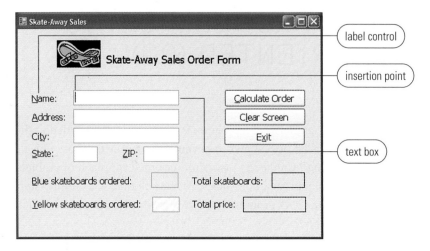

Figure 2-4: Order screen created by the OO application

2 Type **Sport Warehouse** as the customer's name, then press **Tab** twice. The insertion point appears in the City text box.

3 Type **Glendale** as the city, then press **Shift+Tab** (press and hold down the Shift key as you press the Tab key) to move the insertion point to the Address text box. Notice that the OO application allows you to enter the order information in any order.

4 Type **123 Main** as the address, then press **Tab** twice.

5 Type **IL** as the state, then press **Tab**.

6 Type **60134** as the ZIP code, and then press **Tab** to position the insertion point in the Blue skateboards ordered text box.

7 Type **10** as the number of blue skateboards ordered, then click the **Calculate Order** button. The Calculate Order button calculates and displays the total skateboards ordered (10) and the total price ($1,050.00). Notice that the OO application allows you to tell the customer the cost of the blue skateboards before the yellow skateboard order is placed.

8 Click the **Yellow skateboards ordered** text box, type **20**, and then click the **Calculate Order** button. The application recalculates the total skateboards ordered (30) and the total price ($3,150.00).

9 Change the number of blue skateboards ordered from 10 to **20**, then click the **Calculate Order** button. The application recalculates the total skateboards (40) and the total price ($4,200.00). See Figure 2-5.

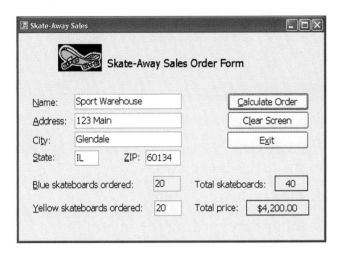

Figure 2-5: Completed order using the OO program

Looking closely at the Skate-Away Sales interface shown in Figure 2-5, you will notice that the captions that identify each button and text box contain an underlined letter, called an access key. An **access key** allows the user to select an object using the Alt key in combination with a letter or number. For example, when the salesperson is finished with an order, he or she can clear the screen either by clicking the Clear Screen button or by pressing the Alt key along with the letter l, which is the Clear Screen button's access key.

To clear the order screen, and then exit the application:

1 Press **Alt + l** (the letter "l") to select the Clear Screen button. The button removes the previous customer's information from the order screen, and it places the insertion point in the Name text box.

> **▶▶HELP?** Pressing Alt + l means to press and hold down the Alt key as you type the letter l. Be sure to type the letter l, and not the number 1.

2 Press **Alt + x** (or click the **Exit** button) to end the application.

Unlike the procedure-oriented program, the OO program gives users a great deal of control. Users can enter information in any order, change what they entered at any time, and calculate a subtotal whenever they like.

In Lesson A, you will learn how a Visual Basic 2005 programmer plans an OO application. Then, in Lessons B and C, you will create the OO application that you just viewed.

LESSON A
OBJECTIVES

AFTER STUDYING LESSON A, YOU SHOULD
BE ABLE TO:

» Plan an OO application in Visual Basic 2005

» Complete a TOE (Task, Object, Event) chart

» Follow the Windows standards regarding the layout and
labeling of controls

PLANNING AN OBJECT-ORIENTED (OO) APPLICATION IN VISUAL BASIC 2005

CREATING AN OO APPLICATION

The process a programmer follows when creating an OO application is similar to the process a builder follows when building a home. Both processes are shown in Figure 2-6.

A builder's process	A programmer's process
1. Meet with the client	1. Meet with the client
2. Plan the home (blueprint)	2. Plan the application (TOE chart)
3. Build the frame	3. Build the user interface
4. Complete the home	4. Code the application
5. Inspect the home and fix any problems	5. Test and debug the application
6. Assemble the documentation	6. Assemble the documentation

Figure 2-6: Processes used by a builder and a programmer

As Figure 2-6 shows, both the builder and the programmer first meet with the client to discuss the client's wants and needs. They then create a plan (blueprint) for the project. After the client approves the plan, the builder builds the home's frame; likewise, the programmer builds the user interface, which is the application's frame. Once the frame is built, the builder completes the home by adding the electrical wiring, walls, and so on. Similarly, the programmer completes the application by adding the necessary code (instructions) to the user interface. When the home is complete, the builder makes a final inspection and corrects any problems before the customer moves in. Likewise, the programmer tests the completed application, and any problems, called **bugs**, are fixed before the application is given to the user. The final step in both processes is to assemble the project's documentation (paperwork), which then is given to the customer/user.

You learn how to plan an OO application in this lesson. Steps three through six of the process are covered in Lessons B and C.

PLANNING AN OO APPLICATION

As any builder will tell you, the most important aspect of a home is not its beauty; rather, it is how closely the home matches the buyer's wants and needs. For example, a large dining room may be appropriate for someone who frequently entertains; for someone who does not, it may be a waste of space. The same is true for an OO application. Therefore, for an application to meet the user's needs, it is essential for the programmer to plan the application jointly with the user. It cannot be stressed enough that the only way to guarantee the success of an application is to actively involve the user in the planning phase. Planning an OO application requires the following four steps:

1. Identify the tasks the application needs to perform.

2. Identify the objects to which you will assign the tasks.

3. Identify the events required to trigger an object into performing its assigned tasks.

4. Draw a sketch of the user interface.

You can use a TOE (Task, Object, Event) chart to record the application's tasks, objects, and events, which are identified in the first three steps of the planning phase. In the next section, you begin completing a TOE chart for the Skate-Away Sales application. The first step is to identify the application's tasks.

IDENTIFYING THE APPLICATION'S TASKS

Realizing that it is essential to involve the user when planning the application, you meet with the sales manager of Skate-Away Sales, Mr. Cousard, to determine his requirements. You ask Mr. Cousard to bring the form the salespeople currently use to record the orders. Viewing the current forms and procedures will help you gain a better understanding of the application. You also can use the current form as a guide when designing the user interface. Figure 2-7 shows the current order form used by Skate-Away Sales.

Skate-Away Sales Order Form

Customer name _____

Address _____

City _____ State _____ ZIP _____

Number of blue skateboards ordered	Number of yellow skateboards ordered	Total number of skateboards ordered	Total price

Figure 2-7: Current order form used by Skate-Away Sales

When identifying the tasks an application needs to perform, it is helpful to ask the following questions:

» What information, if any, will the application need to display on the screen and/or print on the printer?

» What information, if any, will the user need to enter into the user interface to display and/or print the desired information?

» What information, if any, will the application need to calculate to display and/or print the desired information?

» How will the user end the application?

» Will previous information need to be cleared from the screen before new information is entered?

The answers to these questions will help you identify the application's major tasks. The answers for each question for the Skate-Away Sales application are as follows.

What information, if any, will the application need to display on the screen and/or print on the printer? (Notice that "display" refers to the screen, and "print" refers to the printer.) The Skate-Away Sales application should display the customer's name, street address, city, state, ZIP code, the number of blue skateboards ordered, the number of yellow skateboards ordered, the total number of skateboards ordered, and the total price of the order. In this case, the application does not need to print anything on the printer.

What information, if any, will the user need to enter into the user interface to display and/or print the desired information? In the Skate-Away Sales application, the salesperson (the user) must enter the customer's name, street address, city, state, ZIP code, and the number of blue and yellow skateboards ordered.

What information, if any, will the application need to calculate to display and/or print the desired information? The Skate-Away Sales application needs to calculate the total number of skateboards ordered and the total price of the order.

How will the user end the application? In Chapter 1, you learned that all applications should provide a way for the user to end the application. The Skate-Away Sales application will use an Exit button for this task.

»TIP
You can draw a TOE chart by hand, or you can draw one using the table feature in a word processor (such as Microsoft Word).

Will previous information need to be cleared from the screen before new information is entered? After Skate-Away's salesperson enters and calculates an order, he or she will need to clear the customer's information from the screen before entering the next order.

Figure 2-8 shows the Skate-Away Sales application's tasks listed in a TOE chart. Unlike procedure-oriented planning, OO planning does not require the TOE chart tasks to be listed in any particular order. In this case, the data entry tasks are listed first, followed by the calculation tasks, display tasks, application ending task, and screen clearing task.

Task	Object	Event
Get the following order information from the user: Customer's name Street address City State ZIP code Number of blue skateboards ordered Number of yellow skateboards ordered		
Calculate the total skateboards ordered and the total price		
Display the following information: Customer's name Street address City State ZIP code Number of blue skateboards ordered Number of yellow skateboards ordered Total skateboards ordered Total price		
End the application		
Clear the screen for the next order		

Figure 2-8: Tasks entered in a TOE chart

Next, you identify the objects that will perform the tasks listed in the TOE chart.

IDENTIFYING THE OBJECTS

After completing the Task column of the TOE chart, you then assign each task to an object in the user interface. For this application, the only objects you will use, besides the Windows form itself, are the button, label, and text box controls. As you learned in Chapter 1, you use a label control to display information that you do not want the user to change while your application is running, and you use a button control to perform an action immediately after the user clicks it. As you learned earlier, you use a text box to give the user an area in which to enter data.

The first task listed in Figure 2-8 is to get the order information from the user. For each order, the salesperson will need to enter the customer's name, address, city, state, and ZIP code, as well as the number of blue skateboards ordered and the number of yellow skateboards ordered. Because you need to provide the salesperson with areas in which to enter the information, you will assign the first task to seven text boxes—one for each item of information. The names of the text boxes will be xNameTextBox, xAddressTextBox, xCityTextBox, xStateTextBox, xZipTextBox, xBlueTextBox, and xYellowTextBox.

The second task listed in the TOE chart is to calculate both the total number of skateboards ordered and the total price. So that the salesperson can calculate these amounts at any time, you will assign the task to a button named xCalcButton.

The third task listed in the TOE chart is to display the order information, the total number of skateboards ordered, and the total price. The order information will be displayed automatically when the user enters that information in the seven text boxes. The total skateboards ordered and the total price, however, are not entered by the user; rather, those amounts are calculated by the xCalcButton. Because the user should not be allowed to change the calculated results, you will have the xCalcButton display the total skateboards ordered and the total price in two label controls named xTotalBoardsLabel and xTotalPriceLabel. Recall from Chapter 1 that a user cannot access the contents of a label control while the application is running. Notice that the task of displaying the total skateboards ordered involves two objects (xCalcButton and xTotalBoardsLabel). The task of displaying the total price also involves two objects (xCalcButton and xTotalPriceLabel).

The last two tasks listed in the TOE chart are "End the application" and "Clear the screen for the next order." You will assign the tasks to buttons so that the user has control over when the tasks are performed. You will name the buttons xExitButton and xClearButton. Figure 2-9 shows the TOE chart with the Task and Object columns completed.

Task	Object	Event

Get the following order information from the user:
  Customer's name
  Street address
  City
  State
  ZIP code
  Number of blue skateboards ordered
  Number of yellow skateboards ordered
	
	xNameTextBox
	xAddressTextBox
	xCityTextBox
	xStateTextBox
	xZipTextBox
	xBlueTextBox
	xYellowTextBox	

Calculate the total skateboards ordered and the total price	xCalcButton	

Display the following information:
  Customer's name
  Street address
  City
  State
  ZIP code
  Number of blue skateboards ordered
  Number of yellow skateboards ordered
  Total skateboards ordered
  Total price
	
	xNameTextBox
	xAddressTextBox
	xCityTextBox
	xStateTextBox
	xZipTextBox
	xBlueTextBox
	xYellowTextBox
	xCalcButton, xTotalBoardsLabel
	xCalcButton, xTotalPriceLabel	

End the application	xExitButton	
Clear the screen for the next order	xClearButton	

Figure 2-9: Tasks and objects entered in a TOE chart

After defining the application's tasks and assigning the tasks to objects in the user interface, you then determine which event (if any) must occur for an object to do its assigned task.

IDENTIFYING THE EVENTS

The seven text boxes listed in the TOE chart in Figure 2-9 are assigned the task of getting and displaying the order information. Text boxes accept and display information automatically, so no special event is necessary for them to do their assigned task.

The two label controls listed in the TOE chart are assigned the task of displaying the total number of skateboards ordered and the total price of the order. Label controls automatically display their contents; so, here again, no special event needs to occur. (Recall that the two label controls will get their values from the xCalcButton.)

The remaining objects listed in the TOE chart are the three buttons: xCalcButton, xClearButton, and xExitButton. You will have the buttons perform their assigned tasks when the user clicks them. Figure 2-10 shows the TOE chart with the tasks, objects, and events necessary for the Skate-Away Sales application.

Task	Object	Event
Get the following order information from the user:		
Customer's name	xNameTextBox	None
Street address	xAddressTextBox	None
City	xCityTextBox	None
State	xStateTextBox	None
ZIP code	xZipTextBox	None
Number of blue skateboards ordered	xBlueTextBox	None
Number of yellow skateboards ordered	xYellowTextBox	None
Calculate the total skateboards ordered and the total price	xCalcButton	Click
Display the following information:		
Customer's name	xNameTextBox	None
Street address	xAddressTextBox	None
City	xCityTextBox	None
State	xStateTextBox	None
ZIP code	xZipTextBox	None
Number of blue skateboards ordered	xBlueTextBox	None
Number of yellow skateboards ordered	xYellowTextBox	None
Total skateboards ordered	xCalcButton, xTotalBoardsLabel	Click, None
Total price	xCalcButton, xTotalPriceLabel	Click, None
End the application	xExitButton	Click
Clear the screen for the next order	xClearButton	Click

Figure 2-10: Completed TOE chart ordered by task

If the application you are creating is small, as is the Skate-Away Sales application, you can use the TOE chart in its current form to help you write the Visual Basic code. When the application you are creating is large, however, it is helpful to rearrange the TOE chart so that it is ordered by object instead of by task. To do so, you simply list all of the objects in the Object column, being sure to list each object only once. Then list the tasks you have assigned to each object in the Task column, and list the events in the Event column. Figure 2-11 shows the rearranged TOE chart, ordered by object rather than by task.

Task	Object	Event
1. Calculate the total skateboards ordered and the total price 2. Display the total skateboards ordered and the total price in the xTotalBoardsLabel and xTotalPriceLabel	xCalcButton	Click
Clear the screen for the next order	xClearButton	Click
End the application	xExitButton	Click
Display the total skateboards ordered (from xCalcButton)	xTotalBoardsLabel	None
Display the total price (from xCalcButton)	xTotalPriceLabel	None
Get and display the order information	xNameTextBox, xAddressTextBox, xCityTextBox, xStateTextBox, xZipTextBox, xBlueTextBox, xYellowTextBox	None

Figure 2-11: Completed TOE chart ordered by object

After completing the TOE chart, the next step is to draw a rough sketch of the user interface.

DRAWING A SKETCH OF THE USER INTERFACE

Although the TOE chart lists the objects you need to include in the application's user interface, it does not tell you *where* to place those objects in the interface. While the design of an interface is open to creativity, there are some guidelines to which you should adhere so that your application is consistent with the Windows standards. This consistency will make your application easier to both learn and use, because the user interface will have a familiar look to it.

In Western countries, you should organize the user interface so that the information flows either vertically or horizontally, with the most important information always located in the upper-left corner of the screen. In a vertical arrangement, the information flows from top to bottom; the essential information is located in the first column of the screen, while secondary information is placed in subsequent columns. In a horizontal arrangement, on the other hand, the information flows from left to right; the essential information is placed in the first row of the screen, with secondary information placed in subsequent rows.

You can group together related controls using white (empty) space. Or, you can use a control instantiated from one of the tools located in the Containers section of the toolbox. Examples of tools found in the Containers section include the GroupBox tool, Panel tool, and TableLayoutPanel tool. You use these tools to instantiate a group box, a panel, and a table layout panel, respectively. The difference between a panel and a group box is that a panel can have scroll bars, whereas a group box cannot. In addition, a group box has a Text property that you can use to indicate the contents of the control; a panel does not have a Text property. Unlike the panel and group box controls, the table layout panel control provides a table structure in which you place other controls.

Figures 2-12 and 2-13 show two different sketches of the Skate-Away Sales interface. In Figure 2-12, the information is arranged vertically, and white space is used to group together the related controls. In Figure 2-13, the information is arranged horizontally. Related controls are grouped together using a group box, a panel, and a table layout panel.

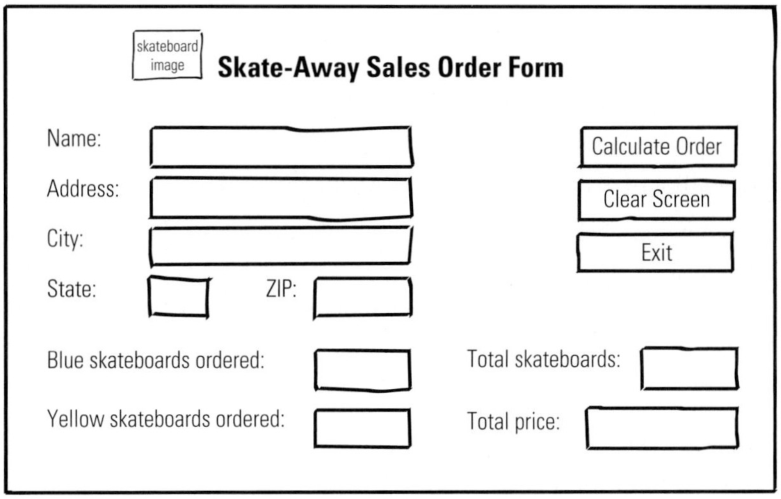

Figure 2-12: Vertical arrangement of the Skate-Away Sales interface

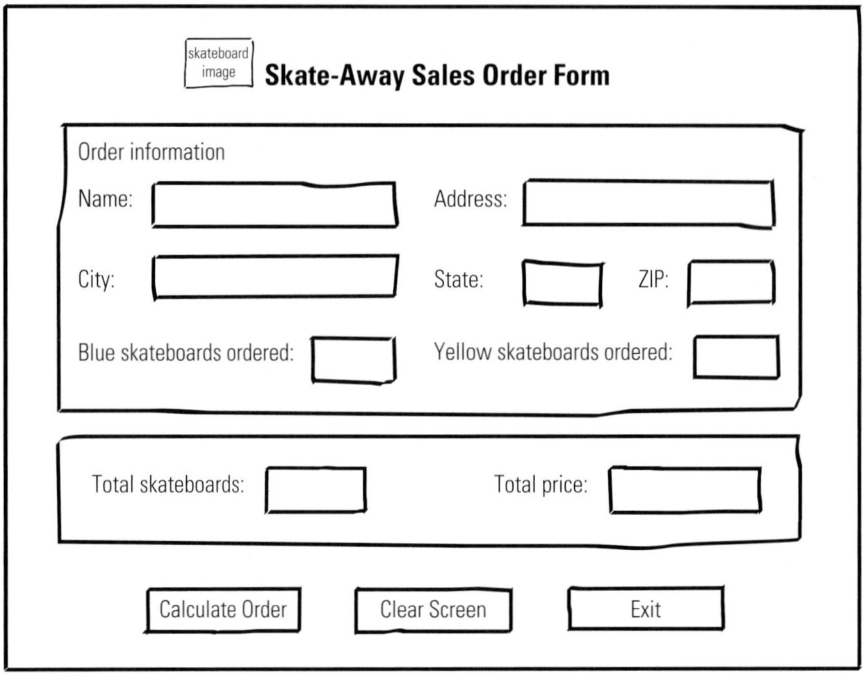

Figure 2-13: Horizontal arrangement of the Skate-Away Sales interface

Each text box and button control in the interfaces shown in Figures 2-12 and 2-13 is labeled so the user knows the control's purpose. For example, the "Name:" label that identifies the xNameTextBox tells the user the type of information to enter in the text box. Similarly, the "Calculate Order" caption on the xCalcButton indicates the action the button will perform when it is clicked.

In many applications, program output (such as the result of calculations) is displayed in a label control in the interface. Label controls that display program output should be labeled so that their contents are obvious to the user. For example, in the interfaces shown in Figures 2-12 and 2-13, the "Total skateboards:" and "Total price:" labels describe the contents of the xTotalBoardsLabel and xTotalPriceLabel controls.

The text contained in identifying label controls should be left-aligned within the label control. In addition, the identifying label should be positioned either above or to the left of the control it identifies. As you learned in Chapter 1, buttons are identified by a caption that appears on the button itself. Identifying labels and button captions should be meaningful. In addition, they should be from one to three words only, and each should appear on one line.

An identifying label should end with a colon (:), as shown in Figures 2-12 and 2-13. The colon distinguishes an identifying label from other text in the user interface, such as the heading text "Skate-Away Sales Order Form." The Windows standard is to use sentence capitalization for identifying labels. **Sentence capitalization** means you capitalize only the first letter in the first word and in any words that are customarily capitalized. The Windows standard for button captions is to use book title capitalization. When using **book title capitalization**, you capitalize the first letter in each word, except for articles, conjunctions, and prepositions that do not occur at either the beginning or the end of the caption.

When positioning the controls, be sure to maintain a consistent margin from the edge of the form. Related controls should be placed close to each other on the form. Typically, controls that are not part of any logical grouping are positioned farther away from other controls.

Always size the buttons in the interface relative to each other. When the buttons are positioned horizontally, as they are in Figure 2-13, all the buttons should be the same height; their widths, however, may vary if necessary. If the buttons are stacked vertically, as they are in Figure 2-12, all the buttons should be the same height and the same width.

In a group of buttons, always place the most commonly used button first. For example, if the buttons are positioned horizontally, the most commonly used button should be the leftmost button in the group, as shown in Figure 2-13. If the buttons are stacked vertically, the most commonly used button should be at the top of the button group, as shown in Figure 2-12.

When laying out the controls in the interface, try to minimize the number of different margins so that the user can more easily scan the information. You can do so by aligning the borders of the controls wherever possible, as shown in Figures 2-12 and 2-13.

In this section, you learned some basic guidelines to follow when sketching a GUI (Graphical User Interface). You will learn more GUI guidelines in subsequent chapters. (You can find a complete list of the GUI guidelines in Appendix A of this book.)

»TIP

Some companies have their own standards for interfaces used within the company. A company's standards supersede the Windows standards.

»GUI DESIGN TIP

Layout and Organization of the User Interface

» Organize the user interface so that the information flows either vertically or horizontally, with the most important information always located in the upper-left corner of the screen. When positioning the controls, maintain a consistent margin from the edge of the form.

» Group together related controls using either white (empty) space or a control instantiated from one of the tools contained in the Containers section of the toolbox.

» Use a meaningful caption in each button. Place the caption on one line and use from one to three words only. Use book title capitalization for button captions.

» Use a label to identify each text box in the user interface. Also use a label to identify other label controls that display program output. The label text should be meaningful. It also should be from one to three words only, and appear on one line. Left-align the text within the label, and position the label either above or to the left of the control it identifies. Follow the label text with a colon (:) and use sentence capitalization.

» Size the buttons in a group of buttons relative to each other, and place the most commonly used button first in the group.

» Align the borders of the controls wherever possible to minimize the number of different margins used in the interface.

You have completed Lesson A. You can either take a break or complete the end-of-lesson questions and exercises before moving on to Lesson B, where you will use the sketch shown in Figure 2-12 as a guide when building the Skate-Away Sales interface.

SUMMARY

TO CREATE AN OO APPLICATION:

Follow these six steps:

1. Meet with the client.

2. Plan the application.

3. Build the user interface.

4. Code the application.

5. Test and debug the application.

6. Assemble the documentation.

TO PLAN AN OO APPLICATION IN VISUAL BASIC 2005:

Follow these four steps:

1. Identify the tasks the application needs to perform.

2. Identify the objects to which you will assign the tasks.

3. Identify the events required to trigger an object into performing its assigned tasks.

4. Draw a sketch of the user interface.

TO ASSIST YOU IN IDENTIFYING THE TASKS AN APPLICATION NEEDS TO PERFORM, ASK THE FOLLOWING QUESTIONS:

» What information, if any, will the application need to display on the screen and/or print on the printer?

» What information, if any, will the user need to enter into the user interface to display and/or print the desired information?

» What information, if any, will the application need to calculate to display and/or print the desired information?

» How will the user end the application?

» Will prior information need to be cleared from the screen before new information is entered?

QUESTIONS

1. You use a _____ control to display information you do not want the user to change.

   a. button   b. label

   c. text box   d. user

2. You use a _____ control to accept or display information you will allow the user to change.

   a. button   b. label

   c. text box   d. user

3. You can use a(n) _____ chart to plan your OO applications.

   a. EOT   b. ETO

   c. OTE   d. TOE

4. When designing a user interface, the most important information should be placed in the _____ of the screen.

   a. lower-left corner   b. lower-right corner

   c. upper-left corner   d. upper-right corner

5. If more than one button appears in an interface, the most commonly used button should be placed _____.

   a. first   b. in the middle

   c. last   d. either first or last

6. A button's caption should be entered using _____.

   a. book title capitalization

   b. sentence capitalization

   c. either book title capitalization or sentence capitalization

7. Which of the following statements is false?

    a. The text contained in identifying labels should be aligned on the left.

    b. An identifying label should be positioned either above or to the left of the control it identifies.

    c. Identifying labels should be entered using book title capitalization.

    d. Identifying labels should end with a colon (:).

8. _____ means you capitalize only the first letter in the first word and in any words that are customarily capitalized.

    a. Book title capitalization   b. Sentence capitalization

9. Listed below are the four steps you should follow when planning an OO application. Put the steps in the proper order by placing a number (1 through 4) on the line to the left of the step.

    _____   Identify the objects to which you will assign the tasks.

    _____   Draw a sketch of the user interface.

    _____   Identify the tasks the application needs to perform.

    _____   Identify the events required to trigger an object into performing its assigned tasks.

10. Listed below are the six steps you should follow when creating an OO application. Put the steps in the proper order by placing a number (1 through 6) on the line to the left of the step.

    _____   Test and debug the application.

    _____   Build the user interface.

    _____   Code the application.

    _____   Assemble the documentation.

    _____   Plan the application.

    _____   Meet with the client.

EXERCISES

1. In this exercise, you prepare a TOE chart and create two sketches of the application's user interface. Use the GUI design guidelines listed in Appendix A to verify that the interface you create adheres to the GUI standards outlined in this book.

   Scenario: Sarah Brimley is the accountant at Paper Products. The salespeople at Paper Products are paid a commission, which is a percentage of the sales they make. Sarah wants you to create an application that will compute the commission after she enters the salesperson's name, sales, and commission rate (expressed as a decimal number). In other words, if Sarah enters 2000 as the sales and .1 (the decimal equivalent of 10%) as the commission rate, the commission amount should be 200.

   a. Prepare a TOE chart ordered by task.

   b. Rearrange the TOE chart created in Step a so that it is ordered by object.

   c. Draw two sketches of the user interface: one using a horizontal arrangement and the other using a vertical arrangement.

2. In this exercise, you prepare a TOE chart and create two sketches of the application's user interface. Use the GUI design guidelines listed in Appendix A to verify that the interface you create adheres to the GUI standards outlined in this book.

   Scenario: RM Sales divides its sales territory into four regions: North, South, East, and West. Robert Gonzales, the sales manager, wants an application in which he can enter the current year's sales for each region and the projected increase (expressed as a decimal number) for each region. He then wants the application to compute the following year's projected sales for each region. For example, if Robert enters 10000 as the current sales for the South region, and then enters .05 (the decimal equivalent of 5%) as the projected increase, the application should display 10500 as the next year's projected sales.

   a. Prepare a TOE chart ordered by task.

   b. Rearrange the TOE chart created in Step a so that it is ordered by object.

   c. Draw two sketches of the user interface: one using a horizontal arrangement and the other using a vertical arrangement.

3. In this exercise, you modify an existing application's user interface so that the interface follows the GUI design guidelines you have learned so far.

a. If necessary, start Visual Studio 2005 or Visual Basic 2005 Express Edition. Open the Time Solution (Time Solution.sln) file, which is contained in the VB2005\Chap02\Time Solution folder. If necessary, open the designer window.

b. Lay out and organize the interface so it follows all of the GUI design guidelines you have learned so far. (Refer to Appendix A for a listing of the guidelines.)

c. Save the solution, then start the application. Click the Exit button to end the application. (The Exit button contains the code to end the application.)

LESSON B
OBJECTIVES

AFTER STUDYING LESSON B, YOU SHOULD BE ABLE TO:

» Build the user interface using your TOE chart and sketch

» Follow the Windows standards regarding the use of graphics, fonts, and color

» Set a control's BorderStyle property

» Add a text box to a form

» Lock the controls on the form

» Assign access keys to controls

» Use the TabIndex property

BUILDING THE USER INTERFACE

PREPARING TO CREATE THE USER INTERFACE

In Lesson A, you completed the second of the six steps involved in creating an OO application: plan the application. You now are ready to tackle the third step, which is to build the user interface. You use the TOE chart and sketch you created in the planning step as guides when building the interface, which involves placing the appropriate controls on the form and setting the applicable properties of the controls. Recall that an object's properties determine the appearance and behavior of the object, such as its font, size, and so on. Some programmers create the entire interface before setting the properties of each object. Other programmers change the properties of each object as it is added to the form. Either way will work, so it's really just a matter of personal preference.

To save you time, the VB2005\Chap02\Skate Away Solution folder contains a partially completed application for Skate-Away Sales. When you open the solution, you will notice that most of the user interface has been created and most of the properties have been set. Only one control—a text box—is missing from the form. You add the missing control and set its properties later in this lesson.

To open the partially completed application:

1 Start Visual Studio 2005 or Visual Basic 2005 Express Edition, if necessary, and close the Start Page window.

2 Open the **Skate Away Solution** (Skate Away Solution.sln) file, which is contained in the VB2005\Chap02\Skate Away Solution folder. If necessary, open the designer window. Figure 2-14 shows the partially completed interface.

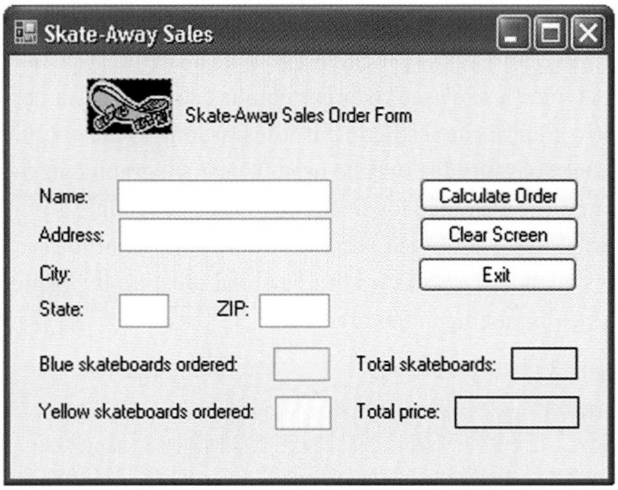

Figure 2-14: Partially completed interface for the Skate-Away Sales application

The user interface shown in Figure 2-14 resembles the sketch shown in Figure 2-12 in Lesson A. Recall that the sketch was created using the GUI guidelines you learned in the lesson. For example, the information in the interface is arranged vertically, with the most important information located in the upper-left corner of the screen. In addition, a consistent margin is maintained from the edge of the form, and the controls are aligned wherever possible to minimize the number of different margins appearing in the interface. Also notice that each text box and button, as well as each label control that displays program output, is labeled so the user knows the control's purpose. The text contained in the identifying labels is entered using sentence capitalization; in addition, it ends with a colon and is left-aligned within the label. The identifying labels are positioned to the left of the controls they identify. The button captions, on the other hand, appear on the button and are entered using book title capitalization. Each caption and identifying label appears on one line, and no caption or identifying label exceeds the three-word limit. Also notice that, because the buttons are stacked in the interface, each button has the same height and width, and the most commonly used button (Calculate Order) is placed at the top of the button group.

When building the user interface, keep in mind that you want to create a screen that no one notices. Snazzy interfaces may get "oohs" and "aahs" during their initial use, but they become tiresome after a while. The most important point to remember is that the interface should not distract the user from doing his or her work. Unfortunately, it is difficult for some application developers to refrain from using the many different graphics, fonts, and colors available in Visual Basic. Actually, using these elements is not the problem—overusing them is. So that you do not overload your user interfaces with too many graphics, too many fonts, and too much color, the next three sections provide some guidelines to follow regarding these elements.

INCLUDING GRAPHICS IN THE USER INTERFACE

The human eye is attracted to pictures before text, so include a graphic in an interface only if it is necessary to do so. Graphics typically are used to either emphasize or clarify a portion of the screen. You also can use a graphic for aesthetic purposes, as long as the graphic is small and placed in a location that does not distract the user. The small graphic in the Skate-Away Sales interface, for example, is included for aesthetics only. The graphic is purposely located in the upper-left corner of the interface, which is where you want the user's eye to be drawn first anyway. The skateboard graphic adds a personal touch to the Skate-Away Sales order form without being distracting to the user.

> **»GUI DESIGN TIP**
>
> **Adding Graphics**
>
> » Include a graphic in an interface only if it is necessary to do so. If the graphic is used solely for aesthetics, use a small graphic and place it in a location that will not distract the user.

INCLUDING DIFFERENT FONTS IN THE USER INTERFACE

As you learned in Chapter 1, you can use an object's Font property to change the type, style, and size of the font used to display the text contained in an object. Recall that Tahoma, Courier, and Microsoft Sans Serif are examples of font types. Font styles include regular, bold, and italic. The numbers 8.25, 10, and 18 are examples of font sizes, which typically are measured in points, with one point equaling $\frac{1}{72}$ of an inch.

»TIP

As you learned in Chapter 1, you should use the Tahoma font for applications that will run on computer systems running Windows 2000 or Windows XP. If the Tahoma font is not available, use either Microsoft Sans Serif or Arial.

Some font types are serif, and some are sans serif. A **serif** is a light cross stroke that appears at the top or bottom of a character. The characters in a serif font have the light strokes, whereas the characters in a sans serif font do not. ("Sans" is a French word meaning "without.") Books use serif fonts, because serif fonts are easier to read on the printed page. Sans serif fonts, on the other hand, are easier to read on the screen, so you should use a sans serif font (preferably the Tahoma font) for the text in a user interface. In addition, you should use only one font type for all of the text in the interface.

You should avoid using italics and underlining in an interface, because both font styles make text difficult to read. You also should limit the use of bold text to titles, headings, and key items that you want to emphasize.

You can use 8-point through 12-point fonts for the elements in the user interface; however, text displayed using a 12-point font is easier to read at high screen resolutions. Be sure to limit, to either one or two, the number of font sizes used in an interface.

The computer automatically assigns the value Microsoft Sans Serif, 8.25 pt ("pt" stands for "point") to a form's Font property when the form is created. When you add a control to the form, the value stored in the form's Font property is automatically assigned to the control's Font property. In other words, using OOP terminology, the control inherits the form's Font property setting. Therefore, one way to change the font used in an interface is to change the form's Font property *before* adding the controls to the form. By doing this, the controls added to the form will inherit the form's Font setting, and you will not need to set each control's Font property separately. You also can change the form's Font property *after* adding the controls. An existing control whose Font property has not been set individually will inherit the form's setting. You will observe how this works in the next set of steps.

To change the Font property of the form and controls:

1 Click the **form**, if necessary, to select it.

First, you will change the font type of the form from Microsoft Sans Serif to Tahoma.

2 Click **Font** in the Properties window, then click the **. . .** (ellipsis) button to open the Font dialog box. Scroll down the Font list box, and then click **Tahoma** in the list. Click the **OK** button to close the Font dialog box. The value contained in the form's Font property changes from Microsoft Sans Serif, 8.25 pt to Tahoma, 8.25 pt. The value contained in the Font property for the existing controls also changes to Tahoma, 8.25 pt. The only exception is the PictureBox1 control, which does not have a Font property.

3 Click the **Calculate Order** button, then view its Font property setting in the Properties window. Notice that the Font property contains the same value as the form's Font property: Tahoma, 8.25 pt.

Next, you will increase the size of the characters contained in the heading text, Skate-Away Sales Order Form.

4 Click the **Label10** control, which contains the heading text. Click **Font** in the Properties window, then click the **. . .** (ellipsis) button to open the Font dialog box. Click **14** in the Size list box, then click the **OK** button to close the Font dialog box. The size of the characters contained in the heading text increases to 14.25 point.

Lastly, you will change the font size of the form from 8.25 point to 12 point.

5 Click the **form** to select it. Open the Font dialog box, then click **12** in the Size list box. Click the **OK** button to close the Font dialog box. The form's Font property setting changes to Tahoma, 12 pt. The Tahoma, 12 pt value is also assigned to the Font properties of all of the existing controls, except the PictureBox1 control (which does not have a Font property) and the Label10 control (whose Font property was set individually). Figure 2-15 shows the interface after selecting the new font type (Tahoma) and font sizes (12 pt and 14.25 pt).

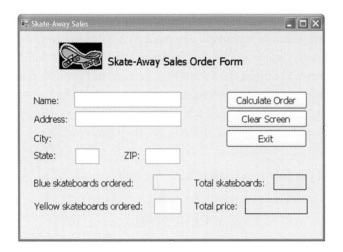

Figure 2-15: New font type and font sizes shown in the interface

6 Save the solution.

≫GUI DESIGN TIP

Selecting Appropriate Font Types, Styles, and Sizes

≫ Use only one font type for all of the text in the interface. Use a sans serif font, preferably the Tahoma font. If the Tahoma font is not available, use either Microsoft Sans Serif or Arial.

≫ Use an 8-, 9-, 10-, 11-, or 12-point font for the text in an interface.

≫ Limit the number of font sizes used to either one or two.

≫ Avoid using italics and underlining, because these font styles make text difficult to read.

≫ Limit the use of bold text to titles, headings, and key items that you want to emphasize.

In addition to overusing graphics and fonts, many application developers make the mistake of using either too much color or too many different colors in the user interface. In the next section, you learn some guidelines pertaining to the use of color.

INCLUDING COLOR IN THE USER INTERFACE

Just as the human eye is attracted to graphics before text, it also is attracted to color before black and white, so you should use color sparingly. It is a good practice to build the interface using black, white, and gray first, then add color only if you have a good reason to do so. Keep the following three points in mind when deciding whether to include color in an interface:

1. Many people have some form of either color blindness or color confusion, so they will have trouble distinguishing colors.

2. Color is very subjective; a pretty color to you may be hideous to someone else.

3. A color may have a different meaning in a different culture.

Usually, it is best to use black text on a white, off-white, or light gray background. This is because dark text on a light background is the easiest to read. The Skate-Away Sales interface, for example, displays black text on a light gray background. You should never use a dark color for the background or a light color for the text, because a dark background is hard on the eyes, and light-colored text can appear blurry.

If you are going to include color in the interface, limit the number of colors to three, not including white, black, and gray. Be sure that the colors you choose complement each other.

Although color can be used to identify an important element in the interface, you should never use it as the only means of identification. In the Skate-Away Sales application, for example, the blue and yellow text boxes help the salesperson quickly identify where to enter the order for blue and yellow skateboards, respectively. However, color is not the only means of identifying those areas in the interface; the labels to the left of the text boxes also tell the user where to enter the orders for blue and yellow skateboards.

In the next set of steps, you will observe how the Skate-Away Sales interface looks with a white background instead of a gray one.

To change the background color of the form:

1 If necessary, click the **form** to select it.

2 Click **BackColor** in the Properties list, then click the **list arrow** button in the **Settings box**. Click the **Custom** tab, then click a **white square**. The background color of the form, as well as the background color of most of the controls on the form, changes to white. Notice that, using OOP terminology, the controls inherit the value contained in the form's BackColor property. The only controls whose background color does not change to white are the xBlueTextBox and xYellowTextBox controls; this is because the BackColor properties of those controls were explicitly set to blue and yellow, respectively. (Although it is not obvious in the interface, the BackColor property of the PictureBox1 control also changes to white; you can use the Properties window to verify that fact. You don't see the white because the image stored in the picture box fills the entire control.)

Next, you will explicitly set the background color of the Calculate Order button.

3 Click the **Calculate Order** button. Click **BackColor** in the Properties list, then click the **list arrow** button in the Settings box. Click the **System** tab, then click **Control**. The background color of the Calculate Order button changes to gray.

If you prefer the way the interface originally looked, you can use the Undo option to cancel the changes you just made.

4 Click **Edit** on the menu bar, then click **Undo** to change the background color of the Calculate Order button to white, which is the color of the form.

5 Click **Edit** on the menu bar, then click **Undo** to change the background color of the form to its original color, gray.

> **►► TIP**
>
> As you learned in Chapter 1, you can reset a property to its default setting by right-clicking the property and then clicking Reset on the context menu.

6 Save the solution.

»GUI DESIGN TIP

Selecting Appropriate Colors

» Build the interface using black, white, and gray first, then add color only if you have a good reason to do so.

» Use white, off-white, or light gray for an application's background, and use black for the text.

» Never use a dark color for the background or a light color for the text. A dark background is hard on the eyes, and light-colored text can appear blurry.

» Limit the number of colors in an interface to three, not including white, black, and gray. The colors you choose should complement each other.

» Never use color as the only means of identification for an element in the user interface.

Next, you learn the Windows standards regarding the border style of the text boxes and labels in an interface.

THE BORDERSTYLE PROPERTY

The **BorderStyle property** determines the style of a control's border and can be set to None, FixedSingle, or Fixed3D. Controls with a BorderStyle property set to None have no border. Setting the BorderStyle property to FixedSingle surrounds the control with a thin line, and setting it to Fixed3D gives the control a three-dimensional appearance.

In most cases, a text box's BorderStyle property should be set to Fixed3D, which is the default setting for a text box. All of the text boxes in the Skate-Away Sales interface, for example, have Fixed3D as the setting for the BorderStyle property. Label controls that identify other controls (such as those that identify text boxes) should have their BorderStyle property left at the default value for labels, which is None. However, you typically set to FixedSingle the BorderStyle property of label controls that display program output, such as those that display the result of a calculation. In the Skate-Away Sales interface, the BorderStyle property for all of the identifying labels is set to None. The BorderStyle property of the xTotalBoardsLabel and xTotalPriceLabel controls, however, is set to FixedSingle, because both controls display calculated results.

»GUI DESIGN TIP

Setting the BorderStyle Property of a Text Box and Label

» Leave the BorderStyle property of text boxes at the default value, Fixed3D.

» Leave the BorderStyle property of labels that identify other controls at the default value, None.

» Set to FixedSingle the BorderStyle property of labels that display program output, such as those that display the result of a calculation.

» In Windows applications, a control that contains data that the user is not allowed to edit does not usually appear three-dimensional. Therefore, you should avoid setting a label control's BorderStyle property to Fixed3D.

ADDING A TEXT BOX CONTROL TO THE FORM

The toolbox contains a TextBox tool, which you use to instantiate a text box control. As you learned in the preview section of this chapter, a text box provides an area in the form where the user can enter data. Notice that the text box in which the user enters the city is missing from the Skate-Away Sales interface.

To add the missing text box to the form:

1 Click the **TextBox tool** in the toolbox, but don't release the mouse button. Drag the mouse pointer to the form. Position the mouse pointer to the right of the City: label, immediately below the Address text box, then release the mouse button. A text box for entering the city appears on the form.

2 Change the TextBox1's **Name** property to **xCityTextBox**.

Next, you will use the Format menu to make the City text box the same size as the Address text box. As you learned in Chapter 1, to size (or align) two or more controls, you first select the reference control, and then select the other controls. Recall that the reference control is the control whose size (or alignment) you want the other controls to match. In this case, for example, you want the City text box to match the size of the Address text box. Therefore, the Address text box is the reference control and must be selected first.

3 Click the **xAddressTextBox**, then press and hold down the **Ctrl** (or Control) key as you click the **xCityTextBox**. The xAddressTextBox and xCityTextBox controls should now be selected. Notice that the xAddressTextBox (the reference control) has white sizing handles, whereas the xCityTextBox has black sizing handles.

4 Click **Format** on the menu bar, point to **Make Same Size**, and then click **Both** to make the xCityTextBox's height and width the same as the xAddressTextBox's height and width.

You also can use the Format menu to align the left border of the City text box with the left border of the Address text box. However, you will align the controls using the snap lines instead.

5 Click the **form** to deselect the City and Address text boxes.

6 Place the mouse pointer on the City text box, then press and hold down the left mouse button as you drag the text box to the location shown in Figure 2-16. Notice the blue snap lines that help you align the City text box with the other controls in the interface.

»TIP

Recall that, in the context of OOP, each tool in the toolbox is a class, which is a pattern from which one or more objects (called controls) are created. Each control you create is an instance of the class. A text box, for example, is an instance of the TextBox class.

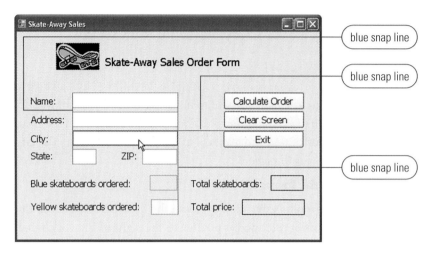

Figure 2-16: Form showing the correct location of the City text box

7 When the City text box is in the correct location, release the mouse button.

LOCKING THE CONTROLS ON A FORM

Once you have placed all of the controls in the desired locations on the form, it is a good idea to lock the controls in their current positions so you do not inadvertently move them. Once the controls are locked, you will not be able to move them until you unlock them; you can, however, delete them. You can lock the controls by clicking the form (or any control on the form), and then clicking Format on the menu bar, and then clicking Lock Controls; you can follow the same procedure to unlock the controls. You also can lock and unlock the controls by right-clicking the form (or any control on the form), and then clicking Lock Controls on the context menu. When a control is locked, a small lock appears in the upper-left corner of the control.

To lock the controls on the form, then save the solution:

1 Right-click the **form** (or any control on the form), then click **Lock Controls** on the context menu.

2 Try dragging one of the controls to a different location on the form. You will not be able to do so.

If you need to move a control after you have locked the controls in place, you can either change the control's Location property setting in the Properties list or unlock the controls by selecting the Lock Controls option again. The Lock Controls option is a toggle option: selecting it once activates it, and selecting it again deactivates it.

3 Save the solution.

> **»GUI DESIGN TIP**
>
> **Locking the Controls**
>
> **»** Lock the controls in place on the form.

In the next section, you learn how to assign access keys to the controls that can accept user input.

ASSIGNING ACCESS KEYS

An **access key** allows the user to select an object using the Alt key in combination with a letter or number. For example, you can select the File menu in Visual Studio by pressing Alt+F, because the letter "F" is the File menu's access key. Access keys are not case sensitive; in other words, you can select the File menu by pressing either Alt+F or Alt+f.

You should assign access keys to each of the controls (in the interface) that can accept user input. Examples of such controls include text boxes and buttons, because the user can enter information in a text box and he or she can click a button. The only exception to this rule is the OK and Cancel buttons, which typically do not have access keys. It is important to assign access keys to controls for the following three reasons:

1. Access keys allow a user to work with the application even when the mouse becomes inoperative.

2. Access keys allow users who are fast typists to keep their hands on the keyboard.

3. Access keys allow people with disabilities, which may prevent them from working with a mouse, to use the application.

> **»TIP**
>
> The ampersand in a label's Text property designates an access key only if the label's UseMnemonic property is set to its default value, True. If you do not want the ampersand to designate an access key—for example, you want the Text property to say, literally, J & M Sales—you need to set the UseMnemonic property to False.

You assign an access key by including an ampersand (&) in the control's caption or identifying label. For example, to assign an access key to a button, you include the ampersand in the button's Text property, which is where a button's caption is stored. To assign an access key to a text box, on the other hand, you include the ampersand in the Text property of the label control that identifies the text box. (As you learn later in this lesson, you also must set the identifying label's TabIndex property to a value that is one number less than the value stored in the text box's TabIndex property.) You enter the ampersand to the immediate left of the character you want to designate as the access key. For example, to assign the letter C as the access key for the Calculate Order button, you enter &Calculate Order in the button's Text property. To assign the letter N as the access key for the xNameTextBox, you enter &Name: in the Text property of its identifying label.

Each access key appearing in the interface should be unique. The first choice for an access key is the first letter of the caption or identifying label, unless another letter provides a more meaningful association. For example, the letter X typically is the access key for an Exit button, because the letter X provides a more meaningful association than does the letter E. If you can't use the first letter (perhaps because it already is used as the access key for another control) and no other letter provides a more meaningful association, then use a distinctive consonant in the caption or label. The last choices for an access key are a vowel or a number.

To assign an access key to each button and text box in the Skate-Away Sales interface:

1 Click the **Calculate Order** button, then click **Text** in the Properties list.

Use the letter C as the access key for the Calculate Order button.

2 Place the mouse pointer in the Text property's Settings box. The mouse pointer becomes an I-bar $\mathcal{I}$.

3 Place the $\mathcal{I}$ to the left of the C in Calculate, then click at that location. The insertion point appears before the word Calculate.

4 Type **&** (ampersand), then press **Enter**. The Text property now contains &Calculate Order, and the interface shows the letter C underlined in the Calculate Order button's caption.

> **»HELP?** If you are using Windows XP and the letter C does not appear underlined in the button's caption, you will need to open the Display Properties dialog box. To open the dialog box, click Start on the Windows taskbar, click Control Panel, click Appearance and Themes, and then click Display. Click the Appearance tab on the dialog box, and then click the Effects button. Deselect the Hide underlined letters for keyboard navigation until I press the Alt key check box. Click the OK button twice, then close the Appearance and Themes window.

Now assign the letter l as the access key for the Clear Screen button. (In this case, you cannot use the letter C for the Clear Screen button, because the letter C is the access key for the Calculate Order button and access keys should be unique.)

5 Click the **Clear Screen** button, then change its Text property to **C&lear Screen**.

As mentioned earlier, the letter X is customarily the access key for an Exit button.

6 Click the **Exit** button, then change its Text property to **E&xit**.

7 Use the information shown in Figure 2-17 to include an access key in the label controls that identify text boxes in the interface.

Control name	Text	Access key
Label1	Name:	N
Label2	Address:	A
Label3	City:	T
Label4	State:	S
Label5	ZIP:	Z
Label6	Blue skateboards ordered:	B
Label7	Yellow skateboards ordered:	Y

Figure 2-17: Access keys included in the label controls that identify text boxes

Notice that you do not include an access key in the Text property of the Total skateboards: and Total price: labels. This is because the labels do not identify text boxes; rather they identify other label controls. Recall that users cannot access label controls while an application is running, so it is inappropriate to assign an access key to the controls.

Most times, the order in which controls are added to a form does not represent the desired tab order, which is the order that each control should receive the focus when the user presses the Tab key. You specify the desired order using the TabIndex property, which you learn about next.

SETTING THE TABINDEX PROPERTY

The **TabIndex property** determines the order in which a control receives the focus when the user presses either the Tab key or an access key while the application is running. A control having a TabIndex of 2, for instance, will receive the focus immediately after the control whose TabIndex is 1. Likewise, a control with a TabIndex of 18 will receive the focus immediately after the control whose TabIndex is 17. When a control has the **focus**, it can accept user input.

When you add to a form a control that has a TabIndex property, the computer sets the control's TabIndex property to a number that represents the order in which the control was added to the form. The TabIndex property for the first control added to a form is 0

>> TIP

When a text box has the focus, an insertion point appears inside it. When a button has the focus, its border is highlighted and a dotted rectangle appears around its caption.

(zero), the TabIndex property for the second control is 1, and so on. In most cases, you will need to change the TabIndex values of the controls, because the order in which controls are added to a form rarely represents the desired tab order.

To determine the appropriate TabIndex settings for an interface, you first make a list of the controls (in the interface) that can accept user input. The list should reflect the order in which the user will want to access the controls. For example, in the Skate-Away Sales interface, the user typically will want to access the xNameTextBox first, then the xAddressTextBox, the xCityTextBox, and so on. If a control that accepts user input is identified by a label control, you also include the label control in the list. (A text box is an example of a control that accepts user input and is identified by a label control.) You place the name of the label control immediately above the name of the control it identifies in the list. For example, in the Skate-Away Sales interface, the Label1 control (which displays Name:) identifies the xNameTextBox control; therefore, Label1 should appear immediately above xNameTextBox in the list. The names of controls that do not accept user input, and those that do not identify controls that accept user input, should be listed at the bottom of the list; these names do not need to appear in any specific order.

After listing the controls, you then assign each control in the list a TabIndex value, beginning with the number 0. If a control does not have a TabIndex property, however, you do not assign it a TabIndex value in the list. You can tell whether a control has a TabIndex property by viewing its Properties list. Figure 2-18 shows the list of controls for the Skate-Away Sales interface, along with the appropriate TabIndex values.

Controls that accept user input, along with their identifying label controls	TabIndex setting
Label1 (Name:)	0
xNameTextBox	1
Label2 (Address:)	2
xAddressTextBox	3
Label3 (City:)	4
xCityTextBox	5
Label4 (State:)	6
xStateTextBox	7

Figure 2-18: List of controls and TabIndex settings *(Continued)*   ▶

Controls that accept user input, along with their identifying label controls	TabIndex setting
Label5 (ZIP:)	8
xZipTextBox	9
Label6 (Blue skateboards ordered:)	10
xBlueTextBox	11
Label7 (Yellow skateboards ordered:)	12
xYellowTextBox	13
xCalcButton	14
xClearButton	15
xExitButton	16
Other controls	**TabIndex setting**
Label10 (Skate-Away Sales Order Form)	17
Label8 (Total skateboards:)	18
Label9 (Total price:)	19
xTotalBoardsLabel	20
xTotalPriceLabel	21
PictureBox1	This control does not have a TabIndex property.

Figure 2-18: List of controls and TabIndex settings

Notice that the first column in the list contains two sections. The first section is titled "Controls that accept user input, along with their identifying label controls." This section contains the names of the seven text boxes and three buttons in the Skate-Away Sales interface, because those controls can accept user input. Notice that each text box in the list is associated with an identifying label control, whose name appears immediately above the text box name in the list. Also notice that the TabIndex value assigned to each text box's identifying label control is one number less than the value assigned to the text box itself. For example, the Label1 control has a TabIndex value of 0, and its corresponding text box (xNameTextBox) has a TabIndex value of 1. Likewise, the Label2 control and its corresponding text box have TabIndex values of 2 and 3, respectively. For a text box's access key (which is defined in the identifying label) to work appropriately, you must be sure to set the identifying label control's TabIndex property to a value that is one number less than the value stored in the text box's TabIndex property.

The second section in the list shown in Figure 2-18 is titled "Other controls." In this section, you list the names of controls that neither accept user input nor identify controls that accept user input.

You can use the Properties window to set the TabIndex property of each control; or, you can use the Tab Order option on the View menu. The Tab Order option is available only when the designer window is the active window.

To use the View menu to set the TabIndex values:

1 Click **View** on the menu bar, then click **Tab Order**. The current TabIndex value for each control that has a TabIndex property appears in blue boxes on the form. The TabIndex values reflect the order in which each control was added to the form.

》HELP? If the Tab Order option does not appear on the View menu, click the form, then repeat Step 1.

You begin specifying the desired tab order by placing the mouse pointer on the first control you want in the tab order. According to the list shown earlier in Figure 2-18, the first control in the tab order should be the Label1 control, which displays the Name: text. Currently, the Label1 control has a TabIndex value of 1, which indicates that it was the second control added to the form.

2 Place the mouse pointer on the blue box that contains the number 1. (You also can place the mouse pointer directly on the Label1 control.) A rectangle surrounds the Label1 control and the mouse pointer becomes a crosshair, as shown in Figure 2-19.

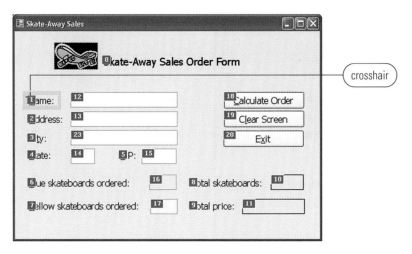

Figure 2-19: Crosshair positioned on the blue box for the Label1 control

3 Click the **blue box that contains the number 1**. (You also can click the Label1 control.) The number 0 replaces the number 1 in the box, and the color of the box changes from blue to white to indicate that you have set the TabIndex value for that control.

According to the list shown earlier in Figure 2-18, the second control in the tab order should be the xNameTextBox, which currently has a TabIndex value of 12.

4 Click the **blue box that contains the number 12**. The number 1 replaces the number 12 in the box, and the color of the box changes from blue to white.

5 Use the information shown in Figure 2-20 to set the TabIndex values for the remaining controls, which have TabIndex values of 2 through 21. Be sure to set the values in numerical order. If you make a mistake, press the Esc key to remove the TabIndex boxes from the form, then repeat Steps 1 through 5. When you have finished setting all of the TabIndex values, the color of the boxes will automatically change from white to blue, as shown in Figure 2-20.

Figure 2-20: Correct TabIndex values shown in the form

» TIP

You also can remove the TabIndex boxes by clicking View, and then clicking Tab Order.

6 Verify that the TabIndex values shown on your screen agree with those shown in Figure 2-20, then press **Esc** to remove the TabIndex boxes from the form.

7 Save the solution.

»GUI DESIGN TIP

Rules for Assigning Access Keys and Controlling the Focus

» Assign a unique access key to each control (in the interface) that can receive user input (for example, text boxes, buttons, and so on).

» When assigning an access key to a control, use the first letter of the caption or identifying label, unless another letter provides a more meaningful association. If you can't use the first letter and no other letter provides a more meaningful association, then use a distinctive consonant. Lastly, use a vowel or a number.

» Assign a TabIndex value (begin with 0) to each control in the interface, except for controls that do not have a TabIndex property. The TabIndex values should reflect the order in which the user will want to access the controls.

» To give users keyboard access to a text box, assign an access key to the text box's identifying label. Set the identifying label's TabIndex property to a value that is one number less than the value stored in the text box's TabIndex property. (In other words, the TabIndex value of the text box should be one number greater than the TabIndex value of its identifying label control.)

In the next set of steps, you will verify that the tab order is working correctly.

To verify that the tab order is working correctly:

1 Start the application. The user interface shown in Figure 2-21 appears on the screen.

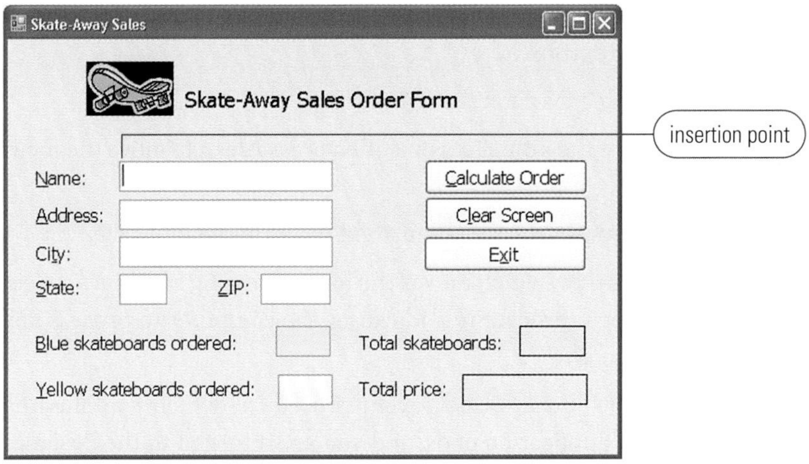

Figure 2-21: Skate-Away Sales interface

When you start an application, the computer sends the focus to the control whose TabIndex value is 0; in this case, that control is the Label1 control, which displays the Name: text. However, because label controls cannot receive the focus, the computer sends the focus to the next control in the tab order sequence. In this case, the next control in the tab order sequence is the xNameTextBox. Notice that an insertion point appears in the xNameTextBox. The insertion point indicates that the text box has the focus and is ready to receive input from you.

2 Type **Sport Warehouse** in the xNameTextBox. Notice that a text box displays the information it receives from you. The information is recorded in the text box's Text property.

In Windows applications, the Tab key moves the focus forward, and the Shift + Tab key combination moves the focus backward.

3 Press **Tab** to move the focus to the xAddressTextBox, then press **Shift + Tab** to move the focus back to the xNameTextBox.

Use the Tab key to verify the tab order of the controls in the interface.

4 Press **Tab**, slowly, seven times. The focus moves to the following controls: xAddressTextBox, xCityTextBox, xStateTextBox, xZipTextBox, xBlueTextBox, xYellowTextBox, and xCalcButton.

Notice that, when the focus moves to the Calculate Order button, the button's border is highlighted and a dotted rectangle appears around its caption. Pressing the Enter key when a button has the focus invokes the button's Click event and causes the computer to process any code contained in the event procedure.

5 Press **Tab** three times. The focus moves to the xClearButton, then to the xExitButton, and finally back to the xNameTextBox.

You also can move the focus using a text box's access key.

6 Press **Alt+b** to move the focus to the xBlueTextBox, then press **Alt+n** to move the focus to the xNameTextBox.

7 On your own, try the access keys for the remaining text boxes in the interface.

Unlike pressing a text box's access key, which moves the focus, pressing a button's access key invokes the button's Click event procedure and causes the computer to process any code contained in the event procedure.

8 Press **Alt+x** to invoke the Exit button's Click event procedure, which contains the `Me.Close()` instruction. The application ends, and you are returned to the designer window.

You have completed Lesson B. You can either take a break or complete the end-of-lesson questions and exercises before moving on to Lesson C, where you complete the remaining steps involved in creating an OO application.

SUMMARY

TO CONTROL THE BORDER AROUND A CONTROL:
» Set the control's BorderStyle property.

TO LOCK/UNLOCK THE CONTROLS ON THE FORM:
» Right-click the form or any control on the form, then select Lock Controls on the context menu. To unlock the controls, simply select the Lock Controls option again. You also can lock/unlock controls by using the Lock Controls option on the Format menu.

TO ASSIGN AN ACCESS KEY TO A CONTROL:
» Type an ampersand (&) in the Text property of the control or identifying label. The ampersand should appear to the immediate left of the letter or number that you want to designate as the access key.

TO GIVE USERS KEYBOARD ACCESS TO A TEXT BOX:
» Assign an access key to the text box's identifying label. Set the identifying label's TabIndex property to a value that is one number less than the text box's TabIndex value.

TO ACCESS A CONTROL THAT HAS AN ACCESS KEY:
» Press and hold down the Alt key as you press the control's access key.

TO SET THE TAB ORDER:

» Set each control's TabIndex property to a number that represents the order in which the control should receive the focus. Remember to begin with 0 (zero). You can use the Properties window to set the TabIndex values. Or, you can use the Tab Order option on the View menu.

QUESTIONS

1. The _____ property determines the order in which a control receives the focus when the user presses the Tab key or an access key.

   a. SetOrder   b. TabIndex

   c. TabOrder   d. TabStop

2. The human eye is attracted to _____.

   a. black and white before color   b. color before black and white

   c. graphics before text   d. both b and c

3. When building an interface, always use _____.

   a. dark text on a light background   b. light text on a dark background

   c. light text on a light background d. either a or b

4. The letter _____ is typically the access key for an Exit button.

   a. E   b. x

   c. i   d. t

5. Use a _____ font for the text in the user interface.

   a. sans serif   b. serif

6. To put a border around a label control, you set the label control's _____ property to FixedSingle.

   a. Appearance   b. BackStyle

   c. Border   d. BorderStyle

7. You use the _____ character to assign an access key to a control.

    a.   b. @

    c. $ d. ^

8. You assign an access key using a control's _____ property.

    a. Access   b. Caption

    c. Key   d. Text

9. Explain the procedure for choosing a control's access key.

10. Explain how you give users keyboard access to a text box.

EXERCISES

1. In this exercise, you finish building a user interface.

    a. If necessary, start Visual Studio 2005 or Visual Basic 2005 Express Edition. Open the Paper Solution (Paper Solution.sln) file, which is contained in the VB2005\Chap02\ Paper Solution folder. If necessary, open the designer window.

    b. Figure 2-22 shows the completed user interface. Finish building the interface by adding a text box named xNameTextBox to the form. Assign access keys to the text boxes and buttons, as shown in the figure. Also set the TabIndex values appropriately.

Figure 2-22

    c. Lock the controls on the form.

d. Save the solution, then start the application. Verify that the tab order is correct, and that the access keys work appropriately. Click the Exit button to end the application. (The Exit button has already been coded for you. You will code the Calculate Commission and Clear Screen buttons in Lesson C's Exercise 1.)

e. Close the solution.

2. In this exercise, you finish building a user interface.

a. If necessary, start Visual Studio 2005 or Visual Basic 2005 Express Edition. Open the RMSales Solution (RMSales Solution.sln) file, which is contained in the VB2005\Chap02\RMSales Solution folder. If necessary, open the designer window.

b. Figure 2-23 shows the completed user interface. Finish building the interface by adding a label control named xNorthSalesLabel to the form. Change the BorderStyle property of the label control to the appropriate setting. Set the TabIndex values appropriately. In this interface, the user typically will enter the North region's sales and increase percentage before entering the South region's sales and increase percentage.

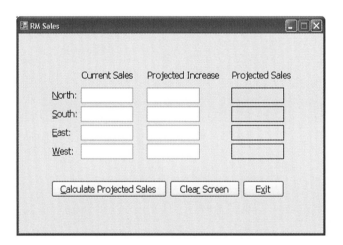

Figure 2-23

c. Lock the controls on the form.

d. Save the solution, then start the application. Verify that the tab order is correct, and that the access keys work appropriately. Click the Exit button to end the application. (The Exit button has already been coded for you. You will code the Calculate Projected Sales and Clear Screen buttons in Lesson C's Exercise 2.)

e. Close the solution.

3. In this exercise, you modify the application that you saved in Lesson A's Exercise 3.

   a. If necessary, start Visual Studio 2005 or Visual Basic 2005 Express Edition. Open the Time Solution (Time Solution.sln) file, which is contained in the VB2005\Chap02\Time Solution folder. If necessary, open the designer window.

   b. Lock the controls on the form.

   c. Assign access keys to the controls that can accept user input.

   d. Set each control's TabIndex property appropriately.

   e. Save the solution, then start the application. Verify that the tab order is correct, and that the access keys work appropriately. Click the Exit button to end the application.

   f. Close the solution.

LESSON C
OBJECTIVES

AFTER STUDYING LESSON C, YOU SHOULD
BE ABLE TO:

» Code an application using its TOE chart

» Plan an object's code using pseudocode or a flowchart

» Write an assignment statement

» Send the focus to a control while an application is
running

» Include internal documentation in the code

» Write arithmetic expressions

» Use the Val and Format functions

CODING, TESTING, DEBUGGING, AND DOCUMENTING THE APPLICATION

CODING THE APPLICATION

After planning an application and building its user interface, you then can begin coding the application so that the objects in the interface perform their assigned tasks when the appropriate event occurs. The objects and events that need to be coded are listed in the application's TOE chart, along with the tasks assigned to each object and event.

In Lessons A and B, you created a TOE chart and a user interface for the Skate-Away Sales application; you will code the application in this lesson. As you may remember, Skate-Away Sales sells skateboards by phone. The skateboards are priced at $100 each and are available in two colors: yellow and blue. Recall that the application should calculate and display the total number of skateboards ordered and the total price of the skateboards, including a 5% sales tax. Figure 2-24 shows the application's user interface, and Figure 2-25 shows its TOE chart.

Figure 2-24: Skate-Away Sales application's interface

Task	Object	Event
1. Calculate the total skateboards ordered and the total price 2. Display the total skateboards ordered and the total price in the xTotalBoardsLabel and xTotalPriceLabel	xCalcButton	Click
Clear the screen for the next order	xClearButton	Click
End the application	xExitButton	Click
Display the total skateboards ordered (from xCalcButton)	xTotalBoardsLabel	None
Display the total price (from xCalcButton)	xTotalPriceLabel	None
Get and display the order information	xNameTextBox, xAddressTextBox, xCityTextBox, xStateTextBox, xZipTextBox, xBlueTextBox, xYellowTextBox	None

Figure 2-25: Skate-Away Sales application's TOE chart (ordered by object)

According to the TOE chart shown in Figure 2-25, only the three buttons require coding, because they are the only objects with an event—in this case, the Click event—listed in the third column of the chart. Before you begin coding an object's event procedure, you should plan the procedure. Programmers commonly use either pseudocode or a flowchart when planning a procedure's code.

USING PSEUDOCODE TO PLAN A PROCEDURE

Pseudocode uses short phrases to describe the steps a procedure needs to take to accomplish its goal. Even though the word *pseudocode* might be unfamiliar to you, you already have written pseudocode without even realizing it. Think about the last time you gave directions to someone. You wrote each direction down on paper, in your own words; your directions were a form of pseudocode. Figure 2-26 shows the pseudocode for the procedures that need to be coded in the Skate-Away Sales application.

---

xCalcButton Click Event Procedure (pseudocode)

1. calculate total skateboards ordered = blue skateboards ordered + yellow skateboards ordered

2. calculate total price = total skateboards ordered * skateboard price * (1 + sales tax rate)

3. display total skateboards ordered and total price in xTotalBoardsLabel and xTotalPriceLabel

xClearButton Click Event Procedure (pseudocode)

1. clear the Text property of the seven text boxes

2. clear the Text property of the xTotalBoardsLabel and xTotalPriceLabel

3. send the focus to the xNameTextBox so the user can begin entering the next order

xExitButton Click Event Procedure (pseudocode)

1. end the application

Figure 2-26: Pseudocode for the Skate-Away Sales application

As the pseudocode indicates, the xCalcButton's Click event procedure is responsible for calculating the total skateboards ordered and the total price, and then displaying the calculated results in the appropriate label controls in the interface. The xClearButton's Click event procedure will prepare the screen for the next order by removing the contents of the text boxes and two label controls, and then sending the focus to the xNameTextBox. The xExitButton's Click event procedure will simply end the application.

USING A FLOWCHART TO PLAN A PROCEDURE

Unlike pseudocode, which consists of short phrases, a **flowchart** uses standardized symbols to show the steps a procedure must follow to reach its goal. Figure 2-27 shows the flowcharts for the procedures that need to be coded in the Skate-Away Sales application. Notice that the logic pictured in the flowcharts is the same as the logic shown in the pseudocode.

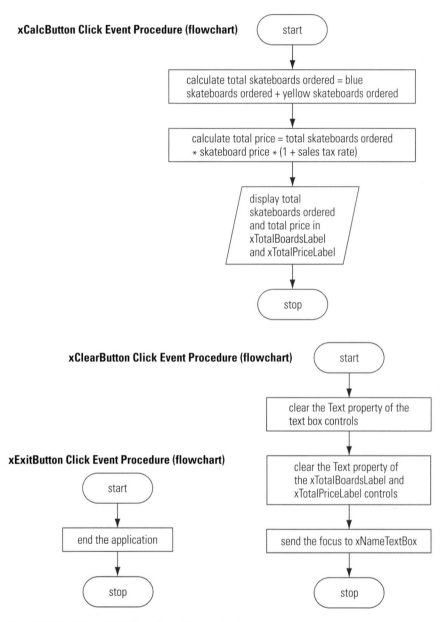

xCalcButton Click Event Procedure (flowchart)

xClearButton Click Event Procedure (flowchart)

xExitButton Click Event Procedure (flowchart)

Figure 2-27 Flowcharts for the Skate-Away Sales application

The flowcharts shown in Figure 2-27 contain three different symbols: an oval, a rectangle, and a parallelogram. The symbols are connected with lines, called **flowlines**. The oval symbol is called the **start/stop symbol**. The start oval indicates the beginning of the flowchart, and the stop oval indicates the end of the flowchart. The rectangles that appear between the start and the stop ovals are called **process symbols**. You use the process symbol to represent tasks such as making calculations.

The parallelogram in a flowchart is called the **input/output symbol** and is used to represent input tasks, such as getting information from the user, and output tasks, such as displaying information. The parallelogram shown in Figure 2-27 represents an output task.

When planning a procedure, you do not need to create both a flowchart and pseudocode; you need to use only one of these planning tools. The tool you use is really a matter of personal preference. For simple procedures, pseudocode works just fine. When a procedure becomes more complex, however, the procedure's steps may be easier to understand in a flowchart. The programmer uses either the procedure's pseudocode or its flowchart as a guide when coding the procedure. In this lesson, you will use the pseudocode shown in Figure 2-26 to code the procedures in the Skate-Away Sales application. First, however, you will need to open the Skate-Away Sales application from Lesson B.

To open the Skate-Away Sales application:

1 Start Visual Studio 2005 or Visual Basic 2005 Express Edition, if necessary, and close the Start Page window.

2 Open the **Skate Away Solution** (Skate Away Solution.sln) file, which is contained in the VB2005\Chap02\Skate Away Solution folder. If necessary, open the designer window. The interface shown earlier in Figure 2-24 appears on the screen.

3 Open the Code Editor window by right-clicking the **form**, and then clicking **View Code**.

»TIP

You also can open the Code Editor window by pressing the F7 key; or you can click View on the menu bar and then click Code.

According to the pseudocode shown in Figure 2-26, the xExitButton's Click event procedure is assigned the task of ending the application. As you learned in Chapter 1, you can use the `Me.Close()` statement to terminate an application. Notice that the statement is already entered in the xExitButton's Click event procedure.

CODING THE CLEAR SCREEN BUTTON

According to the TOE chart shown earlier in Figure 2-25, the xClearButton's Click event procedure is assigned the task of clearing the screen for the next order. The procedure's pseudocode, which is shown in Figure 2-28, indicates that the task involves clearing the Text property of seven text boxes and two labels in the interface, and then sending the focus to the xNameTextBox.

---

xClearButton Click Event Procedure (pseudocode)

1. clear the Text property of the seven text boxes

2. clear the Text property of the xTotalBoardsLabel and xTotalPriceLabel

3. send the focus to the xNameTextBox so the user can begin entering the next order

---

Figure 2-28: Pseudocode for the xClearButton's Click event procedure

You can clear the Text property of an object by assigning a zero-length string to it. A string is simply a group of characters enclosed in quotation marks. The word "Jones," for example, is a string. Likewise, "45" is a string, but 45 is not; 45 is a number. "Jones" is a string with a length of five, because there are five characters between the quotation marks. "45" is a string with a length of two, because there are two characters between the quotation marks. Following this logic, a **zero-length string**, also called an **empty string**, is a set of quotation marks with nothing between them, like this: "". Assigning a zero-length string to the Text property of an object while an application is running removes the contents of the object.

You also can clear an object's Text property by assigning the value **String.Empty** to it while an application is running. When you do this, the computer assigns the empty string ("") to the Text property, thereby removing its contents.

In Chapter 1, you learned how to use the Properties window to set an object's properties during design time, which is when you are building the interface. In the next section, you learn how you can set an object's properties while an application is running.

> **»TIP**
> You also can use the Clear method to clear the contents of a text box while an application is running. You learn about the Clear method in Discovery Exercise 11 at the end of this lesson.

ASSIGNING A VALUE TO A PROPERTY DURING RUN TIME

You use an **assignment statement**, which is one of many different types of Visual Basic instructions, to assign a value to something (such as the property of an object) while an application is running. The syntax of an assignment statement that assigns a value to an object's property is [**Me.**]*object.property* = *expression*. In the syntax, **Me** refers to the current form; however, the square brackets ([ ]) in the syntax indicate that Me. is optional in an assignment statement. *Object* and *property* are the names of the object and property, respectively, to which you want the value of the *expression* assigned. You use a period to separate the form reference (Me) from the object name, and to separate the object name from the property name. You use an equal sign (=) between the [**Me.**]*object.property* information and the *expression*. The equal sign in an assignment statement is called the **assignment operator**.

When the computer processes an assignment statement, it assigns the value of the expression that appears on the right side of the assignment operator to the object and property that appears on the left side of the assignment operator. For example, the

> **»TIP**
> The period that separates each word in Me.xNameTextBox.Text is called the dot member access operator. It tells the computer that what appears to the right of the dot is a member of what appears to the left of the dot. In this case, it indicates that the Text property is a member of the xNameTextBox, which is a member of the current form.

assignment statement `Me.xNameTextBox.Text = ""` assigns a zero-length string to the Text property of the xNameTextBox. (Because the `Me.` is optional, you also could use the instruction `xNameTextBox.Text = ""`.) Similarly, the assignment statement `Me.xStateTextBox.Text = "IL"` assigns the string "IL" to the xStateTextBox's Text property. You will use assignment statements to code the first two steps listed in the xClearButton's pseudocode (shown earlier in Figure 2-28).

To begin coding the Clear Screen button:

1 Click the **Class Name** list arrow in the Code Editor window, and then click **xClearButton** in the list. Click the **Method Name** list arrow, and then click **Click** in the list. The code template for the xClearButton's Click event procedure appears in the Code Editor window.

Step 1 in the procedure's pseudocode is to clear the Text property of the seven text boxes in the interface. You can do so using either the `Me.`*textbox*`.Text = String.Empty` instruction or the `Me.`*textbox*`.Text = ""` instruction, where *textbox* is the name of the appropriate text box. You also can use either the *textbox*`.Text = String.Empty` instruction or the *textbox*`.Text = ""` instruction, because the `Me.` is optional in an assignment statement. As you learned in Chapter 1, you can type the Visual Basic instructions on your own; or you can use the IntelliSense feature that is built into the Code Editor. In this set of steps, you will use the IntelliSense feature.

2 Type **me.** (but don't press Enter). When you type the period, the IntelliSense feature displays a list of choices from which you can select.

3 Type **xn** (but don't press Enter). The IntelliSense feature highlights the xNameTextBox choice in the list, as shown in Figure 2-29.

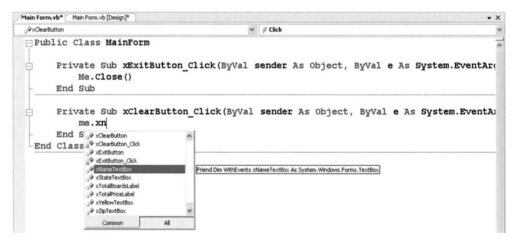

Figure 2-29: xNameTextBox choice highlighted in the list

4 Press the **Tab** key on your keyboard to include the xNameTextBox choice in the assignment statement, then type **.** (a period). The IntelliSense feature highlights the Text property in the list.

5 Press **Tab** to include the Text property in the assignment statement, then type **=** **string.e** to highlight the Empty choice in the list.

6 Press **Tab** to include the Empty choice in the assignment statement, and then press **Enter** to move the insertion point to the next line in the procedure. Figure 2-30 shows the completed assignment statement in the procedure.

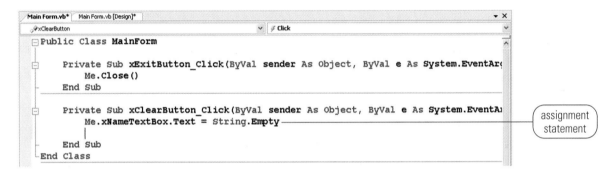

Figure 2-30: First assignment statement entered in the xClearButton's Click event procedure

When entering code, you can type the names of commands, objects, and properties in lowercase letters. When you move to the next line, the Code Editor automatically changes your code to reflect the proper capitalization of those elements. This provides a quick way of verifying that you entered an object's name and property correctly, and that you entered the code using the correct syntax. If the capitalization does not change, then the Code Editor does not recognize the object, command, or property.

Rather than typing Me. to activate the IntelliSense feature, you also can use the Control key along with the spacebar. You will use this method to enter the instruction xAddressTextBox.Text = String.Empty.

7 Press and hold down the **Ctrl** (or Control) key on your keyboard as you press the **spacebar**, then release the Ctrl key. The IntelliSense feature displays the list of choices shown in Figure 2-31.

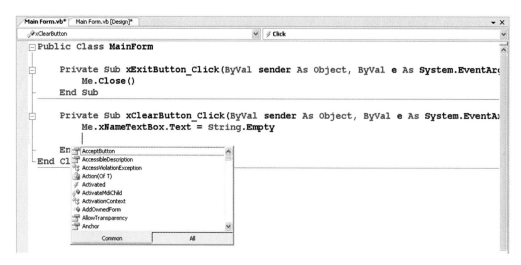

Figure 2-31: Choices displayed when you use Ctrl+spacebar

8   Type **x** (but don't press Enter). The IntelliSense feature highlights the xAddressTextBox choice in the list.

At this point, you can either press the Tab key to enter the xAddressTextBox choice in the assignment statement, or you can simply type a period, which is the character that comes after xAddressTextBox in the assignment statement.

9   Type **.** (a period). Notice that typing the period enters both the xAddressTextBox choice and a period in the assignment statement. The IntelliSense feature highlights the Text property in the list.

At this point, you can either press the Tab key to enter the Text choice in the assignment statement, or you can simply type the assignment operator (=), which is the character that comes after Text in the assignment statement.

10   Type = to enter both the Text choice and the assignment operator in the assignment statement, then type **string.e** and press **Enter**. The completed assignment statement, `xAddressTextBox.Text = String.Empty`, appears in the procedure, as shown in Figure 2-32.

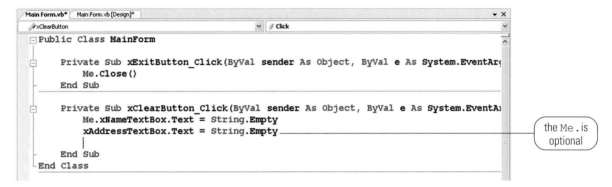

Figure 2-32: Second assignment statement entered in the procedure

Although entering Me. in a Visual Basic statement is optional, in this book you always will be instructed to enter the Me. in your instructions. In addition, you always will be given the complete instruction to enter. Keep in mind that you can type the instruction on your own, or you can use the IntelliSense feature to enter the instruction.

To continue coding the Clear Screen button:

1 Position the insertion point at the beginning of the xAddressTextBox.Text = String.Empty assignment statement. Type **me.** (but don't press Enter). When the IntelliSense feature displays the list of choices, press the **Esc** key on your keyboard to close the list, then click the line below the assignment statement. The statement changes to Me.xAddressTextBox.Text = String.Empty.

2 If necessary, press **Tab** twice to align the insertion point with the letter M in the second assignment statement.

3 Use the IntelliSense feature to enter the following five instructions:

   Me.xCityTextBox.Text = String.Empty

   Me.xStateTextBox.Text = String.Empty

   Me.xZipTextBox.Text = String.Empty

   Me.xBlueTextBox.Text = String.Empty

   Me.xYellowTextBox.Text = String.Empty

The second step in the procedure's pseudocode is to clear the Text property of the xTotalBoardsLabel and xTotalPriceLabel controls.

4 Use the IntelliSense feature to enter the following two instructions:

   Me.xTotalBoardsLabel.Text = String.Empty

   Me.xTotalPriceLabel.Text = String.Empty

The last step in the procedure's pseudocode (shown earlier in Figure 2-28) is to send the focus to the xNameTextBox. You can accomplish this task using the Focus method. As you learned in Chapter 1, a method is a predefined Visual Basic procedure that you can call (or invoke) when needed.

USING THE FOCUS METHOD

You can use the **Focus method** to move the focus to a specified control while the application is running. As you learned in Lesson B, when a control has the focus, it can accept user input. The syntax of the Focus method is [**Me.**]*object*.**Focus()**, where *object* is the name of the object to which you want the focus sent.

To enter the Focus method in the xClearButton's Click event procedure, then save the solution:

1 Type **me.xNameTextBox.focus()** and press **Enter**.

2 Save the solution.

INTERNALLY DOCUMENTING THE PROGRAM CODE

It is a good practice to include some comments as reminders in the Code Editor window. Programmers refer to the comments as **internal documentation**. You create a comment in Visual Basic by placing an apostrophe (') before the text that represents the comment. The computer ignores everything that appears after the apostrophe on that line. Although it is not required, many programmers use a space to separate the apostrophe from the comment.

Many programmers use a comment to document a procedure's purpose. You enter the comment below the `Private Sub` line in the procedure. Here again, although it is not required, many programmers follow the comment with a blank line. You also should include comments that explain various sections of the procedure's code, because comments make the code more readable and easier to understand by anyone viewing it.

To add comments to the xClearButton's Click event procedure, then test the procedure:

1 Position the insertion point at the beginning of the `Me.xNameTextBox.Text = String.Empty` statement in the xClearButton's Click event procedure.

2 Press **Enter** to insert a blank line above the statement.

3 Press the **up arrow** key on your keyboard to position the insertion point in the blank line. Press **Tab** twice to indent the code you are about to type, then type ' **prepare the screen for the next order** (be sure to type the apostrophe, followed by a space) and press **Enter**.

Notice that the comments appear in a different color from the rest of the code. The color-coding helps you easily locate the comments in the Code Editor window.

4 Position the insertion point at the end of the `Me.xTotalPriceLabel.Text = String.Empty` statement. Press **Enter** to insert a blank line below the statement, then type **' send the focus to the Name text box**. Figure 2-33 shows the completed Click event procedure for the xClearButton. Verify that the code shown on your screen agrees with the code shown in the figure.

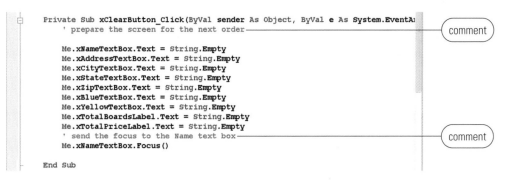

```
Private Sub xClearButton_Click(ByVal sender As Object, ByVal e As System.EventA
    ' prepare the screen for the next order                        comment

    Me.xNameTextBox.Text = String.Empty
    Me.xAddressTextBox.Text = String.Empty
    Me.xCityTextBox.Text = String.Empty
    Me.xStateTextBox.Text = String.Empty
    Me.xZipTextBox.Text = String.Empty
    Me.xBlueTextBox.Text = String.Empty
    Me.xYellowTextBox.Text = String.Empty
    Me.xTotalBoardsLabel.Text = String.Empty
    Me.xTotalPriceLabel.Text = String.Empty
    ' send the focus to the Name text box                          comment
    Me.xNameTextBox.Focus()

End Sub
```

Figure 2-33: Completed Click event procedure for the xClearButton

It is a good programming practice to write the code for one object at a time, and then test and debug that object's code before coding the next object. This way, if something is wrong with the program, you know exactly where to look for the error.

5 Save the solution, then start the application.

6 Enter your name and address information (including the city, state, and ZIP) in the appropriate text boxes, then enter **10** for the number of blue skateboards ordered and **10** for the number of yellow skateboards ordered.

7 Click the **Clear Screen** button. Following the instructions you entered in the xClearButton's Click event procedure, the computer removes the contents of the seven text boxes, as well as the contents of the xTotalBoardsLabel and xTotalPriceLabel controls. It also sends the focus to the Name text box.

8 Click the **Exit** button to end the application. You are returned to the Code Editor window.

Many programmers also use comments to document the project's name and purpose, as well as to document the programmer's name and the date the code was either created or modified. Typically, such comments are placed at the beginning of the application's code, above the `Public Class` statement. The area above the `Public Class` statement in the Code Editor window is called the General Declarations section.

To include comments in the General Declarations section:

1 Position the insertion point at the beginning of the `Public Class MainForm` instruction, then press **Enter** to insert a blank line above the instruction.

2 Press the **up arrow** key on your keyboard to position the insertion point in the blank line.

3 Type the comments shown in Figure 2-34. Replace the <your name> and <current date> text with your name and the current date.

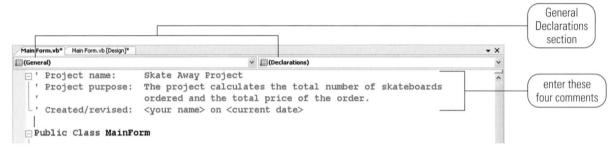

Figure 2-34: Comments entered in the General Declarations section

4 Save the solution.

The Calculate Order button is the only object that still needs to be coded. However, before coding the button, you learn how to write arithmetic expressions in Visual Basic.

WRITING ARITHMETIC EXPRESSIONS

Most applications require the computer to perform one or more calculations. You instruct the computer to perform a calculation by writing an arithmetic expression that contains one or more arithmetic operators. Figure 2-35 lists the most commonly used arithmetic operators available in Visual Basic, along with their precedence numbers. The **precedence numbers** indicate the order in which the computer performs the operation in an expression. Operations with a precedence number of 1 are performed before operations with a precedence number of 2, which are performed before operations with a precedence number of 3, and so on. However, you can use parentheses to override the order of precedence, because operations within parentheses always are performed before operations outside parentheses.

Operator	Operation	Precedence number
^	exponentiation (raises a number to a power)	1
–	negation	2
* , /	multiplication and division	3
\	integer division	4
Mod	modulus arithmetic	5
+, –	addition and subtraction	6
Important Note: You can use parentheses to override the order of precedence. Operations within parentheses are always performed before operations outside parentheses.		

Figure 2-35: Most commonly used arithmetic operators and their order of precedence

The difference between the negation and subtraction operators shown in Figure 2-35 is that the negation operator is unary, whereas the subtraction operator is binary. Unary and binary refer to the number of operands required by the operator. Unary operators require one operand, whereas binary operators require two operands. The expression –7 uses the negation operator to turn the positive number 7 into a negative number. The expression 9 – 4 uses the subtraction operator to subtract the number 4 from the number 9.

Notice that some operators shown in Figure 2-35 have the same precedence number. For example, both the addition and subtraction operators have a precedence number of 6. If an expression contains more than one operator having the same priority, those operators are evaluated from left to right. In the expression 3 + 12 / 3 – 1, for instance, the division (/) is performed first, then the addition (+), and then the subtraction (–). In other words, the computer first divides 12 by 3, then adds the result of the division (4) to 3, and then subtracts 1 from the result of the addition (7). The expression evaluates to 6.

You can use parentheses to change the order in which the operators in an expression are evaluated. For example, the expression 3 + 12 / (3 – 1) evaluates to 9, not 6. This is because the parentheses tell the computer to subtract 1 from 3 first, then divide the result of the subtraction (2) into 12, and then add the result of the division (6) to 3, giving 9.

Two of the arithmetic operators listed in Figure 2-35 might be less familiar to you; these are the integer division operator (\) and the modulus arithmetic operator (Mod). You use the **integer division operator** (\) to divide two integers (whole numbers), and then return the result as an integer. For example, the expression 211\4 results in 52, which is the integer result of dividing 211 by 4. (If you use the standard division operator [/] to divide 211 by 4, the result is 52.75 rather than 52.)

The modulus arithmetic operator also is used to divide two numbers, but the numbers do not have to be integers. After dividing the numbers, the **modulus arithmetic operator** returns the remainder of the division. For example, 211 Mod 4 equals 3, which is the remainder of 211 divided by 4. One use for the modulus arithmetic operator is to determine whether a year is a leap year—one that has 366 days rather than 365 days. As you may know, if a year is a leap year, then its year number is evenly divisible by the number four. In other words, if you divide the year number by 4 and the remainder is zero, then the year is a leap year. You can determine whether the year 2008 is a leap year by using the expression 2008 Mod 4. This expression evaluates to zero (the remainder of 2008 divided by 4), so the year 2008 is a leap year. Similarly, you can determine whether the year 2009 is a leap year by using the expression 2009 Mod 4. This expression evaluates to one (the remainder of 2009 divided by 4), so the year 2009 is not a leap year.

When entering an arithmetic expression in code, you do not enter the dollar sign ($) or the percent sign (%). If you want to enter a percentage in an arithmetic expression, you first must change the percentage to its decimal equivalent; for example, you would change 5% to .05.

In addition to the arithmetic operators, Visual Basic also allows you to use comparison operators and logical operators in an expression. You learn about comparison and logical operators in Chapter 4. To code the Calculate Order button in the Skate-Away Sales application, you need to know only the arithmetic operators.

CODING THE CALCULATE ORDER BUTTON

According to the TOE chart for the Skate-Away Sales application (shown earlier in Figure 2-25), the xCalcButton is responsible for calculating both the total number of skateboards ordered and the total price of the order, and then displaying the calculated amounts in the xTotalBoardsLabel and xTotalPriceLabel controls. The instructions to accomplish the button's tasks should be placed in the button's Click event procedure, because you want the instructions processed when the user clicks the button. Figure 2-36 shows the pseudocode for the xCalcButton's Click event procedure. Recall that the pseudocode lists the steps the button must take to accomplish its tasks.

---

xCalcButton Click Event Procedure (pseudocode)

1. calculate total skateboards ordered = blue skateboards ordered + yellow skateboards ordered

2. calculate total price = total skateboards ordered * skateboard price * (1 + sales tax rate)

3. display total skateboards ordered and total price in xTotalBoardsLabel and xTotalPriceLabel

---

Figure 2-36: Pseudocode for the xCalcButton's Click event procedure

The first step listed in the pseudocode is to calculate the total number of skateboards ordered. This is accomplished by adding the number of blue skateboards ordered to the number of yellow skateboards ordered. Recall that the number of blue skateboards ordered is recorded in the xBlueTextBox's Text property as the user enters that information in the interface. Likewise, the number of yellow skateboards ordered is recorded in the xYellowTextBox's Text property. You can use an assignment statement to first add together the Text property of the two text boxes, and then assign the sum to the Text property of the xTotalBoardsLabel control, which is where the TOE chart indicates the sum should be displayed. The total skateboards ordered calculation is illustrated in Figure 2-37.

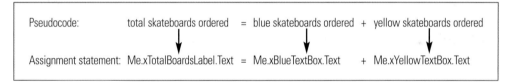

Figure 2-37: Illustration of the total skateboards ordered calculation

The next step shown in the procedure's pseudocode is to compute the total price of the order. You can accomplish this task by multiplying the total number of skateboards ordered (which is recorded in the xTotalBoardsLabel) by the skateboard price ($100), and then adding a 5% sales tax to the result. The TOE chart indicates that the total price of the order should be displayed in the xTotalPriceLabel. The total price calculation is illustrated in Figure 2-38.

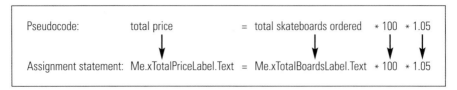

Figure 2-38: Illustration of the total price calculation

The last step in the procedure's pseudocode is to display the total skateboards ordered and total price in the xTotalBoardsLabel and xTotalPriceLabel controls. The assignment statements shown in Figures 2-37 and 2-38 accomplish this task.

To begin coding the xCalcButton's Click event procedure:

1 Open the code template for the xCalcButton's Click event procedure.

> **▶▶HELP?** To open the code template, click the Class Name list arrow, and then click xCalcButton. Click the Method Name list arrow, and then click Click.

2 Type ' **calculates the total number of skateboards ordered and the total price** and press **Enter** twice.

3 Type **me.xTotalBoardsLabel.text = me.xBlueTextBox.text + me.xYellowTextBox. text** and press **Enter**.

4 Type **me.xTotalPriceLabel.text = me.xTotalBoardsLabel.text * 100 * 1.05** and press **Enter**. Figure 2-39 shows the comment and assignment statements entered in the procedure.

```
Private Sub xCalcButton_Click(ByVal sender As Object, ByVal e As System.EventArg
        ' calculates the total number of skateboards ordered and the total price

    Me.xTotalBoardsLabel.Text = Me.xBlueTextBox.Text + Me.xYellowTextBox.Text
    Me.xTotalPriceLabel.Text = Me.xTotalBoardsLabel.Text * 100 * 1.05

End Sub
```

Figure 2-39: Code entered in the xCalcButton's Click event procedure

5 Save the solution, then start the application.

6 Press **Tab** five times to move the focus to the xBlueTextBox control. Type **5** as the number of blue skateboards ordered, then press **Tab**. Type **10** as the number of yellow skateboards ordered, then click the **Calculate Order** button. The xCalcButton's Click event procedure calculates the total number of skateboards ordered and the total price, and displays the results in the xTotalBoardsLabel and xTotalPriceLabel controls. As Figure 2-40 indicates, the results are incorrect.

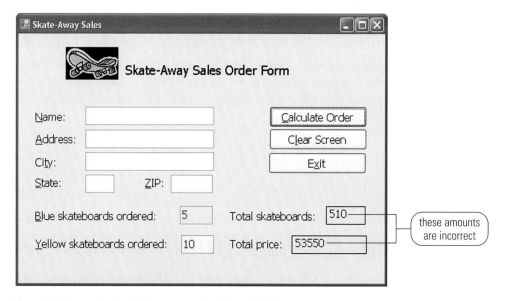

Figure 2-40: Screen showing the incorrect results of the calculations

Notice that the screen shows 510 as the total number of skateboards ordered. Rather than mathematically adding the two order quantities together, which should have resulted in a total of 15, the computer appended the second order quantity to the end of the first order quantity, giving 510. When the total skateboards ordered figure is incorrect, it follows that the total price figure also will be incorrect, because the total skateboards ordered figure is used in the total price calculation.

7 Click the **Exit** button to end the application. You are returned to the Code Editor window.

The `Me.xTotalBoardsLabel.Text = Me.xBlueTextBox.Text + Me.xYellow TextBox.Text` equation you entered in the xCalcButton's Click event procedure is supposed to calculate the total number of skateboards ordered, but the equation is not working correctly. Instead of the plus sign (+) adding the blue skateboard quantity to the yellow skateboard quantity, the plus sign appends the latter quantity to the end of the first one. This occurs because the plus sign in Visual Basic performs two roles: it adds numbers together and it concatenates (links together) strings. You learn about string concatenation in Chapter 3. (Recall that strings are groups of characters enclosed in quotation marks.)

In Visual Basic, a value stored in the Text property of an object is treated as a string rather than as a number, even though you do not see the quotation marks around the value. Adding strings together does not give you the same result as adding numbers together. As you observed in the Skate-Away Sales application, adding the string "5" to the string "10" results in the string "510," whereas adding the number 5 to the number 10 results in the number 15. To fix the problem, you need to instruct the computer to treat the entries in the Text property of both the xBlueTextBox and xYellowTextBox controls as numbers rather than as strings. Visual Basic provides several ways of telling the computer to treat a string as though it were a number. For example, you can use the Val function, or the TryParse method, or the Convert method. In this chapter (and only in this chapter), you will use the Val function, because it is the easiest to learn. However, keep in mind that most programmers now use either the TryParse method or the Convert method, rather than the Val function. You will learn how to use the TryParse and Convert methods in Chapter 3.

THE VAL FUNCTION

A **function** is a predefined procedure that performs a specific task and then returns a value after completing the task. The **Val function**, for instance, temporarily converts a string to a number, and then returns the number. (The number is stored in the computer's memory only while the function is processing.)

The syntax of the Val function is **Val**(*string*), where *string* is the string you want treated as a number. Because the computer must be able to interpret the *string* as a numeric value, the *string* cannot include a letter or a special character, such as the dollar sign, the comma, or the percent sign (%); it can, however, include a period and a space. When the computer encounters an invalid character in the Val function's *string*, it stops converting the *string* to a number at that point. Figure 2-41 shows some examples of how the Val function converts various strings. Notice that the Val function converts the "$56.88", the "Abc", and the "" (zero-length string) to the number 0.

This Val function:	Would be converted to:
Val("456")	456
Val("24,500")	24
Val("123X")	123
Val("25%")	25
Val("$56.88")	0
Val("Abc")	0
Val("")	0

Figure 2-41: Examples of the Val function

You will use the Val function in the assignment statements in the xCalcButton's Click event procedure. The Val function will temporarily convert to numbers the Text property of the controls included in the calculations.

To include the Val function in the xCalcButton's code:

1 Change the `Me.xTotalBoardsLabel.Text = Me.xBlueTextBox.Text + Me.xYellowTextBox.Text` statement to **Me.xTotalBoardsLabel.Text = Val(Me.xBlueTextBox.Text) + Val(Me.xYellowTextBox.Text)**. Be sure to watch the placement of the parentheses in the statement.

2 Change the `Me.xTotalPriceLabel.Text = Me.xTotalBoardsLabel.Text * 100 * 1.05` statement to **Me.xTotalPriceLabel.Text = Val(Me.xTotalBoardsLabel. Text) * 100 * 1.05**. Figure 2-42 shows the Val function entered in the xCalcButton's Click event procedure.

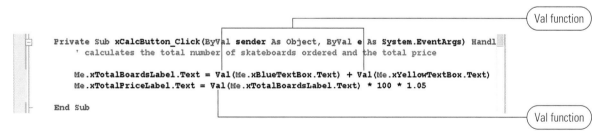

```
Private Sub xCalcButton_Click(ByVal sender As Object, ByVal e As System.EventArgs) Handl
    ' calculates the total number of skateboards ordered and the total price

    Me.xTotalBoardsLabel.Text = Val(Me.xBlueTextBox.Text) + Val(Me.xYellowTextBox.Text)
    Me.xTotalPriceLabel.Text = Val(Me.xTotalBoardsLabel.Text) * 100 * 1.05

End Sub
```

Val function

Val function

Figure 2-42: Val function entered in the xCalcButton's Click event procedure

3 Save the solution, then start the application.

4 Click the **xBlueTextBox** control, type **5** as the number of blue skateboards ordered, then press **Tab**. Type **10** as the number of yellow skateboards ordered, then click the **Calculate Order** button. The application correctly calculates and displays the total number of skateboards ordered (15) and the total price of the order (1575).

In the next section, you will improve the appearance of the interface by including a dollar sign, a comma thousand separator, and two decimal places in the total price amount. You also will center the calculated results within their respective label controls.

5 Click the **Clear Screen** button to clear the screen, then click the **Exit** button. You are returned to the Code Editor window.

USING THE FORMAT FUNCTION TO FORMAT NUMERIC OUTPUT

You can use the **Format function** to improve the appearance of the numbers displayed in an interface. The syntax of the Format function is **Format**(*expression, style*). *Expression* specifies the number, date, time, or string whose appearance you want to format. *Style* is either the name of a predefined Visual Basic format style or, if you want more control over the appearance of the *expression*, a string containing special symbols that indicate how you want the *expression* displayed. (You can display the Help screen for the Format function to learn more about these special symbols.) In this case, you will use one of the predefined Visual Basic format styles, some of which are explained in Figure 2-43.

Format style	Description
Currency	Displays a number with a dollar sign and two decimal places; if appropriate, displays a number with a thousand separator; negative numbers are enclosed in parentheses
Fixed	Displays a number with at least one digit to the left and two digits to the right of the decimal point
Standard	Displays a number with at least one digit to the left and two digits to the right of the decimal point; if appropriate, displays a number with a thousand separator
Percent	Multiplies a number by 100 and displays the number with a percent sign (%); displays two digits to the right of the decimal point

Figure 2-43: Some of the predefined format styles in Visual Basic

You will use the Currency format style to display the total price amount with a dollar sign, a comma thousand separator, and two decimal places.

To format the total price amount:

1 In the blank line below the total price equation, type **me.xTotalPriceLabel.text = format(me.xTotalPriceLabel.text, "currency")** and then press **Enter**. Figure 2-44 shows the Format function entered in the xCalcButton's Click event procedure. (You could have included the Format function in the equation that calculates the total price, but then the equation would be so long that it would be difficult to understand.)

```
Private Sub xCalcButton_Click(ByVal sender As Object, ByVal e As System.EventArgs) Handl
    ' calculates the total number of skateboards ordered and the total price

    Me.xTotalBoardsLabel.Text = Val(Me.xBlueTextBox.Text) + Val(Me.xYellowTextBox.Text)
    Me.xTotalPriceLabel.Text = Val(Me.xTotalBoardsLabel.Text) * 100 * 1.05
    Me.xTotalPriceLabel.Text = Format(Me.xTotalPriceLabel.Text, "currency")

End Sub
```
Format function

Figure 2-44: Format function entered in the xCalcButton's Click event procedure

2 Save the solution, then close the Code Editor window.

ALIGNING THE TEXT WITHIN A CONTROL

You use a control's **TextAlign property** to specify the position of the text within the control. You will use the TextAlign property to center the text contained in the xTotalBoardsLabel and xTotalPriceLabel controls.

To center the text contained in two of the label controls:

1 Click the **xTotalBoardsLabel** control, then Ctrl + click the **xTotalPriceLabel** control. Both controls are now selected.

2 Click **TextAlign** in the Properties list, then click the **list arrow** button in the Settings box, and then click the **rectangle** that appears in the second row, second column. The MiddleCenter value appears in the Settings box.

3 Click the **form** to deselect the controls.

4 Save the solution, then start the application.

5 Enter the following order: **Sport Warehouse, 123 Main, Glendale, IL, 60134, 10 blue skateboards, 15 yellow skateboards**.

6 Click the **Calculate Order** button. The application calculates the total number of skateboards ordered and the total price. The calculated results appear centered within their respective label controls, and the total price appears formatted, as shown in Figure 2-45.

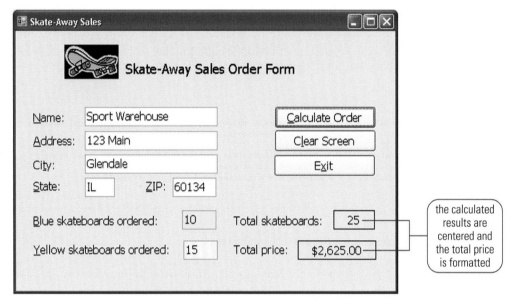

Figure 2-45: Result of calculating the Sport Warehouse order

7 Click the **Exit** button. You are returned to the designer window.

You have completed the first four of the six steps involved in creating an OO application: meeting with the client, planning the application, building the user interface, and coding the application. The fifth step is to test and debug the application.

TESTING AND DEBUGGING THE APPLICATION

You test an application by starting it and entering some sample data. You should use both valid and invalid test data. **Valid data** is data that the application is expecting. For example, the Skate-Away Sales application is expecting the user to enter a numeric value as the number of blue skateboards ordered. **Invalid data**, on the other hand, is data that the application is not expecting. The Skate-Away Sales application, for example, is not expecting the user to enter a letter for the number of either blue or yellow skateboards ordered. You should test the application as thoroughly as possible, because you don't want to give the user an application that ends abruptly when invalid data is entered.

Debugging refers to the process of locating errors in the program. Program errors can be either syntax errors or logic errors. Most **syntax errors** are simply typing errors that occur when entering instructions. For example, typing `Me.Clse()` instead of `Me.Close()` results in a syntax error. The Code Editor detects most syntax errors as you enter the instructions. An example of a much more difficult type of error to find, and one that the Code Editor cannot detect, is a logic error. You create a **logic error** when you enter an instruction that does not give you the expected results. An example of a logic error is the instruction `Me.xAverageLabel.Text = Val(Me.xNum1TextBox.Text) + Val(Me.xNum2TextBox.Text) / 2`, which is supposed to calculate the average of two numbers. Although the instruction is syntactically correct, it is logically incorrect. The instruction to calculate the average of two numbers, written correctly, is `Me.xAverageLabel.Text = (Val(Me.xNum1TextBox.Text) + Val(Me.xNum2TextBox.Text)) / 2`. Because division has a higher precedence number than does addition, you must place parentheses around the `Val(Me.xNum1TextBox.Text) + Val(Me.xNum2TextBox.Text)` part of the expression.

To test and debug the Skate-Away Sales application with both valid and invalid data:

1 Start the application. First, test the application by clicking the **Calculate Order** button without entering any data. The application displays 0 as the total number of skateboards ordered, and $0.00 as the total price. (Recall that the Val function converts the empty string to the number 0.)

2 Click the **Clear Screen** button to clear the calculated results from the label controls.

3 Now enter the letter **r** as the number of blue skateboards ordered and the letter **p** as the number of yellow skateboards ordered. Click the **Calculate Order** button. The application displays 0 as the total number of skateboards ordered, and $0.00 as the total price. (Recall that the Val function converts letters to the number 0.)

4 Click the **Clear Screen** button, then enter an order that is correct. Click the **Calculate Order** button.

5 Click the **Clear Screen** button, then practice with other entries to see how the application responds.

6 When you are finished testing the application, click the **Exit** button to end the application. You are returned to the designer window.

After you have tested the application to verify that it is working correctly, you can move to the last step involved in creating an OO application, which is to assemble the documentation.

ASSEMBLING THE DOCUMENTATION

Assembling the documentation refers to putting your planning tools and a printout of the application's interface and code in a safe place, so you can refer to them if you need to change the application in the future. Your planning tools include the TOE chart, a sketch of the user interface, and either the flowcharts or pseudocode.

To print the application's code:

1 Open the Code Editor window.

2 Click **File** on the menu bar, then click **Print**. When the Print dialog box appears, click the **OK** button to print the code, then close the Code Editor window. Figure 2-46 shows the Skate-Away Sales application's code.

```
' Project name:    Skate Away Project
' Project purpose: The project calculates the total number of skateboards
' ordered and the total price of the order.
' Created/revised: <your name> on <current date>

Public Class MainForm

    Private Sub xExitButton_Click(ByVal sender As Object, ByVal
    e As System.EventArgs) Handles xExitButton.Click
        Me.Close()
    End Sub

    Private Sub xClearButton_Click(ByVal sender As Object, ByVal
    e As System.EventArgs) Handles xClearButton.Click
        ' prepare the screen for the next order
        Me.xNameTextBox.Text = String.Empty
        Me.xAddressTextBox.Text = String.Empty
        Me.xCityTextBox.Text = String.Empty
```

Figure 2-46: Skate-Away Sales application's code *(Continued)* ▶

```
        Me.xStateTextBox.Text = String.Empty
        Me.xZipTextBox.Text = String.Empty
        Me.xBlueTextBox.Text = String.Empty
        Me.xYellowTextBox.Text = String.Empty
        Me.xTotalBoardsLabel.Text = String.Empty
        Me.xTotalPriceLabel.Text = String.Empty
        ' send the focus to the Name text box
        Me.xNameTextBox.Focus()
    End Sub
    Private Sub xCalcButton_Click(ByVal sender As Object, ByVal
    e As System.EventArgs) Handles xCalcButton.Click
        ' calculates the total number of skateboards ordered and the total price

        Me.xTotalBoardsLabel.Text = Val(Me.xBlueTextBox.Text) + Val(Me.xYellowTextBox.Text)
        Me.xTotalPriceLabel.Text = Val(Me.xTotalBoardsLabel.Text) * 100 * 1.05
        Me.xTotalPriceLabel.Text = Format(Me.xTotalPriceLabel.Text, "currency")
    End Sub
End Class
```

Figure 2-46: Skate-Away Sales application's code

To print the application's interface:

1 Start the application. Press **Alt + Print Screen** (or PrtSc) to place a picture of the interface on the Clipboard.

2 Click the **Exit** button to end the application.

3 Start Microsoft Word (or any application that can display a picture) and open a new document (if necessary). Click **Edit** on the Word menu bar, then click **Paste** to paste the contents of the Clipboard in the document. (You also can press Ctrl + v.)

4 Click **File** on the Word menu bar, and then click **Print**. When the Print dialog box appears, click the **OK** button to print the document.

5 Click **File** on the Word menu bar, and then click **Exit**. When you are asked if you want to save the changes made to the document, click the **No** button.

6 Close the solution.

You have completed Lesson C and Chapter 2. You can either take a break or complete the end-of-lesson questions and exercises.

SUMMARY

TO PLAN AN OBJECT'S CODE:
» Use pseudocode or a flowchart.

TO CLEAR THE TEXT PROPERTY OF AN OBJECT WHILE AN APPLICATION IS RUNNING:
» Assign the empty string (""), or the `String.Empty` value, to the object's Text property.

TO ASSIGN A VALUE TO THE PROPERTY OF AN OBJECT WHILE AN APPLICATION IS RUNNING:
» Use an assignment statement that follows the syntax [**Me.**]*object.property = expression*.

TO MOVE THE FOCUS TO AN OBJECT WHILE AN APPLICATION IS RUNNING:
» Use the Focus method. The method's syntax is [**Me.**]*object*. **Focus()**.

TO DOCUMENT VISUAL BASIC CODE WITH COMMENTS:
» Begin the comment text with an apostrophe (').

TO DIVIDE TWO INTEGERS, AND THEN RETURN THE RESULT AS AN INTEGER:
» Use the integer division operator (\).

TO DIVIDE TWO NUMBERS, AND THEN RETURN THE REMAINDER AS AN INTEGER:
» Use the modulus arithmetic operator (Mod).

TO TEMPORARILY CONVERT A STRING TO A NUMBER:
» Use the Val function. The function's syntax is **Val**(*string*).

TO IMPROVE THE APPEARANCE OF NUMBERS IN THE USER INTERFACE:
» Use the Format function. The function's syntax is **Format**(*expression, style*).

TO ALIGN THE TEXT WITHIN A CONTROL:
» Set the control's TextAlign property.

QUESTIONS

1. Which of the following is *not* a valid assignment statement?

   a. `Me.xNameTextBox.Text = ''`

   b. `Me.xNameTextBox.Text = String.Empty`

   c. `Me.xNameTextBox.Text = "Jones"`

   d. `Me.xNameTextBox.Text = "Carol"`

2. Which of the following assignment statements will *not* calculate correctly?

   a. `Me.xTotalLabel.Text = Val(Me.xSales1TextBox.Text) + Val(Me.xSales2TextBox.Text)`

   b. `Me.xTotalLabel.Text = Val(Me.xSales1Label.Text + Me.xSales2Label.Text)`

   c. `Me.xTotalLabel.Text = Val(Me.xRedTextBox.Text) * 2`

   d. `Me.xTotalLabel.Text = Val(Me.xBlueLabel.Text) * 1.1`

3. You use the _____ function to display a dollar sign and a thousand separator in numbers.

   a. Display   b. Format

   c. Style   d. Val

4. The _____ function temporarily converts a string to a number.

   a. Format   b. String

   c. StringToNum   d. Val

5. In a flowchart, the _____ symbol is used to represent a calculation task.

   a. circle   b. oval

   c. parallelogram   d. rectangle

6. The instruction `Me.xTotalLabel.Text = Val(Me.xNumTextbox.Text) / 2`, which should multiply the contents of the xNumTextbox by 2 and then assign the result to the xTotalLabel, is an example of _____.

   a. a logic error   b. a syntax error

   c. a correct instruction

7. The instruction `Me.xSalesLabel.Text = Format(Me.xSalesLabel.Text, "curency")` is an example of _____.

   a. a logic error   b. a syntax error

   c. a correct instruction

8. What value is assigned to the xNumLabel control when the `Me.xNumLabel.Text = 73 / 25` instruction is processed by the computer?

9. What value is assigned to the xNumLabel control when the `Me.xNumLabel.Text = 73 \ 25` instruction is processed by the computer?

10. What value is assigned to the xNumLabel control when the `Me.xNumLabel.Text = 73 Mod 25` instruction is processed by the computer?

EXERCISES

NOTE: In several of the exercises in this lesson, you perform the second through sixth steps involved in creating an OO application. Recall that the six steps are:

1. Meet with the client.

2. Plan the application. (Prepare a TOE chart that is ordered by object, and draw a sketch of the user interface.)

3. Build the user interface. (To help you remember the names of the controls as you are coding, print the application's interface and then write the names next to each object.)

4. Code the application. (Write pseudocode for each of the objects that will be coded, and include appropriate comments in the code.)

5. Test and debug the application. (Use the sample data provided in each of the exercises.)

6. Assemble the documentation (your planning tools and a printout of the interface and code).

1. In this exercise, you complete the application that you saved in Lesson B's Exercise 1.

    a. If necessary, start Visual Studio 2005 or Visual Basic 2005 Express Edition. Open the Paper Solution (Paper Solution.sln) file, which is contained in the VB2005\Chap02\Paper Solution folder. If necessary, open the designer window.

    b. Code the Calculate Commission button appropriately. Be sure to use the Val function. Use the Format function to display the commission with a dollar sign, a comma thousand separator, and two decimal places. Use the Focus method to send the focus to the Clear Screen button.

    c. Code the Clear Screen button appropriately. Send the focus to the Name text box.

    d. Save the solution, then start the application. Test the application using valid and invalid data. Use the following information for the valid data:

    Name: Pat Brown

    Sales: 2000

    Rate: .1

    e. Stop the application, then close the solution.

2. In this exercise, you complete the application that you saved in Lesson B's Exercise 2.

    a. If necessary, start Visual Studio 2005 or Visual Basic 2005 Express Edition. Open the RMSales Solution (RMSales Solution.sln) file, which is contained in the VB2005\Chap02\RMSales Solution folder. If necessary, open the designer window.

    b. Code the Calculate Projected Sales button appropriately. Be sure to use the Val function. Use the Format function to display the projected sales using the Standard format.

    c. Code the Clear Screen button appropriately. Send the focus to the xNorthSalesTextBox.

    d. Save the solution, then start the application. Test the application using valid and invalid data. Use the following information for the valid data:

North sales and percentage:	25000, .1
South sales and percentage:	10000, .05
East sales and percentage:	10000, .04
West sales and percentage:	15000, .11

    e. Stop the application, then close the solution.

3. In this exercise, you complete the application that you saved in Lesson B's Exercise 3.

   a. If necessary, start Visual Studio 2005 or Visual Basic 2005 Express Edition. Open the Time Solution (Time Solution.sln) file, which is contained in the VB2005\Chap02\Time Solution folder. If necessary, open the designer window.

   b. Code the Calculate button appropriately. Be sure to use the Val function. Send the focus to the Monday text box.

   c. Save the solution, then start the application. Test the application using valid and invalid data. Use the following information for the valid data:

Monday hours:	7
Tuesday hours:	8
Wednesday hours:	6
Thursday hours:	5
Friday hours:	4
Saturday hours:	2
Sunday hours:	0

   d. Stop the application, then close the solution.

4. Scenario: John Lee wants an application in which he can enter the following three pieces of information: his cash balance at the beginning of the month, the amount of money he earned during the month, and the amount of money he spent during the month. He wants the application to compute his ending balance.

   a. If necessary, start Visual Studio 2005 or Visual Basic 2005 Express Edition.

   b. Create a Visual Basic Windows-based application. Name the solution JohnLee Solution, and name the project JohnLee Project. Save the application in the VB2005\Chap02 folder.

   c. Assign the filename Main Form.vb to the form file object.

   d. Assign the name MainForm to the form.

   e. Perform the steps involved in creating an OO application. (See the NOTE at the beginning of the Exercises section. Use the GUI design guidelines listed in Appendix A to verify that the interface you create adheres to the GUI standards outlined in this book.)

   f. Test the application using the following valid and invalid data:

Beginning cash balance: 5000	Earnings: 2500	Expenses: 3000
Beginning cash balance: xyz	Earnings: xyz	Expenses: xyz

   g. Stop the application, then close the solution.

5. Scenario: Lana Jones wants an application that will compute the average of any three numbers she enters.

   a. If necessary, start Visual Studio 2005 or Visual Basic 2005 Express Edition.

   b. Create a Visual Basic Windows-based application. Name the solution LanaJones Solution, and name the project LanaJones Project. Save the application in the VB2005\Chap02 folder.

   c. Assign the filename Main Form.vb to the form file object.

   d. Assign the name MainForm to the form.

   e. Perform the steps involved in creating an OO application. (See the NOTE at the beginning of the Exercises section. Use the GUI design guidelines listed in Appendix A to verify that the interface you create adheres to the GUI standards outlined in this book.)

   f. Test the application using the following valid and invalid data:

   First Number: 27   Second Number: 9   Third Number: 18

   First Number: A   Second Number: B   Third Number: C

   g. Stop the application, then close the solution.

6. Scenario: Martha Arenso, manager of Bookworms Inc., needs an inventory application. Martha will enter the title of a book, the number of paperback versions of the book currently in inventory, the number of hardcover versions of the book currently in inventory, the cost of the paperback version, and the cost of the hardcover version. Martha wants the application to compute the value of the paperback versions of the book, the value of the hardcover versions of the book, the total number of paperback and hardcover versions, and the total value of the paperback and hardcover versions.

   a. If necessary, start Visual Studio 2005 or Visual Basic 2005 Express Edition.

   b. Create a Visual Basic Windows-based application. Name the solution Bookworms Solution, and name the project Bookworms Project. Save the application in the VB2005\Chap02 folder.

   c. Assign the filename Main Form.vb to the form file object.

   d. Assign the name MainForm to the form.

   e. Perform the steps involved in creating an OO application. (See the NOTE at the beginning of the Exercises section. Use the GUI design guidelines listed in Appendix A to verify that the interface you create adheres to the GUI standards outlined in this book.)

   f. Format the calculated dollar amounts to show a dollar sign, comma thousand separator, and two decimal places.

g. Test the application using the following valid and invalid data:

Book Title: An Introduction to Visual Basic 2005

Paperback versions: 100   Paperback cost: 40

Hardcover versions: 50   Hardcover cost: 75

Book Title: Advanced Visual Basic 2005

Paperback versions: A   Paperback cost: B

Hardcover versions: C   Hardcover cost: D

h. Stop the application, then close the solution.

7. Scenario: Jackets Unlimited is having a 25% off sale on all its merchandise. The store manager asks you to create an application that requires the clerk simply to enter the original price of a jacket. The application should then compute the discount and new price.

a. If necessary, start Visual Studio 2005 or Visual Basic 2005 Express Edition.

b. Create a Visual Basic Windows-based application. Name the solution Jackets Solution, and name the project Jackets Project. Save the application in the VB2005\Chap02 folder.

c. Assign the filename Main Form.vb to the form file object.

d. Assign the name MainForm to the form.

e. Perform the steps involved in creating an OO application. (See the NOTE at the beginning of the Exercises section. Use the GUI design guidelines listed in Appendix A to verify that the interface you create adheres to the GUI standards outlined in this book.)

f. Format the discount and new price using the Standard format style.

g. Test the application using valid and invalid data.

h. Stop the application, then close the solution.

8. Scenario: Typing Salon charges $.10 per typed envelope and $.25 per typed page. The company accountant wants an application to help her prepare bills. She will enter the customer's name, the number of typed envelopes, and the number of typed pages. The application should compute the total bill.

a. If necessary, start Visual Studio 2005 or Visual Basic 2005 Express Edition.

b. Create a Visual Basic Windows-based application. Name the solution TypingSalon Solution, and name the project TypingSalon Project. Save the application in the VB2005\Chap02 folder.

c. Assign the filename Main Form.vb to the form file object.

d. Assign the name MainForm to the form.

e. Perform the steps involved in creating an OO application. (See the NOTE at the beginning of the Exercises section. Use the GUI design guidelines listed in Appendix A to verify that the interface you create adheres to the GUI standards outlined in this book.)

f. Format the total bill using the Currency format style.

g. Test the application using the following valid and invalid data:

Customer's name: Alice Wong

Number of typed envelopes: 250   Number of typed pages: 200

Customer's name: Alice Wong

Number of typed envelopes: $4   Number of typed pages: AB

h. Stop the application, then close the solution.

9. Scenario: Suman Gadhari, the payroll clerk at Sun Projects, wants an application that will compute the net pay for each of the company's employees. Suman will enter the employee's name, hours worked, and rate of pay. For this application, you do not have to worry about overtime, because this company does not allow anyone to work more than 40 hours. Suman wants the application to compute the gross pay, the federal withholding tax (FWT), the Social Security tax (FICA), the state income tax, and the net pay. Use the following information when computing the three taxes:

FWT: 20% of gross pay

FICA: 8% of gross pay

state income tax: 2% of gross pay

a. If necessary, start Visual Studio 2005 or Visual Basic 2005 Express Edition.

b. Create a Visual Basic Windows-based application. Name the solution Sun Solution, and name the project Sun Project. Save the application in the VB2005\Chap02 folder.

c. Assign the filename Main Form.vb to the form file object.

d. Assign the name MainForm to the form.

e. Perform the steps involved in creating an OO application. (See the NOTE at the beginning of the Exercises section. Use the GUI design guidelines listed in Appendix A to verify that the interface you create adheres to the GUI standards outlined in this book.)

f. Format the calculated amounts using the Standard format style.

g. Test the application using valid and invalid data.

h. Stop the application, then close the solution.

10. In this exercise, you modify the Skate-Away Sales application that you completed in the chapter.

    a. Use Windows to make a copy of the Skate Away Solution folder, which is contained in the VB2005\Chap02 folder. Rename the folder Modified Skate Away Solution.

    b. If necessary, start Visual Studio 2005 or Visual Basic 2005 Express Edition. Open the Skate Away Solution (Skate Away Solution.sln) file contained in the VB2005\Chap02\Modified Skate Away Solution folder. Open the designer window.

    c. Modify the interface so that it allows the user to enter the skateboard price and sales tax rate. Also modify the application's code.

    d. Save the solution, then start the application. Test the application using valid and invalid data. Be sure to use different prices and tax rates.

    e. Stop the application, then close the solution.

DISCOVERY EXERCISE

11. In this exercise, you learn about the TabStop property and the Clear method.

    a. Use Windows to make a copy of the Skate Away Solution folder, which is contained in the VB2005\Chap02 folder. Rename the folder Discovery Skate Away Solution.

    b. If necessary, start Visual Studio 2005 or Visual Basic 2005 Express Edition. Open the Skate Away Solution (Skate Away Solution.sln) file contained in the VB2005\Chap02\Discovery Skate Away Solution folder. Open the designer window.

    c. Most of Skate-Away's customers reside in Illinois. Use the Properties window to set the xStateTextBox's Text property to IL.

    A control's TabStop property allows you to bypass the control in the tab order when the user is tabbing. You can use the TabStop property in the Skate-Away Sales application to bypass the xStateTextBox control. Because the xStateTextBox already contains IL, there is no need for the user to tab into the control when entering data. Should the user want to change the State value, he or she needs simply to click the control or use the control's access key.

    d. Change the xStateTextBox control's TabStop property to False, then save the solution and start the application. Verify that the xStateTextBox control is bypassed when you tab through the controls in the interface.

    e. Click the Clear Screen button. Notice that the button removes the IL from the xStateTextBox. Stop the application.

f. Modify the xClearButton's Click event procedure so that it assigns the string "IL" to the xStateTextBox when the button is clicked.

g. Save the solution, then start the application. Click the xStateTextBox. Delete the IL, then type TX. Click the Clear Screen button. The button should assign the value IL to the xStateTextBox. Stop the application.

h. You can use a text box control's Clear method to remove the contents of the control while an application is running. The method's syntax is `Me.`*textbox*`.Clear()`. Modify the xClearButton's Click event procedure so that it uses the Clear method to remove the contents of the text boxes (except the xStateTextBox). (You cannot use the Clear method to remove the contents of label controls.)

i. Save the solution, then start the application. Verify that the Clear Screen button's code works correctly.

j. Stop the application, then close the solution.

DISCOVERY EXERCISE

12. Scenario: Colfax Industries needs an application that allows the shipping clerk to enter the quantity of an item in inventory and the number of the items that can be packed in a box for shipping. When the shipping clerk clicks a button, the application should compute and display the number of full boxes that can be packed and the number of items left over.

a. If necessary, start Visual Studio 2005 or Visual Basic 2005 Express Edition.

b. Create a Visual Basic Windows-based application. Name the solution Colfax Solution, and name the project Colfax Project. Save the application in the VB2005\Chap02 folder.

c. Assign the filename Main Form.vb to the form file object.

d. Assign the name MainForm to the form.

e. Perform the steps involved in creating an OO application. (See the NOTE at the beginning of the Exercises section. Use the GUI design guidelines listed in Appendix A to verify that the interface you create adheres to the GUI standards outlined in this book.)

f. Test the application using the following information. Colfax has 45 skateboards in inventory. If six skateboards can fit into a box for shipping, how many full boxes could the company ship, and how many skateboards will remain in inventory?

g. Stop the application, then close the solution.

DEBUGGING EXERCISE

13. In this exercise, you introduce a syntax error in an application. You then learn how to debug the application.

   a. Use Windows to make a copy of the Skate Away Solution folder, which is contained in the VB2005\Chap02 folder. Rename the folder Debug Skate Away Solution.

   b. If necessary, start Visual Studio 2005 or Visual Basic 2005 Express Edition. Open the Skate Away Solution (Skate Away Solution.sln) file contained in the VB2005\Chap02\Debug Skate Away Solution folder. Open the designer window.

   c. Open the Code Editor window. In the xExitButton's Click event procedure, change the Me.Close() statement to Me.Clse(), then click in the line above the procedure header. Notice that a jagged blue line appears below the statement. The jagged line indicates that the code contains a syntax error.

   d. Position your mouse pointer on the Me.Clse() statement. The Code Editor displays a box that contains an appropriate error message, as shown in Figure 2-47. In this case, the message indicates that Clse is not a member of the form.

Figure 2-47: Jagged blue line and box indicate a syntax error

At this point, you should correct the error before starting the application. However, observe what happens when you start an application that contains a syntax error.

   e. Save the solution, then start the application. The computer displays the message box shown in Figure 2-48.

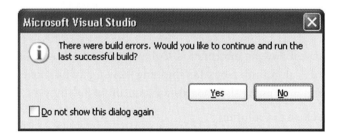

Figure 2-48: Message box indicates that the code contains errors

f. Click the No button. The Error List window shown in Figure 2-49 opens. Notice that the Error List window indicates that the code has one error: 'Clse' is not a member of 'Skate_Away_Project.MainForm'.

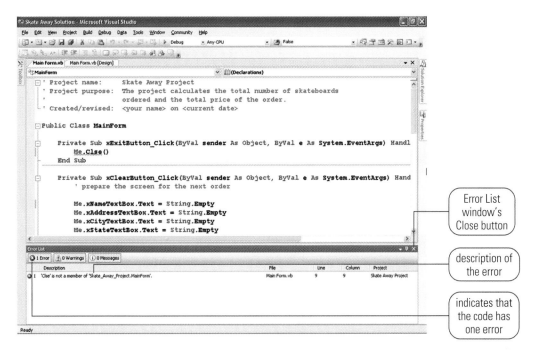

Figure 2-49: Error List window

g. Double-click the description of the error in the Error List window. The Code Editor highlights the error—in this case, the Me.Clse text—in the code, as shown in Figure 2-50.

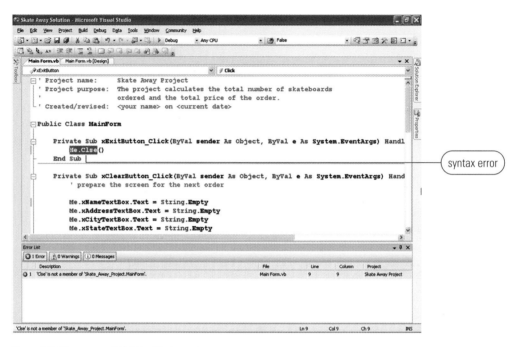

Figure 2-50: Syntax error highlighted in the code

h. Type me.close to correct the syntax error, then click the Code Editor window.

i. Close the Error List window. Save the solution, then start the application. Click the Exit button to end the application.

j. Close the Code Editor window, then close the solution.

3

USING VARIABLES AND CONSTANTS

REVISING THE SKATE-AWAY SALES APPLICATION

Mr. Cousard, the manager of Skate-Away Sales, informs you that he wants to make a change to the Skate-Away Sales application that you created in Chapter 2. He now wants to include a message on the order form. The message should say "The sales tax was", followed by the sales tax amount and the name of the salesperson who recorded the order. In this chapter, you modify the application's code to accommodate this change.

PREVIEWING THE COMPLETED APPLICATION

Before you begin modifying the Skate-Away Sales application, you first preview the completed application.

To preview the completed application:

1 Use the Run command on the Start menu to run the **SkateAway** (SkateAway.exe) file, which is contained in the VB2005\Chap03 folder. An order form similar to the one that you created in Chapter 2 appears on the screen.

2 Enter the following customer information on the order form: **Skaters Inc., 34 Plum Drive, Chicago, IL, 60654**.

3 Enter **25** as the number of blue skateboards ordered, then enter **5** as the number of yellow skateboards ordered.

Although the Calculate Order button does not have the focus, you still can select it by pressing the Enter key, because the Calculate Order button is the default button in the user interface. You learn how to designate a default button in Lesson B.

4 Press **Enter** to calculate the order. A Name Entry dialog box appears and requests the salesperson's name, as shown in Figure 3-1.

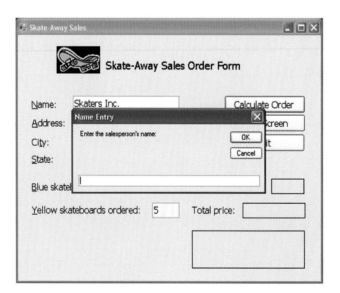

Figure 3-1: Name Entry dialog box

5 Type **Jack Sysmanski** as the salesperson's name and press **Enter**. The application calculates the order. The completed order form is shown in Figure 3-2.

Figure 3-2: Completed order form

Notice that the sales tax amount and the salesperson's name appear on the order form. The application uses string concatenation, which you learn about in Lesson B, to display the information.

6 Change the number of yellow skateboards ordered to **10**. The application clears the contents of the label controls that display the total skateboards ordered, total price, and message. In Lesson C, you learn how to clear the contents of a control when a change is made to the value stored in a different control.

7 Click the **Calculate Order** button to calculate the order. The Name Entry dialog box appears and displays the salesperson's name (Jack Sysmanski) in a text box. Press **Enter** to select the dialog box's OK button. The application recalculates the total skateboards ordered, total price, and sales tax amount.

8 Click the **Clear Screen** button to clear the order information from the form.

9 Click the **Exit** button to end the application.

In Lesson A, you learn how to store information, temporarily, in memory locations inside the computer. You modify the Skate-Away Sales application in Lessons B and C.

LESSON A
OBJECTIVES

AFTER STUDYING LESSON A, YOU SHOULD
BE ABLE TO:

» Declare variables and named constants

» Assign data to an existing variable

» Convert string data to a numeric data type using the
TryParse method

» Convert numeric data to a different data type using the
Convert class methods

» Explain the scope and lifetime of variables and named
constants

» Explain the purpose of the `Option Explicit` and
`Option Strict` statements

CREATING VARIABLES AND NAMED CONSTANTS

USING VARIABLES TO STORE INFORMATION

Recall that all of the skateboard information in the Skate-Away Sales application is temporarily stored in the properties of various controls on the order form. For example, the number of blue skateboards ordered is stored in the Text property of the xBlueTextBox, and the number of yellow skateboards ordered is stored in the Text property of the xYellowTextBox. Also recall that the assignment statement `Me.xTotalBoardsLabel.Text = Val(Me.xBlueTextBox.Text) + Val(Me.xYellowTextBox.Text)` calculates the total skateboards ordered by adding the value stored in the xBlueTextBox's Text property to the value stored in the xYellowTextBox's Text property, and then assigns the sum to the Text property of the xTotalBoardsLabel. Similarly, the total price equation, `Me.xTotalPriceLabel.Text = Val(Me.xTotalBoardsLabel.Text) * 100 * 1.05`, calculates the total price of the order and assigns the result to the xTotalPriceLabel.

Besides storing data in the properties of controls, a programmer also can store data, temporarily, in memory locations inside the computer. The memory locations are called **variables**, because the contents of the locations can change as the application is running. It may be helpful to picture a variable as a small box inside the computer. You can enter and store data in the box, but you cannot actually see the box.

One use for a variable is to hold information that is not stored in a control on the user interface. For example, if you did not need to display the total number of skateboards ordered on the Skate-Away Sales order form, you could eliminate the xTotalBoardsLabel from the form and store the total number of skateboards ordered in a variable instead. You then would use the value stored in the variable, rather than the value stored in the Text property of the xTotalBoardsLabel, in the total price equation.

You also can store, in a variable, the data contained in a control's property. For example, you can store the data contained in the Text property of a text box in a variable. Programmers typically do this when the data is a numeric amount that will be used in a calculation. As you will learn in the next section, assigning numeric data to a variable allows you to control the preciseness of the data. It also makes your code run more efficiently, because the computer can process data stored in a variable much faster than it can process data stored in the property of a control.

Every variable has a data type, name, scope, and lifetime. First, you will learn how to select an appropriate data type for a variable.

SELECTING A DATA TYPE FOR A VARIABLE

Each variable used in an application must be assigned a data type by the programmer. The **data type** determines the type of data the variable can store. Figure 3-3 describes most of the basic data types available in Visual Basic 2005. Each data type is a class, which means that each data type is a pattern from which one or more objects—in this case, variables—are instantiated (created).

»TIP

Also available in Visual Basic 2005 are the SByte, UInteger, ULong, and UShort data types. The "S" in SByte stands for "signed." The "U" in the other data types stands for "Unsigned."

Type	Stores	Memory required	Values
Boolean	logical value	2 bytes	True, False
Byte	binary number	1 byte	0 to 255 (unsigned)
Char	one Unicode character	2 bytes	one Unicode character
Date	date and time information	8 bytes	dates from January 1, 0001 to December 31, 9999, and times from 0:00:00 to 23:59:59
Decimal	fixed-point number	16 bytes	+/− 79,228,162,514,264,337,593,543,950,335 number with no decimal point; +/− 7.9228162514264337593543950335 with a decimal point; smallest non-zero number is +/− 0.0000000000000000000000000001
Double	floating-point number	8 bytes	+/− 4.94065645841247E-324 to 1.79769313486231E308
Integer	integer	4 bytes	−2,147,483,648 to 2,147,483,647
Long	integer	8 bytes	−9,223,372,036,854,775,808 to 9,223,372,036,854,775,807
Object	object reference	4 bytes	N/A
Short	integer	2 bytes	−32,768 to 32,767
Single	floating-point number	4 bytes	+/− 1.401298E-45 to 3.402823E38
String	text	varies	0 to approximately 2 billion characters

Figure 3-3: Basic data types in Visual Basic 2005

As Figure 3-3 indicates, variables assigned the Integer, Long, or Short data type can store integers, which are whole numbers—positive or negative numbers without any decimal places. The differences among these three data types are in the range of integers each type can store and the amount of memory each type needs to store the integer.

Figure 3-3 indicates that Single and Double variables can store a floating-point number, which is a number that is expressed as a multiple of some power of 10. Floating-point numbers are written in E (exponential) notation, which is similar to scientific notation. For example, the number 3,200,000 written in E (exponential) notation is 3.2E6; written in scientific notation it is 3.2×10^6. Notice that exponential notation simply replaces "x 10^6" with the letter E followed by the power number—in this case, 6. Floating-point numbers also can have a negative number after the E. For example, 3.2E-6 means 3.2 divided by 10 to the sixth power, or .0000032.

Floating-point numbers are used to represent both extremely small and extremely large numbers. The differences between the Single and Double types are in the range of numbers each type can store and the amount of memory each type needs to store the numbers. Although a Double variable can store numbers in a Single variable's range, a Double variable takes twice as much memory to do so.

》》TIP

A number such as 4.5 can be written as either 4.5 or 4.5E0.

Variables declared using the Decimal data type store numbers with a fixed decimal point. Unlike floating-point numbers, fixed-point numbers are not expressed as a multiple of some power of 10. To illustrate this point, the number 32000 expressed as a floating-point number is 3.2E4, but that same number expressed as a fixed-point number is simply 32000. Calculations involving fixed-point numbers are not subject to the small rounding errors that may occur when floating-point numbers are used. In most cases, the small rounding errors do not create any problems in an application. One exception, however, is when the application contains complex equations dealing with money, where you need accuracy to the penny. In those cases, the Decimal data type is the best type to use.

Also listed in Figure 3-3 are the Char data type, which can store one Unicode character, and the String data type, which can store from zero to approximately two billion Unicode characters. **Unicode** is the universal coding scheme for characters. It assigns a unique numeric value to each character used in the written languages of the world. For more information, see The Unicode Standard at *www.unicode.org*.

You use a Boolean variable to store the Boolean values True and False, and a Date variable to store date and time information. The Byte data type is used to store binary numbers.

If you do not assign a specific data type to a variable, Visual Basic 2005 assigns the Object type to it. Unlike other variables, an Object variable can store many different types of data, and it also can freely change the type of stored data while the application is running. For example, you can store the number 40 in an Object variable at the beginning of the application and then, later on in the application, store the text "John Smith" in that same variable. Although the Object data type is the most flexible data type, it is less efficient than the other data types. At times it uses more memory than necessary to store a value and, because the computer must determine the type of data currently stored in the variable, your application will run more slowly.

In this book, you will use the Integer data type for variables that will store integers used in calculations, even when the integers are small enough to fit into a Short variable. This is because a calculation containing Integer variables takes less time to process than the equivalent calculation containing Short variables. You will use either the Decimal data type or the Double data type for numbers that contain decimal places and are used in calculations. You will use the String data type for variables that contain text or numbers not used in calculations.

In addition to assigning a data type to the variables used in an application, the programmer also must assign a name to each variable.

SELECTING A NAME FOR A VARIABLE

You should assign a descriptive name to each variable used in an application, and the name should be entered using camel case. The name, also called the **identifier**, should help you remember the variable's purpose. In other words, it should help you remember the meaning of the value stored inside the variable. The names length and width, for example, are much more meaningful than are the names x and y, because length and width remind you that the amounts stored in the variables represent a length and width measurement, respectively.

For many years, most Visual Basic programmers used Hungarian notation when naming variables, and many programmers still follow this practice. As you learned in Chapter 1, Hungarian notation is a naming convention that uses the first three (or more) characters in the name to represent the object's type, and the remaining characters in the name to represent the object's purpose. Using Hungarian notation, a Decimal variable that stores a sales amount might be named decSales. The "dec" identifies the variable as a Decimal variable, and "Sales" reminds the programmer of the variable's purpose—in this case, to store a sales amount.

More recently, a new naming convention for variables has emerged. In the new naming convention, you no longer indicate the data type in a variable's name. Rather, you name the variable by its intended purpose only. Using this naming convention, a programmer

TIP

As you learned in Chapter 1, camel case means you lowercase the first word in the variable's name and then uppercase the first letter of each subsequent word in the name.

might assign the name `sales`, or the name `salesAmount`, to a variable that stores a sales amount. In this book, you will use the new naming convention for variables.

In addition to being descriptive, a variable name must follow the rules listed in Figure 3-4. The figure also includes examples of valid and invalid variable names.

Rules for naming variables
1. The name must begin with a letter or an underscore.
2. The name can contain only letters, numbers, and the underscore character. No punctuation characters or spaces are allowed in the name.
3. Although the name can contain a maximum of 16383 characters, 32 characters is the recommended maximum number of characters to use.
4. The name cannot be a reserved word, such as `Val` or `Print`.

Valid variable names	Invalid variable names	
`printReport`	`print`	(the name cannot be a reserved word)
`sales2007`	`2007Sales`	(the name must begin with a letter or an underscore)
`westRegion`	`west Region`	(the name cannot contain a space)
`firstName`	`first.Name`	(the name cannot contain punctuation)

Figure 3-4: Rules for variable names along with examples of valid and invalid names

»TIP
Although Microsoft recommends the new naming convention for variables, your company (or instructor) may have a different naming convention you are expected to use. Your company's (or instructor's) naming conventions supersede the ones recommended by Microsoft.

Now that you know how to select an appropriate data type and name for a variable, you can learn how to declare a variable in code. Declaring a variable tells the computer to set aside a small section of its internal memory, and it allows you to refer to the section by the variable's name. The size of the section is determined by the variable's data type.

DECLARING A VARIABLE

You use a declaration statement to declare (instantiate) a variable. Figure 3-5 shows the syntax of a declaration statement and includes several examples of declaring variables.

Declaring a variable

Syntax

{**Dim** | **Private** | **Static**} *variablename* **As** *datatype* [= *initialvalue*]

Examples

```
Dim hoursWorked As Double
```

declares a Double variable named `hoursWorked`; the variable is automatically initialized to 0

```
Dim itemPrice As Decimal
Dim discount As Decimal
```

declares two Decimal variables named `itemPrice` and `discount`; the variables are automatically initialized to 0

```
Dim isDataOk As Boolean = True
```

declares a Boolean variable named `isDataOK` and initializes it using the keyword `True`

```
Dim message As String = "Good morning"
```

declares a String variable named `message` and initializes it using the string "Good morning"

Figure 3-5: Syntax and examples of variable declaration statements

The {**Dim** | **Private** | **Static**} portion of the syntax shown in Figure 3-5 indicates that you can select only one of the keywords appearing within the braces. In this case, you can select `Dim`, `Private`, or `Static`. In most instances, you declare a variable using the `Dim` keyword. (You will learn about the `Private` and `Static` keywords later in this lesson.)

Variablename in the syntax is the variable's name, and *datatype* is the variable's data type. As mentioned earlier, a variable is considered an object in Visual Basic and is an instance of the class specified in the *datatype* information. The `Dim hoursWorked as Double` statement, for example, creates an object named `hoursWorked`. The `hoursWorked` object is an instance of the Double class.

Initialvalue in the syntax is the value you want stored in the variable when it is created in the computer's internal memory. The square brackets in the syntax indicate that the "= *initialvalue*" part of a variable declaration statement is optional. If you do not assign an initial value to a variable when it is declared, the computer stores a default value in the variable; the default value depends on the variable's data type. A variable declared using one of the numeric data types is automatically initialized to—in other words, given a beginning value of—the number zero. The computer automatically initializes a Boolean variable using the keyword `False`, and a Date variable to 1/1/0001 12:00:00 AM. Object and String variables are automatically initialized using the keyword `Nothing`. Variables initialized to `Nothing` do not actually contain the word "Nothing"; rather, they contain no data at all.

After a variable is declared, you can use an assignment statement to store other data in the variable.

ASSIGNING DATA TO AN EXISTING VARIABLE

In Chapter 2, you learned how to use an assignment statement to assign a value to a control's property while an application is running. You also can use an assignment statement to assign a value to a variable while an application is running. Figure 3-6 shows the syntax of an assignment statement that assigns a value to a variable. The figure also includes several examples of such assignment statements. Recall that the equal sign that appears in an assignment statement is called the assignment operator.

Assigning a value to a variable

Syntax

variablename **=** *value*

Examples

```
Dim quantityOrdered As Integer
quantityOrdered = 500
```

assigns the integer 500 to an Integer variable named quantityOrdered

```
Dim firstName As String
firstName = "Mary"
```

assigns the string "Mary" to a String variable named firstName

```
Dim zipCode As String
zipCode = Me.xZipTextBox.Text
```

assigns the string contained in the xZipTextBox's Text property to a String variable named zipCode

```
Dim discountRate As Double
discountRate = .03
```

assigns the Double number .03 to a Double variable named discountRate

```
Dim taxRate As Decimal
taxRate = .05D
```

converts the number .05 from Double to Decimal, and then assigns the result to a Decimal variable named taxRate

---

Figure 3-6: Syntax and examples of assignment statements that assign values to variables

When the computer processes an assignment statement, it assigns the value that appears on the right side of the assignment operator to the variable (memory location) whose name appears on the left side of the assignment operator. In other words, the computer stores the value in the variable. The data type of the value should be the same data type as the variable. For example, the `quantityOrdered = 500` assignment statement shown in Figure 3-6 stores the number 500, which is an integer, in an Integer variable named `quantityOrdered`. Similarly, the `firstName = "Mary"` assignment statement stores the string "Mary" in a String variable named `firstName`. As you learned in Chapter 2, a string is a group of characters enclosed in quotation marks. When the computer processes an assignment statement that assigns a string to a String variable, it assigns only the characters that appear between the quotation marks; the computer does not assign the quotation marks.

The number 500 and the string "Mary" are called literal constants. A **literal constant** is an item of data whose value does not change while the application is running. The number 500 is a numeric literal constant, and the string "Mary" is a string literal constant. Notice that you can store literal constants in variables. Also notice that string literal constants are enclosed in quotation marks, but numeric literal constants and variable names are not. The quotation marks differentiate a string from both a number and a variable name. In other words, "500" is a string, but 500 is a number. Similarly, "Mary" is a string, but Mary (without the quotation marks) would be interpreted by the computer as the name of a variable.

As you learned in Chapter 2, the value stored in the Text property of an object is always treated as a string, never as a number. Therefore, the `zipCode = Me.xZipTextBox.Text` assignment statement shown in Figure 3-6 assigns the string contained in the xZipTextBox's Text property to a String variable named `zipCode`.

In Visual Basic, a numeric literal constant that has a decimal place is automatically treated as a Double number. As a result, the `discountRate = .03` assignment statement shown in Figure 3-6 assigns the Double number .03 to a Double variable named `discountRate`. The last assignment statement in the figure, `taxRate = .05D`, shows how you convert a numeric literal constant of the Double data type to the Decimal data type, and then assign the result to a Decimal variable. The D that follows the number .05 in the statement is one of the literal type characters in Visual Basic. A **literal type character** forces a literal constant to assume a data type other than the one its form indicates. In this case, the D forces the Double number .05 to assume the Decimal data type, which causes the computer to store the number with a fixed-point rather than with a floating-point.

Figure 3-7 lists the literal type characters in Visual Basic and includes an example of using each character. Notice that you append the literal type character to the end of the literal constant.

Literal type character	Data type	Example
S	Short	age = 35S
I	Integer	hours = 40I
L	Long	population = 20500L
D	Decimal	rate = .03D
F	Single	payRate = .03F
R	Double	sales = 2356R
C	Char	initial = "A"C

Figure 3-7: Literal type characters

Technically, the I in the hours = 40I example in Figure 3-7 is not necessary. This is because Visual Basic treats a numeric literal constant that does not have a decimal place as an Integer number. The only exception to this treatment is when the number is too large to fit into an Integer variable; in that case, the number is treated as a Long.

Many times, the data type of the value you need to assign to a variable is different from the data type of the variable itself. As you just learned, if the value is a literal constant, you can use a literal type character to change the literal constant's data type to match the variable's data type. If the value is not a literal constant, however, you can use the TryParse method or one of the methods contained in the Convert class to change the value to the appropriate data type. You learn about the TryParse method first.

THE TRYPARSE METHOD

Recall that each data type in Visual Basic is a class. Most classes have one or more methods. A **method** is a specific portion of the class instructions, and its purpose is to perform a task for the class. For example, every numeric data type in Visual Basic 2005 has a **TryParse method** that can be used to convert a string to that numeric data type. Figure 3-8 shows the basic syntax of the TryParse method and includes examples of using the method. (You will learn more about the TryParse method in Chapter 4.)

Using the TryParse method

Basic syntax

datatype.**TryParse**(*string, variable*)

Examples

```
Dim sales As Decimal
Decimal.TryParse(Me.xSalesTextBox.Text, sales)
```

If the string stored in the xSalesTextBox can be converted to a Decimal number, the TryParse method converts the string and stores the result in the `sales` variable; otherwise, it stores the number 0 in the `sales` variable. Examples of strings that the method can convert to Decimal include "34", "12.55", "-4.23", "7.88-", "1,457.99", and " 33 ". The strings will be converted to the numbers 34, 12.55, -4.23, -7.88, 1457.99, and 33, respectively. Examples of strings that the method cannot convert to Decimal include "$5.67", "(4.23)", "7%", "122o", and "1 345".

```
Dim num As Integer
Integer.TryParse(Me.xNumTextBox.Text, num)
```

If the string stored in the xNumTextBox can be converted to an Integer number, the TryParse method converts the string and stores the result in the `num` variable; otherwise, it stores the number 0 in the `num` variable. Examples of strings that the method can convert to Integer include "6", " 7 ", and "–896". The strings will be converted to the numbers 6, 7, and –896, respectively. Examples of strings that the method cannot convert to Integer include "5,889", "$78", "(11)", "4-", and "7.5".

Figure 3-8: Basic syntax and examples of the TryParse method

In the TryParse method's syntax, *datatype* is one of the numeric data types available in Visual Basic—such as Decimal, Double, and Integer. Notice that you use a period to separate the class name (*datatype*) from the method name (TryParse). Recall from Chapter 1 that the period is called the dot member access operator, and it indicates that what appears to the right of the operator is a member of what appears to the left of the operator. In this case, the dot member access operator indicates that the TryParse method is a member of the *datatype* class.

The items within the parentheses in the syntax are called **arguments** and represent information you must provide to the method. In the TryParse method, the *string* argument represents the string you want converted to a number of the *datatype* type; the *string* argument typically is the Text property of a control. The *variable* argument is the name of a numeric variable where the TryParse method can store the number. The numeric variable must have the same data type as specified in the *datatype* portion of the syntax. In other words, when using the TryParse method to convert a string to a Decimal number, you need to provide the method with the name of a decimal variable in which to store the number.

»TIP

The word *parse* means to analyze something by separating it into individual elements. The TryParse method analyzes a string by separating it into individual characters, and determines whether each character can be converted to a number.

The TryParse method parses the string, which means it looks at each character in the string, to determine whether the string can be converted to a number of the specified data type. If the string can be converted, the TryParse method converts the string to a number and stores the number in the variable specified in the *variable* argument. However, if the TryParse method determines that the string cannot be converted to the appropriate data type, the method assigns the number zero to the variable specified in the *variable* argument.

In the first example shown in Figure 3-8, the `Decimal.TryParse(Me.xSalesTextBox.Text, sales)` statement uses the TryParse method to convert the string stored in the xSalesTextBox to a Decimal number. As you learned in Chapter 2, you need to convert the contents of a text box to a number before you can use the contents in a calculation. If the conversion is successful, the TryParse method stores the number in the `sales` variable; otherwise, it stores the number zero in the `sales` variable. As indicated in the figure, the TryParse method in the first example can convert (to Decimal) a string that contains only numbers, as well as one that also contains a decimal point, a leading or trailing sign, a comma, or leading and/or trailing spaces. It cannot, however, convert a string that contains a dollar sign, parentheses, a percent sign, a letter, or a space within the string.

In the second example shown in Figure 3-8, the `Integer.TryParse(Me.xNumTextBox.Text, num)` statement uses the TryParse method to convert the string stored in the xNumTextBox to an Integer. If the string can be converted, the method stores the result in an Integer variable named `num`. If, on the other hand, the string cannot be converted to an Integer, the method stores the number zero in the `num` variable. Notice that, in this example, the TryParse method can convert strings containing numbers, as well as strings that also contain a leading sign, leading spaces, or trailing spaces. It cannot, however, convert a string that contains a comma, a dollar sign, parentheses, a trailing sign, or a decimal point.

At times, you may need to convert a number (rather than a string) from one data type to another. Visual Basic provides several ways of accomplishing this task. For example, you can use the Visual Basic conversion functions, which are listed in Appendix B. You also can use one of the methods defined in the Convert class. In this book, you will use the Convert class methods, because they have an advantage over the conversion functions: the methods can be used in any .NET language, whereas the conversion functions can be used only in Visual Basic.

THE CONVERT CLASS

The **Convert class** contains methods that you can use to convert a numeric value to a specified data type. The most commonly used methods in the Convert class are the ToDecimal, ToDouble, ToInt32, and ToString methods. You use the methods to convert a number to the Decimal, Double, Integer, and String data types, respectively. Figure 3-9 shows the syntax of the Convert class methods, and it includes examples of using the methods. The dot member access operator in the syntax indicates that the *method* is a member of the Convert class.

Using the Convert class methods

Syntax
Convert.*method*(*value*)

Examples

```
Dim sales As Integer = 4500
Dim newSales As Double
newSales = Convert.ToDouble(sales)
```

converts the contents of an Integer variable named `sales` to Double, and assigns the result to a Double variable named `newSales`

```
Dim rate As Decimal = Convert.ToDecimal(.05)
```

converts the Double number .05 to Decimal before storing it in a Decimal variable named `rate`

```
Dim testScore As Integer = 98
Me.xScoreLabel.Text = Convert.ToString(testScore)
```

converts the contents of an Integer variable named `testScore` to String, and assigns the result to the xScoreLabel's Text property

Figure 3-9: Syntax and examples of the Convert class methods

»»TIP

You also can use the Convert methods to convert a String value to a numeric data type. However, the TryParse method is the recommended method to use for that task. This is because, unlike the TryParse method, the Convert methods result in an error when the String value cannot be converted to a number.

In the syntax shown in Figure 3-9, *method* is one of the Convert class methods, and *value* is the numeric value you want to convert to a different data type. In the first example shown in the figure, the `newSales = Convert.ToDouble(sales)` statement converts the contents of an Integer variable named `sales` to Double, and assigns the result to a Double variable named `newSales`. In the second example, the `Dim rate As Decimal = Convert.ToDecimal(.05)` statement converts the Double number .05 to Decimal, and stores the result in a Decimal variable named `rate`. The statement is equivalent to the `Dim rate As Decimal = .05D` statement. However, many programmers would argue that using the Convert.ToDecimal method, rather than the literal type character (D), makes the code clearer. The last assignment statement shown in the figure, `Me.xScoreLabel.Text = Convert.ToString(testScore)`, converts the contents of an Integer variable named `testScore` to String before assigning it to the xScoreLabel's Text property.

USING A VARIABLE IN AN ARITHMETIC EXPRESSION

After data is stored in a variable, you can use the variable in calculations, just as you can with the Text property of a control. When a statement contains the name of a variable, the computer uses the value stored inside the variable to process the statement. Figure 3-10 shows examples of arithmetic expressions in assignment statements.

Examples of variables in expressions

```
Dim age As Integer
age = age + 1
```

adds the integer 1 to the contents of an Integer variable named `age`, then assigns the result to the `age` variable

```
Dim sales As Decimal
Dim bonus As Decimal
Decimal.TryParse(Me.xSalesTextBox.Text, sales)
bonus = sales * Convert.ToDecimal(.05)
```

converts the Double number .05 to Decimal before multiplying it by the contents of a Decimal variable named `sales`, then assigns the result to a Decimal variable named `bonus`

```
Dim totalAmountDue As Double = 250.55
Me.xTotalLabel.Text =
      Convert.ToString(totalAmountDue)
```

line continuation character

converts the contents of a Double variable named `totalAmountDue` to String, and then assigns the result to the xTotalLabel's Text property

```
Dim currentPay As Double = 1500.65
Dim newPay As Double
newPay = currentPay + (currentPay * .02)
```

multiplies the contents of a Double variable named `currentPay` by the Double number .02, then adds the result to the contents of the `currentPay` variable, and then assigns the sum to a Double variable named `newPay`

Figure 3-10: Examples of using variables in arithmetic expressions

》TIP

In the second example in Figure 3-10, you could have used .05D rather than `Convert.ToDecimal(.05)`.

The assignment statement shown in the first example in Figure 3-10 adds the number one (an Integer) to an Integer variable named `age`, and then assigns the result to the `age` variable. Notice that the variable and the literal constant have the same data type, Integer. As you learned earlier, the value assigned to a variable should have the same data type as the variable itself.

The `bonus = sales * Convert.ToDecimal(.05)` assignment statement in the second example converts the Double number .05 to Decimal before multiplying it by the contents of a Decimal variable named `sales`. The statement assigns the result to a Decimal variable named `bonus`. In this case, the variables and literal constant in the assignment statement have the Decimal data type.

The third example in the figure contains the `Me.xTotalLabel.Text = Convert.ToString(totalAmountDue)` assignment statement. The statement first converts the contents of a Double variable named `totalAmountDue` to the String data type, and then assigns the result to the xTotalLabel's Text property. Recall that the Text property of a control has the String data type. The underscore (_) that appears at the end of the second line of code in the third example is called the line continuation character. You use the **line continuation character** to break up a long instruction into two or more physical lines in the Code Editor window. Breaking up an instruction in this manner makes the instruction easier to read and understand. The line continuation character must be immediately preceded by a space, and it must appear at the end of a physical line of code.

》TIP

You also could write the assignment statement shown in the last example in Figure 3-10 as `newPay = currentPay * 1.02`.

In the last example shown in Figure 3-10, the `newPay = currentPay + (currentPay * .02)` assignment statement multiplies the contents of a Double variable named `currentPay` by the Double number .02. The statement adds the result to the contents of the `currentPay` variable, assigning the sum to a Double variable named `newPay`. Here again, notice that the variables and literal constant in the statement have the same data type, Double.

Technically, the parentheses in the `newPay = currentPay + (currentPay * .02)` assignment statement are not necessary, because the computer always performs multiplication before addition. In other words, you could write the statement as `newPay = currentPay + currentPay * .02`. However, many programmers feel that the parentheses make the arithmetic expression easier to understand.

Keep in mind that a variable can store only one item of data at any one time. When you use an assignment statement to assign another item to the variable, the new data replaces the existing data. To illustrate this point, assume that a button's Click event procedure contains the following three lines of code:

```
Dim sales As Integer
sales = 500
sales = sales * 2
```

When you run the application and click the button, the three lines of code are processed as follows:

» The Dim statement creates the `sales` variable in memory and automatically initializes it to the number zero.

» The `sales = 500` assignment statement removes the zero from the `sales` variable and stores the number 500 there instead. The `sales` variable now contains the number 500 only.

» The `sales = sales * 2` assignment statement first multiplies the contents of the `sales` variable (500) by the number two, giving 1000. The assignment statement then replaces the current contents of the `sales` variable (500) with 1000. Notice that the calculation appearing on the right side of the assignment operator is performed first, and then the result is assigned to the variable whose name appears on the left side of the assignment operator.

You now know how to use a variable declaration statement to declare a variable. Recall that the statement allows you to assign a name, data type, and initial value to the variable you are declaring. You also know how to use an assignment statement to store literal constants and the result of arithmetic expressions in an existing variable. There are just two more things about variables that you need to learn to complete this chapter's application: in addition to a name and a data type, every variable also has both a scope and a lifetime.

THE SCOPE AND LIFETIME OF A VARIABLE

A variable's **scope** indicates where in the application's code the variable can be used, and its **lifetime** indicates how long the variable remains in the computer's internal memory. As you will learn in this section, variables can have module scope, procedure scope, or block scope. However, most of the variables used in an application will have procedure scope. This is because fewer unintentional errors occur in applications when the variables are declared using the minimum scope needed, which usually is procedure scope. A variable's scope and lifetime are determined by where you declare the variable—in other words, where you enter the variable's declaration statement. Typically, you enter the declaration statement either in a procedure, such as an event procedure, or in the Declarations section of a form.

» TIP

Variables also can have namespace scope; these variables are referred to as namespace variables, global variables, or public variables. Using namespace variables can lead to unintentional errors in a program and should be avoided, if possible. For this reason, they are not covered in this book.

» TIP

Procedure-level variables are also called local variables, and their scope is sometimes referred to as local scope.

» TIP

As you will learn later in this lesson, you can use the Static keyword to declare a procedure-level variable that remains in the computer's memory even when the procedure in which it is declared ends.

When you declare a variable in a procedure, the variable is called a **procedure-level variable** and it has **procedure scope**, because only that procedure can use the variable. For example, if you enter the Dim number As Integer statement in the xCalcButton's Click event procedure, only the xCalcButton's Click event procedure can use the number variable. No other procedures in the application are allowed to use the number variable. As a matter of fact, no other procedures in the application will even be aware of the number variable's existence. Procedure-level variables remain in the computer's internal memory only while the procedure in which they are declared is running; they are removed from memory when the procedure ends. In other words, a procedure-level variable has the same lifetime as the procedure that declares it. As mentioned earlier, most of the variables in your applications will be procedure-level variables.

The Sales Tax application that you view next illustrates the use of procedure-level variables. Figure 3-11 shows the MainForm in the application, and Figure 3-12 shows the Click event procedures for the Calculate 2% Tax and Calculate 5% Tax buttons. As the MainForm indicates, the application allows the user to enter a sales amount. It then calculates and displays either a 2% sales tax or a 5% sales tax, depending on the button selected by the user.

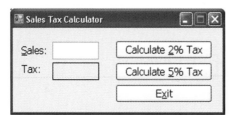

Figure 3-11: The MainForm in the Sales Tax application

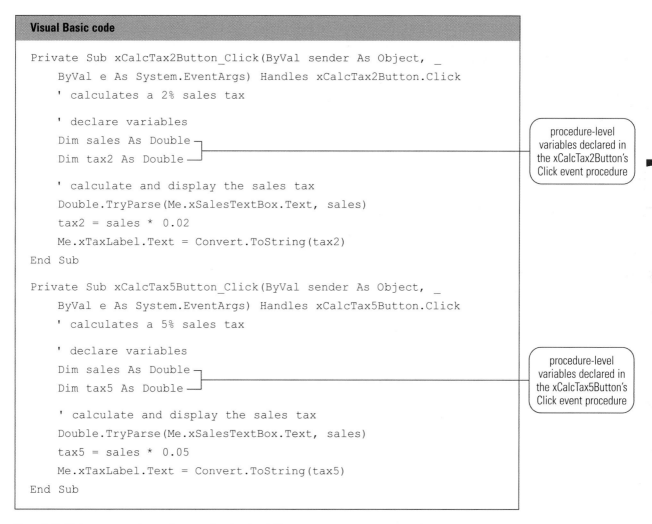

Visual Basic code

```
Private Sub xCalcTax2Button_Click(ByVal sender As Object, _
    ByVal e As System.EventArgs) Handles xCalcTax2Button.Click
    ' calculates a 2% sales tax

    ' declare variables
    Dim sales As Double
    Dim tax2 As Double

    ' calculate and display the sales tax
    Double.TryParse(Me.xSalesTextBox.Text, sales)
    tax2 = sales * 0.02
    Me.xTaxLabel.Text = Convert.ToString(tax2)
End Sub

Private Sub xCalcTax5Button_Click(ByVal sender As Object, _
    ByVal e As System.EventArgs) Handles xCalcTax5Button.Click
    ' calculates a 5% sales tax

    ' declare variables
    Dim sales As Double
    Dim tax5 As Double

    ' calculate and display the sales tax
    Double.TryParse(Me.xSalesTextBox.Text, sales)
    tax5 = sales * 0.05
    Me.xTaxLabel.Text = Convert.ToString(tax5)
End Sub
```

procedure-level variables declared in the xCalcTax2Button's Click event procedure

procedure-level variables declared in the xCalcTax5Button's Click event procedure

Figure 3-12: Click event procedures using procedure-level variables

Notice that both procedures shown in Figure 3-12 declare two procedure-level Double variables. It is customary to enter the declaration statements for procedure-level variables at the beginning of the procedure, as shown in the figure.

When the user enters a sales amount and then clicks the Calculate 2% Tax button, the xCalcTax2Button's Click event procedure creates and initializes the sales and tax2 variables; only the xCalcTax2Button's Click event procedure can use the variables. The procedure then converts the sales amount to Double and stores the result in the sales variable. Then the procedure multiplies the contents of the sales variable by .02 and stores the result in the tax2 variable. Finally, the procedure assigns the contents of the tax2 variable, converted to String, to the xTaxLabel's Text property. When the procedure ends, the computer removes the sales and tax2 procedure-level variables from memory. The variables will be created again the next time the user clicks the Calculate 2% Tax button. A similar process is followed when the user clicks the Calculate 5% Tax button, except the variable that stores the tax amount is named tax5, and the tax is calculated using a rate of .05 rather than .02.

Notice that both procedures shown in Figure 3-12 declare a variable named sales. When you use the same name to declare a variable in more than one procedure, each procedure creates its own variable when the procedure is invoked. Each procedure also destroys its own variable when the procedure ends. In other words, although the sales variables in both procedures have the same name, they are not the same variable. Rather, each refers to a different section in memory, and each is created and destroyed independently from the other.

To code and then test the Sales Tax application:

1 Start Visual Studio 2005 or Visual Basic 2005 Express Edition, if necessary, and close the Start Page window.

2 Open the **Sales Tax Solution** (Sales Tax Solution.sln) file, which is contained in the VB2005\Chap03\Sales Tax Solution folder. If necessary, open the designer window. The user interface shown earlier in Figure 3-11 appears on the screen.

3 Open the Code Editor window. For now, do not be concerned about the two Option statements that appear in the window. You will learn about the Option statements later in this lesson.

4 Replace the <your name> and <current date> text in the comments with your name and the current date.

5 Open the code template for the xCalcTax2Button's Click event procedure. Also open the code template for the xCalcTax5Button's Click event procedure. In the procedures, enter the comments and code shown in Figure 3-12.

6 Close the Code Editor window. Save the solution, then run the application.

7 Enter **1000** as the sales amount, then click the **Calculate 2% Tax** button. The button's Click event procedure calculates and displays a tax of 20.

8 Click the **Calculate 5% Tax** button. The button's Click event procedure calculates and displays a tax of 50.

9 Enter the letter **a** as the sales amount, then click the **Calculate 2% Tax** button. The button's Click event procedure calculates and displays a tax of 0.

10 Click the **Calculate 5% Tax** button. The button's Click event procedure calculates and displays a tax of 0.

11 Click the **Exit** button to end the application. You are returned to the designer window. Close the solution.

In addition to declaring a variable in a procedure, you also can declare a variable in the form's Declarations section, which begins with the `Public Class` statement and ends with the `End Class` statement. When you declare a variable in the form's Declarations section, the variable is called a **module-level variable** and it has **module scope**. You typically use a module-level variable when you need more than one procedure in the same form to use the same variable, because a module-level variable can be used by all of the procedures in the form, including the procedures associated with the controls contained on the form. (The form's Declarations section is not the same as the General Declarations section, which you learned about in Chapter 2. The General Declarations section is located above the `Public Class` statement in the Code Editor window, whereas the form's Declarations section is located within the `Public Class` statement.)

Unlike a procedure-level variable, which you declare using the `Dim` keyword, you declare a module-level variable using the `Private` keyword. For example, when entered in the form's Declarations section, the `Private number As Integer` statement creates a module-level variable named `number`. Because the variable has module scope, it can be used by every procedure in the form. Module-level variables retain their values and remain in the computer's internal memory until the application ends. In other words, a module-level variable has the same lifetime as the application itself.

> **» TIP**
>
> You also can use the `Dim` keyword to declare a module-level variable. However, most Visual Basic programmers use the `Private` keyword, because it makes the scope more obvious to anyone reading the code.

The Total Sales application that you view next illustrates the use of a module-level variable. Figure 3-13 shows the MainForm in the application, and Figure 3-14 shows the application's code. As the MainForm indicates, the application calculates the total of the sales amounts entered by the user.

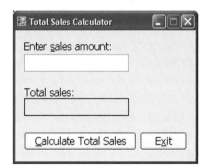

Figure 3-13: The MainForm in the Total Sales application

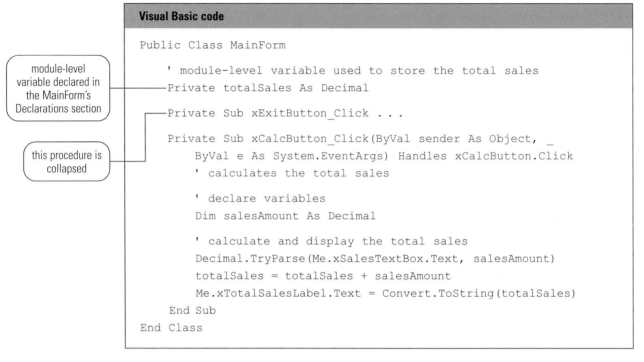

Visual Basic code

```
Public Class MainForm

    ' module-level variable used to store the total sales
    Private totalSales As Decimal

    Private Sub xExitButton_Click . . .

    Private Sub xCalcButton_Click(ByVal sender As Object, _
        ByVal e As System.EventArgs) Handles xCalcButton.Click
        ' calculates the total sales

        ' declare variables
        Dim salesAmount As Decimal

        ' calculate and display the total sales
        Decimal.TryParse(Me.xSalesTextBox.Text, salesAmount)
        totalSales = totalSales + salesAmount
        Me.xTotalSalesLabel.Text = Convert.ToString(totalSales)
    End Sub
End Class
```

module-level variable declared in the MainForm's Declarations section

this procedure is collapsed

Figure 3-14: Total Sales application's code using a module-level variable

The Total Sales application uses a module-level variable named `totalSales` to accumulate (add together) the sales amounts entered by the user. Notice that you place the declaration statement for a module-level variable after the `Public Class` statement, but before the first `Private Sub` statement, in the form's Declarations section.

When the Total Sales application is started, the `Private` statement contained in the MainForm's Declarations section is processed first. The statement creates and initializes (to the number zero) a Decimal variable named `totalSales`. The variable is created and initialized only once, when the application is first started. It remains in the computer's internal memory until the application ends.

Each time the user enters a sales amount in the interface and then clicks the Calculate Total Sales button, the button's Click event procedure creates and initializes (to the number zero) a procedure-level variable named `salesAmount`. The procedure then converts the sales amount entered by the user to Decimal, and stores the result in the `salesAmount` variable. Then the procedure adds the contents of the procedure-level `salesAmount` variable to the contents of the module-level `totalSales` variable. At this point, the `totalSales` variable contains the sum of all of the sales amounts entered so far. The procedure then displays the contents of the `totalSales` variable, converted to String, in the xTotalSalesLabel. When the procedure ends, the computer removes the procedure-level `salesAmount` variable from its memory; however, it does not remove the module-level `totalSales` variable. The `totalSales` variable is removed from the computer's memory only when the application ends.

To code and then test the Total Sales application:

1 Open the **Total Sales Solution** (Total Sales Solution.sln) file, which is contained in the VB2005\Chap03\Total Sales Solution folder. If necessary, open the designer window. The user interface shown earlier in Figure 3-13 appears on the screen.

2 Open the Code Editor window. (Recall that you will learn about the Option statements later in this lesson.)

3 Replace the `<your name>` and `<current date>` text in the comments with your name and the current date.

4 Enter the **Private totalSales As Decimal** statement in the MainForm's Declarations section, as shown in Figure 3-14.

5 Open the code template for the xCalcButton's Click event procedure, then enter the comments and code shown in Figure 3-14.

6 Close the Code Editor window. Save the solution, then run the application.

7 Enter **2000** as the sales amount, then click the **Calculate Total Sales** button. The button's Click event procedure calculates and displays the number 2000 as the total sales.

8 Enter **4000** as the sales amount, then click the **Calculate Total Sales** button. The button's Click event procedure calculates and displays the number 6000 as the total sales.

9 Enter **500** as the sales amount, then click the **Calculate Total Sales** button. The button's Click event procedure calculates and displays the number 6500 as the total sales.

10 Click the **Exit** button to end the application. You are returned to the designer window. Close the solution.

As mentioned earlier, variables also can have **block scope**; such variables are called **block-level variables**. Block-level variables are declared within specific blocks of code, such as within If...Then...Else statements or For...Next statements. Only the block of code in which it is declared can use a block-level variable. You will learn more about block-level variables in Chapter 4.

As the syntax shown earlier in Figure 3-5 indicates, you can declare a variable using the `Dim`, `Private`, or `Static` keywords. You already have learned how to use the `Dim` keyword to declare a procedure-level variable, and how to use the `Private` keyword to declare a module-level variable. Next, you will learn how to use the `Static` keyword to declare a special type of procedure-level variable, called a static variable.

STATIC VARIABLES

A **static variable** is a procedure-level variable that remains in memory and also retains its value even when the procedure in which it is declared ends. Similar to a module-level variable, a static variable is not removed from the computer's internal memory until the application ends. You declare a static variable using the Static keyword.

As mentioned earlier, you can prevent many unintentional errors from occurring in an application by declaring the variables using the minimum scope needed. Because a static variable, which is simply a special type of procedure-level variable, has a narrower scope than does a module-level variable, it is better to use a static variable instead of a module-level variable, if possible.

Earlier you viewed the interface (Figure 3-13) and code (Figure 3-14) for the Total Sales application. Recall that the application used a module-level variable to accumulate the sales amounts entered by the user. Rather than using a module-level variable for that purpose, you also can use a static variable. Figure 3-15 shows the Total Sales application's code using a static variable.

> **» TIP**
> The Static keyword can be used only in a procedure.

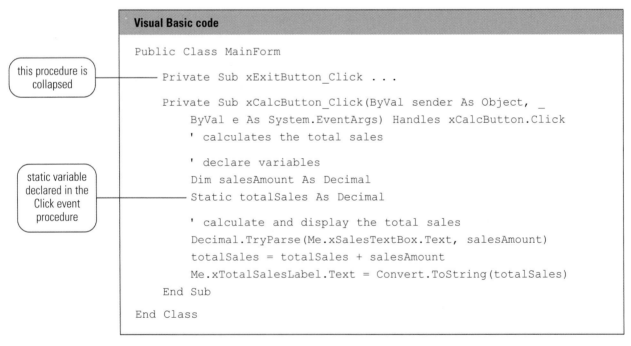

Visual Basic code

```
Public Class MainForm

    Private Sub xExitButton_Click . . .

    Private Sub xCalcButton_Click(ByVal sender As Object, _
        ByVal e As System.EventArgs) Handles xCalcButton.Click
        ' calculates the total sales

        ' declare variables
        Dim salesAmount As Decimal
        Static totalSales As Decimal

        ' calculate and display the total sales
        Decimal.TryParse(Me.xSalesTextBox.Text, salesAmount)
        totalSales = totalSales + salesAmount
        Me.xTotalSalesLabel.Text = Convert.ToString(totalSales)
    End Sub

End Class
```

this procedure is collapsed

static variable declared in the Click event procedure

Figure 3-15: Total Sales application's code using a static variable

The first time the user clicks the Calculate Total Sales button in the interface, the button's Click event procedure creates and initializes (to zero) a procedure-level variable named salesAmount and a static variable named totalSales. The procedure then converts the sales amount entered by the user to Decimal, and stores the result in the salesAmount variable. Then the procedure adds the contents of the salesAmount variable to the contents of the totalSales variable. Lastly, the procedure displays the contents of the totalSales variable, converted to String, in the xTotalSalesLabel. When the procedure ends, the computer removes from its internal memory the variable declared using the Dim keyword (salesAmount). But it does not remove the variable declared using the Static keyword (totalSales).

Each subsequent time the user clicks the Calculate Total Sales button, the computer re-creates and re-initializes the salesAmount variable declared in the button's Click event procedure. However, it does not re-create or re-initialize the totalSales variable because that variable, as well as its current value, is still in the computer's memory. After re-creating and re-initializing the salesAmount variable, the computer processes the remaining instructions contained in the button's Click event procedure. Here again, each time the procedure ends, the salesAmount variable is removed from the computer's internal memory. The totalSales variable is removed only when the application ends.

To use a static variable in the Total Sales application:

1 Use Windows to make a copy of the Total Sales Solution folder, which is contained in the VB2005\Chap03 folder. Rename the folder **Total Sales Static Solution**.

2 Open the **Total Sales Solution** (Total Sales Solution.sln) file contained in the VB2005\Chap03\Total Sales Static Solution folder. Open the designer window. The user interface shown earlier in Figure 3-13 appears on the screen.

3 Open the Code Editor window. Modify the code so that it uses a static variable rather than a module-level variable. Use the code shown in Figure 3-15 as a guide.

4 Close the Code Editor window. Save the solution, then run the application.

5 Enter **2000** as the sales amount, then click the **Calculate Total Sales** button. The button's Click event procedure calculates and displays the number 2000 as the total sales.

6 Enter **4000** as the sales amount, then click the **Calculate Total Sales** button. The button's Click event procedure calculates and displays the number 6000 as the total sales.

7 Enter **500** as the sales amount, then click the **Calculate Total Sales** button. The button's Click event procedure calculates and displays the number 6500 as the total sales.

8 Click the **Exit** button to end the application. You are returned to the designer window. Close the solution.

In addition to using literal constants and variables in your code, you also can use named constants.

NAMED CONSTANTS

Like a variable, a **named constant** is a memory location inside the computer. However, unlike a variable, the contents of a named constant cannot be changed while the application is running. You create a named constant using the **Const statement**. Figure 3-16 shows the syntax of the Const statement and includes several examples of declaring named constants.

Declaring a named constant
Syntax **Const** *constantname* **As** *datatype* = *expression*

Examples
`Const Pi As Double = 3.141593`
declares `Pi` as a Double named constant, and initializes it to the Double number 3.141593
 	
`Const MaxHours As Integer = 40`
declares `MaxHours` as an Integer named constant, and initializes it to the integer 40
 	
`Private Const CoTitle As String = "ABC Company"`
declares `CoTitle` as a String named constant, and initializes it to the string "ABC Company"

Figure 3-16: Syntax and examples of the Const statement

In the syntax shown in Figure 3-16, *constantname* is the name of the named constant. The new naming convention uses Pascal case for the names of named constants. Recall that Pascal case means that you capitalize the first letter in the name, as well as the first letter of each subsequent word in the name. (Recall that Pascal case is also used for the names of forms. Variable names, on the other hand, are entered using camel case rather than Pascal case.)

Datatype in the syntax is the named constant's data type, and *expression* is the value you want stored in the named constant. The *expression* must have the same data type as the named constant. The *expression* can contain a literal constant, or another named constant, or an arithmetic operator. However, it cannot contain a variable.

You can use the Const statements shown in the first two examples in Figure 3-16 to create procedure-level named constants. To do this, you need simply to enter the statements in the appropriate procedure. You would use the Const statement shown in the last example in the figure to create a module-level named constant. Notice that you precede the `Const` keyword with the `Private` keyword when creating a module-level constant. In addition, you need to enter the `Private Const CoTitle As String = "ABC Company"` statement in the form's Declarations section.

Named constants make code more self-documenting and, therefore, easier to modify, because they allow you to use meaningful words in place of values that are less clear. The named constant Pi, for example, is much more meaningful than is the number 3.141593, which is the value of pi rounded to six decimal places. Once you create a named constant, you then can use the constant's name rather than its value in the application's code. Unlike a variable, the value stored in a named constant cannot be inadvertently changed while the application is running. Using a named constant to represent a value has another advantage: if the value changes in the future, you will need to modify only the Const statement in the program, rather than all of the program statements that use the value.

The Area Calculator application that you view next illustrates the use of a named constant. Figure 3-17 shows the MainForm in the application, and Figure 3-18 shows the code for the Calculate Area button's Click event procedure. As the MainForm indicates, the application allows the user to enter the radius of a circle. It then calculates and displays the area of the circle. Recall that the formula for calculating the area of a circle is $\prod r2$, where $\prod$ stands for pi (3.141593).

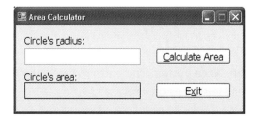

Figure 3-17: The MainForm in the Area Calculator application

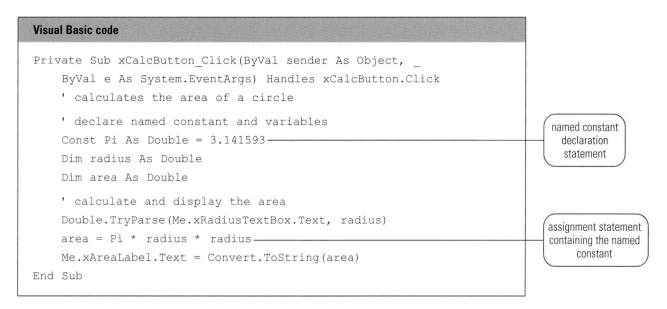

Visual Basic code

```
Private Sub xCalcButton_Click(ByVal sender As Object, _
    ByVal e As System.EventArgs) Handles xCalcButton.Click
    ' calculates the area of a circle

    ' declare named constant and variables
    Const Pi As Double = 3.141593          named constant
    Dim radius As Double                   declaration
    Dim area As Double                     statement

    ' calculate and display the area
    Double.TryParse(Me.xRadiusTextBox.Text, radius)
    area = Pi * radius * radius            assignment statement
    Me.xAreaLabel.Text = Convert.ToString(area)   containing the named
End Sub                                    constant
```

Figure 3-18: Click event procedure using a named constant

The xCalcButton's Click event procedure declares and initializes a named constant (Pi) and two variables (radius and area). It then converts (to Double) the radius value entered by the user, and it stores the result in the radius variable. The area = Pi * radius * radius statement calculates the circle's area using the values stored in the Pi named constant and radius variable, and then assigns the result to the area variable. Lastly, the procedure displays the contents of the area variable (converted to String) in the xAreaLabel. When the procedure ends, the computer removes the named constant and the two variables from its internal memory.

To code and then test the Area Calculator application:

1 Open the **Area Calculator Solution** (Area Calculator Solution.sln) file, which is contained in the VB2005\Chap03\Area Calculator Solution folder. If necessary, open the designer window. The user interface shown earlier in Figure 3-17 appears on the screen.

2 Open the Code Editor window. Replace the <your name> and <current date> text in the comments with your name and the current date.

3 Open the code template for the xCalcButton's Click event procedure, then enter the comments and code shown in Figure 3-18.

4 Close the Code Editor window. Save the solution, then run the application.

5 Enter **10** as the radius, then click the **Calculate Area** button. The button's Click event procedure calculates and displays the number 314.1593 as the area.

6 Click the **Exit** button to end the application. You are returned to the designer window. Close the solution.

OPTION EXPLICIT AND OPTION STRICT

Earlier in the chapter, you learned that it is important to declare the variables used in an application, because it allows you to control their data type. Unfortunately, in Visual Basic you can create variables "on the fly," which means that if your code contains the name of an undeclared variable, Visual Basic creates one for you and assigns the Object data type to it. (An undeclared variable is a variable that does not appear in a declaration statement, such as a Dim statement.) Recall that the Object type is not a very efficient data type. Because it is so easy to forget to declare a variable—and so easy to misspell a variable's name while coding, thereby inadvertently creating an undeclared variable—Visual Basic provides a way that prevents you from using undeclared variables in your code. You simply enter the statement `Option Explicit On` in the General Declarations section of the Code Editor window. Then if your code contains the name of an undeclared variable, the Code Editor informs you of the error.

In this chapter, you also learned that the data type of the value assigned to a memory location (variable or named constant) should be the same as the data type of the memory location itself. If the value's data type does not match the memory location's data type, the computer uses a process called **implicit type conversion** to convert the value to fit the memory location. For example, if you assign the integer 9 to a Decimal memory location, which stores fixed-point numbers, the computer converts the integer to a fixed-point number before storing the value in the memory location. It does this by appending a decimal point and the number 0 to the end of the integer. In this case, for example, the integer 9 is converted to the fixed-point number 9.0, and it is the fixed-point number 9.0 that is assigned to the Decimal memory location. When a value is converted from one data type to another data type that can store larger numbers, the value is said to be **promoted**. In this case, if the Decimal memory location is used subsequently in a calculation, the results of the calculation will not be adversely affected by the implicit promotion of the number 9 to the number 9.0.

However, if you inadvertently assign a Double number—such as 3.2—to a memory location that can store only integers, the computer converts the Double number to an integer before storing the value in the memory location. It does this by rounding the number to the nearest whole number and then truncating (dropping off) the decimal portion of the number. In this case, the computer converts the Double number 3.2 to the integer 3. As a result, the number 3, rather than the number 3.2, is assigned to the memory location. When a value is converted from one data type to another data type that can store only smaller numbers, the value is said to be **demoted**. If the memory location is used subsequently in a calculation, the results of the calculation probably will be adversely affected by the implicit demotion of the number 3.2 to the number 3. More than likely, the demotion will cause the calculated results to be incorrect.

With implicit type conversions, data loss can occur when the value of one data type (for example, Double) is converted to a narrower data type, which is a data type with less precision or smaller capacity (for example, Integer). You can eliminate the problems that occur as a result of implicit type conversions by entering the `Option Strict On` statement in the General Declarations section of the Code Editor window. When the `Option Strict On` statement appears in an application's code, the computer uses the type conversion rules listed in Figure 3-19. The figure also includes examples of implicit type conversions.

»TIP
Recall that the General Declarations section is located above the `Public Class` statement in the Code Editor window.

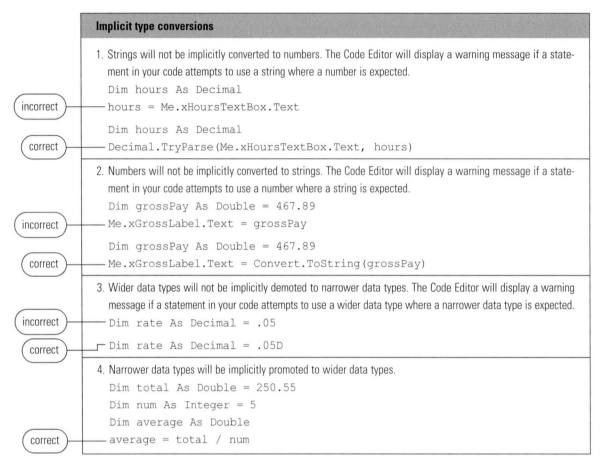

Implicit type conversions

1. Strings will not be implicitly converted to numbers. The Code Editor will display a warning message if a statement in your code attempts to use a string where a number is expected.

incorrect
```
Dim hours As Decimal
hours = Me.xHoursTextBox.Text
```

correct
```
Dim hours As Decimal
Decimal.TryParse(Me.xHoursTextBox.Text, hours)
```

2. Numbers will not be implicitly converted to strings. The Code Editor will display a warning message if a statement in your code attempts to use a number where a string is expected.

incorrect
```
Dim grossPay As Double = 467.89
Me.xGrossLabel.Text = grossPay
```

correct
```
Dim grossPay As Double = 467.89
Me.xGrossLabel.Text = Convert.ToString(grossPay)
```

3. Wider data types will not be implicitly demoted to narrower data types. The Code Editor will display a warning message if a statement in your code attempts to use a wider data type where a narrower data type is expected.

incorrect
```
Dim rate As Decimal = .05
```

correct
```
Dim rate As Decimal = .05D
```

4. Narrower data types will be implicitly promoted to wider data types.

correct
```
Dim total As Double = 250.55
Dim num As Integer = 5
Dim average As Double
average = total / num
```

Figure 3-19: Rules and examples of implicit type conversions

According to the first rule listed in Figure 3-19, the computer will not implicitly convert a string to a number. As a result, the Code Editor will issue a warning if your code contains the `hours = Me.xHoursTextBox.Text` statement, because the statement tells the computer to store a string in a Decimal variable. The warning message will say "Option Strict On disallows implicit conversions from 'String' to 'Decimal'." As you learned earlier, you should use the TryParse method to explicitly convert a string to the Decimal data type before assigning it to a Decimal variable. In this case, for example, the appropriate statement to use is `Decimal.TryParse(Me.xHoursTextBox.Text, hours)`.

According to the second rule, the computer will not implicitly convert a number to a string. Therefore, the Code Editor will issue a warning if your code contains the `Me.xGrossLabel.Text = grossPay` statement, because the statement assigns a number to a string. In this case, the warning message will say "Option Strict On disallows implicit conversions from 'Double to 'String.'" Recall that you can use the Convert class methods to explicitly convert a number to the String data type. The appropriate statement to use here is `Me.xGrossLabel.Text = Convert.ToString(grossPay)`.

The third rule states that wider data types will not be implicitly demoted to narrower data types. A data type is wider than another data type if it can store larger numbers, or store numbers with greater precision. Because of this rule, a Double will not be implicitly demoted to a narrower data type, such as Single, Decimal, or Integer. Similarly, a Long will not be demoted to an Integer or Short. As a result, the Code Editor will issue a warning if your code contains the `Dim rate As Decimal = .05` statement, because the statement assigns a Double number to a Decimal variable. The warning will say "Option Strict On disallows implicit conversions from 'Double to 'Decimal.'" The correct statement to use in this case is `Dim rate As Decimal = .05D`. However, you also can use the statement `Dim rate As Decimal = Convert.ToDecimal(.05)`.

According to the last rule listed in Figure 3-19, the computer will implicitly convert narrower data types to wider data types. For example, when processing the `average = total / num` statement, the computer will implicitly promote the `num` variable from Integer to Double before dividing it into the Double variable named `total`. It then will assign the result to the Double variable named `average`.

Figure 3-20 shows the `Option Explicit On` and `Option Strict On` statements entered in the General Declarations section of the Code Editor window for the Area Calculator application, which you viewed earlier in Figures 3–17 and 3–18. The statements typically are entered below the comments that document the project's name, the project's purpose, the programmer's name, and the date the code was either created or modified.

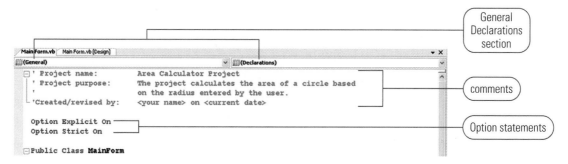

Figure 3-20: Option statements entered in the General Declarations section

Rather than turning on the settings for Option Explicit and Option Strict from code, as shown in Figure 3-20, you also can use either the Project Designer window or the Options dialog box. Following are the various ways you can turn on Option Explicit and Option Strict:

» Enter the `Option Explicit On` and `Option Strict On` statements in the General Declarations section of the Code Editor window. If a project contains more than one form, the statements must be entered in each form's Code Editor window.

» To turn the settings on for an entire project, open the solution that contains the project, then right-click My Project in the Solution Explorer window. Click Open to open the Project Designer window, then click the Compile tab. Use the Option explicit and Option strict boxes to turn on the settings.

» To turn the settings on for all of the projects you create, click Tools on the menu bar, and then click Options. When the Options dialog box opens, expand the Projects and Solutions node, then click VB Defaults. Use the Option Explicit and Option Strict boxes to turn on the settings.

Although you can use the Project Designer window or the Options dialog box to turn on the Option Explicit and Option Strict settings, it is strongly recommended that you enter the `Option Explicit On` and `Option Strict On` statements in your code. Entering the statements in your code ensures that the options are set to On, and it makes the code more self-documenting.

You have completed Lesson A. You can either take a break or complete the end-of-lesson questions and exercises before moving on to Lesson B.

»TIP

In Visual Basic 2005, the default setting for Option Explicit is On, whereas the default setting for Option Strict is Off.

SUMMARY

TO CREATE A VARIABLE:

» The syntax of a variable declaration statement is {**Dim** | **Private** | **Static**} *variablename* **As** *datatype* [= *initialvalue*]. Use camel case for a variable's name.

» To create a procedure-level variable, enter the variable declaration statement, using the `Dim` keyword, in a procedure.

» To create a module-level variable, enter the variable declaration statement, using the `Private` keyword, in a form's Declarations section.

» To create a static variable, enter the variable declaration statement, using the `Static` keyword, in a procedure.

TO USE AN ASSIGNMENT STATEMENT TO ASSIGN DATA

TO A VARIABLE:

» Use the syntax *variablename = value*.

TO FORCE A LITERAL CONSTANT TO ASSUME A DIFFERENT

DATA TYPE:

» Use one of the literal type characters listed in Figure 3-7.

TO CONVERT A STRING TO A NUMERIC DATA TYPE:

» Use the TryParse method, whose syntax is *datatype*.**TryParse**(*string, variable*).

TO CONVERT A NUMERIC VALUE TO A DIFFERENT DATA TYPE:

» Use one of the Convert methods, whose syntax is **Convert.***method*(*value*).

TO CREATE A NAMED CONSTANT:

» Use the Const statement, whose syntax is **Const** *constantname* **As** *datatype = expression*. Use Pascal case for a named constant's name.

» To create a procedure-level named constant, enter the Const statement in a procedure.

» To create a module-level named constant, enter the Const statement, preceded by the keyword `Private`, in a form's Declarations section.

TO PREVENT THE COMPUTER FROM CREATING

AN UNDECLARED VARIABLE:

» Enter the `Option Explicit On` statement in the General Declarations section of the Code Editor window.

TO PREVENT THE COMPUTER FROM MAKING IMPLICIT TYPE

CONVERSIONS THAT MAY RESULT IN A LOSS OF DATA:

» Enter the `Option Strict On` statement in the General Declarations section of the Code Editor window.

QUESTIONS

1. _____ are computer memory locations in which you store information, temporarily.

   a. Literal constants   b. Named constants

   c. Variables   d. Both b and c.

2. A _____ is a data item whose value does not change while the application is running.

    a. literal constant   b. literal variable

    c. named constant   d. variable

3. If you do not provide a data type in a variable declaration statement, Visual Basic 2005 assigns the _____ data type to the variable.

    a. Decimal   b. Integer

    c. Object   d. String

4. You use the _____ keyword to declare a module-level variable.

    a. `Dimension`   b. `Global`

    c. `Module`   d. `Private`

5. Which of the following statements declares a procedure-level variable that retains its value until the application ends?

    a. `Dim score As Integer`

    b. `Dim Static score As Integer`

    c. `Static Dim score As Integer`

    d. `Static score As Integer`

6. Which of the following declares a procedure-level String variable?

    a. `Dim String city`   b. `Dim city As String`

    c. `Private city As String`   d. `String city`

7. Which of the following assigns the contents of the xSalesTextBox control to a Double variable named `sales`? (The application contains the `Option Strict On` statement.)

    a. `sales = Me.xSalesTextBox.Text`

    b. `sales = Me.xSalesTextBox.Text.Convert.ToDouble`

    c. `TryParse.Double(Me.xSalesTextBox.Text, sales)`

    d. `Double.TryParse(Me.xSalesTextBox.Text, sales)`

8. Which of the following declares a Double named constant?

   a. `Const Rate As Double = .09`

   b. `Const Rate As Double = .09D`

   c. `Constant Rate = .09`

   d. Both a and b.

9. Which of the following assigns the sum of two Integer variables to the Text property of the xTotalLabel? (The application contains the `Option Strict On` statement.)

   a. `Me.xTotalLabel.Text = Convert.ToInteger(num1 + num2)`

   b. `Me.xTotalLabel.Text = Convert.ToInt32(num1 + num2)`

   c. `Me.xTotalLabel.Text = Convert.ToString(num1) + Convert.ToString(num2)`

   d. None of the above.

10. The _____ statement prevents data loss due to implicit type conversions.

   a. `Option Explicit On`

   b. `Option Strict On`

   c. `Option Implicit Off`

   d. `Option Convert Off`

EXERCISES

1. A procedure needs to store an item's name and its price. The price may have decimal places. Write the appropriate Dim statements to create the necessary procedure-level variables.

2. A procedure needs to store the name of an item in inventory and its height and weight. The height may have decimal places; the weight will be whole numbers only. Write the appropriate Dim statements to create the necessary procedure-level variables.

3. A procedure needs to store the name of an inventory item, the number of units in stock at the beginning of the current month, the number of units purchased during the current month, the number of units sold during the current month, and the number of

units in stock at the end of the current month. (The number of units is always a whole number.) Write the appropriate Dim statements to create the necessary procedure-level variables.

4. An application needs to store the part number of an item and its cost. (An example of a part number for this application is A103.) Write the appropriate Private statements to create the necessary module-level variables.

5. Write an assignment statement that assigns Miami to an existing String variable named `city`.

6. Write an assignment statement that assigns the word Desk to a String variable named `itemName`. Also write an assignment statement that assigns the number 40 to an Integer variable named `quantityInStock`, and an assignment statement that assigns the number 20 to an Integer variable named `quantityOnOrder`.

7. Write an assignment statement that adds together the contents of two Double variables (`northSales` and `southSales`), and then assigns the sum to a Double variable named `totalSales`.

8. Write an assignment statement that multiplies the contents of a Decimal variable named `salary` by the number 1.5, and then assigns the result to the `salary` variable.

9. A form contains two buttons named xSalaryButton and xBonusButton. Both buttons' Click event procedures need to use the same variable, which is a String variable named `employeeName`. Write the appropriate statement to declare the `employeeName` variable. Also specify where you will need to enter the statement and whether the variable is a procedure-level or module-level variable.

10. Write the statement to declare a procedure-level named constant named `TaxRate` whose value is .05. The named constant should have the Decimal data type.

11. Write the statement to assign the contents of the xUnitsTextBox to an Integer variable named `numberOfUnits`. (The application contains the `Option Strict On` statement.)

12. Write the statement to assign, to the xUnitsLabel, the contents of an Integer variable named `numberOfUnits`.

13. Write the statement to assign, to a String variable named `totalSales`, the sum of the values stored in two Decimal variables named `westSales` and `eastSales`.

DISCOVERY EXERCISE

14. In this exercise, you experiment with procedure-level and module-level variables.

    a. If necessary, start Visual Studio 2005 or Visual Basic 2005 Express Edition. Open the Scope Solution (Scope Solution.sln) file, which is contained in the VB2005\Chap03\Scope Solution folder. The Scope application allows the user to calculate either a 5% or a 10% commission on a sales amount. It displays the sales and commission amounts in the xSalesLabel and xCommissionLabel controls, respectively.

    b. Open the Code Editor window, then open the code template for the xSalesButton's Click event procedure. Code the procedure so that it declares a procedure-level Double variable named `sales`. The procedure also should use an assignment statement to assign the number 500.0 to the `sales` variable. In addition, the procedure should display the contents of the `sales` variable in the xSalesLabel control on the form.

    c. Save the solution, then start the application. Click the Display Sales button. What does the xSalesButton's Click event procedure display in the xSalesLabel control? When the Click event procedure ends, what happens to the procedure-level `sales` variable?

    d. Click the Exit button to end the application.

    e. Open the code template for the xComm5Button's Click event procedure. In the procedure, enter an assignment statement that multiplies a variable named `sales` by .05, and then assigns the result to the xCommissionLabel on the form. When you press the Enter key after typing the assignment statement, notice that a jagged line appears below the variable's name (`sales`) in the instruction. The jagged line indicates that there is something wrong with the code. To determine the problem, you need simply to rest your mouse pointer somewhere on the word (or words) immediately above the jagged line. In this case, for example, you need to rest your mouse pointer on the variable name, `sales`. The message in the box indicates that the `sales` variable is not declared. In other words, the xComm5Button's Click event procedure cannot locate the variable's declaration statement, which you previously entered in the xSalesButton's Click event procedure. As you learned in Lesson A, only the procedure in which a variable is declared can use the variable. No other procedure is even aware that the variable exists.

    f. Now observe what happens when you use the same name to declare a variable in more than one procedure. Insert a blank line above the assignment statement in the xComm5Button's Click event procedure. In the blank line, type a statement that declares a procedure-level Double variable named sales, then click the assignment statement to move the insertion point away from the current line. Notice that the jagged line disappears from the assignment statement.

g. Save the solution, then start the application. Click the Display Sales button. The contents of the sales variable declared in the xSalesButton's Click event procedure (500) appears in the xSalesLabel control.

h. Click the 5% Commission button. Why does the number 0 appear in the xCommissionLabel control? What happens to the sales variable declared in the xComm5Button's Click event procedure when the procedure ends?

i. Click the Exit button to end the application. As this example shows, when you use the same name to declare a variable in more than one procedure, each procedure creates its own procedure-level variable. Although the variables have the same name, each refers to a different location in memory.

j. Next, you use a module-level variable in the application. Position the insertion point above the xExitButton's Click event procedure. MainForm appears in the Class Name list box, and (Declarations) appears in the Method Name list box. Press Enter to insert a blank line. In the blank line, type a statement that declares a module-level Double variable named sales.

k. Delete the Dim statement from the xSalesButton's Click event procedure. Also delete the Dim statement from the xComm5Button's Click event procedure.

l. Open the code template for the xComm10Button's Click event procedure. In the procedure, enter an assignment statement that multiplies the sales variable by .1, and then assigns the result to the xCommissionLabel on the form.

m. Save the solution, and then start the application. The variable declaration statement in the form's Declarations section creates and initializes (to the number 0) a Double variable named sales.

n. Click the Display Sales button. The xSalesButton's Click event procedure stores the number 500 in the sales variable, and then displays the contents of the variable (500) in the xSalesLabel.

o. Click the 5% Commission button. The xComm5Button's Click event procedure multiplies the contents of the sales variable (500) by .05, and then displays the result (25) in the xCommissionLabel.

p. Click the 10% Commission button. The xComm10Button's Click event procedure multiplies the contents of the sales variable (500) by .1, and then displays the result (50) in the xCommissionLabel. As this example shows, any procedure in the form can use a module-level variable.

q. Click the Exit button to end the application. What happens to the `sales` variable when the application ends?

r. Close the Code Editor window, then close the solution.

DEBUGGING EXERCISE

15. In this exercise, you debug an existing application.

a. If necessary, start Visual Studio 2005 or Visual Basic 2005 Express Edition. Open the Count Solution (Count Solution.sln) file, which is contained in the VB2005\Chap03\Count Solution folder. The application is supposed to count the number of times the Count button is pressed, but it is not working correctly.

b. Start the application. Click the Count button. The message indicates that you have pressed the Count button once, which is correct.

c. Click the Count button several more times. Notice that the message still displays the number 1.

d. Click the Exit button to end the application.

e. Open the Code Editor window and study the code.

f. What are the two ways that you can correct the code? Which way is the preferred way? Modify the code using the preferred way.

g. Save the solution, then start the application.

h. Click the Count button several times. Each time you click the Count button, the message changes to indicate the number of times the button was clicked.

i. Click the Exit button to end the application. Close the Code Editor window, then close the solution.

LESSON B
OBJECTIVES

AFTER STUDYING LESSON B, YOU SHOULD
BE ABLE TO:

- » Include a procedure-level and module-level variable in an application
- » Concatenate strings
- » Get user input using the InputBox function
- » Include the `ControlChars.NewLine` constant in code
- » Designate the default button for a form
- » Format numbers using the ToString method

MODIFYING THE SKATE-AWAY SALES APPLICATION

REVISING THE APPLICATION'S DOCUMENTS

Recall that Mr. Cousard, the manager of Skate-Away Sales, has asked you to modify the order form that you created in Chapter 2. The order form should now display the message "The sales tax was" followed by the sales tax amount and the name of the salesperson who recorded the order. Before making modifications to an application's existing code, you should review the application's documentation and revise the necessary documents. In this case, you need to revise the Skate-Away Sales application's TOE chart and also the pseudocode for the Calculate Order button, which is responsible for making the application's calculations. The revised TOE chart is shown in Figure 3-21. Changes made to the original TOE chart, which is shown in Chapter 2's Figure 2-11, are shaded in the figure. (You will view the revised pseudocode for the Calculate Order button later in this lesson.)

Task	Object	Event
1. Calculate the total skateboards ordered and the total price 2. Display the total skateboards ordered and the total price in the xTotalBoardsLabel and xTotalPriceLabel 3. Calculate the sales tax 4. Display the message, sales tax, and salesperson's name in the xMessageLabel	xCalcButton	Click
Clear the screen for the next order	xClearButton	Click
End the application	xExitButton	Click
Display the total skateboards ordered (from xCalcButton)	xTotalBoardsLabel	None
Display the total price (from xCalcButton)	xTotalPriceLabel	None
Get and display the order information	xNameTextBox, xAddressTextBox, xCityTextBox, xStateTextBox, xZipTextBox, xBlueTextBox, xYellowTextBox	None
Get the salesperson's name	MainForm	Load
Show the message, sales tax, and salesperson's name (from xCalcButton)	xMessageLabel	None

Figure 3-21: Revised TOE chart for the Skate-Away Sales application

Notice that the xCalcButton's Click event procedure now has two more tasks to perform: it must calculate the sales tax and also display the message, sales tax, and salesperson's name in the xMessageLabel control. Two additional objects (MainForm and xMessageLabel) also are included in the revised TOE chart. The MainForm's Load event procedure, which occurs before the MainForm is displayed the first time, is responsible for getting the salesperson's name when the application is started. The xMessageLabel control will show the message, sales tax, and salesperson's name. As the revised TOE chart indicates, you need to change the code in the xCalcButton's Click event procedure, and you also need to code the form's Load event procedure. The xMessageLabel control, however, does not need to be coded.

Before you can begin modifying its code, you need to open the Skate-Away Sales application.

To open the Skate-Away Sales application, and then enter your name and the current date:

1 Start Visual Studio 2005 or Visual Basic 2005 Express Edition, if necessary, and close the Start Page window.

2 Open the **Skate Away Solution** (Skate Away Solution.sln) file, which is contained in the VB2005\Chap03\Skate Away Solution folder. Auto-hide the Toolbox, Solution Explorer, and Properties windows, if necessary. Figure 3-22 shows the Skate-Away Sales interface.

Figure 3-22: Skate-Away Sales interface

Two minor modifications were made to the application that you created in Chapter 2. First, the xMessageLabel was added to the interface. The label's Name and Text properties were set to xMessageLabel; its AutoSize and BorderStyle properties were set to False and FixedSingle, respectively. Second, the instruction `Me.xMessageLabel.Text = String.Empty` was added to the xClearButton's Click event procedure. The instruction will remove the contents of the xMessageLabel when the user clicks the Clear Screen button.

3 Click the **xMessageLabel** control to select it.

The control should be empty when the interface first appears on the screen.

4 Delete the contents of the xMessageLabel's Text property.

> **▶▶HELP?** To delete the contents of the Text property, double-click Text in the Properties list; this will highlight the contents of the Text property in the Settings box. Press either the Delete key or the Backspace key to delete the highlighted text, then press Enter.

5 Click the **form's title bar** to select the form.

6 Open the Code Editor window.

7 Replace the `<your name>` and `<current date>` text with your name and the current date, respectively.

MODIFYING THE CALCULATE ORDER BUTTON'S CODE

Currently, the Calculate Order button calculates the amount of sales tax as part of the total price equation. Recall that the total price equation from Chapter 2 is `Me.xTotalPriceLabel.Text = Val(Me.xTotalBoardsLabel.Text) * 100 * 1.05`. Now that Mr. Cousard wants the sales tax amount to appear on the order form, you need to include a separate equation for the sales tax amount in the Calculate Order button's code. In this lesson, you will remove the existing code from the xCalcButton's Click event procedure, and then code the procedure using variables (rather than control properties) in the equations. Because you will be using variables, you will enter the `Option Explicit On` and `Option Strict On` statements in the Code Editor window. As you learned in Lesson A, the `Option Explicit On` statement prevents the computer from creating an undeclared variable. The `Option Strict On` statement, on the other hand, prevents the computer from making implicit type conversions that may result in a loss of data. After entering the Option statements, you will review and then delete the code currently contained in the xCalcButton's Click event procedure.

To enter the Option statements, and then review and delete the xCalcButton's Click event procedure:

1 Position the insertion point in the blank line above the `Public Class MainForm` statement, then press **Enter** to insert a blank line.

2 Type **option explicit on** and press **Enter**, then type **option strict on** and press **Enter**.

3 Scroll down the Code Editor window until the entire xCalcButton Click event procedure is visible. Notice that jagged blue lines appear below the expressions in the two calculations. The jagged lines indicate that the expressions contain an error.

4 Position your mouse pointer on the first jagged blue line, as shown in Figure 3-23. An explanation of the error appears in a box, as shown in the figure. In this case, the message says "Option Strict On disallows implicit conversions from 'Double' to 'String'."

```
Private Sub xCalcButton_Click(ByVal sender As Object, ByVal e As System.EventArgs) Handles xCalcButton.
    ' calculates the total number of skateboards ordered and the total price
                              Option Strict On disallows implicit conversions from 'Double' to 'String'.
    Me.xTotalBoardsLabel.Text = Val(Me.xBlueTextBox.Text) + Val(Me.xYellowTextBox.Text)
    Me.xTotalPriceLabel.Text = Val(Me.xTotalBoardsLabel.Text) * 100 * 1.05
    Me.xTotalPriceLabel.Text = Format(Me.xTotalPriceLabel.Text, "currency")

End Sub
```

mouse pointer

Figure 3-23: Jagged blue lines shown in the xCalcButton's Click event procedure

HELP? The font used to display the text in the Code Editor window shown in Figure 3-23 was changed to 14-point Courier New so that you could view more of the code in the figure. It is not necessary for you to change the font.

In Chapter 2, you learned that the Val function returns the numeric equivalent of a string. However, the chapter did not mention that the number returned by the Val function always has a Double data type. When the computer processes the Val(Me.xBlueTextBox.Text) + Val(Me.xYellowTextBox.Text) expression shown in Figure 3-23, it first converts the strings stored in both text boxes to Double numbers, and then adds together both numbers; the sum also has a Double data type. The assignment statement that contains the Val(Me.xBlueTextBox.Text) + Val(Me.xYellowTextBox.Text) expression assigns the sum to the xTotalBoardsLabel's Text property, whose data type is String. The message shown in Figure 3-23 warns you that, when Option Strict is set to On, the computer will not implicitly convert a Double to a String. The same message will appear when you place your mouse pointer on the second jagged blue line.

5 Select the three lines of code and the blank line that appears below them, as shown in Figure 3-24.

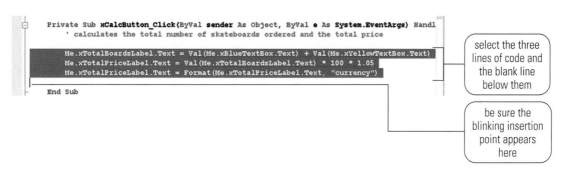

select the three lines of code and the blank line below them

be sure the blinking insertion point appears here

Figure 3-24: Instructions highlighted in the xCalcButton's Click event procedure

6 Press **Delete** to remove the selected code and blank line.

»HELP? If you inadvertently deleted the `Private Sub` and `End Sub` instructions, click the Class Name list arrow, then click xCalcButton in the list. Click the Method Name list arrow, and then click Click in the list.

Figure 3-25 shows the revised pseudocode for the xCalcButton's Click event procedure. Changes made to the original pseudocode, which is shown in Chapter 2's Figure 2-36, are shaded in the figure.

---

xCalcButton Click event procedure

---

1. calculate total skateboards ordered = blue skateboards ordered + yellow skateboards ordered

2. calculate subtotal = total skateboards ordered * skateboard price

3. calculate   sales tax = subtotal * sales tax rate

4. calculate   total price = subtotal + sales tax

5. display total skateboards ordered and total price in xTotalBoardsLabel and xTotalPriceLabel

6. display "The sales tax was" message, sales tax, and salesperson's name in xMessageLabel

---

Figure 3-25: Revised pseudocode for the xCalcButton's Click event procedure

Notice that the Click event procedure now includes two additional calculations: one for a subtotal and the other for the sales tax. The subtotal amount is computed by multiplying the total number of skateboards ordered by the skateboard price. The sales tax amount is computed by multiplying the subtotal amount by the sales tax rate. Also notice that the total price equation has changed: it now adds the subtotal amount to the sales tax amount. Lastly, the Click event procedure displays a message, the sales tax amount, and the salesperson's name in the xMessageLabel.

Before you begin coding a procedure, you first study the procedure's pseudocode to determine the variables and named constants (if any) the procedure will use. When determining the named constants, look for items whose value will be the same each time the procedure is invoked. In the xCalcButton's Click event procedure, for instance, the skateboard price and sales tax rate will always be $100 and .05 (the decimal equivalent of 5%), respectively; therefore, you will assign both values to named constants. You will declare the named constants using the names `BoardPrice` and `TaxRate`, and the Decimal data type. At this point, you may be wondering why the `BoardPrice` named constant will be declared using the Decimal data type rather than the Integer data type. Although the price of a skateboard does not currently contain any decimal places, it is possible that the price may include a decimal place in the future. By using the Decimal data type now, you can change the constant's value to include a decimal place without having to remember to also change its data type.

When determining the variables a procedure will need to use, look in the pseudocode for items whose value probably will change each time the procedure is processed. In the xCalcButton's Click event procedure, for instance, the numbers of blue and yellow skateboards ordered, as well as the total number of skateboards ordered, the subtotal, the sales tax, and the total price, probably will be different each time the procedure is processed; therefore, you will assign those values to variables. You will use Integer variables to store the number of blue skateboards ordered, the number of yellow skateboards ordered, and the total number of skateboards ordered. The Integer data type is the appropriate type to use for this information, because a customer can order only a whole number of skateboards, and the number of skateboards ordered is typically under 1,000 for each color. You will use Decimal variables to store the subtotal, sales tax, and total price, because these amounts may contain a decimal place. Figure 3-26 lists the names and data types of the two named constants and six variables you will use in the xCalcButton's Click event procedure.

Named constant/variable	Data type
BoardPrice	Decimal
TaxRate	Decimal
blueBoards	Integer
yellowBoards	Integer
totalBoards	Integer
subtotal	Decimal
salesTax	Decimal
totalPrice	Decimal

Figure 3-26: Named constants and variables for the xCalcButton's Click event procedure

To enter the named constant and variable declaration statements:

1 Press **Tab** twice, if necessary, to align the blinking insertion point with the apostrophe in the comment.

2 Type **const BoardPrice as decimal = 100d** and press **Enter**. For now, don't be concerned about the green jagged line that appears below the Const statement.

You should type the named constant's name in the Const statement, as well as the variable's name in the Dim statement, using the exact capitalization you want. Then, any time you want to refer to the named constant or variable in the code, you can enter its name using any case and the Code Editor will adjust the name to match the case used in the declaration statement.

3 Type **const TaxRate as decimal = .05d** and press **Enter**.

4 Enter the following six variable declaration statements. Press **Enter** twice after typing the last statement.

dim blueBoards as integer

dim yellowBoards as integer

dim totalBoards as integer

dim subtotal as decimal

dim salesTax as decimal

dim totalPrice as decimal

5 Notice the green jagged lines that appear below the Const and Dim statements. Place your mouse pointer on the last green jagged line. A box containing a message appears, as shown in Figure 3-27.

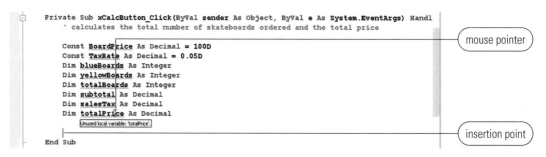

Figure 3-27: Const and Dim statements entered in the procedure

The message indicates that, although the totalPrice variable has been declared, it has not been used yet. In other words, the variable name does not appear in any other statement in the code. The green jagged line will disappear when you include the variable name in another statement in the procedure.

After declaring the named constants and variables, you can begin coding each step in the procedure's pseudocode (shown earlier in Figure 3-25). Keep in mind that some steps may require more than one line of code. The first step in the pseudocode is to calculate the total number of skateboards ordered. The calculation is made by adding the number of blue skateboards ordered (which is stored in the Text property of the xBlueTextBox) to the number of yellow skateboards ordered (which is stored in the Text property of the xYellowTextBox). You will use the TryParse method to convert the Text properties of both text boxes to integers, which you will store in the `blueBoards` and `yellowBoards` variables. You then will use an assignment statement to add together the contents of both variables, assigning the sum to the `totalBoards` variable.

To continue coding the xCalcButton's Click event procedure:

1 The insertion point should be positioned as shown earlier in Figure 3-27. Type **' calculate the total number of skateboards ordered** and press **Enter**.

2 Type **integer.tryparse(me.xBlueTextBox.text, blueboards)** and press **Enter**. Notice that a green jagged line no longer appears below the `Dim blueBoards As Integer` statement. (You can type the control name—in this case, xBlueTextBox—using all lowercase letters, like this: xbluetextbox. However, to improve readability, the steps in this book will always use the exact capitalization for the control names.)

3 Type **integer.tryparse(me.xYellowTextBox.text, yellowboards)** and press **Enter**.

4 Type **totalboards = blueboards + yellowboards** and press **Enter** twice. Notice that all of the variables in the assignment statement have the same data type, Integer.

The second step in the pseudocode is to calculate the subtotal by multiplying the total number of skateboards ordered (which is stored in the `totalBoards` variable) by the skateboard price (which is stored in the `BoardPrice` named constant). You will assign the subtotal to the `subtotal` variable.

5 Type **' calculate the subtotal** and press **Enter**, then type **subtotal = totalboards * boardprice** and press **Enter** twice. When processing the assignment statement, the computer will implicitly convert the integer stored in the `totalBoards` variable to Decimal before multiplying it by the decimal number stored in the `BoardPrice` named constant. It then will assign the result to the Decimal variable named `subtotal`.

The third step in the pseudocode is to calculate the sales tax by multiplying the subtotal stored in the `subtotal` variable by the sales tax rate stored in the `TaxRate` named constant. You will assign the sales tax to the `salesTax` variable.

6 Type **' calculate the sales tax** and press **Enter**, then type **salestax = subtotal * taxrate** and press **Enter** twice.

The fourth step in the pseudocode is to calculate the total price by adding together the subtotal and the sales tax. The subtotal is stored in the `subtotal` variable, and the sales tax is stored in the `salesTax` variable. You will assign the total price to the `totalPrice` variable.

7 Type **' calculate the total price** and press **Enter**, then type **totalprice = subtotal + salestax** and press **Enter** twice. Notice that all of the variables in the assignment statement have the same data type, Decimal.

Step 5 in the pseudocode is to display the total skateboards ordered and the total price in the xTotalBoardsLabel and xTotalPriceLabel controls on the form. The total number of skateboards ordered is stored in the `totalBoards` variable, and the total price is stored in the `totalPrice` variable. Because both variables have a numeric data type, you will need to convert their contents to the String data type before assigning the contents to the Text property of the label controls. You can use the ToString method of the Convert class to make the conversions.

8 Type **' display total amounts** and press **Enter**.

9 Type **me.xTotalBoardsLabel.text = convert.tostring(totalboards)** and press **Enter**, then type **me.xTotalPriceLabel.text = convert.tostring(totalprice)** and press **Enter** twice.

The last step in the pseudocode is to display a message, the sales tax, and the salesperson's name in the xMessageLabel. For now, you will only display the sales tax.

10 Type **' display message, tax, and name** and press **Enter**, then type **me.xMessageLabel.text = convert.tostring (salestax)** and press **Enter**. Figure 3-28 shows the code entered in the xCalcButton's Click event procedure.

```
Private Sub xCalcButton_Click(ByVal sender As Object, _
    ByVal e As System.EventArgs) Handles xCalcButton.Click
    ' calculates the total number of skateboards ordered and the
    total price

    Const BoardPrice As Decimal = 100D
    Const TaxRate As Decimal = 0.05D
    Dim blueBoards As Integer
    Dim yellowBoards As Integer
    Dim totalBoards As Integer
    Dim subtotal As Decimal
    Dim salesTax As Decimal
    Dim totalPrice As Decimal
```

Figure 3-28: Code entered in the xCalcButton's Click event procedure *(Continued)*   ▶

```
' calculate the total number of skateboards ordered
Integer.TryParse(Me.xBlueTextBox.Text, blueBoards)
Integer.TryParse(Me.xYellowTextBox.Text, yellowBoards)
totalBoards = blueBoards + yellowBoards

' calculate the subtotal
subtotal = totalBoards * BoardPrice

' calculate the sales tax
salesTax = subtotal * TaxRate

' calculate the total price
totalPrice = subtotal + salesTax

' display total amounts
Me.xTotalBoardsLabel.Text = Convert.ToString(totalBoards)
Me.xTotalPriceLabel.Text = Convert.ToString(totalPrice)

' display message, tax, and name
Me.xMessageLabel.Text = Convert.ToString(salesTax)
End Sub
```

Figure 3-28: Code entered in the xCalcButton's Click event procedure

Now you will save the solution and then start the application to verify that the code is working correctly.

To save the solution, then start and test the application:

1 Save the solution, then start the application.

2 Enter **10** as the number of blue skateboards ordered, and enter **10** as the number of yellow skateboards ordered.

3 Click the **Calculate Order** button. The application displays the total number of skateboards ordered, the total price, and the sales tax in the xTotalBoardsLabel, xTotalPriceLabel, and xMessageLabel controls, as shown in Figure 3-29.

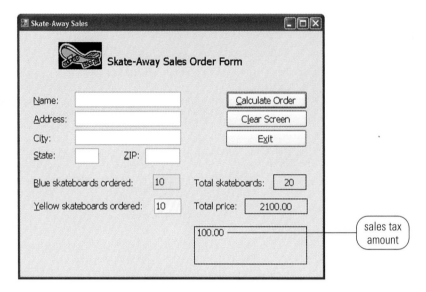

Figure 3-29: Calculated amounts shown in the interface

4 Click the **Clear Screen** button to clear the order form, then click the **Exit** button to end the application.

In addition to displaying the sales tax, the xMessageLabel also must display the message "The sales tax was" and the name of the salesperson recording the order. Before you can accomplish this task, you need to learn how to concatenate (link together) strings.

CONCATENATING STRINGS

TIP

You also can use the plus sign (+) to concatenate strings. To avoid confusion, however, you should use the plus sign for addition and use the ampersand for concatenation.

You use the **concatenation operator**, which is the ampersand (&), to concatenate (connect or link) strings together. When concatenating strings, you must be sure to include a space before and after the ampersand; otherwise, the Visual Basic compiler will not recognize the ampersand as the concatenation operator. Figure 3-30 shows some examples of string concatenation. As the last example shows, you do not need to use the Convert class's ToString method when concatenating a numeric value to a string. This is because the Visual Basic compiler automatically converts, to a string, a numeric value preceded by the concatenation operator.

Concatenating strings		
Variable name	**Data type**	**Contents**
firstName	String	Sue
lastName	String	Chen
age	Integer	21
Using the above variables, this concatenated string:		**Would result in:**
firstName & lastName		SueChen
firstName & " " & lastName		Sue Chen
lastName & ", " & firstName		Chen, Sue
"She is " & Convert.ToString(age) & "!"		She is 21!
"She is " & age & "!"		She is 21!

Figure 3-30: Examples of string concatenation

You will use the concatenation operator to link the string "The sales tax was " to the sales tax stored in the salesTax variable, and then concatenate the sales tax to a period, which will mark the end of the sentence. Using the examples shown in Figure 3-30 as a guide, the correct syntax for the assignment statement is Me.xMessageLabel.Text = "The sales tax was " & Convert.ToString(salesTax) & ".".

To concatenate a message, the sales tax amount, and a period, and then save the solution and start the application:

1 Change the Me.xMessageLabel.Text = Convert.ToString(salesTax) assignment statement as shown in Figure 3-31.

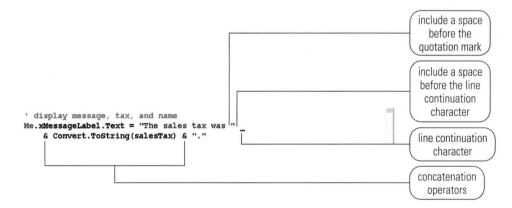

Figure 3-31: Modified assignment statement entered in the procedure

2 Save the solution, and then start the application.

3 Enter **10** as the number of blue skateboards ordered, and enter **10** as the number of yellow skateboards ordered.

4 Click the **Calculate Order** button. The application displays the total number of skateboards ordered, the total price, and the message, including the sales tax, as shown in Figure 3-32.

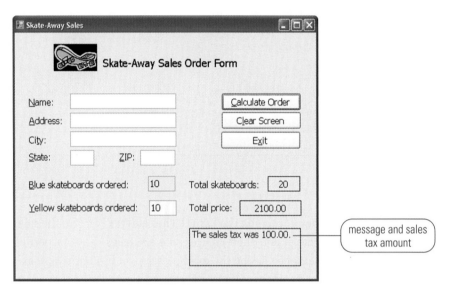

Figure 3-32: Order form showing the message and sales tax amount

5 Click the **Exit** button to end the application.

Now that you have the message and sales tax amount displaying correctly in the xMessageLabel, you just need to get the salesperson's name and then concatenate it to the end of the message. You can use the InputBox function to obtain the name from the user.

THE INPUTBOX FUNCTION

The **InputBox function** displays one of the Visual Basic predefined dialog boxes. The dialog box contains a message along with an OK button, a Cancel button, and an input area in which the user can enter information. Figure 3-33 shows an example of a dialog box created by the InputBox function.

Figure 3-33: Example of a dialog box created by the InputBox function

The message that you display in the dialog box should prompt the user to enter the appropriate information in the input area of the dialog box. The user then needs to click either the OK button or the Cancel button to continue working in the application. Figure 3-34 shows the syntax of the InputBox function and includes several examples of using the function.

Using the InputBox function

Syntax
InputBox(*prompt*[, *title*][, *defaultResponse*])

Examples
```
firstName = InputBox("Enter your first name")
```
displays a dialog box that shows "Enter your first name" as the prompt, the project's name as the title, and an empty input area; assigns the user's response to a String variable named `firstName`

```
city = InputBox("City name:", "City")
```
displays a dialog box that shows "City name:" as the prompt, "City" as the title, and an empty input area; assigns the user's response to a String variable named `city`

```
state = InputBox("State name:", "State", "Alaska")
```
displays a dialog box that shows "State name:" as the prompt, "State" as the title, and "Alaska" in the input area; assigns the user's response to a String variable named `state`

```
state = InputBox("State name:",, "Alaska")
```
displays a dialog box that shows "State name:" as the prompt, the project's name as the title, and "Alaska" in the input area; assigns the user's response to a String variable named `state`

```
Const InputPrompt As String = "Enter the rate:"
Const InputTitle As String = "Rate Entry"
rate = InputBox(InputPrompt, InputTitle, "0.0")
```
displays a dialog box that shows the contents of the `InputPrompt` constant as the prompt, the contents of the `InputTitle` constant as the title, and "0.0" in the input area; assigns the user's response to a String variable named `rate`

Figure 3-34: Syntax and examples of the InputBox function

In the syntax for the InputBox function, *prompt* is the message to display inside the dialog box, *title* is the text to display in the dialog box's title bar, and *defaultResponse* is the text you want displayed in the input area of the dialog box. In Figure 3-33, "Enter the number of hours worked:" is the *prompt*, "Hours Entry" is the *title*, and "40" is the *defaultResponse*.

When entering the InputBox function in the Code Editor window, the *prompt*, *title*, and *defaultResponse* arguments must be enclosed in quotation marks, unless that information is stored in a String named constant or String variable. The Windows standard is to use sentence capitalization for the *prompt*, but book title capitalization for the *title*. The capitalization (if any) you use for the *defaultResponse* depends on the text itself.

Notice that the *title* and *defaultResponse* arguments are optional, as indicated by the square brackets in the syntax. If you omit the *title* argument, the project name appears in the title bar. If you omit the *defaultResponse* argument, a blank input area appears when the dialog box opens.

As you learned in Chapter 2, a function is a predefined procedure that performs a specific task and then returns a value after completing the task. The task performed by the InputBox function is to display a dialog box. The value returned by the InputBox function depends on whether the user clicks the dialog box's OK button, Cancel button, or Close button. If the user clicks the OK button, the InputBox function returns the value contained in the input area of the dialog box; this value is always treated as a string. However, if the user clicks either the Cancel button in the dialog box or the Close button on the dialog box's title bar, the InputBox function returns an empty (or zero-length) string.

»GUI DESIGN TIP

InputBox Function's Prompt and Title Capitalization

» In the InputBox function, use sentence capitalization for the *prompt*, and book title capitalization for the *title*.

You will use the InputBox function in the Skate-Away Sales application to prompt the salesperson to enter his or her name. The InputBox function should be entered in the MainForm's Load event procedure because, according to the revised TOE chart (shown earlier in Figure 3-21), that is the procedure responsible for getting the salesperson's name. Recall that a form's Load event occurs before the form is displayed the first time. After the Load event procedure obtains the salesperson's name, you then will have the xCalcButton's Click event procedure concatenate the name to the message displayed in the xMessageLabel.

Before entering the InputBox function in the Load event procedure, you must decide where to declare the String variable that will store the function's return value. In other words, should the variable have procedure scope or module scope? When deciding, consider the fact that the form's Load event procedure needs to assign to the variable the value returned by the InputBox function. The Calculate Order button's Click event procedure also needs to use the variable, because the procedure must concatenate the variable to the message displayed in the xMessageLabel. Recall from Lesson A that when two procedures in the same form need to use the same variable, you declare the variable as a module-level variable. You do this by entering the variable declaration statement in the form's Declarations section.

To continue coding the Skate-Away Sales application, then save the solution and start the application:

1 Scroll to the top of the Code Editor window. Position the mouse pointer in the blank line immediately below the `Public Class MainForm` line, then click at that location. When you do so, the Class Name list box will say MainForm and the Method Name list box will say (Declarations).

First, you will declare a module-level String variable named `salesPerson`.

2 Press **Enter** to insert a blank line, then type **' declare module-level variable** and press **Enter**.

3 Type **private salesPerson as string** and press **Enter**. See Figure 3-35.

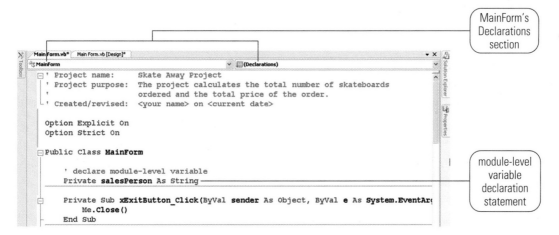

Figure 3-35: Module-level variable declared in the form's Declarations section

Now you will enter the InputBox function in the form's Load event procedure, so the function will be processed as soon as the salesperson starts the application. You access the form's procedures by selecting (MainForm Events) in the Class Name list box.

4 Click the **Class Name** list arrow, and then click **(MainForm Events)** in the list. Click the **Method Name** list arrow to view a list of the form's procedures. Scroll down the list until you see Load, then click **Load** in the list. The MainForm's Load event procedure appears in the Code Editor window.

To make the assignment statement that contains the InputBox function shorter and easier to understand, you will create named constants for the function's *prompt* ("Enter the salesperson's name:") and *title* ("Name Entry") arguments, and then use the named constants rather than the longer strings in the function. You are using named constants rather than variables because the *prompt* and *title* arguments will not change as the application is running.

5 Type the comments and code shown in Figure 3-36.

```
Private Sub MainForm_Load(ByVal sender As Object, ByVal e As System.EventArgs) |
    ' gets the salesperson's name

    Const InputPrompt As String = "Enter the salesperson's name:"
    Const InputTitle As String = "Name Entry"
    ' assign the name to the module-level salesPerson variable
    salesPerson = InputBox(InputPrompt, InputTitle)

End Sub
End Class
```

enter these comments and lines of code

Figure 3-36: MainForm's Load event procedure

The InputBox function shown in Figure 3-36 will prompt the user to enter the salesperson's name, and then store the response in the module-level salesPerson variable. Recall that module-level variables remain in memory until the application ends. Next, you will concatenate the salesPerson variable to the message assigned to the xMessageLabel.

6 Locate the xCalcButton's Click event procedure in the Code Editor window, then modify the xMessageLabel's assignment statement as shown in Figure 3-37.

```
' display message, tax, and name
Me.xMessageLabel.Text = "The sales tax was " _
    & Convert.ToString(salesTax) & "." & salesPerson
```

add the concatenation operator and variable name to the assignment statement

Figure 3-37: Modified assignment statement

7 Save the solution and then start the application. The Name Entry dialog box created by the InputBox function appears first. See Figure 3-38.

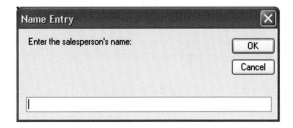

Figure 3-38: Dialog box created by the InputBox function

8 Type your name in the input area of the dialog box, then click the **OK** button. The order form appears.

9 Enter **10** as the number of blue skateboards ordered, and enter **10** as the number of yellow skateboards ordered.

10 Click the **Calculate Order** button. Notice that your name appears much too close to the period in the xMessageLabel.

11 Click the **Exit** button to end the application.

You can correct the spacing problem in the xMessageLabel by replacing the period (".") in the assignment statement with a period and two spaces (". "). Or, you can use the `ControlChars.NewLine` constant to display the salesperson's name on the next line in the xMessageLabel.

THE CONTROLCHARS.NEWLINE CONSTANT

The **ControlChars.NewLine constant** instructs the computer to issue a carriage return followed by a line feed, which advances the insertion point to the next line in a control, or in a file, or on the printer. Whenever you want to start a new line, you simply type the `ControlChars.NewLine` constant at the appropriate location in your code. In this case, for example, you want to advance to a new line after displaying the period—in other words, before displaying the salesperson's name.

To display the salesperson's name on a separate line:

1 Modify the xMessageLabel's assignment statement as indicated in Figure 3-39.

»TIP

The `ControlChars.NewLine` constant is an intrinsic constant, which is a named constant built into Visual Basic.

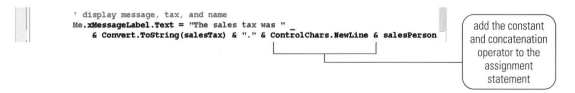

```
' display message, tax, and name
Me.xMessageLabel.Text = "The sales tax was " _
    & Convert.ToString(salesTax) & "." & ControlChars.NewLine & salesPerson
```

add the constant and concatenation operator to the assignment statement

Figure 3-39: `ControlChars.NewLine` constant added to the assignment statement

2 Save the solution and then start the application. The Name Entry dialog box created by the InputBox function appears first. See Figure 3-40.

default button has a highlighted border

input area has the focus

Figure 3-40: Focus and default button shown in the dialog box

Notice that the OK button in the dialog box has a highlighted border, even though it does not have the focus; the input area has the focus, as indicated by the position of the insertion point. In Windows terminology, a button that has a highlighted border when it does not have the focus is called the default button. You can select a default button by pressing Enter at any time. You will try this next.

3 Type **Mary Jones** in the input area of the dialog box. Then, instead of clicking the OK button, simply press **Enter**. The order form appears.

4 Enter **10** as the number of blue skateboards ordered, and enter **10** as the number of yellow skateboards ordered.

5 Click the **Calculate Order** button. The salesperson's name now appears on a separate line in the xMessageLabel, as shown in Figure 3-41.

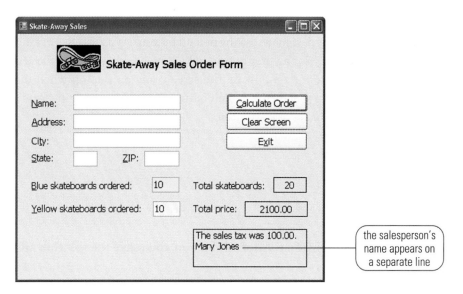

Figure 3-41: Order form showing the message, sales tax, and salesperson's name

6 Click the **Exit** button to end the application.

In the next section, you designate a default button for the order form.

DESIGNATING A DEFAULT BUTTON

As you already know from using Windows applications, you can select a button by click-ing it or by pressing the Enter key when the button has the focus. If you make a button the **default button**, you also can select it by pressing the Enter key even when the but-ton does not have the focus. When a button is selected, the computer processes the code contained in the button's Click event procedure.

An interface does not have to have a default button. However, if one is used, it should be the button that is most often selected by the user, except in cases where the tasks performed by the button are both destructive and irreversible. For example, a button that deletes information should not be designated as the default button. If you assign a default button in an interface, it typically is the first button, which means that it is on the left when the buttons are positioned horizontally on the screen, and on the top when the buttons are stacked vertically. You specify the default button (if any) by setting the form's **AcceptButton property** to the name of the button.

> ## »GUI DESIGN TIP
>
> **Rules for Assigning the Default Button**
>
> » The default button should be the button that is most often selected by the user, except in cases where the tasks performed by the button are both destructive and irreversible. The default button typically is the first button.

»TIP

A form can have only one default button.

»TIP

A Windows form also has a CancelButton property, which determines which button's Click event procedure is processed when the user presses the Esc key. A form can have only one cancel button.

To make the Calculate Order button the default button, then save the solution and start the application:

1 Click the **Main Form.vb [Design]** tab to return to the designer window.

2 Set the form's **AcceptButton** property to **xCalcButton**. A highlighted border appears around the Calculate Order button.

3 Save the solution, and then start the application.

4 Type your name in the Name Entry dialog box and press **Enter**. The order form appears.

5 Enter **5** as the number of blue skateboards ordered, and enter **20** as the number of yellow skateboards ordered. Press **Enter** to select the Calculate Order button. The numbers 25 and 2625.00 appear as the number of skateboards ordered and total price, respectively. In addition, "The sales tax was 125.00." message and your name appear in the xMessageLabel.

6 Click the **Exit** button.

Lastly, you will modify the xCalcButton's Click event procedure so that it displays a dollar sign and comma (if necessary) in the total price amount.

USING THE TOSTRING METHOD TO FORMAT NUMBERS

Numbers representing monetary amounts typically are displayed with either zero or two decimal places and usually include a dollar sign and a thousands separator. Similarly, numbers representing percentage amounts usually are displayed with zero or more decimal places and a percent sign. Specifying the number of decimal places and the special characters to display in a number is called **formatting**. In Chapter 2, you learned how to use the Format function to format a number for output as a string. Although you can still use the Format function in Visual Basic 2005, most programmers now use the **ToString method**. Figure 3-42 shows the syntax of the ToString method and includes several examples of using the method to format a number for output as a string.

Using the ToString method to format a number for output as a string
<u>Syntax</u>
variablename.**ToString**(*formatString*)
<u>Examples</u>
`Me.xCommissionLabel.Text = commission.ToString("C")`
if the `commission` variable contains the number 1250, the statement assigns the string "$1,250.00" to the Text property of the xCommissionLabel
`Me.xTotalLabel.Text = total.ToString("N2")`
if the `total` variable contains the number 123.675, the statement assigns the string "123.68" to the Text property of the xTotalLabel; however, if the variable contains the number 123.674, the statement assigns the string "123.67" to the Text property
`Me.xRateLabel.Text = rate.ToString("P0")`
if the `rate` variable contains the number .06, the statement assigns the string "6 %" to the Text property of the xRateLabel control

Figure 3-42: Syntax and examples of the ToString method

In the syntax shown in Figure 3-42, *variablename* is the name of a numeric variable, and ToString is a method that can be used with any of the numeric data types. The *formatString* argument in the syntax is a string that specifies the format you want to use. The *formatString* argument, which must be enclosed in double quotation marks, takes the form *Axx*, where *A* is an alphabetic character called the **format specifier**, and *xx* is a sequence of digits called the **precision specifier**. The format specifier must be one of the built-in format characters; the most commonly used format characters are listed in Figure 3-43. The precision specifier controls the number of significant digits or zeros to the right of the decimal point in the formatted number. As the second example shown in Figure 3-42 indicates, the ToString method rounds the number up when the number to its right is 5 or greater; otherwise, it truncates the excess digits.

Format specifier	Name	Description
C or c	Currency	displays a number with a dollar sign; the precision specifier indicates the desired number of decimal places; if appropriate, displays a number with a thousands separator; negative numbers are enclosed in parentheses
D or d	Decimal	formats only integers; the precision specifier indicates the minimum number of digits desired; if required, the number is padded with zeros to its left to produce the number of digits specified by the precision specifier; negative numbers are preceded by a minus sign
F or f	Fixed-point	the precision specifier indicates the desired number of decimal places; negative numbers are preceded by a minus sign
N or n	Number	the precision specifier indicates the desired number of decimal places; if appropriate, displays a number with a thousands separator; negative numbers are preceded by a minus sign
P or p	Percent	the precision specifier indicates the desired number of decimal places; multiplies the number by 100 and displays the number with a percent sign; negative numbers are preceded by a minus sign

Figure 3-43: Most commonly used format specifiers

Notice that you can use either an uppercase letter or a lowercase letter as the format specifier. Figure 3-44 shows the results of using various *formatStrings* to format numeric values.

formatString	Value	Result
C	3764	$3,764.00
C0	3764	$3,764
C2	3764	$3,764.00
C2	456.783	$456.78
C2	456.785	$456.79
C2	−75.31	($75.31)
D	3764	3764
D	−53	−53
D3	8	008
D3	15	015
F	3764	3764.00
F0	3764	3764
F2	3764	3764.00
F2	456.783	456.78
F2	456.785	456.79
F2	−75.31	−75.31
N	3764	3,764.00
N0	3764	3,764
N2	3764	3,764.00
N2	456.783	456.78
N2	456.785	456.79
N2	−75.31	−75.31
P	.364	36.40 %
P	−.05	−5.00 %
P1	.3645	36.5 %
P2	1.1	110.00 %

Figure 3-44: Results of using various *formatStrings*

>> TIP

To learn how to create custom *formatStrings*, click Help on the menu bar, and then click Index. Click Visual Basic in the Filtered by list box, type *custom numeric format strings* in the Look for text box, and then press Enter.

In the Skate-Away Sales application, the xCalcButton's Click event procedure displays the total price of the order in the xTotalPriceLabel. You can include a dollar sign, thousands separator, and two decimal places when displaying the total price by changing the `Me.xTotalPriceLabel.Text = Convert.ToString(totalPrice)` statement in the procedure to `Me.xTotalPriceLabel.Text = totalPrice.ToString("C2")`. You also can use the `Me.xTotalPriceLabel.Text = totalPrice.ToString("C")` statement, because the default precision specifier for the Currency format is two decimal places. However, including the precision specifier in the `formatString` makes the statement more self-documenting.

To format the total price:

1 Click the **Main Form.vb** tab to return to the Code Editor window.

2 In the xCalcButton's Click event procedure, change the `Me.xTotalPriceLabel.Text = Convert.ToString(totalPrice)` statement to **Me.xTotalPriceLabel.Text = totalPrice.ToString("C2")**.

Figure 3-45 shows the Skate-Away Sales application's code.

```
Visual Basic code

' Project name:        Skate Away Project
' Project purpose:     The project calculates the total number of skateboards
                       ordered and the total price of the order.
' Created/revised:     <your name> on <current date>

Option Explicit On
Option Strict On

Public Class MainForm

    ' declare module-level variable
    Private salesPerson As String

    Private Sub xExitButton_Click(ByVal sender As Object, _
        ByVal e As System.EventArgs) Handles xExitButton.Click
        Me.Close()
    End Sub
```

Figure 3-45: Skate-Away Sales application's code *(continued)*

```
Private Sub xClearButton_Click(ByVal sender As Object, _
    ByVal e As System.EventArgs) Handles xClearButton.Click
    ' prepare the screen for the next order

    Me.xNameTextBox.Text = String.Empty
    Me.xAddressTextBox.Text = String.Empty
    Me.xCityTextBox.Text = String.Empty
    Me.xStateTextBox.Text = String.Empty
    Me.xZipTextBox.Text = String.Empty
    Me.xBlueTextBox.Text = String.Empty
    Me.xYellowTextBox.Text = String.Empty
    Me.xTotalBoardsLabel.Text = String.Empty
    Me.xTotalPriceLabel.Text = String.Empty
    Me.xMessageLabel.Text = String.Empty
    ' send the focus to the Name text box
    Me.xNameTextBox.Focus()

End Sub

Private Sub xCalcButton_Click(ByVal sender As Object, _
    ByVal e As System.EventArgs) Handles xCalcButton.Click
    ' calculates the total number of skateboards ordered and the
       total price

    Const BoardPrice As Decimal = 100D
    Const TaxRate As Decimal = 0.05D
    Dim blueBoards As Integer
    Dim yellowBoards As Integer
    Dim totalBoards As Integer
    Dim subtotal As Decimal
    Dim salesTax As Decimal
    Dim totalPrice As Decimal

    ' calculate the total number of skateboards ordered
    Integer.TryParse(Me.xBlueTextBox.Text, blueBoards)
    Integer.TryParse(Me.xYellowTextBox.Text, yellowBoards)
    totalBoards = blueBoards + yellowBoards

    ' calculate the subtotal
    subtotal = totalBoards * BoardPrice
```

Figure 3-45: Skate-Away Sales application's code *(Continued)*

▶

```
        ' calculate the sales tax
        salesTax = subtotal * TaxRate

        ' calculate the total price
        totalPrice = subtotal + salesTax

        ' display total amounts
        Me.xTotalBoardsLabel.Text = Convert.ToString(totalBoards)
        Me.xTotalPriceLabel.Text = totalPrice.ToString("C2")

        ' display message, tax, and name
        Me.xMessageLabel.Text = "The sales tax was " _
            & Convert.ToString(salesTax) & "." & ControlChars.NewLine
            & salesPerson
    End Sub

    Private Sub MainForm_Load(ByVal sender As Object, _
        ByVal e As System.EventArgs) Handles Me.Load
        ' gets the salesperson's name

        Const InputPrompt As String = "Enter the salesperson's name:"
        Const InputTitle As String = "Name Entry"
        ' assign the name to the module-level salesPerson variable
        salesPerson = InputBox(InputPrompt, InputTitle)

    End Sub
End Class
```

Figure 3-45: Skate-Away Sales application's code

Now you will save the solution and then start and test the application.

To save the solution, then start and test the application:

1 Close the Code Editor window.

2 Save the solution, then start the application.

3 Type **Perry Hormel** in the input area of the dialog box, then press **Enter**. The order form appears.

4 Enter **15** as the number of blue skateboards ordered, and enter **9** as the number of yellow skateboards ordered.

5 Click the **Calculate Order** button. The total price appears with a dollar sign, a thousands separator, and two decimal places, as shown in Figure 3-46.

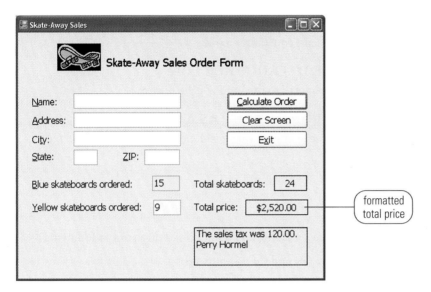

Figure 3-46: Order form showing the formatted total price

6 Click the **Exit** button to end the application, then close the solution.

You have completed Lesson B. You can either take a break or complete the end-of-lesson questions and exercises before moving on to Lesson C.

SUMMARY

TO CONCATENATE STRINGS:

» Use the concatenation operator, which is the ampersand (&). Be sure to include a space before and after the ampersand.

TO DISPLAY A DIALOG BOX CONTAINING A PROMPT, AN INPUT AREA, AN OK BUTTON, AND A CANCEL BUTTON:

» Use the InputBox function, whose syntax is **InputBox**(*prompt*[, *title*][, *defaultResponse*]). The *prompt*, *title*, and *defaultResponse* arguments must be enclosed in quotation marks, unless the information is stored in a String named constant or String variable. Use sentence capitalization for the *prompt*, but book title capitalization for the *title*.

» If the user clicks the OK button, the InputBox function returns the value contained in the input area of the dialog box; this value is always treated as a string. If the user clicks either the Cancel button in the dialog box or the Close button on the dialog box's title bar, the InputBox function returns an empty (or zero-length) string.

TO ADVANCE THE INSERTION POINT TO THE NEXT LINE:

» Use the `ControlChars.NewLine` constant in code.

TO MAKE A BUTTON THE DEFAULT BUTTON:

» Set the form's AcceptButton property to the name of the button.

TO FORMAT A NUMBER FOR OUTPUT AS A STRING:

» Use the ToString method, whose syntax is *variablename*.**ToString**(*formatString*).

QUESTIONS

1. The InputBox function displays a dialog box containing which of the following?

   a. input area   b. OK and Cancel buttons

   c. prompt   d. All of the above.

2. Which of the following is the concatenation operator?

   a. @   b. #

   c. $ d. &

3. The `region1` variable contains the string "North", and the `region2` variable contains the string "West". Which of the following will display the string "NorthWest" (one word) in the xRegionLabel?

   a. `Me.xRegionLabel.Text = region1 & region2`

   b. `Me.xRegionLabel.Text = "region1" & "region2"`

   c. `Me.xRegionLabel.Text = region1 @ region2`

   d. `Me.xRegionLabel.Text = region1 # region2`

4. The `cityName` variable contains the string "Boston", and the `stateName` variable contains the string "MA". Which of the following will display the string "Boston, MA" (the city, a comma, a space, and the state) in the xAddressLabel?

   a. `Me.xAddressLabel.Text = cityName #, & stateName`

   b. `Me.xAddressLabel.Text = "cityName" & "," & "stateName"`

   c. `Me.xAddressLabel.Text = cityName & "," & stateName`

   d. None of the above.

5. Which of the following Visual Basic constants advances the insertion point to the next line?

   a. `Advance`

   b. `ControlChars.Advance`

   c. `ControlChars.NewLine`

   d. `ControlChars.NextLine`

6. The form's _____ property allows the user to select a specific button by pressing the Enter key, even when the button does not have the focus.

   a. AcceptButton

   b. DefaultButton

   c. EnterButton

   d. FocusButton

7. Which of the following statements prompts the user for a number, and then correctly assigns the user's response to a Double variable named `number`?

   a. `Double.TryParse(InputBox("Enter a number:", "Number") , number)`

   b. `number = Double.TryParse(InputBox("Enter a number:", "Number"))`

   c. `number = InputBox("Enter a number:", "Number")`

   d. `TryParse.Double(InputBox("Enter a number:", "Number"), number)`

8. Which of the following statements prompts the user for the name of a city, and then correctly assigns the user's response to a String variable named `cityName`?

   a. `String.TryParse(InputBox("Enter the city:", "City"), cityName)`

   b. `cityName = String(InputBox("Enter the city:", "City"))`

   c. `cityName = InputBox("Enter the city:", "City")`

   d. None of the above.

9. The InputBox function's *prompt* argument should be entered using _____.

   a. book title capitalization

   b. sentence capitalization

10. If the `sales` variable contains the number 12345.89, which of the following statements displays the number as 12,345.89?

    a. `Me.xSalesLabel.Text = sales.ToString("C2")`

    b. `Me.xSalesLabel.Text = sales.ToString("N2")`

    c. `Me.xSalesLabel.Text = sales.ToString("D2")`

    d. `Me.xSalesLabel.Text = sales.ToString("F2")`

EXERCISES

1. In this exercise, you modify the Skate-Away Sales application that you coded in the lesson.

   a. Use Windows to make a copy of the Skate Away Solution folder, which is contained in the VB2005\Chap03 folder. Rename the folder Modified Skate Away Solution.

   b. If necessary, start Visual Studio 2005 or Visual Basic 2005 Express Edition. Open the Skate Away Solution (Skate Away Solution.sln) file contained in the VB2005\Chap03\Modified Skate Away Solution folder. Open the designer window.

   c. Modify the xCalcButton's Click event procedure so that it displays the sales tax amount with a dollar sign, two decimal places, and a thousands separator (if necessary).

   d. Save the solution, then start and test the application.

   e. Click the Exit button to end the application.

   f. Close the Code Editor window, then close the solution.

2. In this exercise, you modify the code in an existing application so that it uses a named constant and variables rather than control properties. The application calculates the commission earned on a salesperson's sales using a commission rate of 10%.

   a. If necessary, start Visual Studio 2005 or Visual Basic 2005 Express Edition. Open the Commission Solution (Commission Solution.sln) file, which is contained in the VB2005\Chap03\Commission Solution folder. If necessary, open the designer window.

   b. Make the Calculate Commission button the default button.

   c. Review the code in the Calculate Commission button's Click event procedure. Recode the procedure so that it uses variables. Also use a named constant for the commission rate, which is 10%. Be sure to enter the `Option Explicit On` and `Option Strict On` statements in the General Declarations section.

   d. Use the ToString method to display the commission amount with a dollar sign, two decimal places, and a thousands separator (if necessary).

   e. Save the solution, then start the application. Test the application by calculating the commission for sales of 7500. The commission should be $750.00.

   f. Click the Exit button to end the application. Close the Code Editor window, then close the solution.

3. In this exercise, you code an application for Mingo Sales. The application allows the sales manager to enter the sales made in three states. It should calculate both the total sales made and the total commission earned in the three states.

   a. If necessary, start Visual Studio 2005 or Visual Basic 2005 Express Edition. Open the Mingo Solution (Mingo Solution.sln) file, which is contained in the VB2005\Chap03\Mingo Solution folder.

   b. Make the Calculate button the default button.

   c. Enter the Option Explicit On and Option Strict On statements in the Code Editor window.

   d. Code the Exit button so that it ends the application when it is clicked.

   e. Use the pseudocode shown in Figure 3-47 to code the Calculate button's Click event procedure. (Be sure to use variables.) Use the ToString method to display a thousands separator (if necessary) and two decimal places in the total sales and commission amounts.

---

xCalcButton Click event procedure

1. calculate the total sales = New York sales + Maine sales + Florida sales
2. calculate the commission = total sales * 5%
3. display the total sales and commission in the xTotalSalesLabel and xCommissionLabel controls
4. send the focus to the New York sales text box

Figure 3-47

   f. Save the solution, then start the application. Test the application by calculating the total sales and commission for the following sales amounts:

   New York sales: 15000

   Maine sales: 25000

   Florida sales: 10500

   g. Click the Exit button to end the application. Close the Code Editor window, then close the solution.

4. In this exercise, you modify the Mingo Sales application that you coded in Exercise 3.

   a. Use Windows to make a copy of the Mingo Solution folder, which is contained in the VB2005\Chap03 folder. Rename the folder Modified Mingo Solution.

    b. If necessary, start Visual Studio 2005 or Visual Basic 2005 Express Edition. Open the Mingo Solution (Mingo Solution.sln) file contained in the VB2005\Chap03\Modified Mingo Solution folder. Open the designer window.

    c. Code the form's Load event procedure so that it uses the InputBox function to ask the user for the commission rate before the form appears. Modify the code in the xCalcButton's Click event procedure so that it uses the commission rate entered by the user.

    d. Save the solution, then start the application. When you are prompted to enter the commission rate, type .1 (the decimal equivalent of 10%) and then click the OK button. Test the application by calculating the total sales and commission for the following sales amounts:

New York sales:	26000
Maine sales:	34000
Florida sales:	17000

    e. Click the Exit button to end the application. Close the Code Editor window, then close the solution.

5. In this exercise, you code an application for IMY Industries. The application should calculate the new hourly pay for each of three job codes, given the current hourly pay for each job code and the raise percentage (entered as a decimal number). The application should display the message "Raise percentage: XX" in a label control on the form. The XX in the message should be replaced by the actual raise percentage, formatted using the "P0" *formatString*.

    a. If necessary, start Visual Studio 2005 or Visual Basic 2005 Express Edition. Open the IMY Solution (IMY Solution.sln) file, which is contained in the VB2005\Chap03\IMY Solution folder.

    b. Code the Exit button so that it ends the application when it is clicked.

    c. Before the form appears, use the InputBox function to prompt the personnel clerk to enter the raise percentage. You will use the raise percentage to calculate the new hourly pay for each job code.

    d. Use the pseudocode shown in Figure 3-48 to code the Calculate button's Click event procedure. Create a named constant for the "Raise percentage:" message. Format the new hourly pay using the "N2" *formatString*. Format the raise rate (in the message) using the "P0" *formatString*.

---

xCalcButton Click event procedure

1. calculate the new hourly pays = current hourly pays * raise rate + current hourly pays
2. display new hourly pays in appropriate label controls
3. display the message and raise rate in the xMessageLabel
4. send the focus to the Job Code 1 text box

Figure 3-48

e. Save the solution, then start the application. When you are prompted to enter the raise percentage, type .05 (the decimal equivalent of 5%) and then click the OK button. Use the following information to calculate the new hourly pay for each job code:

Current hourly pay for job code 1:   5

Current hourly pay for job code 2:   6.5

Current hourly pay for job code 3:   8.75

f. Click the Exit button to end the application. Close the Code Editor window, then close the solution.

6. In this exercise, you modify the IMY Industries application that you coded in Exercise 5. The application now will allow the user to enter a separate raise percentage for each job code.

a. Use Windows to make a copy of the IMY Solution folder, which is contained in the VB2005\Chap03 folder. Rename the folder Modified IMY Solution.

b. If necessary, start Visual Studio 2005 or Visual Basic 2005 Express Edition. Open the IMY Solution (IMY Solution.sln) file contained in the VB2005\Chap03\Modified IMY Solution folder. Open the designer window.

c. Modify the application's code so that it asks the personnel clerk to enter the raise for each job code separately. (*Hint*: Use three InputBox functions in the form's Load event procedure.)

d. Display the following information on separate lines in the xMessageLabel control (be sure to replace the XX in each line with the appropriate raise percentage):

Job Code 1:   XX %

Job Code 2:   XX %

Job Code 3:   XX %

e. Save the solution, then start the application. When you are prompted to enter the raise percentages for the job codes, use .03 for job code 1, .05 for job code 2, and .04 for job code 3.

f. Use the following information to calculate the new hourly pay for each job code:

Current hourly pay for job code 1:   5

Current hourly pay for job code 2:   6.5

Current hourly pay for job code 3:   8.75

g. Click the Exit button to end the application. Close the Code Editor window, then close the solution.

Use the information shown in Figure 3-49 to complete Exercises 7 through 9.

Variable/named constant	Contents
cityName	Madison
stateName	WI
zipCode	53711
Message	The capital of

Figure 3-49

7. Using the information shown in Figure 3-49, write an assignment statement that displays the string "Madison, WI" in the xAddressLabel.

8. Using the information shown in Figure 3-49, write an assignment statement that displays the string "The capital of WI is Madison." in the xAddressLabel.

9. Using the information shown in Figure 3-49, write an assignment statement that displays the string "My ZIP code is 53711." in the xAddressLabel. (The zipCode variable is a String variable.)

DISCOVERY EXERCISE

10. In this exercise, you learn about the CancelButton property of a Windows form.

    a. If necessary, start Visual Studio 2005 or Visual Basic 2005 Express Edition. Open the Cancel Solution (Cancel Solution.sln) file, which is contained in the VB2005\Chap03\Cancel Solution folder.

    b. Open the Code Editor window and view the existing code.

    c. Start the application. Type your first name in the text box, then press Enter to select the Clear button, which is the form's default button. The Clear button removes your name from the text box.

    d. Click the Undo button. Your name reappears in the text box.

    e. Click the Exit button to end the application.

    f. Return to the designer window. Set the form's CancelButton property to xUndoButton. This tells the computer to process the code in the Undo button's Click event procedure when the user presses the Esc key.

    g. Save the solution, then start the application.

    h. Type your first name in the text box, then press Enter to select the Clear button.

    i. Press Esc to select the Undo button. Your name reappears in the text box.

    j. Click the Exit button to end the application. Close the Code Editor window, then close the solution.

LESSON C
OBJECTIVES

AFTER STUDYING LESSON C, YOU SHOULD
BE ABLE TO:

» Include a static variable in code

» Code the TextChanged event procedure

» Create a procedure that handles more than one event

MODIFYING THE SKATE-AWAY SALES APPLICATION'S CODE

MODIFYING THE CODE IN THE MAINFORM'S LOAD AND XCALCBUTTON CLICK PROCEDURES

Mr. Cousard, the sales manager at Skate-Away Sales, asks you to make an additional change to the application that you completed in Lesson B. Currently, the application allows the user to enter the salesperson's name only once, when the application first starts. Mr. Cousard would like to have the application ask for the salesperson's name each time an order is calculated. This way, while a salesperson is at lunch or on a break, another salesperson can use the same computer to take an order, without having to start the application again.

As you learned in Lesson B, before making modifications to an application's existing code, you should review the application's documentation and revise the necessary documents. Figure 3-50 shows the revised TOE chart. Changes made to the TOE chart from Lesson B are shaded in the figure. (Lesson B's TOE chart is shown in Figure 3-21.) Notice that the Calculate Order button's Click event procedure, rather than the MainForm's Load event procedure, now is responsible for getting the salesperson's name.

Task	Object	Event
1. Get the salesperson's name 2. Calculate the total skateboards ordered and the total price 3. Display the total skateboards ordered and the total price in the xTotalBoardsLabel and xTotalPriceLabel 4. Calculate the sales tax 5. Display the message, sales tax, and salesperson's name in the xMessageLabel	xCalcButton	Click
Clear the screen for the next order	xClearButton	Click
End the application	xExitButton	Click
Display the total skateboards ordered (from xCalcButton)	xTotalBoardsLabel	None
Display the total price (from xCalcButton)	xTotalPriceLabel	None
Get and display the order information	xNameTextBox, xAddressTextBox, xCityTextBox, xStateTextBox, xZipTextBox, xBlueTextBox, xYellowTextBox	None
~~Get the salesperson's name~~	~~MainForm~~	~~Load~~
Display the message, sales tax, and salesperson's name (from xCalcButton)	xMessageLabel	None

Figure 3-50: Revised TOE chart

Figure 3-51 shows the revised pseudocode for the Calculate Order button's Click event procedure. Changes made to the pseudocode from Lesson B are shaded in the figure. (Lesson B's pseudocode is shown in Figure 3-25.)

First, you will open the Skate-Away Sales application from Lesson B. You then will move the code contained in the MainForm's Load event procedure to the xCalcButton's Click event procedure.

xCalcButton Click event procedure
1. get the salesperson's name
2. calculate total skateboards ordered = blue skateboards ordered + yellow skateboards ordered
3. calculate subtotal = total skateboards ordered * skateboard price
4. calculate sales tax = subtotal * sales tax rate
5. calculate total price = subtotal + sales tax
6. display total skateboards ordered and total price in xTotalBoardsLabel and xTotalPriceLabel
7. display "The sales tax was" message, sales tax, and salesperson's name in xMessageLabel

Figure 3-51: Revised pseudocode for the Calculate Order button

To open the Skate-Away Sales application and then move some of the code:

1 Start Visual Studio 2005 or Visual Basic 2005 Express Edition, if necessary, and close the Start Page window.

2 Open the **Skate Away Solution** (Skate Away Solution.sln) file, which is contained in the VB2005\Chap03\Skate Away Solution folder. Auto-hide the Toolbox, Solution Explorer, and Properties windows, if necessary.

3 Open the Code Editor window, then locate the MainForm Load event procedure. Highlight the two Const statements in the procedure. (The Const statements declare the `InputPrompt` and `InputTitle` named constants.) Click **Edit** on the menu bar, and then click **Cut** to remove the two Const statements from the procedure.

4 Locate the xCalcButton Click event procedure. Position the insertion point in the blank line above the first Const statement in the procedure, then press **Enter** to insert a new blank line. With the insertion point in the new blank line, click **Edit** on the menu bar, and then click **Paste**. The two Const statements that you cut from the Load event procedure now appear in the Click event procedure.

5 Return to the MainForm Load event procedure. Highlight the second comment and the assignment statement. Click **Edit** on the menu bar, and then click **Cut** to remove the comment and the assignment statement from the procedure.

6 Return to the xCalcButton Click event procedure. Position the insertion point in the blank line below the last Dim statement, then press **Enter** to insert a new blank line. With the insertion point in the new blank line, click **Edit** on the menu bar, and then click **Paste**. The comment and assignment statement that you cut from the Load event procedure now appear in the Click event procedure. Press **Enter** to insert a new blank line below the assignment statement.

7 Remove the word `module-level` from the comment. Figure 3-52 shows the current status of the xCalcButton Click event procedure.

Visual Basic code

```
Private Sub xCalcButton_Click(ByVal sender As Object, _
    ByVal e As System.EventArgs) Handles xCalcButton.Click
    ' calculates the total number of skateboards ordered and the
      total price

    Const InputPrompt As String = "Enter the salesperson's name:"
    Const InputTitle As String = "Name Entry"
    Const BoardPrice As Decimal = 100D
    Const TaxRate As Decimal = 0.05D
    Dim blueBoards As Integer
    Dim yellowBoards As Integer
    Dim totalBoards As Integer
    Dim subtotal As Decimal
    Dim salesTax As Decimal
    Dim totalPrice As Decimal

    ' assign the name to the salesPerson variable
    salesPerson = InputBox(InputPrompt, InputTitle)

    ' calculate the total number of skateboards ordered
    Integer.TryParse(Me.xBlueTextBox.Text, blueBoards)
    Integer.TryParse(Me.xYellowTextBox.Text, yellowBoards)
    totalBoards = blueBoards + yellowBoards

    ' calculate the subtotal
    subtotal = totalBoards * BoardPrice

    ' calculate the sales tax
    salesTax = subtotal * TaxRate

    ' calculate the total price
    totalPrice = subtotal + salesTax

    ' display total amounts
    Me.xTotalBoardsLabel.Text = Convert.ToString(totalBoards)
    Me.xTotalPriceLabel.Text = totalPrice.ToString("C2")

    ' display message, tax, and name
    Me.xMessageLabel.Text = "The sales tax was " _
        & Convert.ToString(salesTax) & "." & ControlChars.NewLine & 
          salesPerson
End Sub
```

from the MainForm's Load event procedure

from the MainForm's Load event procedure

Figure 3-52: Current status of the xCalcButton Click event procedure

8 Return to the MainForm Load event procedure. Highlight the remaining lines in the procedure, beginning with the `Private Sub` line and ending with the `End Sub` line. Press **Delete** to delete the lines from the Code Editor window.

Now that you have moved the InputBox function from the MainForm's Load event procedure to the xCalcButton's Click event procedure, only one procedure—the xCalcButton's Click event procedure—needs to use the `salesPerson` variable. Therefore, you can move the statement that declares the `salesPerson` variable from the form's Declarations section to the xCalcButton's Click event procedure. In addition, you will need to change the keyword `Private` in the declaration statement to the keyword `Dim`. Recall that you use the `Private` keyword to create module-level variables, but you use the `Dim` keyword to create procedure-level variables.

To move the declaration statement, then modify the statement, and then save the solution and start the application:

1 Locate the form's Declarations section. Highlight the `' declare module-level variable` comment, then press **Delete** to delete the comment.

2 Highlight the `Private salesPerson As String` statement in the Declarations section. Click **Edit** on the menu bar, and then click **Cut**.

3 Locate the xCalcButton's Click event procedure. Position the insertion point in the blank line below the last Dim statement in the procedure. Click **Edit** on the menu bar, and then click **Paste** to paste the Private statement in the procedure, then press **Enter** to insert a blank line below the statement.

Notice that a blue jagged line appears below the `Private` keyword in the declaration statement. The blue jagged line indicates that there is something wrong with the statement. You can determine the problem by resting your mouse pointer somewhere on the word (or words) immediately above the jagged line.

4 Rest your mouse pointer on the `Private` keyword. A message appears in a box. The message indicates that the `Private` keyword is not valid on a local variable declaration.

5 Change `Private` in the variable declaration statement to **Dim**.

Now save the solution and start it to verify that the application works correctly.

6 Save the solution, then start the application. The order form appears. Click the **Calculate Order** button. The Name Entry dialog box created by the InputBox function appears.

7 Type your name in the Name Entry dialog box, then press **Enter**. "The sales tax was 0.00." message and your name appear in the xMessageLabel.

8 Click the **Calculate Order** button again. Notice that the Name Entry dialog box requires the user to enter the salesperson's name again. It would be more efficient for the user if the salesperson's name appeared as the default response the second and subsequent times the Calculate Order button is clicked.

9 Click the **Cancel** button in the dialog box. Notice that no name appears in the xMessageLabel; this is because the InputBox function returns a zero-length (empty) string when you click the Cancel button in the dialog box.

10 Click the **Exit** button on the order form.

Recall that the InputBox function allows you to specify a default response, which appears in the input area of the dialog box when the dialog box is opened. In the next set of steps, you will observe the effect of using the salesPerson variable as the *defaultResponse* argument in the InputBox function.

To modify the InputBox function:

1 Change the salesPerson = InputBox(InputPrompt, InputTitle) statement in the xCalcButton's Click event procedure to **salesPerson = InputBox(InputPrompt, InputTitle, salesPerson)**. The green jagged line indicates that there is a problem with the salesPerson entry in the InputBox function.

2 Position your mouse pointer on the green jagged line. A message explaining the problem appears in a box, as shown in Figure 3-53. The message says "Variable 'salesPerson' is used before it has been assigned a value. A null reference exception could result at runtime."

```
' assign the name to the salesPerson variable
salesPerson = InputBox(InputPrompt, InputTitle, salesPerson)
                                                 ┌────────────────────────────────────────────────────────────────────────────────┐
                                                 │Variable 'salesPerson' is used before it has been assigned a value. A null reference exception could result at runtime.│
                                                 └────────────────────────────────────────────────────────────────────────────────┘
```

Figure 3-53: Message explaining the problem

In this case, the InputBox function is attempting to use the salesPerson variable before the variable has been assigned a value. (Recall that the computer processes the expression that appears on the right side of the assignment operator before assigning the result to the variable whose name appears on the left side of the assignment operator.) But, you might be wondering, doesn't the Dim salesPerson As String statement provide an initial value for the variable? As you learned in Lesson A, String variables are automatically initialized using the Nothing keyword. However, recall that variables initialized to `Nothing` do not actually contain the word "Nothing"; rather, they contain no data at all. You can fix the problem by assigning an initial value to the `salesPerson` variable. In this case, you will assign the empty string.

3 Change the `Dim salesPerson As String` statement in the xCalcButton's Click event procedure to **Dim salesPerson As String = String.Empty**, then click a different line in the procedure. Notice that the green jagged line disappears.

4 Save the solution, then start the application.

5 Click the **Calculate Order** button. Type your name in the Name Entry dialog box, then press **Enter**. "The sales tax was 0.00." message and your name appear in the xMessageLabel.

6 Click the **Calculate Order** button again. Notice that your name still does not appear in the input area of the dialog box. This is because the `salesPerson` variable is both created in and removed from the computer's internal memory each time you click the Calculate Order button. (Recall that the Dim statement creates the variable in memory, and the variable is removed from memory when the `End Sub` statement is processed.)

7 Click the **Cancel** button in the dialog box, then click the **Exit** button on the order form to end the application.

To display the salesperson's name in the dialog box when the Calculate Order button is clicked the second and subsequent times, you can declare the `salesPerson` variable as either a module-level variable or a static variable. In this case, a static variable is a better choice, because static variables have a lesser scope than module-level variables. Recall that a static variable is really just a special type of procedure-level variable. As you learned in Lesson A, fewer unintentional errors occur in applications when variables are declared using the minimum scope needed. In this case, for example, only the xCalcButton's Click event procedure needs to use the `salesPerson` variable, so a variable with procedure scope is a much better choice than one with module scope.

USING A STATIC VARIABLE

As you learned in Lesson A, a static variable is a procedure-level variable that retains its value even when the procedure in which it is declared ends. Similar to a module-level variable, a static variable is not removed from memory until the application ends.

To declare the `salesPerson` variable as a static variable, then test the application:

1 Change the `Dim salesPerson As String` statement in the xCalcButton's Click event procedure to **Static salesPerson As String**. Figure 3-54 shows the code entered in the xCalcButton's Click event procedure.

USING VARIABLES AND CONSTANTS

Visual Basic code

```vb
Private Sub xCalcButton_Click(ByVal sender As Object, _
    ByVal e As System.EventArgs) Handles xCalcButton.Click
    ' calculates the total number of skateboards ordered and the
        total price

    Const InputPrompt As String = "Enter the salesperson's name:"
    Const InputTitle As String = "Name Entry"
    Const BoardPrice As Decimal = 100D
    Const TaxRate As Decimal = 0.05D
    Dim blueBoards As Integer
    Dim yellowBoards As Integer
    Dim totalBoards As Integer
    Dim subtotal As Decimal
    Dim salesTax As Decimal
    Dim totalPrice As Decimal
    Static salesPerson As String = String.Empty

    ' assign the name to the salesPerson variable
    salesPerson = InputBox(InputPrompt, InputTitle, salesPerson)

    ' calculate the total number of skateboards ordered
    Integer.TryParse(Me.xBlueTextBox.Text, blueBoards)
    Integer.TryParse(Me.xYellowTextBox.Text, yellowBoards)
    totalBoards = blueBoards + yellowBoards

    ' calculate the subtotal
    subtotal = totalBoards * BoardPrice

    ' calculate the sales tax
    salesTax = subtotal * TaxRate

    ' calculate the total price
    totalPrice = subtotal + salesTax

    ' display total amounts
    Me.xTotalBoardsLabel.Text = Convert.ToString(totalBoards)
    Me.xTotalPriceLabel.Text = totalPrice.ToString("C2")

    ' display message, tax, and name
    Me.xMessageLabel.Text = "The sales tax was" _
        & Convert.ToString(salesTax) & "." & ControlChars.NewLine &
            salesPerson
End Sub
```

Static variable → (points to the `Static salesPerson As String = String.Empty` line)

Figure 3-54: Code entered in the xCalcButton's Click event procedure

2 Save the solution, then start the application.

3 Enter **5** as the number of blue skateboards ordered, and enter **5** as the number of yellow skateboards ordered.

4 Press **Enter** to calculate the order. Type your name in the Name Entry dialog box, and then press **Enter**. The application calculates and displays the total skateboards ordered (10) and total price ($1,050.00). In addition, "The sales tax was 50.00." message and your name appear in the xMessageLabel.

5 Enter **20** as the number of blue skateboards ordered. Notice that, at this point, the total skateboards ordered, the total price, and the sales tax amounts shown on the order form are incorrect, because they do not reflect the change in the order of blue skateboards. To display the correct amounts, you will need to recalculate the order by selecting the Calculate Order button.

6 Press **Enter** to recalculate the order. Notice that your name appears highlighted in the input area of the Name Entry dialog box. Press **Enter** to select the OK button in the Name Entry dialog box. The application calculates and displays the total skateboards ordered (25) and total price ($2,625.00). "The sales tax was 125.00." message and your name appear in the xMessageLabel.

7 Click the **Exit** button to end the application.

Having the previously calculated figures remain on the screen when a change is made to the interface could be misleading. A better approach is to clear the total skateboards ordered, total price, and sales tax message when a change is made to either the number of blue skateboards ordered or the number of yellow skateboards ordered.

CODING THE TEXTCHANGED EVENT PROCEDURE

A control's **TextChanged event** occurs when a change is made to the contents of the control's Text property. This can happen as a result of either the user entering data into the control, or the application's code assigning data to the control's Text property. In the next set of steps, you code the xBlueTextBox's TextChanged event procedure so that it clears the contents of the xTotalBoardsLabel, xTotalPriceLabel, and xMessageLabel controls when the user changes the number of blue skateboards ordered.

To code the xBlueTextBox's TextChanged event procedure, then test the procedure:

1 Open the code template for the xBlueTextBox's TextChanged event procedure.

2 Type **' clears the total boards, total price, and message** and press **Enter** twice.

3 Type **me.xTotalBoardsLabel.Text** = **string.empty** and press **Enter**.

4 Type **me.xTotalPriceLabel.Text** = **string.empty** and press **Enter**.

5 Type **me.xMessageLabel.text** = **string.empty** and press **Enter**.

6 Save the solution, then start the application.

7 Enter **5** as the number of blue skateboards ordered, and enter **15** as the number of yellow skateboards ordered. Press **Enter** to calculate the order.

8 Type your name in the Name Entry dialog box, then press **Enter** to select the OK button. The application calculates and displays the total skateboards ordered (20), total price ($2,100.00), and sales tax (100.00).

9 Change the number of blue skateboards ordered to **3**. Notice that when you make a change to the number of blue skateboards ordered, the xBlueTextBox's TextChanged event procedure clears the total skateboards ordered, total price, and message information from the form.

10 Click the **Exit** button to end the application.

Recall that you also want to clear the total skateboards ordered, total price, and message information when a change is made to the number of yellow skateboards ordered. You could code the TextChanged event procedure for the xYellowTextBox control separately, as you did with the xBlueTextBox control. However, an easier way is simply to create one procedure for the computer to process when the TextChanged event of either of the two controls occurs.

ASSOCIATING A PROCEDURE WITH DIFFERENT OBJECTS AND EVENTS

As you learned in Chapter 1, the `Handles` keyword appears in an event procedure's header and indicates the object and event associated with the procedure. For example, the `Handles xBlueTextBox.TextChanged` clause that appears at the end of the procedure header shown in Figure 3-55 indicates that the xBlueTextBox_TextChanged procedure is associated with the TextChanged event of the xBlueTextBox. In other words, the xBlueTextBox_TextChanged procedure will be processed when the xBlueTextBox's TextChanged event occurs.

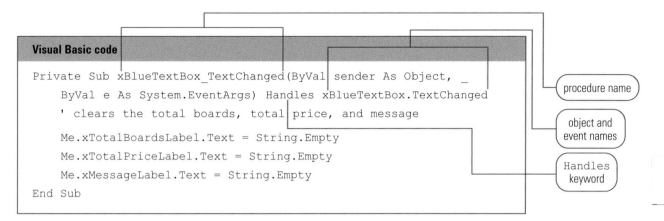

Visual Basic code

```
Private Sub xBlueTextBox_TextChanged(ByVal sender As Object, _
    ByVal e As System.EventArgs) Handles xBlueTextBox.TextChanged
    ' clears the total boards, total price, and message
    Me.xTotalBoardsLabel.Text = String.Empty
    Me.xTotalPriceLabel.Text = String.Empty
    Me.xMessageLabel.Text = String.Empty
End Sub
```

procedure name

object and event names

Handles keyword

Figure 3-55: xBlueTextBox's TextChanged event procedure

Although the name of an event procedure includes both the object name and the event name, both of which appear after the `Handles` keyword, that is not a requirement. You can change the name of an event procedure to almost anything you like. For example, you can change the name xBlueTextBox_TextChanged in Figure 3-55 to simply Clear and the procedure will still work correctly. This is because the Handles clause, rather than the event procedure's name, determines when the procedure is invoked.

Keep in mind that the name you assign to a procedure must follow certain rules. The rules for naming procedures are the same as those for naming variables and constants. Like constants, procedure names are entered using Pascal case.

You also can associate a procedure with more than one object and event, as long as each event contains the same parameters in its procedure header. To do so, you simply list each object and event, separated by commas, in the Handles section of the procedure header. In the Skate-Away Sales application, you will change the name of the xBlueTextBox_TextChanged procedure to ClearControls. You then will associate the ClearControls procedure with the xBlueTextBox.TextChanged and xYellowTextBox.TextChanged events.

To change the procedure's name, and then associate the procedure with different objects and events:

1 Change `xBlueTextBox_TextChanged`, which appears after `Private  Sub` in the procedure header, to **ClearControls**.

2 In the ClearControls procedure header, position the insertion point immediately before the letter H in the word `Handles`. Type _ (the underscore, which is the line continuation character). Be sure there is a space between the ending parentheses and the underscore.

3 Press **Enter** to move the Handles portion of the procedure header to the next line in the procedure, then press **Tab** to indent the line.

4 Position the insertion point immediately after `Handles xBlueTextBox.TextChanged`.

The ClearControls procedure is already associated with the xBlueTextBox.TextChanged event. You just need to associate it with the xYellowTextBox.TextChanged event.

5 Type **,** (a comma). Scroll the list of object names until you see xYellowTextBox. Click **xYellowTextBox** in the list, and then press **Tab** to enter the object name in the procedure.

6 Type **.** (a period), then scroll the list of event names (if necessary) until you see TextChanged. Click **TextChanged**, and then press **Tab**. Figure 3-56 shows the completed ClearControls procedure.

```
Private Sub ClearControls(ByVal sender As Object, ByVal e As System.EventArgs) _
    Handles xBlueTextBox.TextChanged, xYellowTextBox.TextChanged ──────────  Handles clause
    ' clears the total boards, total price, and message

    Me.xTotalBoardsLabel.Text = String.Empty
    Me.xTotalPriceLabel.Text = String.Empty
    Me.xMessageLabel.Text = String.Empty

End Sub
```

Figure 3-56: Completed ClearControls procedure

Now you will test the ClearControls procedure to verify that it is working correctly.

To test the ClearControls procedure:

1 Save the solution, then start the application.

2 Enter **5** as the number of blue skateboards ordered, and enter **10** as the number of yellow skateboards ordered.

3 Press **Enter** to select the Calculate Order button.

4 Type your name in the Name Entry dialog box, then press **Enter** to select the OK button. The application calculates the total skateboards ordered (15), total price ($1,575.00), and sales tax (75.00).

5 Change the number of yellow skateboards ordered to **4**. When you do this, the ClearControls procedure clears the total skateboards ordered, total price, and message information from the form.

6 Press **Enter** to select the Calculate Order button, then press **Enter** to select the OK button in the Name Entry dialog box. The application calculates the total skateboards ordered (9), total price ($945.00), and sales tax (45.00).

7 Change the number of blue skateboards ordered to **2**. When you do this, the ClearControls procedure clears the total skateboards ordered, total price, and message information from the form.

8 Click the **Exit** button to end the application.

9 Close the Code Editor window, then close the solution.

You have completed Lesson C and Chapter 3. You can either take a break or complete the end-of-lesson questions and exercises.

SUMMARY

TO PROCESS CODE WHEN A CHANGE IS MADE TO THE CONTENTS OF A CONTROL'S TEXT PROPERTY:

» Enter the code in the control's TextChanged event procedure.

TO CREATE A PROCEDURE FOR MORE THAN ONE OBJECT OR EVENT:

» List each object and event (using the syntax *object.event*) after the Handles keyword in the procedure header.

QUESTIONS

1. A _____ variable is a procedure-level variable that retains its value after the procedure in which it is declared ends.

    a. constant   b. static

    c. stationary   d. term

2. Which of the following statements declares a procedure-level variable that retains its value after the procedure in which it is declared ends?

    a. Const counter As Integer   b. Dim counter As Constant

    c. Dim counter As Integer   d. Static counter As Integer

3. The _____ event occurs when the contents of a text box have changed.

    a. Change   b. Changed

    c. TextChange   d. TextChanged

4. Which of the following procedure headers indicates that the GetNumber procedure should be processed when the user clicks either the xNum1TextBox or the xNum2TextBox?

a. ```
Private Sub GetNumber(ByVal sender As Object, ByVal e As
System.EventArgs) Handles xNum1TextBox.Click, xNum2TextBox.Click
```

b. ```
Private Sub GetNumber(ByVal sender As Object, ByVal e As
System.EventArgs) Handles xNum1TextBox, xNum2TextBox
```

c. ```
Private Sub GetNumber(ByVal sender As Object, ByVal e As
System.EventArgs) Handles xNum1TextBox.Click and
xNum2TextBox.Click
```

d. None of the above.

# EXERCISES

1. In this exercise, you code an application that allows the user to enter a person's first name and last name, and then uses string concatenation to display the last name, a comma, a space, and the first name in a label control.

   a. If necessary, start Visual Studio 2005 or Visual Basic 2005 Express Edition. Open the Name Solution (Name Solution.sln) file, which is contained in the VB2005\Chap03\Name Solution folder.

   b. Code the form's Load event procedure so that it uses two InputBox functions to prompt the user to enter his or her first name and last name. Assign the results of both functions to variables.

   c. Code the Display button's Click event procedure so that it displays the user's last name, a comma, a space, and the user's first name in the xNameLabel.

   d. Save the solution, then start the application. Test the application by entering your first and last names, and then clicking the Display button.

   e. Click the Exit button to end the application. Close the Code Editor window, then close the solution.
```

2. In this exercise, you create an application that allows the user to enter the number of pennies he has in a jar. The application then calculates the number of dollars, quarters, dimes, nickels, and pennies that he will receive when he cashes in the pennies at a bank.

   a. If necessary, start Visual Studio 2005 or Visual Basic 2005 Express Edition.

   b. Create a Visual Basic Windows-based application. Name the solution Pennies Solution, and name the project Pennies Project. Save the application in the VB2005\Chap03 folder.

   c. Assign the filename Main Form.vb to the form file object.

   d. Assign the name MainForm to the form.

   e. The design of the interface is up to you. Use the GUI design guidelines listed in Appendix A to verify that the interface you create adheres to the GUI standards outlined in this book. Code the application appropriately. (*Hint*: It might be helpful to review the arithmetic operators listed in Figure 2–35 in Chapter 2.)

   f. Save the solution, then start the application. Test the application twice, using the following data: 2311 pennies and 7333 pennies.

   g. Stop the application. Close the Code Editor window, then close the solution.

3. In this exercise, you create an application that can help students in grades 1 through 6 learn how to make change. The application should allow the student to enter the amount of money a customer owes and the amount of money the customer paid. It then should calculate the amount of change, as well as the number of dollars, quarters, dimes, nickels, and pennies to return to the customer. For now, you do not have to worry about the situation where the amount owed is greater than the amount paid. You can assume that the customer pays either the exact amount or more than the exact amount.

   a. If necessary, start Visual Studio 2005 or Visual Basic 2005 Express Edition.

   b. Create a Visual Basic Windows-based application. Name the solution Change Solution, and name the project Change Project. Save the application in the VB2005\Chap03 folder.

   c. Assign the filename Main Form.vb to the form file object.

   d. Assign the name MainForm to the form.

   e. The design of the interface is up to you. Use the GUI design guidelines listed in Appendix A to verify that the interface you create adheres to the GUI standards outlined in this book. Code the application appropriately. (*Hint*: It may be helpful to review the arithmetic operators listed in Figure 2–35 in Chapter 2.)

f. Save the solution, then start the application. Test the application three times, using the following data:

75.33 as the amount owed and 80.00 as the amount paid

39.67 as the amount owed and 50.00 as the amount paid

45.55 as the amount owed and 45.55 as the amount paid

g. Stop the application. Close the Code Editor window, then close the solution.

4. In this exercise, you create an application that allows the user to enter the number of American dollars that she wants to convert to both British pounds and Mexican pesos. The application should make the appropriate calculations and then display the results on the screen.

a. If necessary, start Visual Studio 2005 or Visual Basic 2005 Express Edition.

b. Create a Visual Basic Windows-based application. Name the solution Currency Calculator Solution, and name the project Currency Calculator Project. Save the application in the VB2005\Chap03 folder.

c. Assign the filename Main Form.vb to the form file object.

d. Assign the name MainForm to the form.

e. The design of the interface is up to you. Use the GUI design guidelines listed in Appendix A to verify that the interface you create adheres to the GUI standards outlined in this book. Code the application appropriately. Calculate the number of British pounds by multiplying the number of American dollars by .571505. Calculate the number of Mexican pesos by multiplying the number of American dollars by 10.7956.

f. Save the solution, then start and test the application.

g. Stop the application. Close the Code Editor window, then close the solution.

DISCOVERY EXERCISE

5. In this exercise, you experiment with the Visual Basic conversion functions listed in Appendix B.

a. If necessary, start Visual Studio 2005 or Visual Basic 2005 Express Edition. Open the Conversion Functions Solution (Conversion Functions Solution.sln) file, which is contained in the VB2005\Chap03\Conversion Functions Solution folder.

b. Test the application by entering a letter as the item price and number purchased. Record the results on a piece of paper.

c. Modify the code so that it uses the Visual Basic conversion functions listed in Appendix B rather than the TryParse and Convert methods.

d. Save the solution, then start the application. Test the application by entering a letter as the item price and number purchased. What is the difference between the methods and conversion functions?

e. Click the Exit button to end the application. Close the Code Editor window, then close the solution.

DEBUGGING EXERCISE

6. In this exercise, you debug an existing application.

   a. If necessary, start Visual Studio 2005 or Visual Basic 2005 Express Edition. Open the Debug Solution (Debug Solution.sln) file, which is contained in the VB2005\Chap03\Debug Solution folder.

   b. Start the application, then test the application.

   c. Locate and correct any errors.

   d. Save the solution, then start and test the application. When the application is working correctly, close the Code Editor window, then close the solution.

4

THE SELECTION STRUCTURE

CREATING A MONTHLY PAYMENT CALCULATOR APPLICATION

After weeks of car shopping, Herman Juarez still has not decided what car to purchase. Recently, Herman has noticed that many auto dealers, in an effort to boost sales, are offering buyers a choice of either a large cash rebate or an extremely low financing rate, much lower than the rate Herman would pay by financing the car through his local credit union. Herman is not sure whether to take the lower financing rate from the dealer, or take the rebate and then finance the car through the credit union. He has asked you to create an application that he can use to calculate and display the monthly payment on a car loan.

PREVIEWING THE COMPLETED APPLICATION

Before creating the Monthly Payment Calculator application, you first preview the completed application.

To preview the completed application:

1 Use the Run command on the Windows Start menu to run the **Monthly Payment** (**Monthly Payment.exe**) file, which is contained in the VB2005\Chap04 folder. The Monthly Payment Calculator application's user interface appears on the screen.

First, you will calculate the monthly payment on a $9,000 loan at 5% interest for 3 years.

2 Type **9000** in the Principal text box, and then press **Tab**. Type **5** in the Rate text box, and then click the **Calculate Monthly Payment** button. A message box containing the message "The term must be greater than or equal to 1." appears on the screen, as shown in Figure 4-1. You learn how to create a message box in Lesson B.

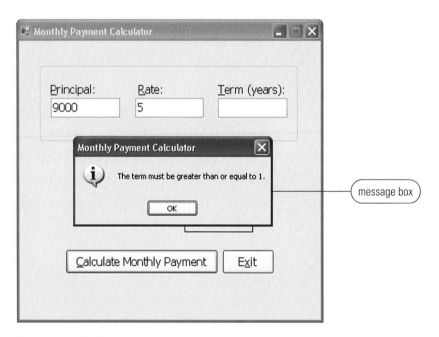

Figure 4-1: Monthly Payment Calculator application's user interface

3 Click the **OK** button in the message box. The message box closes.

4 Press **Tab** to move the insertion point into the Term text box. Type **3** as the term, then click the **Calculate Monthly Payment** button. The application calculates and displays a monthly payment amount of $269.74, as shown in Figure 4-2.

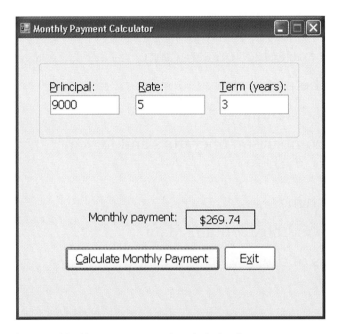

Figure 4-2: Monthly payment amount shown in the interface

5 Click the **Exit** button to end the application.

Before you can begin coding the Monthly Payment Calculator application, you need to learn about the selection structure; you learn that structure in Lesson A. In Lesson B, you complete the Monthly Payment Calculator application's interface as you learn how to use a GroupBox control. You begin coding the application in Lesson B, and complete the application in Lesson C.

LESSON A
OBJECTIVES

AFTER STUDYING LESSON A, YOU SHOULD
BE ABLE TO:

» Write pseudocode for the selection structure

» Create a flowchart to help you plan an application's code

» Write an If...Then...Else statement

» Write code that uses comparison operators and logical
operators

» Change the case of a string

» Determine whether a text box contains data

» Determine the success of the TryParse method

THE IF...THEN...ELSE STATEMENT

THE SELECTION STRUCTURE

The applications you created in the previous three chapters used the sequence programming structure only, where a procedure's instructions are processed, one after another, in the order in which each appears in the procedure. In many applications, however, the next instruction processed depends on the result of a decision or comparison that the program must make. For example, a payroll program typically compares the number of hours the employee worked with the number 40 to determine whether the employee should receive overtime pay in addition to regular pay. Based on the result of that comparison, the program then selects either an instruction that computes regular pay only or an instruction that computes regular pay plus overtime pay.

You use the **selection structure**, also called the **decision structure**, when you want a program to make a decision or comparison and then select one of two paths, depending on the result of that decision or comparison. Although the idea of using the selection structure in a program is new, the concept of the selection structure is already familiar to you, because you use it each day to make hundreds of decisions. For example, every morning you have to decide whether you are hungry and, if you are, what you are going to eat. Figure 4-3 shows other examples of selection structures you might use today.

»TIP

As you may remember from Chapter 1, the selection structure is one of the three programming structures. The other two programming structures are sequence (which you used in the previous chapters) and repetition (which is covered in Chapter 6).

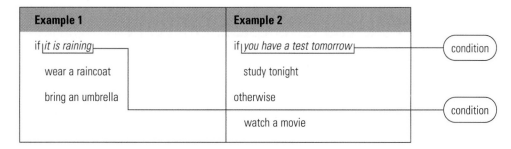

Figure 4-3: Selection structures you might use today

In the examples shown in Figure 4-3, the portion in *italics*, called the **condition**, specifies the decision you are making and is phrased so that it results in either a true or false answer only. For example, it is either raining (true) or not raining (false); either you have a test tomorrow (true) or you do not have a test tomorrow (false).

If the condition is true, you perform a specific set of tasks. If the condition is false, on the other hand, you might or might not need to perform a different set of tasks. For instance, look at the first example shown in Figure 4-3. If it is raining (a true condition), then you will wear a raincoat and bring an umbrella. Notice that you do not have anything in particular to do if it is not raining (a false condition). Compare this with the second example shown in Figure 4-3. If you have a test tomorrow (a true condition), then you will study tonight. However, if you do not have a test tomorrow (a false condition), then you will watch a movie.

Like you, the computer also can evaluate a condition and then select the appropriate tasks to perform based on that evaluation. When using the selection structure in a program, the programmer must be sure to phrase the condition so that it results in either a true or a false answer only. The programmer also must specify the tasks to be performed when the condition is true and, if necessary, the tasks to be performed when the condition is false.

Visual Basic provides four forms of the selection structure: If, If/Else, If/ElseIf/Else, and Case. You will learn about the If and If/Else selection structures in this chapter. The If/ElseIf/Else and Case selection structures are covered in Chapter 5. (Chapter 5 also covers nested selection structures. A nested selection structure is a selection structure that is contained entirely within another selection structure.)

WRITING PSEUDOCODE FOR IF AND IF/ELSE SELECTION STRUCTURES

An **If selection structure** contains only one set of instructions, which are processed when the condition is true. An **If/Else selection structure**, on the other hand, contains two sets of instructions: one set is processed when the condition is true and the other set is processed when the condition is false. Figure 4-4 shows examples of the If and the If/Else structures written in pseudocode.

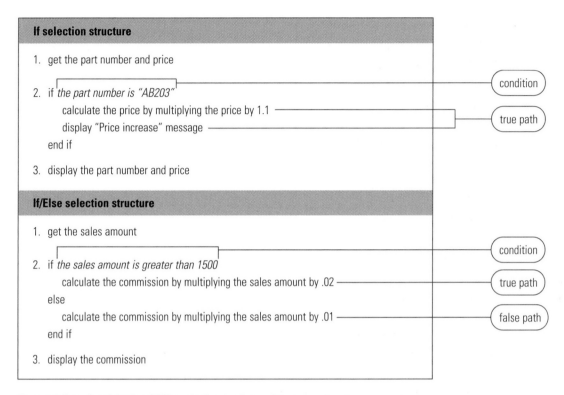

Figure 4-4: Examples of the If and If/Else selection structures written in pseudocode

Although pseudocode is not standardized—every programmer has his or her own version—you will find some similarities among the various versions. For example, many programmers begin the selection structure with the word "if" and end the structure with the two words "end if." They also use the word "else" to designate the instructions to be performed when the condition is false.

In the examples shown in Figure 4-4, the italicized portion of the instruction indicates the condition to be evaluated. Notice that each condition results in either a true or a false answer only. In Example 1, either the part number is "AB203" or it isn't. In Example 2, either the sales amount is greater than the number 1500 or it isn't.

When the condition is true, the set of instructions following the condition is selected for processing. The instructions following the condition are referred to as the **true path**—the path you follow when the condition is true. The true path ends when you come to the "else" or, if there is no "else", when you come to the end of the selection structure (the "end if"). After the true path instructions are processed, the instruction following the "end if" is processed. In the examples shown in Figure 4-4, the display instructions are processed after the instructions in the true path.

The instructions processed when the condition is false depend on whether the selection structure contains an "else". When there is no "else", as in the first example shown in Figure 4-4, the selection structure ends when its condition is false, and processing continues with the instruction following the "end if". In the first example, for instance, the "display the part number and price" instruction is processed when the part number is not "AB203". In cases where the selection structure contains an "else", as in the second example shown in Figure 4-4, the instructions between the "else" and the "end if"—referred to as the **false path**—are processed before the instruction after the "end if" is processed. In the second example, the "calculate the commission by multiplying the sales amount by .01" instruction is processed first, followed by the "display the commission" instruction.

FLOWCHARTING THE IF AND IF/ELSE SELECTION STRUCTURES

Recall from Chapter 2 that, in addition to using pseudocode to plan a procedure's code, programmers also use flowcharts. Unlike pseudocode, which consists of short phrases, a flowchart uses standardized symbols to show the steps the computer must take to accomplish a task. Figure 4-5 shows Figure 4-4's examples in flowchart form.

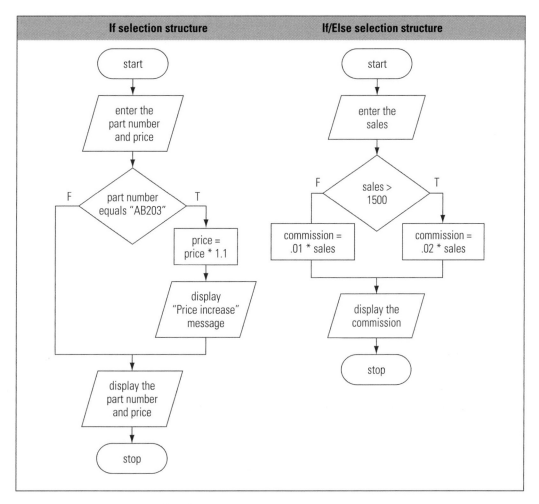

Figure 4-5: Examples of the If and If/Else selection structures drawn in flowchart form

As you learned in Chapter 2, the oval in the flowcharts shown in Figure 4-5 is the start/stop symbol, the rectangle is the process symbol, and the parallelogram is the input/output symbol. The new symbol in the flowcharts, the diamond, is called the **selection/repetition symbol**, because it is used to represent both selection and repetition. In Figure 4-5's flowcharts, the diamonds represent the selection structure. (You will learn how to use the diamond to represent the repetition structure in Chapter 6.) Notice that inside each diamond is a comparison that evaluates to either true or false only. Each diamond also has one flowline entering the symbol and two flowlines leaving the symbol. The two flowlines leading out of the diamond should be marked so that anyone reading the flowchart can distinguish the true path from the false path. You mark the flowline leading to the true path with a "T" (for true), and you mark the flowline leading to the false path with an "F" (for false).

》 TIP

You also can mark the flowlines leading out of the diamond with a "Y" and an "N" (for yes and no).

CODING THE IF AND IF/ELSE SELECTION STRUCTURES

You use the **If...Then...Else statement** to code the If and If/Else selection structures in Visual Basic. Figure 4-6 shows the syntax of the If...Then...Else statement and includes two examples of using the statement.

If...Then...Else statement used to code the If and If/Else selection structures

Syntax

If *condition* **Then**

> *statement block containing one or more statements to be processed when the condition is true*

[Else

> *statement block containing one or more statements to be processed when the condition is false]*

End If

Examples

```
If partNumber = "AB203" Then
      price = price * 1.1
      Me.xMessageLabel.Text = "Price increase"
End If
```

If the partNumber variable contains the string "AB203", the first instruction in the true path multiplies the contents of the price variable by 1.1 and assigns the result to the price variable. The second instruction in the true path displays the message "Price increase" in the xMessageLabel.

```
If sales > 1500 Then
      commission = .02 * sales
Else
      commission = .01 * sales
End If
```

If the sales variable contains a number that is greater than 1500, the instruction in the true path multiplies the contents of the sales variable by .02 and assigns the result to the commission variable; otherwise, the instruction in the false path multiplies the contents of the sales variable by .01 and assigns the result to the commission variable.

Figure 4-6: Syntax and examples of the If...Then...Else statement used to code the If and If/Else selection structures

The items in square brackets in the syntax are optional. For example, you do not always need to include the Else portion of the syntax, referred to as the **Else clause**, in an If...Then...Else statement. Words in **bold**, however, are essential components of the statement. The words If, Then, and End If, for instance, must be included in the If...Then...Else statement. The word Else must be included only when the programmer needs to use the false path of the selection structure.

Items in *italics* indicate where the programmer must supply information pertaining to the current application. For instance, the programmer must supply the *condition* to be evaluated. The *condition* must be a Boolean expression, which is an expression that results in a Boolean value (True or False). In addition to supplying the *condition*, the programmer must supply the statements to be processed in the true path and, if used, the false path. The set of statements contained in the true path, as well as the set of statements contained in the false path, is referred to as a **statement block**.

The If...Then...Else statement's *condition* can contain variables, literal constants, named constants, properties, functions, methods, arithmetic operators, comparison operators, and logical operators. You already know about variables, literal constants, named constants, properties, functions, methods, and arithmetic operators from previous chapters. You will learn about comparison operators and logical operators in this chapter.

> **» TIP**
>
> In Visual Basic, a statement block is a set of statements terminated by an Else, End If, Loop, or Next clause.

COMPARISON OPERATORS

Visual Basic provides nine **comparison operators**, also referred to as **relational operators**. Figure 4-7 lists the six most commonly used comparison operators and includes examples of using the operators in the If...Then...Else statement's *condition*. (The remaining three comparison operators are covered in Chapter 5.) Notice that the expression contained in each *condition* shown in the figure evaluates to one of two Boolean values—either True or False. All expressions containing a comparison operator will result in an answer of either True or False only.

Comparison operators

Operator	Operation
=	equal to
>	greater than
>=	greater than or equal to
<	less than
<=	less than or equal to
<>	not equal to

Examples

```
If sales1 = sales2 Then
```

Compares the contents of the `sales1` variable with the contents of the `sales2` variable. The *condition* evaluates to True when the contents of both variables are equal; otherwise, it evaluates to False.

```
If age >= 21 Then
```

Compares the contents of the `age` variable with the number 21. The *condition* evaluates to True when the `age` variable contains a number that is greater than or equal to 21; otherwise, it evaluates to False.

```
If price < 67.89 Then
```

Compares the contents of the `price` variable with the number 67.89. The *condition* evaluates to True when the `price` variable contains a number that is less than 67.89; otherwise, it evaluates to False.

```
If state <> "TN" Then
```

Compares the contents of the `state` variable with the string "TN". The *condition* evaluates to True when the `state` variable does not contain the string "TN"; otherwise, it evaluates to False.

Figure 4-7: Listing and examples of commonly used comparison operators

Unlike arithmetic operators, comparison operators do not have an order of precedence. If an expression contains more than one comparison operator, the computer evaluates the comparison operators from left to right in the expression. Keep in mind, however, that comparison operators are evaluated after any arithmetic operators in the expression. In other words, in the expression $5 - 2 > 1 + 2$, the two arithmetic operators $(-, +)$ are evaluated before the comparison operator $(>)$ is evaluated. The result of the expression is the Boolean value False, as shown in Figure 4-8.

Evaluation steps	Result
Original expression	$5 - 2 > 1 + 2$
$5 - 2$ is evaluated first	$3 > 1 + 2$
$1 + 2$ is evaluated second	$3 > 3$
$3 > 3$ is evaluated last	False

Figure 4-8: Evaluation steps for an expression containing arithmetic and comparison operators

Next, you will view two examples of procedures that contain a comparison operator in an If...Then...Else statement. The first procedure uses the If selection structure, and the second procedure uses the If/Else selection structure.

USING COMPARISON OPERATORS—SWAPPING NUMERIC VALUES

Figures 4-9 and 4-10 show the pseudocode and flowchart, respectively, for a procedure that displays both the lowest and highest of two numbers entered by the user. Figure 4-11 shows the corresponding Visual Basic code for the procedure, and Figure 4-12 shows a sample run of the application that contains the procedure.

xDisplayButton Click event procedure - pseudocode

1. store the text box values in the num1 and num2 variables

2. if the number contained in the num1 variable is greater than the number contained in the num2 variable
    swap the numbers so that the num1 variable contains the smaller number
   end if

3. display (in xMessageLabel) a message stating the lowest number and the highest number

Figure 4-9: Pseudocode showing the If selection structure

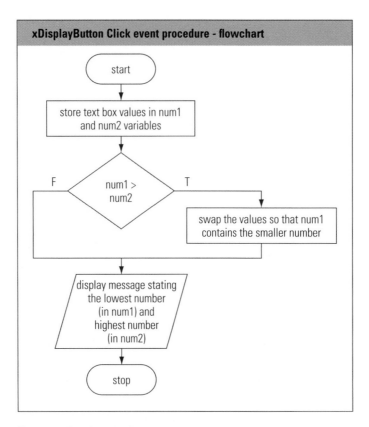

Figure 4-10: Flowchart showing the If selection structure

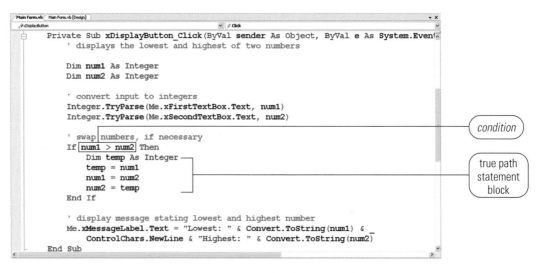

Figure 4-11: The If selection structure shown in the xDisplayButton's Click event procedure

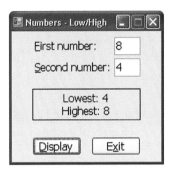

Figure 4-12: Sample run of the application that contains the xDisplayButton's Click event procedure

The code shown in Figure 4-11 first declares two procedure-level Integer variables named num1 and num2. It then converts the contents of two text boxes to integers and assigns the integers to the num1 and num2 variables. The num1 > num2 *condition* in the If...Then...Else statement compares the contents of the num1 variable with the contents of the num2 variable. If the *condition* evaluates to True, it means that the value in the num1 variable is greater than the value in the num2 variable. In that case, the four instructions contained in the If...Then...Else statement's true path swap the values contained in those variables. Swapping the values places the smaller number in the num1 variable, and places the larger number in the num2 variable. If the num1 > num2 *condition* evaluates to False, on the other hand, the true path instructions are skipped over. The instructions do not need to be processed because the num1 variable already contains a number that is smaller than (or possibly equal to) the one stored in the num2 variable. The last statement in the code displays a message that indicates the lowest number (which is contained in the num1 variable) and the highest number (which is contained in the num2 variable).

Study closely the instructions used to swap the values stored in the num1 and num2 variables. The first instruction, Dim temp As Integer, declares a variable named temp. Like the variables declared at the beginning of a procedure, variables declared within a statement block remain in memory until the procedure ends. However, unlike variables declared at the beginning of a procedure, variables declared within a statement block have block scope rather than procedure scope. Recall that when a variable has procedure scope, it can be used anywhere within the procedure. A variable that has **block scope**, on the other hand, can be used only within the statement block in which it is declared. In this case, for example, the num1 and num2 variables can be used anywhere within the xDisplayButton's Click event procedure, but the temp variable can be used only within the If...Then...Else statement's true path. You may be wondering why the temp variable was not declared at the beginning of the procedure, along with the num1 and num2 variables. Although there is nothing wrong with declaring all variables at the beginning of a procedure, in this case the `temp` variable is not needed unless a swap is necessary, so there is no reason to create the variable until it is needed.

The second instruction in the If...Then...Else statement's true path, `temp = num1`, assigns the value in the `num1` variable to the `temp` variable. The `temp` variable is necessary to store the contents of the `num1` variable temporarily so that the swap can be made. If you did not store the `num1` variable's value in the `temp` variable, the `num1` variable's value would be lost when the computer processes the next statement, `num1 = num2`, which replaces the contents of the `num1` variable with the contents of the `num2` variable. Finally, the `num2 = temp` instruction assigns the value in the `temp` variable to the `num2` variable. Figure 4-13 illustrates the concept of swapping, assuming the user enters the numbers eight and four in the xFirstTextBox and xSecondTextBox controls, respectively.

	temp	num1	num2
values stored in the variables immediately before the `temp = num1` instruction is processed	0	8	4
result of the `temp = num1` instruction	8	8	4
result of the `num1 = num2` instruction	8	4	4
result of the `num2 = temp` instruction, which completes the swapping process	8	4	8

values were swapped

Figure 4-13: Illustration of the swapping process

To code and then test the Number Swap application:

1 Start Visual Studio 2005 or Visual Basic 2005 Express Edition, if necessary, and close the Start Page window.

2 Open the **Number Swap Solution** (Number Swap Solution.sln) file, which is contained in the VB2005\Chap04\Number Swap Solution folder. If necessary, open the designer window.

3 Open the Code Editor window. Replace the `<your name>` and `<current date>` text in the comments with your name and the current date.

4 Open the code template for the xDisplayButton's Click event procedure, then enter the comments and code shown in Figure 4-11.

5 Close the Code Editor window. Save the solution, then start the application.

6 Enter **8** as the first number, then enter **4** as the second number. Click the **Display** button. The button's Click event procedure displays the message shown earlier in Figure 4-12.

7 Click the **Exit** button to end the application. You are returned to the designer window. Close the solution.

USING COMPARISON OPERATORS—DISPLAYING THE SUM OR DIFFERENCE

Figures 4-14 and 4-15 show the pseudocode and flowchart, respectively, for a procedure that displays either the sum of or the difference between two numbers entered by the user. Figure 4-16 shows the corresponding Visual Basic code for the procedure, and Figure 4-17 shows a sample run of the application that contains the procedure.

---

xCalcButton Click event procedure - pseudocode

1. store text box values in operation, number1, and number2 variables

2. if the operation variable contains "1"

    calculate the sum by adding together the numbers contained in the number1 and number2 variables

    display (in xAnswerLabel) the "Sum:" message along with the sum

  else

    calculate the difference by subtracting the number contained in the number2 variable from the number contained in the number1 variable

    display (in xAnswerLabel) the "Difference:" message along with the difference

  end if

Figure 4-14: Pseudocode showing the If/Else selection structure

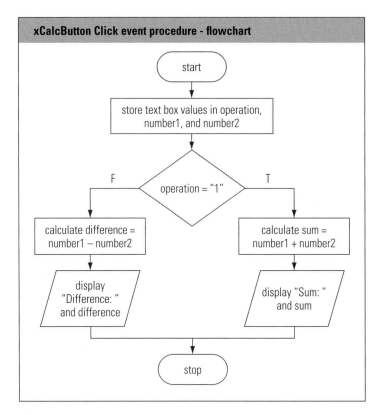

Figure 4-15: Flowchart showing the If/Else selection structure

```
Main Form.vb    Main Form.vb [Design]                                                    ▼ ×
  xCalcButton                                          ▼   Click                          ▼
      Private Sub xCalcButton_Click(ByVal sender As Object, ByVal e As System.EventArgs) Han
          ' calculates either the sum of or the difference between two numbers

          Dim operation As String
          Dim number1 As Integer
          Dim number2 As Integer
          Dim answer As Integer

          ' assign operation input to a variable
          operation = Me.xOperationTextBox.Text

          ' convert number input to integers
          Integer.TryParse(Me.xFirstTextBox.Text, number1)
          Integer.TryParse(Me.xSecondTextBox.Text, number2)                           ──── condition

          ' calculate and display the sum or the difference
          If operation = "1" Then
              answer = number1 + number2
              Me.xAnswerLabel.Text = "Sum: " & Convert.ToString(answer)
          Else
              answer = number1 - number2
              Me.xAnswerLabel.Text = "Difference: " & Convert.ToString(answer)
          End If
      End Sub
```

Figure 4-16: The If/Else selection structure shown in the xCalcButton's Click event procedure

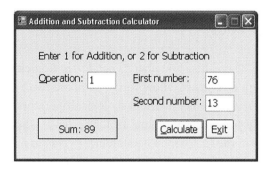

Figure 4-17: Sample run of the application that contains the xCalcButton's Click event procedure

The code shown in Figure 4-16 declares four procedure-level variables: a String variable named `operation` and three Integer variables named `number1`, `number2`, and `answer`. The code then assigns the user's input to the `operation`, `number1`, and `number2` variables. The `operation = "1"` *condition* in the If...Then...Else statement compares the contents of the `operation` variable with the string "1". If the *condition* is true, the instructions in the selection structure's true path calculate and display the sum of the two numbers entered by the user. If the *condition* is false, on the other hand, the instructions in the selection structure's false path calculate and display the difference between the two numbers.

To code and then test the Addition and Subtraction application:

1 Open the **AddSub Solution** (AddSub Solution.sln) file, which is contained in the VB2005\Chap04\AddSub Solution folder. If necessary, open the designer window.

2 Open the Code Editor window. Replace the `<your name>` and `<current date>` text in the comments with your name and the current date.

3 Open the code template for the xCalcButton's Click event procedure, then enter the comments and code shown in Figure 4-16.

4 Close the Code Editor window. Save the solution, then start the application.

5 Enter the number **1** as the operation, **76** as the first number, and **13** as the second number. Click the **Calculate** button. The button's Click event procedure displays the sum of both numbers, as shown earlier in Figure 4-17.

6 Click the **Exit** button to end the application. You are returned to the designer window. Close the solution.

LOGICAL OPERATORS

You also can use logical operators in an If...Then...Else statement's *condition*. **Logical operators**, sometimes referred to as **Boolean operators**, allow you to combine two or more *conditions* into one compound *condition*. Visual Basic provides six logical operators, which are listed along with their order of precedence in Figure 4-18. The figure also contains examples of using logical operators in the If...Then...Else statement's *condition*. Like expressions containing comparison operators, expressions containing logical operators always evaluate to a Boolean value.

Logical operators		
Operator	Operation	Precedence number
Not	reverses the truth-value of the *condition*; True becomes False, and False becomes True	1
And	all conditions must be true for the compound condition to be true	2
AndAlso	same as the And operator, except performs short-circuit evaluation	2
Or	only one of the conditions must be true for the compound condition to be true	3
OrElse	same as the Or operator, except performs short-circuit evaluation	3
Xor	one and only one condition can be true for the compound condition to be true	4

Examples

```
If Not isInsured Then
```

The condition evaluates to True when the isInsured variable contains the Boolean value False; otherwise, it evaluates to False.

```
If hours > 0 And hours <= 40 Then
```

The compound condition evaluates to True when the hours variable contains a number that is greater than zero but less than or equal to 40; otherwise, it evaluates to False.

Figure 4-18: Listing and examples of logical operators *(Continued)* ▶

```
If state = "TN" AndAlso sales > 50000D Then
```

The compound condition evaluates to True when the `state` variable contains the string "TN" and, at the same time, the `sales` variable contains a number that is greater than 50000; otherwise, it evaluates to False.

```
If rating = "A" Or rating = "B" Then
```

The compound condition evaluates to True when the `rating` variable contains either the string "A" or the string "B"; otherwise, it evaluates to False.

```
If state = "TN" OrElse sales > 50000D Then
```

The compound condition evaluates to True when the `state` variable contains the string "TN" or when the `sales` variable contains a number that is greater than 50000; otherwise, it evaluates to False.

```
If coupon1 = "USED" Xor coupon2 = "USED" Then
```

The compound condition evaluates to True when only one of the variables contains the string "USED"; otherwise, it evaluates to False.

Figure 4-18: Listing and examples of logical operators

The tables shown in Figure 4-19, called **truth tables**, summarize how the computer evaluates the logical operators in an expression.

Truth table for the Not operator		
value of *condition*	value of Not *condition*	
True	False	
False	True	
Truth table for the And operator		
value of *condition1*	value of *condition2*	value of *condition1* And *condition2*
True	True	True
True	False	False
False	True	False
False	False	False
Truth table for the AndAlso operator		
value of *condition1*	value of *condition2*	value of *condition1* AndAlso *condition2*
True	True	True
True	False	False
False	(not evaluated)	False

Figure 4-19: Truth tables for the logical operators *(Continued)* ▶

Truth table for the Or operator		
value of *condition1*	value of *condition2*	value of *condition1* Or *condition2*
True	True	True
True	False	True
False	True	True
False	False	False
Truth table for the OrElse operator		
value of *condition1*	value of *condition2*	value of *condition1* OrElse *condition2*
True	(not evaluated)	True
False	True	True
False	False	False
Truth table for the Xor operator		
value of *condition1*	value of *condition2*	value of *condition1* Xor *condition2*
True	True	False
True	False	True
False	True	True
False	False	False

Figure 4-19: Truth tables for the logical operators

As Figure 4-19 indicates, the Not operator reverses the truth-value of the *condition*. If the value of the *condition* is True, then the value of Not *condition* is False. Likewise, if the value of the *condition* is False, then the value of Not *condition* is True.

Now look at the truth tables for the And and AndAlso logical operators. When you use the And or AndAlso operators to combine two conditions, the resulting compound condition is True only when both conditions are True. If either condition is False or if both conditions are False, then the compound condition is False. The difference between the And and AndAlso operators is that the And operator always evaluates both conditions, while the AndAlso operator performs a **short-circuit evaluation**, which means that it does not always evaluate *condition2*. Because both conditions combined with the AndAlso operator need to be True for the compound condition to be True, the AndAlso operator does not evaluate *condition2* when *condition1* is False. Although the And and AndAlso operators produce the same results, the AndAlso operator is more efficient.

Now look at the truth tables for the Or and OrElse logical operators. When you combine conditions using the Or or OrElse operators, the compound condition is False only when both conditions are False. If either condition is True or if both conditions are True, then the compound condition is True. The difference between the Or and OrElse operators is that the Or operator always evaluates both conditions, while the OrElse operator performs a short-circuit evaluation. In this case, because only one of the conditions combined with the OrElse operator needs to be True for the compound condition to be True, the OrElse operator does not evaluate *condition2* when *condition1* is True. Although the Or and OrElse operators produce the same results, the OrElse operator is more efficient.

Finally, look at the truth table for the Xor operator. When you combine conditions using the Xor operator, the compound condition is True only when one and only one condition is True. If both conditions are True or both conditions are False, then the compound condition is False. In the next section, you will use the truth tables to determine the appropriate logical operator to use in the If...Then...Else statement's compound condition.

USING THE TRUTH TABLES

An application needs to calculate a bonus for each A-rated salesperson whose monthly sales total more than $10,000. To receive a bonus, the salesperson must be rated A and he or she must sell more than $10,000 in product. The procedure that calculates the bonus uses a String variable named `rating` and an Integer variable named `sales` to store the salesperson's rating and sales amount, respectively. Therefore, you can phrase *condition1* as `rating = "A"` and *condition2* as `sales > 10000`. Now the question is, which logical operator should you use to combine both conditions into one compound condition? You can use the truth tables shown in Figure 4-19 to answer the question.

For a salesperson to receive a bonus, remember that both *condition1* (`rating = "A"`) and *condition2* (`sales > 10000`) must be True at the same time. If either condition is False, or if both conditions are False, then the compound condition should be False and the salesperson should not receive a bonus. According to the truth tables, the And, AndAlso, Or, and OrElse operators evaluate the compound condition as True when both conditions are True. However, only the And and AndAlso operators evaluate the compound condition as False when either one or both of the conditions are False. The Or and OrElse operators, you will notice, evaluate the compound condition as False only when *both* conditions are False. Therefore, the correct compound condition to use here is either `rating = "A" And sales > 10000` or `rating = "A" AndAlso sales > 10000`. Recall, however, that the AndAlso operator is more efficient than the And operator.

Now assume that you want to send a letter to all A-rated salespeople and all B-rated salespeople. If the rating is stored in the `rating` variable, you can phrase *condition1* as `rating = "A"` and *condition2* as `rating = "B"`. Now which logical operator should you use to combine both conditions? At first it might appear that either the And or the AndAlso operator is the correct one to use, because the example says to send the letter to "all A-rated salespeople and all B-rated salespeople." In everyday conversations, you will find that people sometimes use the word *and* when what they really mean is *or*. Although both words do not mean the same thing, using *and* instead of *or* generally does not cause a problem because we are able to infer what another person means. Computers, however, cannot infer anything; they simply process the directions you give them, word for word. In this case, you actually want to send a letter to all salespeople with either an A or a B rating (a salesperson cannot have both an A rating and a B rating), so you will need to use either the Or or the OrElse operator. As the truth tables indicate, the Or and OrElse operators are the only operators that evaluate the compound condition as True when one or more of the conditions is True. Therefore, the correct compound condition to use here is either `rating = "A" Or rating = "B"` or `rating = "A" OrElse rating = "B"`. Recall, however, that the OrElse operator is more efficient than the Or operator.

Finally, assume that when placing an order, a customer is allowed to use only one of two coupons. If a procedure uses the variables `coupon1` and `coupon2` to keep track of the coupons, you can phrase *condition1* as `coupon1 = "USED"` and *condition2* as `coupon2 = "USED"`. Now which operator should you use to combine both conditions? According to the truth tables, the Xor operator is the only operator that evaluates the compound condition as True when one and only one condition is True. Therefore, the correct compound condition to use here is `coupon1 = "USED" Xor coupon2 = "USED"`.

Figure 4-20 shows the order of precedence for the arithmetic, comparison, and logical operators you have learned so far.

Operator	Operation	Precedence number
^	exponentiation	1
−	negation	2
*, /	multiplication and division	3
\	integer division	4
Mod	modulus arithmetic	5
+, −	addition and subtraction	6
&	concatenation	7
=, >, >=, <, <=, <>	equal to, greater than, greater than or equal to, less than, less than or equal to, not equal to	8
Not	reverses the truth-value of the condition	9
And, AndAlso	all conditions must be true for the compound condition to be true	10
Or, OrElse	only one condition needs to be true for the compound condition to be true	11
Xor	one and only one condition can be true for the compound condition to be true	12

Figure 4-20: Order of precedence for arithmetic, comparison, and logical operators

Notice that logical operators are evaluated after any arithmetic operators or comparison operators in an expression. In other words, in the expression 12 > 0 AndAlso 12 < 10 * 2, the arithmetic operator (*) is evaluated first, followed by the two comparison operators (> and <), followed by the logical operator (AndAlso). The expression evaluates to True, as shown in Figure 4-21.

Evaluation steps	Result
Original expression	12 > 0 AndAlso 12 < 10 * 2
10 * 2 is evaluated first	12 > 0 AndAlso 12 < 20
12 > 0 is evaluated second	True AndAlso 12 < 20
12 < 20 is evaluated third	True AndAlso True
True AndAlso True is evaluated last	True

Figure 4-21: Evaluation steps for an expression containing arithmetic, comparison, and logical operators

In the next section, you will view the Visual Basic code for a procedure that contains a logical operator in an If...Then...Else statement.

USING LOGICAL OPERATORS: CALCULATING GROSS PAY

An application needs a procedure that calculates and displays an employee's gross pay. To keep this example simple, assume that no one at the company works more than 40 hours per week, and everyone earns the same hourly rate, $8.35. Before making the gross pay calculation, the program should verify that the number of hours entered by the user is greater than or equal to zero, but less than or equal to 40. Programmers refer to the process of verifying that the input data is within the expected range as **data validation**. In this case, if the number of hours is valid, the program should calculate and display the gross pay; otherwise, it should display an error message alerting the user that the input data is incorrect. Figure 4-22 shows two ways of writing the Visual Basic code for the procedure. Notice that the If...Then...Else statement in the first example uses the AndAlso logical operator, whereas the If...Then...Else statement in the second example uses the OrElse logical operator.

Example 1: using the AndAlso operator

```
Dim hoursWorked As Double
Dim grossPay As Double

Double.TryParse(Me.xHoursTextBox.Text, hoursWorked)

If hoursWorked >= 0.0 AndAlso hoursWorked <= 40.0 Then
    ' calculate and display the gross pay
    grossPay = hoursWorked * 8.35
    Me.xGrossLabel.Text = grossPay.ToString("C2")
Else
    ' display an error message
    Me.xGrossLabel.Text = "Error"
End If
```

Example 2: using the OrElse operator

```
Dim hoursWorked As Double
Dim grossPay As Double

Double.TryParse(Me.xHoursTextBox.Text, hoursWorked)

If hoursWorked < 0.0 OrElse hoursWorked > 40.0 Then
    ' display an error message
    Me.xGrossLabel.Text = "Error"
Else
    ' calculate and display the gross pay
    grossPay = hoursWorked * 8.35
    Me.xGrossLabel.Text = grossPay.ToString("C2")
End If
```

Figure 4-22: AndAlso and OrElse logical operators in the If...Then...Else statement

> **»TIP**
>
> As you learned in Chapter 3, a numeric literal constant that has a decimal place is automatically treated as a Double number.

The compound condition in the first example shown in Figure 4-22 determines whether the value stored in the hoursWorked variable is greater than or equal to the number 0.0 and, at the same time, less than or equal to the number 40.0. If the compound condition evaluates to True, the selection structure calculates and displays the gross pay; otherwise, it displays the "Error" message. The compound condition in the second example, on the other hand, determines whether the value stored in the hoursWorked variable is less than the number 0.0 or greater than the number 40.0. If the compound condition evaluates to True, the selection structure displays the "Error" message; otherwise, it calculates and displays the gross pay. Both If...Then...Else statements shown in Figure 4-22 produce the same results and simply represent two different ways of performing the same task.

To code and then test the Gross Pay application:

1 Open the **Gross Pay Solution** (Gross Pay Solution.sln) file, which is contained in the VB2005\Chap04\Gross Pay Solution folder. If necessary, open the designer window.

2 Open the Code Editor window. Replace the `<your name>` and `<current date>` text in the comments with your name and the current date.

3 In the xCalcButton's Click event procedure, enter the comments and code shown in either of the two examples in Figure 4-22.

4 Close the Code Editor window. Save the solution, then start the application.

5 Type **20** in the Hours worked text box, then press **Enter** to select the Calculate button. The button's Click event procedure calculates the gross pay amount and displays it in the xGrossLabel. See Figure 4-23.

Figure 4-23: Gross pay amount shown in the interface

6 Change the number of hours worked to **52**, then press **Enter** to select the Calculate button. The button's Click event procedure displays the "Error" message in the xGrossLabel.

7 Click the **Exit** button to end the application. You are returned to the designer window. Close the solution.

In the procedures shown so far in this lesson, the *condition* in the If...Then...Else statement compared either numeric values or numbers treated as strings. The *condition* also can compare strings that contain letters, as well as compare Boolean values. First, you will learn how to compare strings containing letters.

COMPARING STRINGS CONTAINING LETTERS

A procedure needs to display the word "Pass" when the user enters the letter P in the xLetterTextBox, and the word "Fail" when the user enters anything else. Figure 4-24 shows four ways of writing the Visual Basic code for the procedure.

Example 1: using the OrElse operator

```
Dim letter As String
letter = Me.xLetterTextBox.Text
If letter = "P" OrElse letter = "p" Then
    Me.xResultLabel.Text = "Pass"
Else
    Me.xResultLabel.Text = "Fail"
End if
```

Example 2: using the AndAlso operator

```
Dim letter As String
letter = Me.xLetterTextBox.Text
If letter <> "P" AndAlso letter <> "p" Then
    Me.xResultLabel.Text = "Fail"
Else
    Me.xResultLabel.Text = "Pass"
End if
```

Example 3: correct, but less efficient, solution

```
Dim letter As String
letter = Me.xLetterTextBox.Text
If letter = "P" OrElse letter = "p" Then
    Me.xResultLabel.Text = "Pass"
End If
If letter <> "P" AndAlso letter <> "p" Then
    Me.xResultLabel.Text = "Fail"
End if
```

Example 4: using the ToUpper method

```
Dim letter As String
letter = Me.xLetterTextBox.Text
If letter.ToUpper = "P" Then
    Me.xResultLabel.Text = "Pass"
Else
    Me.xResultLabel.Text = "Fail"
End if
```

Figure 4-24: Visual Basic code showing string comparisons in the If...Then...Else statement's *condition*

The first statement in each example shown in Figure 4-24 creates and initializes a String variable named `letter`. The second statement assigns the contents of the xLetterTextBox to the `letter` variable. The `letter = "P" OrElse letter = "p"` compound condition in the first example determines whether the value stored in the `letter` variable is either the uppercase letter P or the lowercase letter p. When the variable contains one of those two letters, the compound condition evaluates to true and the selection structure displays the word "Pass" on the screen; otherwise, it displays the word "Fail". You may be wondering why you need to compare the contents of the `letter` variable with both the uppercase and lowercase version of the letter P. As is true in many programming languages, string comparisons in Visual Basic are case sensitive, which means that the uppercase version of a letter is not the same as its lowercase counterpart. So, although a human being recognizes P and p as being the same letter, a computer does not; to a computer, a P is different from a p. The reason for this differentiation is that each character on the computer keyboard is stored differently in the computer's internal memory. In this case, for example, the uppercase letter P is stored using a Unicode value of 56, whereas the lowercase letter p is stored using a Unicode value of 76. As you learned in Chapter 3, Unicode is the universal coding scheme for characters.

The `letter <> "P" AndAlso letter <> "p"` compound condition in the second example shown in Figure 4-24 determines whether the value stored in the `letter` variable is *not* equal to either the uppercase letter P or the lowercase letter p. When the variable does not contain either of those two letters, the compound condition evaluates to true and the selection structure displays the word "Fail" on the screen; otherwise, it displays the word "Pass".

Rather than using one If...Then...Else statement with an Else clause, as in Examples 1 and 2, Example 3 in Figure 4-24 uses two If...Then...Else statements with no Else clause in either one. Although the If...Then...Else statements in Example 3 produce the same results as the If...Then...Else statement in Examples 1 and 2, they do so less efficiently. To illustrate this point, assume that the user enters the letter P in the xLetterTextBox. The compound condition in the first If...Then...Else statement shown in Example 3 determines whether the value stored in the `letter` variable is equal to either P or p. In this case, the compound condition evaluates to true, because the `letter` variable contains the letter P. As a result, the first If...Then...Else statement's true path displays the word "Pass" in the xResultLabel, and then the first If...Then...Else statement ends. Although the appropriate word ("Pass") already appears in the xResultLabel, the procedure still evaluates the second If...Then...Else statement's compound condition to determine whether to display the "Fail" message. The second evaluation is unnecessary and makes Example 3's code less efficient than the code shown in Examples 1 and 2.

The If...Then...Else statement shown in Example 4 in Figure 4-24 also contains a string comparison in its *condition*, but notice that the *condition* does not use a logical operator; rather, it uses the ToUpper method. You learn about the ToUpper method next.

CONVERTING A STRING TO UPPERCASE OR LOWERCASE

As you learned earlier, string comparisons in Visual Basic are case-sensitive, which means that the string "Yes" is not the same as the string "YES" or the string "yes". A problem occurs when a comparison needs to include a string that is either entered by the user or read from a file, because you cannot always control the case of the string. Although you can change a text box's **CharacterCasing property** from its default value of Normal to either Upper (which converts the user's entry to uppercase) or Lower (which converts the user's entry to lowercase), you may not want to change the case of the user's entry as he or she is typing it. And it's entirely possible that you may not be aware of the case of strings read from a file. Before using a string in a comparison, you can use either the **ToUpper method** or the **ToLower method** to convert the string to uppercase or lowercase, respectively, and then use the converted string in the comparison. Figure 4-25 shows the syntax of both methods and includes several examples of using the methods.

» TIP

You will use the CharacterCasing property in Discovery Exercise 18 at the end of this lesson.

Using the ToUpper and ToLower methods

Syntax
string.**ToUpper**

string.**ToLower**

Examples
```
If letter.ToUpper = "P" Then
```
compares the uppercase version of the string stored in the `letter` variable to the uppercase letter "P"

```
If state.ToLower = "ca" Then
```
compares the lowercase version of the string stored in the `state` variable to the lowercase letters "ca"

```
If item1.ToUpper <> item2.ToUpper Then
```
compares the uppercase version of the string stored in the `item1` variable to the uppercase version of the string stored in the `item2` variable

```
If "reno" = Me.xCityTextBox.Text.ToLower Then
```
compares the lowercase letters "reno" to the lowercase version of the string stored in the xCityTextBox

```
Me.xNameLabel.Text = companyName.ToUpper
```
assigns the uppercase version of the string stored in the `companyName` variable to the Text property of the xNameLabel

```
newName = newName.ToUpper
```
changes the contents of the `newName` variable to uppercase

```
Me.xNameTextBox.Text = Me.xNameTextBox.Text.ToLower
```
changes the contents of the xNameTextBox to lowercase

Figure 4-25: Syntax and examples of the ToUpper and ToLower methods

In each syntax shown in Figure 4-25, *string* typically is the name of a String variable that contains the string you want to convert. However, as the fourth and last examples show, *string* also can be the property of an object. Both methods temporarily convert the string to the appropriate case. For example, `letter.ToUpper` temporarily converts the contents of the `letter` variable to uppercase, and `state.ToLower` temporarily converts the contents of the `state` variable to lowercase.

You also can use the ToUpper and ToLower methods to permanently convert the contents of a String variable or property to uppercase or lowercase, respectively. To do so, you simply include the variable or property, along with the appropriate method, in an assignment statement. For example, to permanently change the contents of the `newName` variable to uppercase, you use the assignment statement `newName = newName.ToUpper`. You use the assignment statement `Me.xNameTextBox.Text = Me.xNameTextBox.Text.ToLower` to convert the contents of the xNameTextBox's Text property to lowercase.

When using the ToUpper method in a comparison, be sure that everything you are comparing is uppercase. In other words, the clause `If letter.ToUpper = "p" Then` will not work correctly: the *condition* will always evaluate to False, because the uppercase version of a letter will never be equal to its lowercase counterpart. Likewise, when using the ToLower method in a comparison, be sure that everything you are comparing is lowercase.

In the next section, you view the Visual Basic code for a procedure that uses the ToUpper and ToLower methods.

USING THE TOUPPER AND TOLOWER METHODS: DISPLAYING A MESSAGE

A procedure needs to display the message "We have a store in this state." when the user enters any of the following three state IDs: Il, In, Ky. When the user enters an ID other than these, the procedure should display the message "We do not have a store in this state." Figure 4-26 shows three ways of writing the Visual Basic code for this procedure.

> **» TIP**
>
> The ToUpper and ToLower methods affect only characters that represent letters of the alphabet, as these are the only characters that have uppercase and lowercase forms.

Example 1: using the ToUpper method

```
Dim state As String
state = Me.xStateTextBox.Text
If state.ToUpper = "IL" OrElse state.ToUpper = "IN" _
        OrElse state.ToUpper = "KY"
   Me.xMsgLabel.Text = "We have a store in this state."
Else
   Me.xMsgLabel.Text = "We do not have a store in this state."
End If
```

Example 2: using the ToUpper method

```
Dim state As String
state = Me.xStateTextBox.Text.ToUpper
If state = "IL" OrElse state = "IN" OrElse state = "KY"
   Me.xMsgLabel.Text = "We have a store in this state."
Else
   Me.xMsgLabel.Text = "We do not have a store in this state."
End If
```

Example 3: using the ToLower method

```
Dim state As String
state = Me.xStateTextBox.Text.ToLower
If state <> "il" AndAlso state <> "in" AndAlso state <> "ky"
   Me.xMsgLabel.Text = "We do not have a store in this state."
Else
   Me.xMsgLabel.Text = "We have a store in this state."
End If
```

Figure 4-26: Examples of using the ToUpper and ToLower methods in a procedure

When the computer processes the `state.ToUpper = "IL" OrElse state.ToUpper =
"IN" OrElse state.ToUpper = "KY"` compound condition shown in Example 1 in
Figure 4-26, it first temporarily converts the contents of the `state` variable to uppercase, and
then compares the result to the string "IL". If the comparison evaluates to False, the computer
again temporarily converts the contents of the `state` variable to uppercase, this time comparing the result to the string "IN". If the comparison evaluates to False, it again converts the
contents of the `state` variable to uppercase, and compares the result to the string "KY". Notice
that, depending on the result of each *condition*, the computer might need to convert the

contents of the state variable to uppercase three times. A more efficient way of writing Example 1's code is shown in Example 2 in Figure 4-26.

The state = Me.xStateTextBox.Text.ToUpper statement in Example 2 assigns to the state variable the uppercase equivalent of the xStateTextBox's Text property. The state = "IL" OrElse state = "IN" OrElse state = "KY" compound condition compares the contents of the state variable (which now contains uppercase letters) to the string "IL". If the comparison evaluates to False, the computer compares the contents of the state variable to the string "IN". If this comparison evaluates to False, the computer compares the contents of the state variable to the string "KY". Notice that, in this case, the contents of the state variable is converted to uppercase only once, rather than three times. However, keep in mind that, although the code shown in Example 2 is more efficient than the code shown in Example 1, there may be times when you will not want to change the case of the string stored in a variable. For example, you may need to display (on the screen or in a printed report) the variable's contents using the exact case entered by the user.

The state = Me.xStateTextBox.Text.ToLower statement in Example 3 assigns to the state variable the lowercase equivalent of the xStateTextBox's Text property. The compound condition in Example 3 is processed similarly to the compound condition in Example 2. However, the comparisons are made using lowercase letters rather than uppercase letters, and the comparisons test for inequality rather than equality. The three examples shown in Figure 4-26 produce the same results and simply represent different ways of performing the same task.

To code and then test the State application:

1 Open the **State Solution** (State Solution.sln) file, which is contained in the VB2005\Chap04\State Solution folder. If necessary, open the designer window.

2 Open the Code Editor window. Replace the <your name> and <current date> text in the comments with your name and the current date.

3 Open the code template for the xToUpperButton's Click event procedure. Also open the code template for the xToLowerButton's Click event procedure.

4 In the xToUpperButton's Click event procedure, enter the code shown in either of the first two examples in Figure 4-26.

5 In the xToLowerButton's Click event procedure, enter the code shown in the last example in Figure 4-26.

6 Close the Code Editor window. Save the solution, then start the application.

7 Type **ky** in the State ID text box, then click the **ToUpper** button. The button's Click event procedure displays the message "We have a store in this state." in the xMsgLabel, as shown in Figure 4-27.

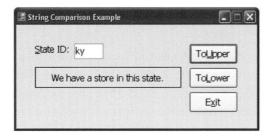

Figure 4-27: Message shown in the interface

8 Change the text entered in the State ID text box to **tn**, then click the **ToUpper** button. The button's Click event procedure displays the message "We do not have a store in this state." in the xMsgLabel.

9 On your own, test the ToLower button's code to verify that it is working correctly.

10 Click the **Exit** button to end the application. You are returned to the designer window. Close the solution.

COMPARING BOOLEAN VALUES

As mentioned earlier, you also can use the *condition* in an If...Then...Else statement to compare Boolean values; Figure 4-28 shows examples of such *conditions*. Notice that each *condition* contains a Boolean variable named isInsured. As you learned in Chapter 3, Boolean variables can contain only the Boolean value True or the Boolean value False. The new naming convention for variables recommends that you begin Boolean variable names with the word "is" to denote the True/False value.

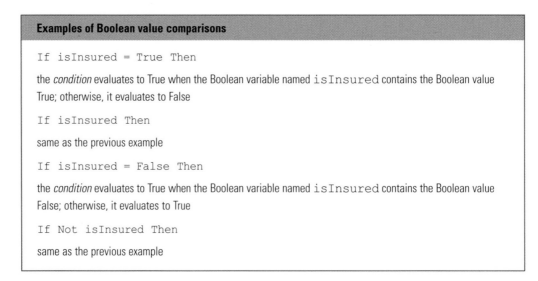

Figure 4-28: Examples of Boolean values compared in an If...Then...Else statement's *condition*

As Figure 4-28 indicates, the `isInsured = True` *condition* in the first example and the `isInsured` *condition* in the second example produce the same result: both *conditions* evaluate to True when the `isInsured` variable contains the Boolean value True. In the last two examples, the `isInsured = False` *condition* and the `Not isInsured` *condition* also produce the same result: in this case, both evaluate to True when the `isInsured` variable contains the Boolean value False.

» TIP

As you learned earlier in the lesson, the Not operator reverses the truth-value. Therefore, if the `isInsured` variable contains False, then `Not isInsured` evaluates to True.

COMPARING BOOLEAN VALUES: DETERMINING WHETHER A TEXT BOX CONTAINS DATA

A procedure needs to display the message "Please enter your first name." in the xMsgLabel when the xNameTextBox does not contain any data; otherwise, it should display the message "Hello" followed by the text box data. You can determine whether the text box contains data by comparing its Text property to either the empty string ("") or the `String.Empty` value. You also can use the String.IsNullOrEmpty method, as shown in Figure 4-29.

Using the String.IsNullOrEmpty method

Syntax

String.IsNullOrEmpty(*string***)**

Examples

```
If String.IsNullOrEmpty(Me.xNameTextBox.Text) Then
     Me.xMsgLabel.Text = "Please enter your first name."
Else
     Me.xMsgLabel.Text = "Hello " & Me.xNameTextBox.Text
End If

If Not String.IsNullOrEmpty(Me.xNameTextBox.Text) Then
     Me.xMsgLabel.Text = "Hello " & Me.xNameTextBox.Text
Else
     Me.xMsgLabel.Text = "Please enter your first name."
End If
```

Figure 4-29: Syntax and examples of the String.IsNullOrEmpty method

In the syntax, *string* is the item whose contents you want to verify. The **String.IsNullOrEmpty method** returns the Boolean value True when the *string* does not contain any data; otherwise, it returns the Boolean value False.

To code and then test the Empty Text Box application:

1 Open the **Empty Text Box Solution** (Empty Text Box Solution.sln) file, which is contained in the VB2005\Chap04\Empty Text Box Solution folder. If necessary, open the designer window.

2 Open the Code Editor window. Replace the <your name> and <current date> text in the comments with your name and the current date.

3 Open the code template for the xDisplayButton's Click event procedure, then enter the code shown in either of the two examples in Figure 4-29.

4 Close the Code Editor window. Save the solution, then start the application.

5 Click the **Display** button. Because the text box does not contain any data, the xDisplayButton's Click event procedure displays the "Please enter your first name." message in the xMsgLabel, as shown in Figure 4-30.

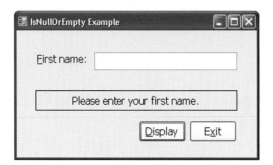

Figure 4-30: Message displayed in the xMsgLabel

6 Type your name in the First name text box, then click the **Display** button. This time, because the text box contains data, the xDisplayButton's Click event procedure displays the "Hello" message and your name.

7 Click the **Exit** button to end the application. You are returned to the designer window. Close the solution.

COMPARING BOOLEAN VALUES: DETERMINING WHETHER A STRING CAN BE CONVERTED TO A NUMBER

In Chapter 3, you learned how to use the TryParse method to convert a string to a specific numeric data type. Recall that if the string can be converted, the TryParse method stores the number in the numeric variable specified in the method's *variable* argument. However, if the TryParse method determines that the string cannot be converted to the appropriate data type, the method assigns the number zero to the numeric variable. In addition to assigning a value to the numeric variable, the TryParse method also returns a Boolean value that indicates whether the conversion was successful. It returns the Boolean value True when the string can be converted to the specified numeric data type, and returns the Boolean value False when it cannot be converted. You can assign the value returned by the TryParse method to a Boolean variable, and then use an If...Then...Else statement to determine the result of the conversion, as shown in Figure 4-31.

Using the Boolean value returned by the TryParse method

Syntax

booleanVariable = *datatype*.**TryParse(***string, variable***)**

Example

```
Dim oldPay As Double
Dim raiseRate As Double
Dim newPay As Double
Dim isOldOk As Boolean
Dim isRateOk As Boolean

' try to convert the string input to numbers
isOldOk = Double.TryParse(Me.xOldTextBox.Text, oldPay)
isRateOk = Double.TryParse(Me.xRateTextBox.Text, raiseRate)

' determine whether the conversions were successful
If isOldOk AndAlso isRateOk Then
     newPay = oldPay + oldPay * raiseRate
     Me.xNewPayLabel.Text = newPay.ToString("C2")
Else
     Me.xNewPayLabel.Text = "Invalid data"
End If
```

Figure 4-31: Syntax and an example of using the Boolean value returned by the TryParse method

> **» TIP**
> You also can phrase the condition in Figure 4-31 as `If isOldOk = True AndAlso isRateOk = True Then`.

The code shown in Figure 4-31 displays either an employee's new pay amount or an "Invalid data" message. First the code declares three Double variables and two Boolean variables. The `isOldOk = Double.TryParse(Me.xOldTextBox.Text, oldPay)` statement then uses the TryParse method to convert the contents of the xOldTextBox to the Double data type. If the conversion is successful, the TryParse method stores the Double number in the `oldPay` variable. In addition, the method returns the Boolean value True to indicate that the conversion was successful. However, if the conversion was not successful, the method stores the number zero in the `oldPay` variable, and it returns the Boolean value False. The statement assigns the method's return value to the Boolean `isOldOk` variable. The computer processes the next statement in the code, `isRateOk = Double.TryParse(Me.xRateTextBox.Text, raiseRate)`, in a similar manner. The `isOldOk AndAlso isRateOk` *condition* in the If...Then...Else statement determines whether the TryParse methods were successful. If both Boolean variables contain True, the code calculates and displays the new pay amount; otherwise, it displays the "Invalid data" message.

To test and then modify the New Pay Calculator application:

1 Open the **New Pay Solution** (New Pay Solution.sln) file, which is contained in the VB2005\Chap04\New Pay Solution folder. If necessary, open the designer window.

2 Open the Code Editor window. Replace the `<your name>` and `<current date>` text in the comments with your name and the current date.

3 Locate the xCalcButton's Click event procedure. Notice that the code does not contain any Boolean variables. Before modifying the code, you will observe how the procedure currently works.

4 Start the application. Type **10** as the old pay, then click the **Calculate** button. Even though no raise rate was entered, the xCalcButton's Click event procedure displays a new pay amount in the xNewPayLabel. In this case, it displays the old pay amount ($10.00) as the new pay amount, as shown in Figure 4-32.

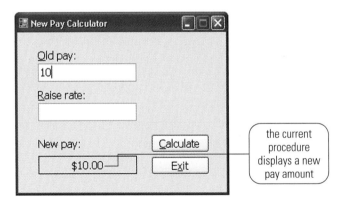

Figure 4-32: Result displayed by the current procedure

5 Type **a** in the Raise rate text box, then click the **Calculate** button. Here again, the procedure displays a new pay amount ($10.00) even though the raise rate you entered is invalid.

6 Change the raise rate to **.05**, then click the **Calculate** button. The procedure calculates and displays $10.50 as the new pay amount, which is correct.

7 Click the **Exit** button to end the application.

8 Use the code shown in Figure 4-31 to modify the xCalcButton's Click event procedure. You will need to enter the two Boolean variable declaration statements, as well as modify the statements containing the TryParse methods. You also will need to enter the comment above the If...Then...Else statement and the If...Then...Else statement itself. (Be sure to enter the statement in its false path.)

9 Close the Code Editor window. Save the solution, then start the application.

10 Type **10** as the old pay, then click the **Calculate** button. Because no raise rate was entered, the procedure displays the "Invalid data" message in the xNewPayLabel, as shown in Figure 4-33.

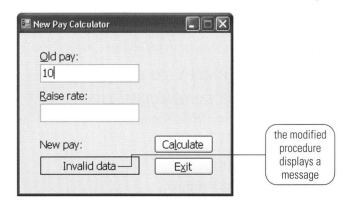

Figure 4-33: Result displayed by the modified procedure

11 Type **a** in the Raise rate text box, then click the **Calculate** button. Notice that the procedure displays the "Invalid data" message when the raise rate you entered is invalid.

12 Change the raise rate to **.05**, then click the **Calculate** button. The procedure calculates and displays $10.50 as the new pay amount, which is correct.

13 Click the **Exit** button to end the application. You are returned to the designer window. Close the solution.

You have completed Lesson A. You can either take a break or complete the end-of-lesson questions and exercises before moving on to Lesson B.

SUMMARY

TO EVALUATE AN EXPRESSION CONTAINING ARITHMETIC, COMPARISON, AND LOGICAL OPERATORS:

» Evaluate the arithmetic operators first, then evaluate the comparison operators, and then evaluate the logical operators. Figure 4-20 shows the order of precedence for the arithmetic, comparison, and logical operators.

TO CODE A SELECTION STRUCTURE:

» Use the If...Then...Else statement, whose syntax is shown in Figure 4-6.

TO COMPARE TWO VALUES:

» Use the comparison operators listed in Figure 4-7.

TO SWAP THE VALUES CONTAINED IN TWO VARIABLES:

» Assign the value stored in the first variable to a temporary variable, then assign the value stored in the second variable to the first variable, and then assign the value stored in the temporary variable to the second variable.

TO CREATE A COMPOUND CONDITION:

» Use the logical operators listed in Figure 4-18, and the truth tables listed in Figure 4-19.

TO CONVERT THE USER'S TEXT BOX ENTRY TO EITHER UPPER-CASE OR LOWERCASE AS THE USER IS TYPING THE TEXT:

» Change the text box's CharacterCasing property from Normal to either Upper or Lower.

TO CONVERT A STRING TO UPPERCASE:

» Use the ToUpper method, whose syntax is *string*.**ToUpper**.

TO CONVERT A STRING TO LOWERCASE:

» Use the ToLower method, whose syntax is *string*.**ToLower**.

TO DETERMINE WHETHER A STRING CONTAINS DATA:

» Use the String.IsNullOrEmpty method, whose syntax is **String.IsNullOrEmpty (***string***)**. The method returns the Boolean value True when the *string* does not contain any data; otherwise, it returns the Boolean value False.

TO DETERMINE WHETHER THE TRYPARSE METHOD CONVERTED A STRING TO THE SPECIFIED NUMERIC DATA TYPE:

» Use the syntax *booleanVariable* = *datatype*.**TryParse(***string***,** *variable***)**. The TryParse method returns the Boolean value True when the string can be converted to the numeric *datatype*; otherwise, it returns the Boolean value False.

QUESTIONS

1. What is the scope of variables declared in an If...Then...Else statement's false path?

   a. the entire application

   b. the procedure in which the If...Then...Else statement appears

   c. the entire If...Then...Else statement

   d. only the false path in the If...Then...Else statement

2. Which of the following is a valid *condition* for an If...Then...Else statement? (The `sales` and `cost` variables have the Integer data type, and the `state` variable has the String data type.)

   a. `sales > 500 AndAlso < 800`

   b. `cost > 100 AndAlso cost <= 1000`

   c. `state.ToUpper = "Alaska" OrElse state.ToUpper = "Hawaii"`

   d. None of the above.

3. Which of the following *conditions* should you use in an If...Then...Else statement to compare the string contained in the xNameTextBox with the name Bob? (Be sure the *condition* will handle Bob, BOB, bob, and so on.)

   a. `Me.xNameTextBox.Text = ToUpper("BOB")`

   b. `Me.xNameTextBox.Text = ToUpper("Bob")`

   c. `ToUpper(Me.xNameTextBox.Text) = "BOB"`

   d. `Me.xNameTextBox.Text.ToUpper = "BOB"`

4. The six logical operators are listed below. Indicate their order of precedence by placing a number (1, 2, and so on) on the line to the left of the operator. (If two or more operators have the same precedence, assign the same number to each.)

   _____ Xor   _____ And

   _____ Not   _____ Or

   _____ AndAlso   _____ OrElse

5. An expression can contain arithmetic, comparison, and logical operators. Indicate the order of precedence for the three types of operators by placing a number (1, 2, or 3) on the line to the left of the operator type.

_____ Arithmetic

_____ Logical

_____ Comparison

6. The expression 3 > 6 AndAlso 7 > 4 evaluates to _____.

   a. True   b. False

7. The expression 4 > 6 OrElse 10 < 2 * 6 evaluates to _____.

   a. True   b. False

8. The expression 7 >= 3 + 5 OrElse 6 < 4 AndAlso 2 < 5 evaluates to _____.

   a. True   b. False

9. The expression 5 * 2 > 5 * 3 AndAlso True evaluates to _____.

   a. True   b. False

10. The expression 5 * 3 > 3 ^ 2 evaluates to _____.

   a. True   b. False

11. The expression 5 * 3 > 3 ^ 2 AndAlso True OrElse False evaluates to _____.

   a. True   b. False

Use the following selection structure to answer Questions 12 and 13:

```
If number <= 100 Then
    number = number * 2
Else
    number = number * 3
End If
```

12. The number variable contains the number 90. What value will be in the number variable after the above selection structure is processed?

   a. 0   b. 90

   c. 180   d. 270

13. The `number` variable contains the number 1000. What value will be in the `number` variable after the above selection structure is processed?

   a. 0   b. 1000

   c. 2000   d. 3000

14. If the xPriceTextBox is empty, the `String.IsNullOrEmpty(Me.xPriceTextBox.Text)` method returns _____.

   a. False   b. True

   c. 0 (zero)   d. "" (the empty string)

15. If the xPriceTextBox contains the value 75, the `Decimal.TryParse(Me.xPriceTextBox.Text, price)` method returns _____.

   a. False   b. True

   c. 75   d. 75.00

EXERCISES

1. Draw the flowchart that corresponds to the following pseudocode:

   if hours are greater than 40
            display "Overtime pay"
   else
            display "Regular pay"
   end if

2. Write an If...Then...Else statement that displays the string "Pontiac" in the xCarMakeLabel when the xCarTextBox contains the string "Grand Am" (in any case).

3. Write an If...Then...Else statement that displays the string "Please enter your ZIP code" in the xMsgLabel when the xZipTextBox does not contain any data.

4. A procedure contains the `isSalesOk = Double.TryParse(Me.xSalesTextBox.Text, sales)` statement. Write an If...Then...Else statement that displays the string "Please enter a number" in the xMsgLabel when the contents of the xSalesTextBox cannot be converted to a number; otherwise, multiply the contents of the text box by 10% and display the result in the xMsgLabel.

5. Write an If...Then...Else statement that displays the string "Entry error" in the xMessageLabel when the units variable contains a number that is less than 0; otherwise, display the string "Valid Number".

6. Write an If...Then...Else statement that displays the string "Reorder" in the xMessageLabel when the quantity variable contains a number that is less than 10; otherwise, display the string "OK".

7. Write an If...Then...Else statement that assigns the number 10 to the bonus variable when the sales variable contains a number that is less than or equal to $250; otherwise, assign the number 15.

8. Write an If...Then...Else statement that displays the value 25 in the xShippingLabel when the state variable contains the string "Hawaii" (in any case); otherwise, display the value 50.

9. A procedure should calculate a 3% sales tax when the state variable contains the string "Colorado" (in any case); otherwise, it should calculate a 4% sales tax. The sales tax is calculated by multiplying the tax rate by the contents of the sales variable. Display the sales tax amount in the xSalesTaxLabel. The sales variable is a Double variable. Draw the flowchart, then write the Visual Basic code.

10. A procedure should calculate an employee's gross pay. Employees working more than 40 hours receive overtime pay (time and one-half) for the hours over 40. Use the variables hours, hourRate, and gross. Display the contents of the gross variable in the xGrossLabel. The variables are Decimal variables. Write the pseudocode, then write the Visual Basic code.

11. Write the If...Then...Else statement that displays the string "Dog" in the xAnimalLabel when the animal variable contains the letter "D" (in any case); otherwise, display the string "Cat". Draw the flowchart, then write the Visual Basic code.

12. A procedure should calculate a 10% discount on desks sold to customers in Colorado. Use the variables item, state, sales, and discount. The item and state variables are String variables. The sales and discount variables are Double variables. Format the discount using the "C2" format and display it in the xDiscountLabel. Write the pseudocode, then write the Visual Basic code.

13. A procedure should calculate a 2% price increase on all red shirts, but a 1% price increase on all other items. In addition to calculating the price increase, the procedure also should calculate the new price. You can use the variables itemColor, item, origPrice, increase, and newPrice. The itemColor and item variables are String variables; the remaining variables are Decimal variables. Format the original price, price increase, and new price using the "N2" format. Display the original price, price increase, and new price in the xOriginalLabel, xIncreaseLabel, and xNewLabel controls, respectively. Write the Visual Basic code.

14. Write the Visual Basic code that swaps the values stored in two Decimal variables named marySales and jeffSales, but only if the value stored in the marySales variable is less than the value stored in the jeffSales variable.

15. In this exercise, you modify the Addition and Subtraction application you coded in the lesson.

    a. Use Windows to make a copy of the AddSub Solution folder, which is contained in the VB2005\Chap04 folder. Rename the folder Modified AddSub Solution.

    b. Open the AddSub Solution (AddSub Solution.sln) file contained in the VB2005\Chap04\Modified AddSub Solution folder. Open the designer window.

    c. Change the Label1's text from "Enter 1 for Addition, or 2 for Subtraction" to "Enter A for Addition, or S for Subtraction".

    d. Open the Code Editor window. Make the appropriate modifications to the xCalcButton's Click event procedure. (The user should be able to enter the operation letter in either uppercase or lowercase.)

    e. Save the solution, then start and test the application.

    f. Click the Exit button to end the application. Close the Code Editor window, then close the solution.

16. In this exercise, you code an application that calculates the amount of a salesperson's bonus.

    a. Open the Bonus Solution (Bonus Solution.sln) file, which is contained in the VB2005\Chap04\Bonus Solution folder. If necessary, open the designer window.

    b. The xCalcButton's Click event procedure should calculate a 5% bonus amount and display the result (formatted using the "C2" format) in the xBonusLabel. Calculate and display the bonus amount only when the xSalesTextBox contains data; otherwise, display the message "No sales" in the xBonusLabel. Code the procedure appropriately.

   c. Save the solution, then start and test the application.

   d. Click the Exit button to end the application. Close the Code Editor window, then close the solution.

17. In this exercise, you code an application that calculates the sum of two numbers.

   a. Open the Sum Solution (Sum Solution.sln) file, which is contained in the VB2005\Chap04\Sum Solution folder. If necessary, open the designer window.

   b. The xCalcButton's Click event procedure should calculate the sum of the two values entered by the user, and then display the result in the xSumLabel. Calculate and display the sum only when both values can be converted to the Integer data type; otherwise, display the message "Please enter two integers" in the xSumLabel. Code the procedure appropriately.

   c. Save the solution, then start and test the application.

   d. Click the Exit button to end the application. Close the Code Editor window, then close the solution.

DISCOVERY EXERCISE

18. In this exercise, you learn how to use a text box's CharacterCasing property.

   a. Open the CharCase Solution (CharCase Solution.sln) file, which is contained in the VB2005\Chap04\CharCase Solution folder. If necessary, open the designer window.

   b. Open the Code Editor window and study the code contained in the xDisplayButton's Click event procedure. Notice that the code compares the contents of the xStateTextBox with the strings "IL", "IN", and "KY". However, it does not convert the contents of the text box to uppercase.

   c. Start the application. Enter ky as the state ID, then click the Display button. The button's Click event procedure displays the "We do not have a store in this state." message, which is incorrect.

   d. Click the Exit button.

   e. Use the Properties window to change the xStateTextBox's CharacterCasing property to Upper.

   f. Save the solution, then start the application. Enter ky as the state ID. Notice that the letters appear in uppercase in the text box. Click the Display button. The button's Click event procedure displays the "We have a store in this state." message, which is correct.

   g. Click the Exit button to end the application. Close the Code Editor window, then close the solution.

LESSON B
OBJECTIVES

AFTER STUDYING LESSON B,
YOU SHOULD BE ABLE TO:

» Group objects using a GroupBox control

» Calculate a periodic payment using the Financial.Pmt method

» Create a message box using the MessageBox.Show method

» Determine the value returned by a message box

THE MONTHLY PAYMENT CALCULATOR APPLICATION

COMPLETING THE USER INTERFACE

Recall that Herman Juarez wants an application that calculates the monthly payment on a car loan. To make the calculation, the application must know the loan amount (principal), the annual percentage rate (APR) of interest, and the life of the loan (term) in years. A sketch of the application's user interface is shown in Figure 4-34.

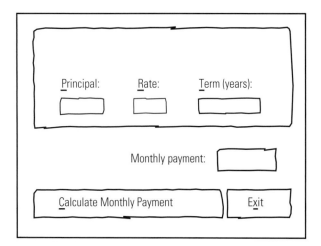

Figure 4-34: Sketch of the Monthly Payment Calculator user interface

The user interface contains a group box, three text boxes, five labels, and two buttons. To save you time, the VB2005\Chap04 folder contains a partially completed Monthly Payment Calculator application.

To open the partially completed application:

1 Start Visual Studio 2005 or Visual Basic 2005 Express Edition, if necessary, and close the Start Page window.

2 Open the **Payment Solution** (**Payment Solution.sln**) file, which is contained in the VB2005\Chap04\Payment Solution folder. Auto-hide the Toolbox, Solution Explorer, and Properties windows, if necessary. Figure 4-35 shows the partially completed user interface. Only the group box control is missing from the interface.

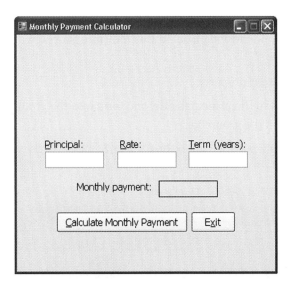

Figure 4-35: Partially completed user interface for the Monthly Payment Calculator application

ADDING A GROUP BOX TO THE FORM

You use the **GroupBox tool** to add a group box to the interface. The GroupBox tool is located in the Containers section of the toolbox, because a **group box** serves as a container for other controls. You can use a group box to visually separate related controls from other controls on the form. In the Monthly Payment Calculator interface, for example, the group box will visually separate the controls relating to the principal, rate, and term information from the rest of the controls. The group box and the controls contained in the group box are treated as one unit. When you move the group box, the controls inside the group box also move. Likewise, when you delete the group box, the controls inside the group box also are deleted. You can include an identifying label on a group box by setting the group box's Text property. Labeling a group box is optional; but if you do label it, the label should be entered using sentence capitalization.

To add a group box to the interface, and then drag several of the existing controls into the group box:

1 Click the **GroupBox** tool in the toolbox, and then drag the mouse pointer to the form. (You do not need to worry about the exact location.) Release the mouse button. The GroupBox1 control appears on the form.

2 Set the group box's **Location** property to **30, 25**. Set its **Size** property to **375, 115**.

The group box control will not need an identifying label in this interface, so you will delete the contents of its Text property.

3 Delete the contents of the group box's Text property.

Next, you will drag the controls related to the principal, rate, and term into the group box, and then center the controls within the group box.

4 Select the following six controls: Label1, xPrincipalTextBox, Label2, xRateTextBox, Label3, and xTermTextBox.

»HELP? As you learned in Chapter 1, you can select more than one control by clicking the first control and then pressing and holding down the Ctrl (Control) key as you click the other controls you want to select.

5 Place your mouse pointer on one of the selected controls. The mouse pointer turns into ✛. Press and hold down the left mouse button as you drag the selected controls into the group box, then release the mouse button.

6 Click **Format** on the menu bar, point to **Center in Form**, and then click **Horizontally**. Click **Format** on the menu bar, point to **Center in Form**, and then click **Vertically**. Notice that the selected controls are centered within the group box.

7 Click the **form** to deselect the controls. Figure 4-36 shows the completed user interface.

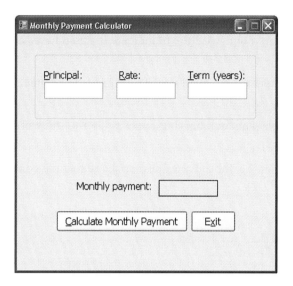

Figure 4-36: Completed user interface

»GUI DESIGN TIP

Labeling a Group Box

» Use sentence capitalization for the optional identifying label, which is entered in the group box's Text property.

Now that you have completed the user interface, you can lock the controls in place and then set each control's TabIndex property appropriately.

LOCKING THE CONTROLS AND SETTING THE TABINDEX PROPERTY

As you learned in Chapter 2, when you have completed a user interface, you should lock the controls in place and then set each control's TabIndex property.

To lock the controls, and then set each control's TabIndex property:

1 Right-click the **form**, and then click **Lock Controls** on the context menu.

2 Click **View** on the menu bar, and then click **Tab Order**. The current TabIndex value for each control appears in blue boxes on the form.

Notice that the TabIndex values of the controls contained within the group box begin with the number 10, which is the TabIndex value of the group box itself. The TabIndex value indicates that the controls belong to the group box rather than to the form. As mentioned earlier, if you move or delete the group box, the controls that belong to the group box also will be moved or deleted. The numbers that appear after the period in the controls' TabIndex values indicate the order in which each control was added to the group box.

3 Click the **GroupBox1** control. The number 0 replaces the number 10 in the TabIndex box, and the color of the box changes from blue to white to indicate that you have set the TabIndex value.

4 Click the **Label1** control, which contains the Principal: text. The number 0.0 appears in the control's TabIndex box.

5 Click the **xPrincipalTextBox** control. The number 0.1 appears in the control's TabIndex box.

6 Use the information in Figure 4-37 to set the TabIndex values for the remaining controls on the form.

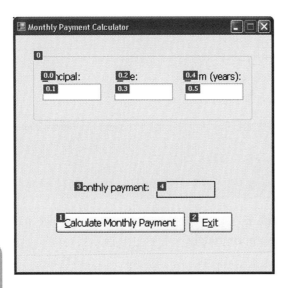

Figure 4-37: Correct TabIndex values

▶▶TIP
You also can remove the TabIndex boxes by clicking View on the menu bar and then clicking Tab Order.

7 Press **Esc** to remove the TabIndex boxes from the form, then save the solution.

CODING THE MONTHLY PAYMENT CALCULATOR APPLICATION

The TOE chart for the Monthly Payment Calculator application is shown in Figure 4-38.

Task	Object	Event
1. Calculate the monthly payment amount 2. Display the monthly payment amount in the xPaymentLabel	xCalcButton	Click
End the application	xExitButton	Click
Display the monthly payment amount (from xCalcButton)	xPaymentLabel	None
Get and display the principal, rate, and term amounts	xPrincipalTextBox, xRateTextBox, xTermTextBox	None
Clear the contents of the xPaymentLabel		TextChanged
Allow the text box to accept only numbers, the period, and the Backspace key		KeyPress
Select the contents of the text box		Enter

Figure 4-38: TOE chart for the Monthly Payment Calculator application

According to the TOE chart, the Click event procedures for the two buttons, as well as the TextChanged, KeyPress, and Enter events for the three text boxes, need to be coded. When you open the Code Editor window, you will notice that the xExitButton's Click event procedure and the TextChanged event procedures for the three text boxes have been coded for you. In this lesson, you will code the xCalcButton's Click event procedure. You will code the KeyPress and Enter event procedures in Lesson C.

CODING THE XCALCBUTTON'S CLICK EVENT PROCEDURE

According to the TOE chart shown in Figure 4-38, the xCalcButton's Click event procedure is responsible for calculating the monthly payment amount, and then displaying the result in the xPaymentLabel. The pseudocode for the xCalcButton's Click event procedure is shown in Figure 4-39.

---

xCalcButton Click event procedure (pseudocode)

---

1. if the interest rate >= 1
    divide the interest rate by 100 to get its decimal equivalent
   end if

2. if the term >= 1
    calculate the monthly payment using the principal, rate, and term entered by the user
    display the monthly payment in the xPaymentLabel
   else
    display the message "The term must be greater than or equal to 1." in a message box
   end if

Figure 4-39: Pseudocode for the xCalcButton's Click event procedure

To begin coding the xCalcButton's Click event procedure:

1 Right-click the **form**, and then click **View Code** to open the Code Editor window. See Figure 4-40.

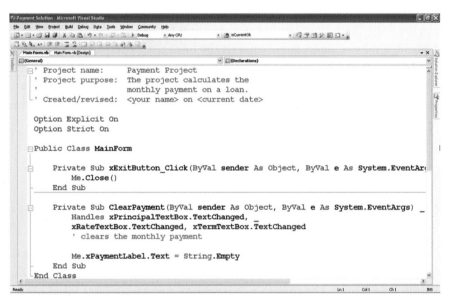

Figure 4-40: Current contents of the Code Editor window

Notice that the xExitButton's Click event procedure already contains the `Me.Close()` statement. Also notice that the ClearPayment procedure is associated with each text box's TextChanged event. The procedure uses the `Me.xPaymentLabel.Text = String.Empty` statement to clear the contents of the xPaymentLabel when a change is made to any of the text boxes.

2 Replace the `<your name>` and `<current date>` text with your name and the current date.

3 Open the code template for the xCalcButton's Click event procedure.

4 Type **' calculates and displays a monthly payment** and press **Enter** twice.

Recall that before you begin coding a procedure, you first study the procedure's pseudocode to determine the variables and named constants (if any) the procedure will use. When determining the named constants, look for items whose value will be the same each time the procedure is invoked. In the xCalcButton's Click event procedure, the number 1 that appears in Steps 1 and 2, as well as the number 100 that appears in Step 1 and the message that appears in Step 2, will be the same each time the procedure is invoked. Although you could create named constants for the numbers 1 and 100, doing so is unnecessary because those values are already self-documenting and are unlikely to change. You will, however, create a named constant for the message; doing this will make your code easier to understand and will allow you to quickly locate the message should it need to be changed in the future.

When determining the variables a procedure will need to use, look in the pseudocode for items whose value probably will change each time the procedure is processed. In this case, the principal, rate, term, and monthly payment amounts probably will be different each time the xCalcButton's Click event procedure is processed; therefore, you will assign the values to variables.

To continue coding the xCalcButton's Click event procedure:

1 Enter the following Const and Dim statements. Press **Enter** twice after typing the last Dim statement.

Const Message As String = "The term must be greater than or equal to 1."

Dim principal As Double

Dim interestRate As Double

Dim loanTerm As Double

Dim monthlyPayment As Double

Now you will assign the principal, rate, and term information to the appropriate variables.

2 Type **double.tryparse(me.xPrincipalTextBox.text, principal)** and press **Enter**.

3 Type **double.tryparse(me.xRateTextBox.text, interestrate)** and press **Enter**.

4 Type **double.tryparse(me.xTermTextBox.text, loanterm)** and press **Enter** twice.

Next, you will use a selection structure to handle Step 1 in the pseudocode (shown earlier in Figure 4-39): determining whether the application needs to convert the interest rate entered by the user to its decimal equivalent. This is necessary because the user might enter the rate as either a whole number or as a decimal number. For example, an interest rate of 5% might be entered as either 5 or .05.

5 Type ' **convert the rate to decimal form, if necessary** and press **Enter**.

6 Type **if interestrate >= 1.0 then** and press **Enter**. Notice that when you press Enter, the Code Editor automatically enters the End If statement in the window. Type **interestrate = interestrate / 100.0** between the If and End If statements.

7 Position the insertion point at the end of the End If statement, and then press **Enter** twice to insert two blank lines after the statement.

The second step in the pseudocode is to determine whether the term amount entered by the user is valid. To be valid, the term must be greater than or equal to one year.

8 Type ' **verify that the term is valid** and press **Enter**.

9 Type **if loanterm >= 1.0 then** and press **Enter**. Figure 4-41 shows the code currently entered in the procedure.

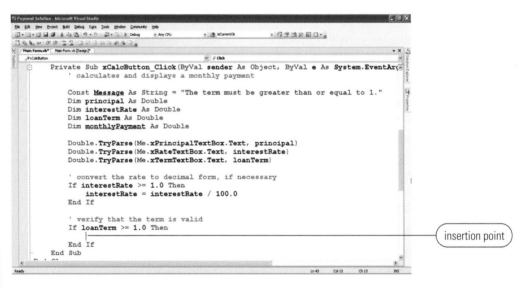

Figure 4-41: Code currently entered in the xCalcButton's Click event procedure

If the term is valid, the procedure should calculate the monthly payment and then display the result in the xPaymentLabel. You can calculate the monthly payment using the Financial.Pmt method.

USING THE FINANCIAL.PMT METHOD

You can use the **Financial.Pmt method** to calculate a periodic payment on either a loan or an investment. ("Pmt" stands for "Payment.") The method returns the periodic payment as a Double type number. Figure 4-42 shows the syntax of the Financial.Pmt method and lists the meaning of each argument. The figure also includes three examples of using the method.

Using the Financial.Pmt method

Syntax

Financial.Pmt(Rate, NPer, PV[, FV, Due]**)**

Argument	Meaning
Rate	interest rate per period
NPer	total number of payment periods (the term)
PV	present value of the loan or investment; the present value of a loan is the loan amount, whereas the present value of an investment is zero
FV	future value of the loan or investment; the future value of a loan is zero, whereas the future value of an investment is the amount you want to accumulate; if omitted, the number 0 is assumed
Due	due date of payments; can be either the constant DueDate.EndOfPeriod or the constant DueDate.BegOfPeriod; if omitted, DueDate.EndOfPeriod is assumed

---

Example 1 – Calculates the annual payment for a loan of $9,000 for 3 years at 5% interest. The payments are due at the end of each period (year).

Rate: .05
NPer: 3

PV: 9000

FV: 0

Due: DueDate.EndOfPeriod

Method: Financial.Pmt(.05, 3, 9000, 0, DueDate.EndOfPeriod)

                              or

    Financial.Pmt(.05, 3, 9000)

Annual payment (rounded to the nearest cent): −3,304.88

Figure 4-42: Syntax, arguments, and examples of the Financial.Pmt method *(Continued)*   ▶

Example 2 – Calculates the monthly payment for a loan of $12,000 for 5 years at 6% interest. The payments are due at the beginning of each period (month).

Rate: .06/12

NPer: 5 * 12

PV: 12000

FV: 0

Due: `DueDate.BegOfPeriod`

Method: `Financial.Pmt(.06/12, 5 * 12, 12000, 0, DueDate.BegOfPeriod)`

Monthly payment (rounded to the nearest cent): -230.84

Example 3 – Calculates the amount you need to save each month to accumulate $40,000 at the end of 20 years. The interest rate is 6%, and deposits are due at the beginning of each period (month).

Rate: .06/12

NPer: 20 * 12

PV: 0

FV: 40000

Due: `DueDate.BegOfPeriod`

Method: `Financial.Pmt(.06/12, 20 * 12, 0, 40000, DueDate.BegOfPeriod)`

Monthly payment (rounded to the nearest cent): -86.14

Figure 4-42: Syntax, arguments, and examples of the Financial.Pmt method

Notice that the Financial.Pmt method contains five arguments. Three of the arguments (*Rate*, *NPer*, and *PV*) are required, and two (*FV* and *Due*) are optional. If the *FV* (future value) argument is omitted, the Financial.Pmt method uses the default value, 0. If the *Due* argument is omitted, the Financial.Pmt method uses the constant `DueDate.EndOfPeriod` as the default value. The `DueDate.EndOfPeriod` constant indicates that payments are due at the end of each period.

The *Rate* and *NPer* (number of periods) arguments in the Financial.Pmt method must be expressed using the same units. In other words, if *Rate* is a monthly interest rate, then *NPer* must specify the number of monthly payments. Likewise, if *Rate* is an annual interest rate, then *NPer* must specify the number of annual payments.

Study the three examples shown in Figure 4-42. Example 1 uses the Financial.Pmt method to calculate the annual payment for a loan of $9,000 for 3 years at 5% interest, where payments are due at the end of each period; in this case, a period is a year. As the example indicates, the annual payment returned by the Financial.Pmt method and rounded to the nearest cent is –3,304.88. In other words, if you borrow $9,000 for 3 years at 5% interest, you would need to make three annual payments of $3,304.88 to pay off the loan.

When calculating an annual payment, the *Rate* argument should specify the annual interest rate, and the *NPer* argument should specify the life of the loan or investment in years. In Example 1, the *Rate* argument is .05, which is the annual interest rate, and the *NPer* argument is the number 3, which is the number of years you have to pay off the loan. As the example indicates, you can use the `Financial.Pmt(.05, 3, 9000, 0, DueDate. EndOfPeriod)` method to calculate the annual payment. You also can use the `Financial.Pmt(.05, 3, 9000)` method, because the default values for the optional *FV* and *Due* arguments are 0 and `DueDate.EndOfPeriod`, respectively.

Notice that the Financial.Pmt method returns a negative number. To change the negative number to a positive number, you can precede the Financial.Pmt method with the negation operator, like this: `-Financial.Pmt(.05, 3, 9000)`. As you learned in Chapter 2, the negation operator is one of the arithmetic operators. Its purpose is to reverse the sign of a number: A negative number preceded by the negation operator becomes a positive number. Likewise, a positive number preceded by the negation operator becomes a negative number.

The Financial.Pmt method shown in Example 2 in Figure 4-42 calculates the monthly payment for a loan of $12,000 for 5 years at 6% interest, where payments are due at the beginning of each period; in this case, a period is a month. Notice that the *Rate* and *NPer* arguments are expressed in monthly terms rather than in annual terms. The monthly payment for this loan, rounded to the nearest cent, is –230.84.

In addition to using the Financial.Pmt method to calculate the payments required for paying off a loan, you also can use the Financial.Pmt method to calculate the amount you need to save each period to accumulate a specific sum. The `Financial.Pmt(.06/12, 20 * 12, 0, 40000, DueDate.BegOfPeriod)` method shown in Example 3 in Figure 4-42, for instance, indicates that you need to save 86.14 (rounded to the nearest cent) each month to accumulate $40,000 at the end of 20 years, assuming a 6% interest rate and the appropriate amount deposited at the beginning of each period.

In the current application, you will use the Financial.Pmt method to calculate a monthly payment on a car loan. When entering the method, you must convert to a monthly rate the annual interest rate stored in the `interestRate` variable; you do this by dividing the annual rate by 12. You also must convert the term of the loan, which is expressed in years and stored in the `loanTerm` variable, to months. To convert an annual term to a monthly term, you simply multiply the annual term by 12. In addition, you will precede the Financial.Pmt method with the negation operator to display the monthly payment amount as a positive number.

To continue coding the xCalcButton's Click event procedure:

1 The insertion point should be positioned in the blank line below the `If loanTerm >= 1.0 Then` instruction, as shown earlier in Figure 4-41. Type **' calculate and display the monthly payment** and press **Enter**.

2 Type **monthlypayment = _** and press **Enter**. (Be sure to include a space before the line continuation character.) Press **Tab**, then type **-financial.pmt(interestrate/12, loanterm * 12, principal)** and press **Enter**.

Next, you will format the monthly payment amount to show a dollar sign and two decimal places, and then display the formatted amount in the xPaymentLabel.

3 Type **me.xPaymentLabel.text = monthlypayment.tostring("C2")** and press **Enter**.

4 Save the solution. Figure 4-43 shows the selection structure's true path coded in the procedure.

```
' verify that the term is valid
If loanTerm >= 1.0 Then
    ' calculate and display the monthly payment ──────────┐
    monthlyPayment = _                                    │
        -Financial.Pmt(interestRate / 12, loanTerm * 12, principal)  ├── true path
    Me.xPaymentLabel.Text = monthlyPayment.ToString("C2") ┘

End If  ────────────────────────────────────────────────── insertion point
```

Figure 4-43: Selection structure's true path coded in the procedure

According to the pseudocode (shown earlier in Figure 4-39), when the term entered by the user is not greater than or equal to 1, the xCalcButton's Click event procedure should display an appropriate message in a message box. You can display the message using the MessageBox.Show method.

THE MESSAGEBOX.SHOW METHOD

You can use the **MessageBox.Show method** to display a message box that contains text, one or more buttons, and an icon. Figure 4-44 shows the syntax of the MessageBox.Show method. It also lists the meaning of each argument, and includes two examples of using the method to create a message box.

Using the MessageBox.Show method

Syntax

MessageBox.Show(*text, caption, buttons, icon*[, *defaultButton*]**)**

Argument	Meaning
text	text to display in the message box
caption	text to display in the title bar of the message box

buttons	buttons to display in the message box; can be one of the following constants:
	`MessageBoxButtons.AbortRetryIgnore`
	`MessageBoxButtons.OK`
	`MessageBoxButtons.OKCancel`
	`MessageBoxButtons.RetryCancel`
	`MessageBoxButtons.YesNo`
	`MessageBoxButtons.YesNoCancel`

icon	icon to display in the message box; typically, one of the following constants: `MessageBoxIcon.Exclamation` ⚠ `MessageBoxIcon.Information` ⓘ `MessageBoxIcon.Stop` ⊗

defaultButton	button automatically selected when the user presses Enter;
	can be one of the following constants:
	`MessageBoxDefaultButton.Button1` (default setting)
	`MessageBoxDefaultButton.Button2`
	`MessageBoxDefaultButton.Button3`

Example 1 – Displays an informational message box that contains the message "Record deleted."

```
MessageBox.Show("Record deleted.", "Payroll", _
      MessageBoxButtons.OK, MessageBoxIcon.Information)
```

Example 2 – Displays a warning message box that contains the message "Delete this record?"

```
MessageBox.Show("Delete this record?", "Payroll", _
      MessageBoxButtons.YesNo, MessageBoxIcon.Exclamation, _
      MessageBoxDefaultButton.Button2)
```

Figure 4-44: Syntax, arguments, and examples of the MessageBox.Show method

As Figure 4-44 indicates, the *text* argument specifies the text to display in the message box. The *text* argument can be a String literal constant, String named constant, or String variable. The message in the *text* argument should be concise but clear, and should be entered using sentence capitalization. It is recommended that you avoid using the words "error," "warning," or "mistake" in the message, as these words imply that the user has done something wrong.

The *caption* argument specifies the text to display in the title bar of the message box, and typically is the application's name. Like the *text* argument, the *caption* argument can be a String literal constant, String named constant, or String variable. Unlike the *text* argument, however, the *caption* argument is entered using book title capitalization.

The *buttons* argument indicates the buttons to display in the message box and can be one of six different constants. For example, a *buttons* argument of `MessageBoxButtons.AbortRetryIgnore` displays the Abort, Retry, and Ignore buttons in the message box. A *buttons* argument of `MessageBoxButtons.OK`, on the other hand, displays only the OK button in the message box.

The *icon* argument specifies the icon to display in the message box and typically is one of the following constants: `MessageBoxIcon.Exclamation`, `MessageBoxIcon.Information`, or `MessageBoxIcon.Stop`. A message box's icon indicates the type of message being sent to the user. The `MessageBoxIcon.Exclamation` constant, for example, displays the Warning Message icon, which alerts the user to a condition or situation that requires him or her to make a decision before the application can proceed. The message to the user can be phrased as a question, such as "Save changes to the document?"

The `MessageBoxIcon.Information` constant displays the Information Message icon. This icon indicates that the message in the message box is for information only and does not require the user to make a decision. An example of an informational message is "The changes were saved." A message box with an Information Message icon should contain only an OK button. In other words, you always use `MessageBoxButtons.OK` for the *buttons* argument when using `MessageBoxIcon.Information` for the *icon* argument. The user acknowledges the informational message by clicking the OK button.

The `MessageBoxIcon.Stop` constant displays the Stop Message icon, which alerts the user to a serious problem that requires intervention or correction before the application can continue. You would use the Stop Message icon in a message box that alerts the user that the disk in the disk drive is write-protected.

The *defaultButton* argument in the MessageBox.Show method identifies the default button, which is the button that is selected automatically when the user presses the Enter key on the computer keyboard. To designate the first button in the message box as the default button, you either set the *defaultButton* argument to `MessageBoxDefaultButton.Button1`, or you simply omit the argument. To have the second or third button be the default button, you set the *defaultButton* argument to `MessageBoxDefaultButton.Button2` or `MessageBoxDefaultButton.Button3`, respectively. The default button should be the button that represents the user's most likely action, as long as that action is not destructive.

Study the two examples shown in Figure 4-44. In the first example, the `MessageBox.Show("Record deleted.", "Payroll", MessageBoxButtons.OK, MessageBoxIcon.Information)` instruction displays the informational message box shown in Figure 4-45. The user can close the message box by clicking either the OK button or the Close button. The `MessageBox.Show("Delete this record?", "Payroll", MessageBoxButtons.YesNo, MessageBoxIcon.Exclamation, MessageBoxDefaultButton.Button2)` instruction in the second example displays the warning message box shown in Figure 4-46. Notice that the Close button in a warning message box is automatically disabled. In this case, the user must select either the Yes button or the No button (which is the default button) to close the message box.

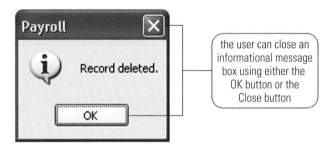

Figure 4-45: Message box displayed by the first example shown in Figure 4-44

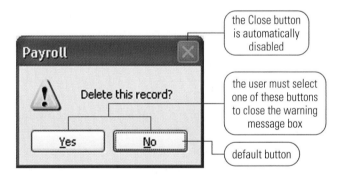

Figure 4-46: Message box displayed by the second example shown in Figure 4-44

MessageBox.Show Method Standards

» Use sentence capitalization for the *text* argument, but book title capitalization for the *caption* argument. The name of the application typically appears in the *caption* argument.

» Avoid using the words "error," "warning," or "mistake" in the message, as these words imply that the user has done something wrong.

» Display the Warning Message icon ⚠ in a message box that alerts the user that he or she must make a decision before the application can continue. You can phrase the message as a question.

» Display the Information Message icon ⓘ in a message box that displays an informational message along with an OK button only.

» Display the Stop Message icon ✖ when you want to alert the user of a serious problem that must be corrected before the application can continue.

» The default button in the dialog box should be the one that represents the user's most likely action, as long as that action is not destructive.

After displaying the message box, the MessageBox.Show method waits for the user to choose one of the buttons displayed in the message box. It then closes the message box and returns an integer that indicates which button the user chose. Sometimes you are not interested in the value returned by the MessageBox.Show method. This is the case when the message box is for informational purposes only, like the message box shown in Figure 4-45. Recall that the only button in an informational message box is the OK button. Many times, however, the button selected by the user determines the next task performed by an application. For example, selecting the Yes button in the message box shown in Figure 4-46 tells the application to delete the record, whereas selecting the No button tells the application not to delete the record.

Figure 4-47 lists the integer values returned by the MessageBox.Show method; each value is associated with a button that can appear in a message box. The figure also lists the DialogResult values assigned to each integer, and the meaning of the integers and DialogResult values. In addition, the figure contains three examples of using the value returned by the MessageBox.Show method.

Values returned by the MessageBox.Show method		
<u>Number</u>	<u>DialogResult value</u>	<u>Meaning</u>
1	Windows.Forms.DialogResult.OK	user chose the OK button
2	Windows.Forms.DialogResult.Cancel	user chose the Cancel button
3	Windows.Forms.DialogResult.Abort	user chose the Abort button
4	Windows.Forms.DialogResult.Retry	user chose the Retry button
5	Windows.Forms.DialogResult.Ignore	user chose the Ignore button
6	Windows.Forms.DialogResult.Yes	user chose the Yes button
7	Windows.Forms.DialogResult.No	user chose the No button

<u>Example 1</u>
```
Dim button As DialogResult
button = MessageBox.Show("Delete this record?", _
      "Payroll", MessageBoxButtons.YesNo, _
      MessageBoxIcon.Exclamation, _
      MessageBoxDefaultButton.Button2)
If button = Windows.Forms.DialogResult.Yes Then
      instructions to delete the record
End If
```

<u>Example 2</u>
```
If MessageBox.Show("Delete this record?", _
      "Payroll", MessageBoxButtons.YesNo, _
      MessageBoxIcon.Exclamation, _
      MessageBoxDefaultButton.Button2) _
      = Windows.Forms.DialogResult.Yes Then
      instructions to delete the record
End If
```

<u>Example 3</u>
```
Dim button As DialogResult
button = MessageBox.Show("Play another game?", _
      "Math Monster", MessageBoxButtons.YesNo, _
      MessageBoxIcon.Exclamation)
If button = Windows.Forms.DialogResult.Yes Then
      instructions to start another game
Else ' Windows.Forms.DialogResult.No
      instructions to close the game application
End If
```

Figure 4-47: Values returned by the MessageBox.Show method

As Figure 4-47 indicates, the MessageBox.Show method returns the integer 6 when the user selects the Yes button. The integer 6 is represented by the DialogResult value, `Windows.Forms.DialogResult.Yes`. When referring to the MessageBox.Show method's return value in code, you should use the DialogResult values listed in Figure 4-47 rather than the integers, because the values make the code easier to understand.

In the first example shown in Figure 4-47, the value returned by the MessageBox.Show method is assigned to a DialogResult variable named `button`. If the user selects the Yes button in the message box, the integer 6 is stored in the `button` variable; otherwise, the integer 7 is stored in the variable to indicate that the user selected the No button. The selection structure in the example compares the contents of the `button` variable to the `Windows.Forms.DialogResult.Yes` value. If the `button` variable contains the integer 6, which is the value of `Windows.Forms.DialogResult.Yes`, then the instructions to delete the record are processed; otherwise, the deletion instructions are skipped.

You do not have to store the value returned by the MessageBox.Show method in a variable, although doing so can make your code more readable. For instance, in the second example shown in Figure 4-47, the method's return value is not stored in a variable. Instead, the method appears in the selection structure's *condition*, where its return value is compared to `Windows.Forms.DialogResult.Yes`.

The selection structure shown in the third example in Figure 4-47 performs one set of tasks when the user selects the Yes button in the message box, but a different set of tasks when the user selects the No button. It is a good programming practice to document the Else portion of the selection structure as shown in the figure, because it makes it clear that the Else portion is processed only when the user selects the No button.

In the current application, the xCalcButton's Click event procedure should display a message box when the term entered by the user is not greater than or equal to 1. The message box is for informational purposes only. Therefore, it should contain the Information Message icon and the OK button, and you do not need to be concerned with its return value. Recall that the message to display in the message box is stored in the `Message` named constant.

To complete the xCalcButton's Click event procedure:

1 The insertion point should be positioned in the blank line above the `End If` instruction, as shown earlier in Figure 4-43. Type **else** and press **Enter**.

2 Type **messagebox.show(message, "Monthly Payment Calculator",** _ and press **Enter**. (Be sure to include a space before the line continuation character.)

3 Press **Tab**, then type **messageboxbuttons.ok, messageboxicon.information)**.

4 Save the solution. Figure 4.48 shows the completed xCalcButton's Click event procedure.

```
Private Sub xCalcButton_Click(ByVal sender As Object, _
    ByVal e As System.EventArgs) Handles xCalcButton.Click
    ' calculates and displays a monthly payment

  Const Message As String = "The term must be greater than or equal
  to 1."
  Dim principal As Double
  Dim interestRate As Double
  Dim loanTerm As Double
  Dim monthlyPayment As Double

  Double.TryParse(Me.xPrincipalTextBox.Text, principal)
  Double.TryParse(Me.xRateTextBox.Text, interestRate)
  Double.TryParse(Me.xTermTextBox.Text, loanTerm)

  ' convert the rate to decimal form, if necessary
  If interestRate >= 1.0 Then
      interestRate = interestRate / 100.0
  End If

  ' verify that the term is valid
  If loanTerm >= 1.0 Then
      ' calculate and display the monthly payment
      monthlyPayment = _
          -Financial.Pmt(interestRate / 12, loanTerm * 12, principal)
      Me.xPaymentLabel.Text = monthlyPayment.ToString("C2")
  Else
      MessageBox.Show(Message, "Monthly Payment Calculator", _
          MessageBoxButtons.OK, MessageBoxIcon.Information)
  End If
End Sub
```

Figure 4-48: Completed xCalcButton's Click event procedure

In the next set of steps, you will test the xCalcButton's Click event procedure to verify that it is working correctly.

To test the xCalcButton's Click event procedure:

1 Start the application. The Monthly Payment Calculator user interface appears on the screen.

First, you will calculate the monthly payment for a loan of $12,000 for 5 years at 6% interest.

2 Type **12000** in the Principal text box and press **Tab**. Type **6** in the Rate text box and press **Tab**. Type **5** in the Term text box and then click the **Calculate Monthly Payment** button. The xCalcButton's Click event procedure calculates and displays the monthly payment amount, as shown in Figure 4-49.

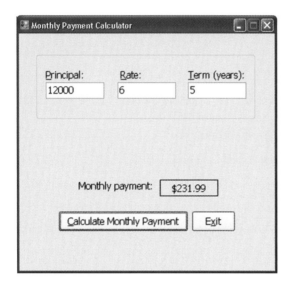

Figure 4-49: Monthly payment amount displayed in the interface

Next, you will verify that the application works correctly when the user enters an incorrect term.

3 Change the term from 5 to **0**, then click the **Calculate Monthly Payment** button. The application displays the message box shown in Figure 4-50.

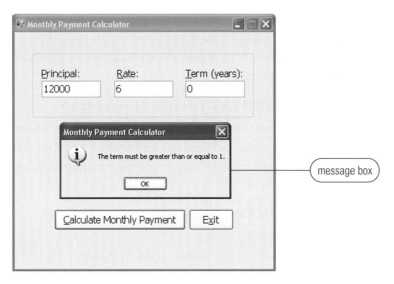

Figure 4-50: Message box created by the MessageBox.Show method

4 Click the **OK** button in the message box. The message box closes.

Now you will verify that the application works correctly when the user enters the interest rate as a decimal number.

5 Change the rate from 6 to **.06**, and change the term from 0 to **5**. Click the **Calculate Monthly Payment** button. The xCalcButton's Click event procedure calculates and displays a monthly payment of $231.99, which is the same monthly payment shown in Figure 4-49.

6 Click the **Exit** button to end the application.

7 Close the Code Editor window, then close the solution.

You have completed Lesson B. You can either take a break or complete the end-of-lesson questions and exercises before moving on to Lesson C.

SUMMARY

TO USE A GROUP BOX TO GROUP CONTROLS TOGETHER:

» Use the GroupBox tool to add a group box to the form. Drag controls from either the form or the Toolbox window into the group box.

» To include an optional identifying label on a group box, set the group box's Text property.

» The TabIndex value of a control contained within a group box is composed of two numbers separated by a period. The number to the left of the period is the TabIndex value of the group box itself. The number to the right of the period indicates the order in which the control was added to the group box.

TO CALCULATE A PERIODIC PAYMENT ON EITHER A LOAN OR AN INVESTMENT:

» Use the Financial.Pmt method, whose syntax is **Financial.Pmt(***Rate*, *NPer*, *PV*[, *FV*, *Due*]**).** Refer to Figure 4-42 for a description of each argument and examples of using the method to calculate a periodic payment.

TO DISPLAY A MESSAGE BOX THAT CONTAINS TEXT, ONE OR MORE BUTTONS, AND AN ICON:

» Use the MessageBox.Show method, whose syntax is **MessageBox.Show(***text*, *caption*, *buttons*, *icon*[, *defaultButton*]**)**. Refer to Figure 4-44 for a description of each argument and examples of using the method to display a message box. Refer to Figure 4-47 for a listing and description of the values returned by the MessageBox.Show method.

QUESTIONS

1. Which of the following statements is false?

   a. When you delete a group box, the controls contained within the group box remain on the form.

   b. Use sentence capitalization for the group box's identifying label.

   c. You can include an identifying label on a group box by setting the group box control's Text property.

   d. You can drag a control from the form into a group box.

2. Assume that the TabIndex value of a group box is 5. If the xNameTextBox was the first control added to the group box, then its TabIndex value will be _____.

   a. 1   b. 1.5

   c. 5.0   d. 5.1

3. Which of the following calculates the monthly payment on a loan of $5,000 for 2 years at 4% interest? Payments are due at the end of the month and should be expressed as a positive number.

   a. `-Financial.Pmt(.04/12, 2 * 12, 5000)`

   b. `-Financial.Pmt(.04/12, 24, 5000)`

   c. `-Financial.Pmt(.04/12, 2 * 12, 5000, 0, DueDate.EndOfPeriod)`

   d. All of the above.

4. Which of the following calculates the quarterly payment on a loan of $6,000 for 3 years at 9% interest? Payments are due at the beginning of the quarter and should be expressed as a negative number.

   a. `Financial.Pmt(.09/4, 3 * 12, 6000, 0, DueDate.BegOfPeriod)`

   b. `Financial.Pmt(.09/4, 3 * 4, 6000, 0, DueDate.BegOfPeriod)`

   c. `Financial.Pmt(.09/12, 3 * 12, 6000, 0, DueDate.BegOfPeriod)`

   d. None of the above.

5. Which of the following calculates the amount you need to save each month to accumulate $50,000 at the end of 10 years? The interest rate is 3% and deposits, which should be expressed as a positive number, are due at the beginning of the month.

   a. `Financial.Pmt(.03/12, 10 * 12, 0, 50000, DueDate.BegOfPeriod)`

   b. `-Financial.Pmt(.03/12, 120, 0, 50000, DueDate.BegOfPeriod)`

   c. `-Financial.Pmt(.03/12, 10 * 12, 50000, 0)`

   d. `-Financial.Pmt(.03/12, 120, 50000, 0, DueDate.BegOfPeriod)`

6. A message box's _____ argument indicates the type of message being sent.

   a. *buttons*   b. *caption*

   c. *icon*   d. *text*

7. You use the _____ constant to include the Warning Message icon in a message box.

   a. `MessageBox.Exclamation`   b. `MessageBox.IconExclamation`

   c. `MessageBoxIcon.Exclamation`   d. `MessageBox.WarningIcon`

8. If a message is for informational purposes only and does not require the user to make a decision, the message box should display which of the following?

   a. an OK button and the Information Message icon

   b. an OK button and the Warning Message icon

   c. a Yes button and the Information Message icon

   d. any button and the Information Message icon

9. You can use the _____ method to display a message in a message box.

   a. MessageBox.Display

   b. MessageBox.Open

   c. Message.Show

   d. None of the above.

10. If the user clicks the OK button in a message box, the message box returns the number 1, which is equivalent to which constant?

    a. `Windows.Forms.DialogResult.OK`

    b. `Windows.Forms.DialogResult.OKButton`

    c. `MessageBox.OK`

    d. `MessageResult.OK`

EXERCISES

1. In this exercise, you code an application that uses the Financial.Pmt method to calculate the amount of money you need to save each week to accumulate a specific sum.

   a. If necessary, start Visual Studio 2005 or Visual Basic 2005 Express Edition. Open the Weekly Savings Solution (Weekly Savings Solution.sln) file, which is contained in the VB2005\Chap04\Weekly Savings Solution folder. If necessary, open the designer window.

   b. Add a group box to the interface. Drag the Label1, Label2, Label3, xGoalTextBox, xRateTextBox, and xTermTextBox controls into the group box. Position the controls appropriately. Delete the contents of the group box's Text property.

c. Lock the controls, and then set the TabIndex property appropriately.

d. The user will enter the amount he wants to accumulate in the xGoalTextBox. He will enter the annual interest rate and term (in years) in the xRateTextBox and xTermTextBox controls, respectively. Code the xCalcButton's Click event procedure so that it calculates the amount of money the user will need to save each week. Assume that each year has exactly 52 weeks, and that deposits are made at the end of the week. The weekly payment should show two decimal places and be displayed in the xSavingsLabel.

e. Save the solution, then start the application. Test the application by calculating the amount the user needs to save to accumulate $10,000 at the end of two years, assuming a 4.5% interest rate.

f. Click the Exit button to end the application. Close the Code Editor window, then close the solution.

2. In this exercise, you code an application for Mingo Sales. The application calculates the total amount a customer owes.

a. If necessary, start Visual Studio 2005 or Visual Basic 2005 Express Edition. Open the Mingo Solution (Mingo Solution.sln) file, which is contained in the VB2005\Chap04\Mingo Solution folder. If necessary, open the designer window.

b. The user will enter the quantity ordered and price per unit in the xQuantityTextBox and xPriceTextBox controls, respectively. Code the xCalcButton's Click event procedure so that it calculates and displays the total amount a customer owes. The procedure should display the message "Are you a wholesaler?" in a message box. If the customer is a wholesaler, calculate a 10% discount on the total amount owed, and then display the discount with two decimal places in the xDiscountLabel; otherwise, display 0.00 in the xDiscountLabel. Display the total amount owed with a dollar sign and two decimal places in the xTotalLabel.

c. Have the application remove the contents of the xDiscountLabel and xTotalLabel controls when a change is made to the contents of a text box on the form.

d. Save the solution, then start the application. Test the application by calculating the total due for a wholesaler ordering four units of product at $10 per unit. Then test the application by calculating the total due for a non-wholesaler ordering two units of product at $5 per unit.

e. Click the Exit button to end the application. Close the Code Editor window, then close the solution.

DISCOVERY EXERCISE

3. In this exercise, you research the constants you can use to display an icon in a message box.

   a. If necessary, start Visual Studio 2005 or Visual Basic 2005 Express Edition. Click View on the menu bar, and then click Object Browser to open the Object Browser window.

   b. Type MessageBoxIcon in the Object Browser Search box, then press Enter. See Figure 4-51.

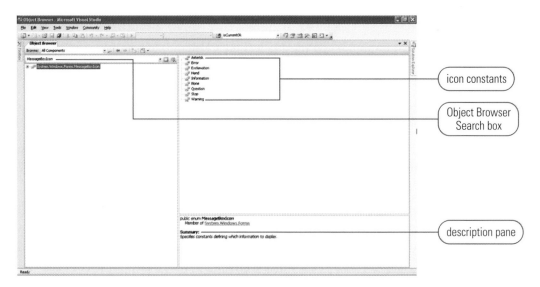

Figure 4-51: Object Browser window

   c. Click Exclamation in the list of icon constants. The description pane indicates that the constant displays a symbol consisting of an exclamation point in a triangle with a yellow background; the icon is called the Warning Message icon. What other icon constant displays the Warning Message icon?

   d. Which icon constants display the Information Message icon?

   e. Which icon constants display the Stop Message icon?

   f. What icon does the Question constant display?

   g. Close the Object Browser window.

LESSON C
OBJECTIVES

AFTER STUDYING LESSON C, YOU SHOULD
BE ABLE TO:

» Specify the keys that a text box will accept

» Select the existing text in a text box

COMPLETING THE MONTHLY PAYMENT CALCULATOR APPLICATION

CODING THE KEYPRESS EVENT PROCEDURES

Recall that to complete the Monthly Payment Calculator application, you still need to code the KeyPress and Enter event procedures for the three text boxes. You will code the KeyPress event procedures first.

To open the Monthly Payment Calculator application from Lesson B:

1 Start Visual Studio 2005 or Visual Basic 2005 Express Edition, if necessary, and close the Start Page window.

2 Open the **Payment Solution** (**Payment Solution.sln**) file, which is contained in the VB2005\Chap04\Payment Solution folder. Auto-hide the Toolbox, Solution Explorer, and Properties windows, if necessary.

3 Open the Code Editor window, and then open the code template for the xPrincipalTextBox's KeyPress event procedure. See Figure 4-52. The items contained within parentheses in the procedure are called **parameters** and represent information passed to the procedure when the event occurs.

```
Private Sub xPrincipalTextBox_KeyPress(ByVal sender As Object, ByVal e As System

    End Sub
```

e parameter

sender parameter

Figure 4-52: Code template for the xPrincipalTextBox's KeyPress event procedure

A control's **KeyPress event** occurs when the user presses a key while the control has the focus. When the KeyPress event occurs, a character corresponding to the key that was pressed is sent to the KeyPress event's e parameter, which appears in the procedure header in every event procedure. For example, when you press the period (.) on your keyboard, a period is sent to the e parameter. Similarly, when you press the Shift key along with a letter key on your keyboard, the uppercase version of the letter is sent to the e parameter.

One popular use for the KeyPress event is to prevent users from entering inappropriate characters in a text box. For instance, a text box for entering a person's age should contain numbers only; it should not contain letters or special characters, such as the dollar sign or percent sign. To prevent a text box from accepting an inappropriate character, you first use the e parameter's **KeyChar property** to determine the key that the user pressed. (KeyChar stands for "key character.") You then use the e parameter's **Handled property** to cancel the key if it is an inappropriate one. Figure 4-53 shows examples of using the KeyChar and Handled properties in the KeyPress event procedure.

Using the KeyChar and Handled properties in the KeyPress event procedure

Example 1 – prevents the text box from accepting the dollar sign

```
Private Sub xSalesTextBox_KeyPress(ByVal sender As Object, _
        ByVal e As System.Windows.Forms.KeyPressEventArgs) _
        Handles xSalesTextBox.KeyPress
    If e.KeyChar = "$" Then
        e.Handled = True
    End If
End Sub
```

Example 2 – allows the text box to accept only numbers

```
Private Sub xAgeTextBox_KeyPress(ByVal sender As Object, _
        ByVal e As System.Windows.Forms.KeyPressEventArgs) _
        Handles xAgeTextBox.KeyPress
    If e.KeyChar < "0" OrElse e.KeyChar > "9" Then
        e.Handled = True
    End If
End Sub
```

Example 3 – allows the text box to accept only numbers and the Backspace key

```
Private Sub xAgeTextBox_KeyPress(ByVal sender As Object, _
        ByVal e As System.Windows.Forms.KeyPressEventArgs) _
        Handles xAgeTextBox.KeyPress
    If (e.KeyChar < "0" OrElse e.KeyChar > "9") _
        AndAlso e.KeyChar <> ControlChars.Back Then
        e.Handled = True
    End If
End Sub
```

Figure 4-53: Examples of using the KeyChar and Handled properties

The selection structure shown in Example 1 in Figure 4-53 prevents the xSalesTextBox from accepting the dollar sign. The e.KeyChar = "$" *condition* in the selection structure compares the contents of the e parameter's KeyChar property with a dollar sign ($). If the *condition* evaluates to True, it means that a dollar sign is stored in the KeyChar property. In that case, the e.Handled = True instruction cancels the key before it is entered in the xSalesTextBox.

You can use the selection structure shown in Example 2 to prevent a text box from accepting a character that is not a number. However, keep in mind that Example 2's selection structure also prevents the text box from accepting the Backspace key. Therefore, you will not be able to use the Backspace key to delete a character from the text box. You can, however, use the left and right arrow keys to position the insertion point immediately before the character you want to delete, and then use the Delete key to delete the character.

Like Example 2's selection structure, the selection structure shown in Example 3 in Figure 4-53 also prevents the xAgeTextBox from accepting a character that is not a number. However, unlike Example 2's selection structure, Example 3's selection structure allows the user to employ the Backspace key, which is represented by the **ControlChars.Back constant**. Basically, Example 3's selection structure cancels any key that is not a number and, at the same time, is not the Backspace key.

According to the TOE chart for the Monthly Payment Calculator application, each text box's KeyPress event procedure should allow the text box to accept only the numbers 0 through 9, the period, and the Backspace key. All other keys should be canceled. (The TOE chart is shown in Figure 4-38 in Lesson B.)

To allow the three text boxes to accept numbers, the Backspace key, and the period:

1 Change xPrincipalTextBox_KeyPress in the procedure header to **CancelKeys**.

2 Position the insertion point immediately before the letter H in the word Handles in the procedure header. Type _ (the underscore, which is the line continuation character), and then press **Enter** to move the Handles xPrincipalTextBox.KeyPress text to the next line in the procedure.

3 Press **Tab** twice to indent the Handles line.

4 Position the insertion point at the end of the Handles xPrincipalTextBox.KeyPress line, then type , _ (a comma, a space, and the underscore) and press **Enter**.

5 Type **xRateTextBox.KeyPress, xTermTextBox.KeyPress** and press **Enter**.

6 Type ' **allows numbers, the Backspace key, and the period** and press **Enter** twice.

7 Type **if (e.keychar < "0" orelse e.keychar > "9")** _ and press **Enter**. (Be sure to include a space before the line continuation character.)

8 Press **Tab** to indent the line. Type **andalso e.keychar <> controlchars.back _** and press **Enter**, then type **andalso e.keychar <> "." then** and press **Enter**.

9 Type **' cancel the key** and press **Enter**, then type **e.handled = true**.

10 Save the solution. Figure 4-54 shows the completed CancelKeys procedure, which is associated with each text box's KeyPress event.

```
Private Sub CancelKeys(ByVal sender As Object, ByVal e As System.Windows.Forms.F
        Handles xPrincipalTextBox.KeyPress, _
        xRateTextBox.KeyPress, xTermTextBox.KeyPress
    ' allows numbers, the Backspace key, and the period

    If (e.KeyChar < "0" OrElse e.KeyChar > "9") _
        AndAlso e.KeyChar <> ControlChars.Back _
        AndAlso e.KeyChar <> "." Then
        ' cancel the key
        e.Handled = True
    End If

End Sub
```

Figure 4-54: Completed CancelKeys procedure

In the next set of steps, you will test the CancelKeys procedure to verify that it allows the text boxes to accept only numbers, the Backspace key, and the period.

To test the CancelKeys procedure:

1 Start the application. Try entering a letter in the Principal text box, and then try entering a dollar sign.

2 Type **30000** in the Principal text box, then press **Backspace** to delete the last zero. The text box now contains 3000.

3 Try entering a letter in the Rate text box, then try entering a percent sign.

4 Type **.045** in the Rate text box, then press **Backspace** to delete the number 5. The text box now contains .04.

5 Try entering a letter in the Term text box, then try entering an ampersand.

6 Type **20** in the Term text box, then press **Backspace** to delete the zero. The text box now contains 2.

7 Click the **Calculate Monthly Payment** button. A monthly payment amount of $130.27 appears in the xPaymentLabel.

8 Press **Tab** twice to move the focus to the xPrincipalTextBox. See Figure 4-55.

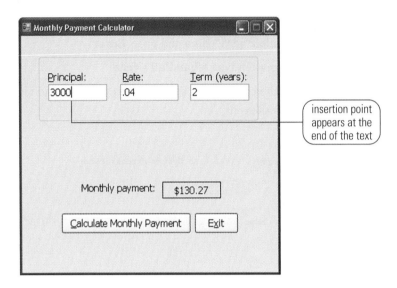

Figure 4-55: Insertion point shown in the xPrincipalTextBox

Notice that the insertion point appears at the end of the text box entry in Figure 4-55. It is customary in Windows applications to have a text box's existing text selected (highlighted) when the text box receives the focus. You will learn how to select the existing text in the next section.

9 Click the **Exit** button to end the application. You are returned to the Code Editor window.

CODING THE ENTER EVENT PROCEDURE

To complete the current application, you just need to code the Enter event procedures for the three text boxes. A text box's **Enter event** occurs when the text box receives the focus. This can happen as a result of the user tabbing to the control or using the control's access key. It also occurs when the Focus method is used in code to send the focus to the control. The Enter event procedure for each text box in the current application is responsible for selecting the contents of the text box. Selecting the existing text allows the user to remove the text simply by pressing a key—for example, the letter n on the keyboard. The key that is pressed—in this case, the letter n—replaces the selected text. You can use the **SelectAll method** to select all of the text contained in a text box. Figure 4-56 shows the syntax of the SelectAll method and includes an example of using the method. In the syntax, *textbox* is the name of the text box whose contents you want to select. The Me.xNameTextBox.SelectAll() statement in the figure tells the computer to select, or highlight, the contents of the xNameTextBox.

Using the SelectAll method

Syntax

Me._textbox_**.SelectAll()**

Example

```
Me.xNameTextBox.SelectAll()
```

Figure 4-56: Syntax and an example of the SelectAll method

You will use the SelectAll method to select the contents of the text boxes in the Monthly Payment Calculator application. You will enter the method in each text box's Enter event procedure so that the method is processed when the text box receives the focus.

To code each text box's Enter event procedure, then test the procedures:

1 Open the code template for the xPrincipalTextBox's Enter event procedure. Type **' selects the contents when the text box receives the focus** and press **Enter** twice. Type **me.xPrincipalTextBox.selectall()** and press **Enter**.

2 Open the code template for the xRateTextBox's Enter event procedure. Type **' selects the contents when the text box receives the focus** and press **Enter** twice. Type **me.xRateTextBox.selectall()** and press **Enter**.

3 Open the code template for the xTermTextBox's Enter event procedure. Type **' selects the contents when the text box receives the focus** and press **Enter** twice. Type **me.xTermTextBox.selectall()** and press **Enter**.

4 Save the solution, then start the application. Enter **10000** as the principal, **8** as the rate, and **5** as the term. Click the **Calculate Monthly Payment** button. A monthly payment amount of $202.76 appears in the xPaymentLabel.

5 Press **Tab** twice to move the focus to the xPrincipalTextBox. The xPrincipalTextBox's Enter event procedure selects the contents of the text box, as shown in Figure 4-57.

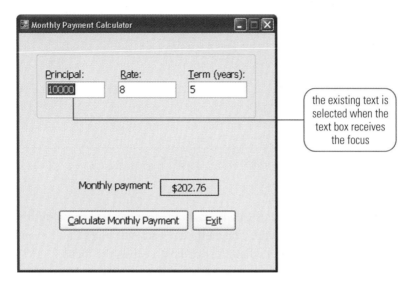

Figure 4-57: Existing text selected in the xPrincipalTextBox

6 Press **Tab** to move the focus to the xRateTextBox. The xRateTextBox's Enter event procedure selects the contents of the text box.

7 Press **Tab** to move the focus to the xTermTextBox. The xTermTextBox's Enter event procedure selects the contents of the text box.

8 Click the **Exit** button to end the application.

9 Close the Code Editor window, then close the solution. Figure 4-58 shows the Monthly Payment Calculator application's code.

```
' Project name:    Payment Project
' Project purpose: The project calculates the
'                  monthly payment on a loan.
' Created/revised: <your name> on <current date>

Option Explicit On
Option Strict On

Public Class MainForm

    Private Sub xExitButton_Click(ByVal sender As Object, _
        ByVal e As System.EventArgs) Handles xExitButton.Click
        Me.Close()
    End Sub
```

Figure 4-58: Monthly Payment Calculator application's code *(Continued)* ▶

```
Private Sub xPrincipalTextBox_Enter(ByVal sender As Object, _
    ByVal e As System.EventArgs) Handles xPrincipalTextBox.Enter
    ' selects the contents when the text box receives the focus

    Me.xPrincipalTextBox.SelectAll()

End Sub

Private Sub xRateTextBox_Enter(ByVal sender As Object, _
    ByVal e As System.EventArgs) Handles xRateTextBox.Enter
    ' selects the contents when the text box receives the focus

    Me.xRateTextBox.SelectAll()

End Sub

Private Sub xTermTextBox_Enter(ByVal sender As Object, _
    ByVal e As System.EventArgs) Handles xTermTextBox.Enter
    ' selects the contents when the text box receives the focus

    Me.xTermTextBox.SelectAll()

End Sub

Private Sub CancelKeys(ByVal sender As Object, _
    ByVal e As System.Windows.Forms.KeyPressEventArgs) _
        Handles xPrincipalTextBox.KeyPress, _
        xRateTextBox.KeyPress, xTermTextBox.KeyPress
    ' allows numbers, the Backspace key, and the period

    If (e.KeyChar < "0" OrElse e.KeyChar > "9") _
        AndAlso e.KeyChar <> ControlChars.Back _
        AndAlso e.KeyChar <> "." Then
        ' cancel the key
        e.Handled = True

    End If
End Sub

Private Sub ClearPayment(ByVal sender As Object, _
    ByVal e As System.EventArgs) _
    Handles xPrincipalTextBox.TextChanged, _
    xRateTextBox.TextChanged, xTermTextBox.TextChanged
    ' clears the monthly payment

    Me.xPaymentLabel.Text = String.Empty
End Sub
```

Figure 4-58: Monthly Payment Calculator application's code *(Continued)* ▶

```
    Private Sub xCalcButton_Click(ByVal sender As Object, _
        ByVal e As System.EventArgs) Handles xCalcButton.Click
        ' calculates and displays a monthly payment

        Const Message As String = "The term must be greater than or ⌐
            equal to 1."

        Dim principal As Double
        Dim interestRate As Double
        Dim loanTerm As Double
        Dim monthlyPayment As Double

        Double.TryParse(Me.xPrincipalTextBox.Text, principal)
        Double.TryParse(Me.xRateTextBox.Text, interestRate)
        Double.TryParse(Me.xTermTextBox.Text, loanTerm)

        ' convert the rate to decimal form, if necessary
        If interestRate >= 1.0 Then
            interestRate = interestRate / 100.0
        End If

        ' verify that the term is valid
        If loanTerm >= 1.0 Then
            ' calculate and display the monthly payment
            monthlyPayment = _
                -Financial.Pmt(interestRate / 12, loanTerm * 12, principal)
            Me.xPaymentLabel.Text = monthlyPayment.ToString("C2")
        Else
            MessageBox.Show(Message, "Monthly Payment Calculator", _
                MessageBoxButtons.OK, MessageBoxIcon.Information)
        End If
    End Sub
End Class
```

Figure 4-58: Monthly Payment Calculator application's code

You now have completed Lesson C and Chapter 4. You can either take a break or complete the end-of-lesson questions and exercises.

SUMMARY

TO ALLOW A TEXT BOX TO ACCEPT ONLY CERTAIN KEYS:

» Code the text box's KeyPress event. The key the user pressed is stored in the e.KeyChar property. You use the `e.Handled = True` instruction to cancel the key pressed by the user.

TO SELECT THE EXISTING TEXT IN A TEXT BOX:

» Use the SelectAll method, whose syntax is **Me.***textbox***.SelectAll()**.

QUESTIONS

1. A control's _____ event occurs when a user presses a key while the control has the focus.

   a. Key

   b. KeyPress

   c. Press

   d. PressKey

2. When entered in the appropriate event, which of the following statements cancels the key pressed by the user?

   a. `Cancel = True`

   b. `e.Cancel = True`

   c. `e.Handled = True`

   d. `Key = Null`

3. Which of the following can be used in an If...Then...Else statement to determine whether the user pressed the Backspace key?

   a. `If ControlChars.Back = True Then`

   b. `If e.KeyChar = Backspace Then`

   c. `If e.KeyChar = ControlChars.Backspace Then`

   d. `If e.KeyChar = ControlChars.Back Then`

4. Which of the following can be used in an If...Then...Else statement to determine whether the user pressed the $ (dollar sign) key?

   a. `If ControlChars.DollarSign = True Then`

   b. `If e.KeyChar = "$" Then`

   c. `If e.KeyChar = Chars.DollarSign Then`

   d. `If KeyChar.ControlChars = "$" Then`

5. When a user tabs to a text box, the text box's _____ event occurs.

    a. Access   b. Enter

    c. TabOrder   d. TabbedTo

6. Which of the following highlights all of the text contained in the xCityTextBox?

    a. `Me.xCityTextBox.SelectAll()`

    b. `Me.xCityTextBox.HighlightAll()`

    c. `Highlight(Me.xCityTextBox.Text)`

    d. `SelectAll(Me.xCityTextBox.Text)`

EXERCISES

1. In this exercise, you create an application for Micro Seminars. The application displays the total amount a company owes for a seminar. The seminar charge is $80 per person.

    a. If necessary, start Visual Studio 2005 or Visual Basic 2005 Express Edition.

    b. Create a Visual Basic Windows-based application. Name the solution Micro Solution, and name the project Micro Project. Save the application in the VB2005\Chap04 folder.

    c. Assign the filename Main Form.vb to the form file object.

    d. Assign the name MainForm to the form.

    e. When designing the interface, provide a text box into which the user can enter the number of seminar registrants, and a label for displaying the total owed. Use the GUI design guidelines listed in Appendix A to verify that the interface you create adheres to the GUI standards outlined in this book.

    f. Code the application appropriately. The number of registrants should be greater than 0 but less than 50. Display an appropriate message when the number of registrants is invalid.

    g. Allow the user to press only numeric keys and the Backspace key when entering the number of registrants.

    h. When a change is made to the number of registrants entered in the text box, clear the contents of the label control that displays the total owed.

    i. When the text box receives the focus, select its existing text.

j. Center the total owed in the label control, and display it with a dollar sign and two decimal places.

k. Save the solution, then start the application. Test the application with both valid and invalid data.

l. End the application. Close the Code Editor window, then close the solution.

2. In this exercise, you code an application that allows the user to enter a state ID.

a. If necessary, start Visual Studio 2005 or Visual Basic 2005 Express Edition. Open the State ID Solution (State ID Solution.sln) file, which is contained in the VB2005\Chap04\State ID Solution folder. If necessary, open the designer window.

b. Code the application so that it allows the user to enter only letters in the xStateTextBox. Also allow the user to use the Backspace key.

c. When the text box receives the focus, select its existing text.

d. Save the solution, then start the application. Test the application with both valid data (uppercase and lowercase letters and the Backspace key) and invalid data (numbers and special characters).

e. Click the Exit button to end the application. Close the Code Editor window, then close the solution.

3. In this exercise, you code an application for the Allenton water department. The application calculates a customer's water bill.

a. If necessary, start Visual Studio 2005 or Visual Basic 2005 Express Edition. Open the Allenton Solution (Allenton Solution.sln) file, which is contained in the VB2005\Chap04\Allenton Solution folder. If necessary, open the designer window.

b. Code the application so that it calculates and displays the gallons of water used and the water charge. Display the water charge with a dollar sign and two decimal places. The charge for water is $1.75 per 1000 gallons, or .00175 per gallon. Before making the calculations, verify that the meter readings entered by the user are valid. To be valid, the current meter reading must be greater than or equal to the previous meter reading. Display an appropriate message if the meter readings are not valid.

c. Allow the user to enter only numbers in the xCurrentTextBox and xPreviousTextBox controls. Also allow the user to press the Backspace key when entering data in those two text boxes.

d. Clear the contents of the xGalUsedLabel and xChargeLabel controls when a change is made to the contents of a text box on the form.

e. When a text box receives the focus, select its existing text.

    f. Save the solution, then start the application. Test the application with both valid and invalid data.

    g. Click the Exit button to end the application. Close the Code Editor window, then close the solution.

4. In this exercise, you modify the Skate-Away Sales application from Chapter 3.

    a. Use Windows to make a copy of the Skate Away Solution folder, which is contained in the VB2005\Chap04 folder. Rename the folder Skate Away Solution – Ex4.

    b. If necessary, start Visual Studio 2005 or Visual Basic 2005 Express Edition. Open the Skate Away Solution (Skate Away Solution.sln) file contained in the VB2005\Chap04\Skate Away Solution – Ex4 folder. Open the designer window.

    c. Code the application so that it allows the xBlueTextBox and xYellowTextBox controls to accept only numbers and the Backspace key.

    d. When a text box in the user interface receives the focus, select its existing text.

    e. Save the solution, then start the application. Test the application appropriately.

    f. Click the Exit button to end the application. Close the Code Editor window, then close the solution.

5. In this exercise, you modify the Skate-Away Sales application from Chapter 3.

    a. Use Windows to make a copy of the Skate Away Solution folder, which is contained in the VB2005\Chap04 folder. Rename the folder Skate Away Solution – Ex5.

    b. If necessary, start Visual Studio 2005 or Visual Basic 2005 Express Edition. Open the Skate Away Solution (Skate Away Solution.sln) file contained in the VB2005\Chap04\Skate Away Solution – Ex5 folder. Open the designer window.

    c. Open the Code Editor window. If the xBlueTextBox does not contain any data, the xCalcButton's Click event procedure should assign a zero to the text box's Text property. Likewise, if the xYellowTextBox does not contain any data, the xCalcButton's Click event procedure should assign a zero to the text box's Text property. Add the appropriate code to the procedure.

    d. Before making the appropriate calculations and displaying the results, the xCalcButton's Click event procedure should determine whether the contents of the xBlueTextBox and xYellowTextBox controls can be converted to integers. If they cannot, the procedure should display an appropriate message in a message box.

    e. When a text box in the user interface receives the focus, select its existing text.

    f. Save the solution, then start the application. Test the application appropriately.

    g. Click the Exit button to end the application. Close the Code Editor window, then close the solution.

6. In this exercise, you use the MessageBox.Show method's return value.

   a. If necessary, start Visual Studio 2005 or Visual Basic 2005 Express Edition. Open the MessageBox Value Solution (MessageBox Value Solution.sln) file contained in the VB2005\Chap04\MessageBox Value Solution folder. If necessary, open the designer window.

   b. Open the Code Editor window. Modify the xCalcButton's Click event procedure so that it asks the user whether he or she wants to include a dollar sign in the gross pay amount. Use the MessageBox.Show method to display the message. Include Yes and No buttons in the message box. If the user clicks the Yes button, the procedure should display the gross pay amount using the "C2" format. If the user clicks the No button, the procedure should display the gross pay amount using the "N2" format.

   c. When a text box in the user interface receives the focus, select its existing text.

   d. Save the solution, then start the application. Test the application appropriately.

   e. Click the Exit button to end the application. Close the Code Editor window, then close the solution.

DISCOVERY EXERCISE

7. In this exercise, you code an application that calculates a bonus.

   a. If necessary, start Visual Studio 2005 or Visual Basic 2005 Express Edition. Open the Discovery Bonus Solution (Discovery Bonus Solution.sln) file, which is contained in the VB2005\Chap04\Discovery Bonus Solution folder. If necessary, open the designer window.

   b. The user will enter the sales amount in the xSalesTextBox. Because the sales amount should always be an integer, the text box should accept only numbers and the Backspace key.

   c. Code the xCalcButton's Click event procedure so that it calculates the salesperson's bonus. Display the bonus with a dollar sign and two decimal places in the xBonusLabel. The following rates should be used when calculating the bonus:

Sales amount ($)	Bonus
0–5000	1% of the sales amount
5001–10000	3% of the sales amount
Over 10000	7% of the sales amount

   (*Hint*: You can nest an If...Then...Else statement, which means you can place one If...Then...Else statement within another If...Then...Else statement.)

    d. Clear the contents of the xBonusLabel when a change is made to the contents of the xSalesTextBox.

    e. Save the solution, then start the application. Test the application with both valid and invalid data.

    f. Click the Exit button to end the application. Close the Code Editor window, then close the solution.

DISCOVERY EXERCISE

8. In this exercise, you learn how to specify the maximum number of characters that can be entered in a text box.

    a. If necessary, start Visual Studio 2005 or Visual Basic 2005 Express Edition. Open the Zip Solution (Zip Solution.sln) file, which is contained in the VB2005\Chap04\Zip Solution folder. If necessary, open the designer window.

    b. Click the xZipTextBox. Scan the Properties list, looking for a property that allows you to specify the maximum number of characters that can be entered in the text box. When you locate the property, set its value to 10.

    c. Save the solution, then start the application. Test the application by trying to enter more than 10 characters in the text box.

    d. Click the Exit button to end the application. Close the Code Editor window, then close the solution.

DEBUGGING EXERCISE

9. In this exercise, you debug an existing application. The purpose of this exercise is to demonstrate operator order of precedence.

    a. If necessary, start Visual Studio 2005 or Visual Basic 2005 Express Edition. Open the Debug Solution (Debug Solution.sln) file, which is contained in the VB2005\Chap04\Debug Solution folder. If necessary, open the designer window.

    b. Open the Code Editor window and review the existing code. The xCalcButton's Click event procedure should calculate a 10% bonus when the code entered by the user is either 1 or 2 and, at the same time, the sales amount is greater than $10,000; otherwise, the bonus rate is 5%. Also, the CancelKeys procedure should allow the two text boxes to accept only numbers and the Backspace key.

    c. Start the application. Type the number 1 in the Code text box, then press Backspace. Notice that the Backspace key is not working correctly.

    d. Click the Exit button to end the application.

e. Make the appropriate change to the CancelKeys procedure.

f. Save the solution, then start the application. Type the number 12 in the Code text box, then press Backspace to delete the 2. The Code text box now contains the number 1. Type 200 in the Sales amount text box, then click the Calculate Bonus button. A message box appears and indicates that the bonus amount is $20.00 (10% of $200), which is incorrect; it should be $10.00 (5% of $200).

g. Click the OK button to close the message box. Click the Exit button to end the application.

h. Make the appropriate change to the xCalcButton's Click event procedure.

i. Save the solution, then start the application. Type the number 1 in the Code text box. Type 200 in the Sales amount text box, then click the Calculate Bonus button. The message box should indicate that the bonus amount is $10.00.

j. Click the Exit button to end the application. Close the Code Editor window, then close the solution.

5

MORE ON THE SELECTION STRUCTURE

CREATING A MATH PRACTICE APPLICATION

On Monday you meet with Susan Chen, the principal of a local primary school. Ms. Chen needs an application that the first and second grade students can use to practice both adding and subtracting numbers. The application should display the addition or subtraction problem on the screen, allow the student to enter the answer, and then verify that the answer is correct. If the student's answer is not correct, the application should give him or her as many chances as necessary to answer the problem correctly.

The problems displayed for the first grade students should use numbers from 1 through 10 only. The problems for the second grade students should use numbers from 10 through 99. Because the first and second grade students have not learned about negative numbers yet, the subtraction problems should never ask them to subtract a larger number from a smaller one.

Ms. Chen also wants the application to keep track of the number of correct and incorrect responses made by the student; this information will help her assess the student's math ability. Finally, she wants to be able to control the display of this information to keep students from being distracted or pressured by the number of right and wrong answers.

PREVIEWING THE COMPLETED APPLICATION

Before you begin creating the Math Practice application, you will preview the completed application.

To preview the completed application:

1 Use the Run command on the Windows Start menu to run the **Math** (Math.exe) file, which is contained in the VB2005\Chap05 folder. The Math Practice application's user interface appears on the screen. See Figure 5-1. Do not worry if the numbers on your screen do not match the ones shown in the figure. This application uses the Random object and the Random.Next method to display random numbers in the two label controls. You learn how to use the Random object and the Random.Next method in Lesson B.

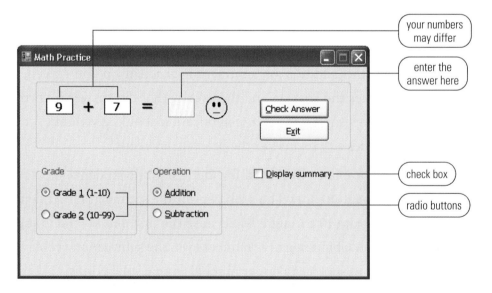

Figure 5-1: Math Practice application's user interface

The Math Practice application contains two new controls—radio buttons and a check box. You learn about these controls in Lesson B.

2 Type the correct answer to the addition problem appearing in the interface, then press **Enter** to select the Check Answer button, which is the default button on the form. When you answer the math problem correctly, a happy face icon appears in the picture box located to the left of the Check Answer button, and a new problem appears in the interface.

3 Click the **Display summary** check box to select it. A check mark appears inside the check box, and a group box appears below the check box. The label controls contained in the group box display the number of correct and incorrect responses, as shown in Figure 5-2. In this case, you have made one correct response and zero incorrect responses.

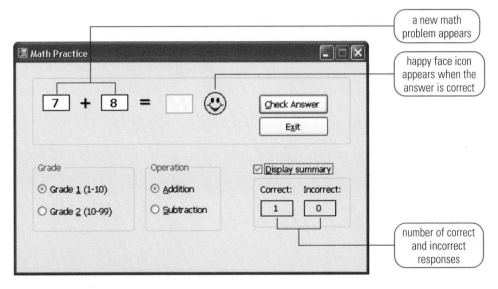

Figure 5-2: Interface showing that a correct response was made to the previous problem

4 Click the **Subtraction** radio button. A colored dot appears in the center of the Subtraction radio button to indicate that the radio button is selected, and the math problem changes to one involving subtraction.

5 Click inside the text box in which you enter the answer. Type an incorrect answer to the subtraction problem appearing on the screen, and then press **Enter**. The application replaces the happy face icon in the picture box with an icon whose facial expression is neutral. It also displays the "Try again!" message in a message box.

6 Press **Enter** to close the message box. The application highlights the incorrect answer in the text box and gives you another chance to enter a correct response. The interface shows that you have made one correct response and one incorrect response.

7 Type the correct answer to the subtraction problem, then press **Enter**. The happy face icon reappears in the picture box, and the number of correct responses now says 2. In addition, a new math problem appears in the interface.

8 Click the **Display summary** check box to deselect it. The application removes the check mark from the check box and hides the group box that contains the summary information.

9 Click the **Exit** button. The application ends.

Before you can begin coding the Math Practice application, you need to learn how to write nested and extended selection structures, as well as how to use the Is, TypeOf...Is, and Like comparison operators. You learn about those structures and operators in Lesson A. In Lesson B you complete the Math Practice application's interface as you learn how to include radio button and check box controls in an interface. You begin coding the application in Lesson B, and complete the application in Lesson C.

LESSON A
OBJECTIVES

AFTER STUDYING LESSON A, YOU SHOULD
BE ABLE TO:

» Include a nested selection structure in pseudocode and
in a flowchart

» Code a nested selection structure

» Desk-check an algorithm

» Recognize common logic errors in selection structures

» Code an If/ElseIf/Else selection structure

» Include a Case selection structure in pseudocode and in a
flowchart

» Code a Case selection structure

» Write code that uses the Is, TypeOf...Is, and Like
comparison operators

NESTED, IF/ELSEIF/ELSE, AND CASE SELECTION STRUCTURES

NESTED SELECTION STRUCTURES

As you learned in Chapter 4, you use the selection structure when you want a procedure to make a decision or comparison and then select one of two paths, depending on the result of that decision or comparison. Both paths in a selection structure can include instructions that declare variables, perform calculations, and so on. Both paths also can include other selection structures. When either a selection structure's true path or its false path contains another selection structure, the inner selection structure is referred to as a **nested selection structure**, because it is contained (nested) within the outer selection structure. You use a nested selection structure when more than one decision must be made before the appropriate action can be taken. For example, assume you want to create a procedure that determines voter eligibility and displays one of three messages. The messages and the criteria for displaying each message are shown in the following chart:

Message	Criteria
You are too young to vote.	person is younger than 18 years old
You can vote.	person is at least 18 years old and is registered to vote
You need to register before you can vote.	person is at least 18 years old but is not registered to vote

As the chart indicates, the person's age and voter registration status determine the appropriate message to display. If the person is younger than 18 years old, the procedure should display the message "You are too young to vote." However, if the person is at least 18 years old, the program should display one of two different messages. The correct message to display is determined by the person's voter registration status. If the person is registered, then the appropriate message is "You can vote."; otherwise, it is "You need to register before you can vote." Notice that determining the person's voter registration status is important only *after* his or her age is determined. You can think of the decision regarding the age as being the **primary decision**, and the decision regarding the registration status as being the **secondary decision**, because whether the registration decision needs to be made depends on the result of the age decision. The primary decision is always made by the outer selection structure, while the secondary decision is always made by the inner (nested) selection structure.

Figures 5-3 and 5-4 show the pseudocode and flowchart, respectively, for the xDisplayButton's Click event procedure, which displays the appropriate message based on a person's voter eligibility. Figure 5-5 shows the corresponding Visual Basic code. In the figures, the outer selection structure determines the age (the primary decision), and the nested selection structure determines the voter registration status (the secondary decision). Notice that the nested selection structure appears in the outer selection structure's true path in the figures. (The lines connecting the selection structures in the pseudocode and code are included to help you see the clauses that are related to each other.)

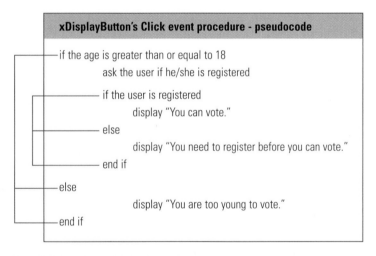

Figure 5-3: Pseudocode showing the nested selection structure in the true path

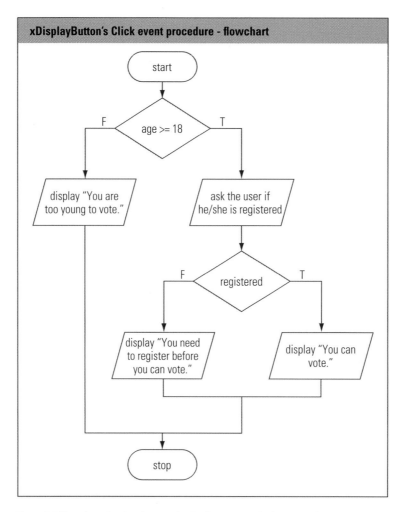

xDisplayButton's Click event procedure - flowchart

Figure 5-4: Flowchart showing the nested selection structure in the true path

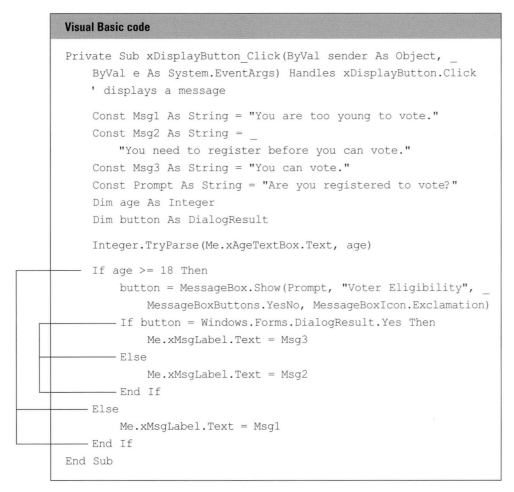

Visual Basic code

```
Private Sub xDisplayButton_Click(ByVal sender As Object, _
    ByVal e As System.EventArgs) Handles xDisplayButton.Click
    ' displays a message

    Const Msg1 As String = "You are too young to vote."
    Const Msg2 As String = _
        "You need to register before you can vote."
    Const Msg3 As String = "You can vote."
    Const Prompt As String = "Are you registered to vote?"
    Dim age As Integer
    Dim button As DialogResult

    Integer.TryParse(Me.xAgeTextBox.Text, age)

    If age >= 18 Then
        button = MessageBox.Show(Prompt, "Voter Eligibility", _
            MessageBoxButtons.YesNo, MessageBoxIcon.Exclamation)
        If button = Windows.Forms.DialogResult.Yes Then
            Me.xMsgLabel.Text = Msg3
        Else
            Me.xMsgLabel.Text = Msg2
        End If
    Else
        Me.xMsgLabel.Text = Msg1
    End If
End Sub
```

Figure 5-5: The xDisplayButton's Click event procedure showing the nested selection structure in the true path

Look closely at the xDisplayButton's Click event procedure shown in Figure 5-5. The procedure declares four named constants and two variables. It then uses the TryParse method to convert the contents of the xAgeTextBox to an integer. The condition in the outer selection structure checks whether the integer stored in the age variable is greater than or equal to 18. If the condition is false, it means that the person is not old enough to vote. In that case, only one message—the "You are too young to vote." message—is appropriate. After the message is displayed, both the outer selection structure and the procedure end.

If the outer selection structure's condition is true, on the other hand, it means that the person *is* old enough to vote. In that case, the outer selection structure's true path displays a message box that asks the user whether he or she is registered. Notice that the message box contains Yes and No buttons. A nested selection structure then is used to determine which of the message box buttons the user chose. If the user selected the Yes button, the instruction in the nested selection structure's true path displays the "You can vote." message. Alternately, if the user selected the No button, the instruction in the nested selection structure's false path displays the "You need to register before you can vote." message. After the appropriate message is displayed, both selection structures and the procedure end. Notice that the nested selection structure in this procedure is processed only when the outer selection structure's condition is true.

Figures 5-6 and 5-7 show the pseudocode and flowchart for a different version of the voter eligibility procedure, and Figure 5-8 shows the corresponding Visual Basic code. As in the previous version, the outer selection structure in this version determines the age (the primary decision), and the nested selection structure determines the voter registration status (the secondary decision). In this version of the procedure, however, the nested selection structure appears in the false path of the outer selection structure.

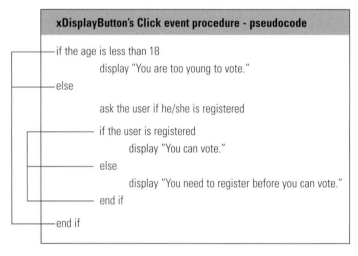

Figure 5-6: Pseudocode showing the nested selection structure in the false path

xDisplayButton's Click event procedure - flowchart

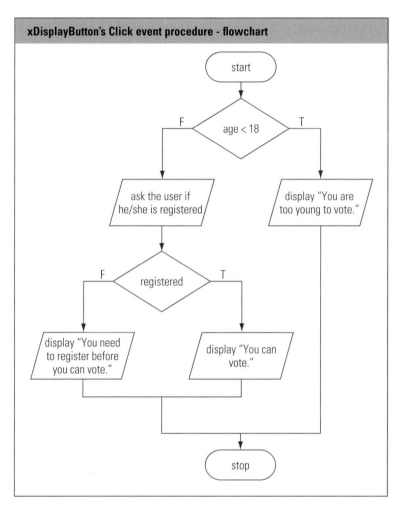

Figure 5-7: Flowchart showing the nested selection structure in the false path

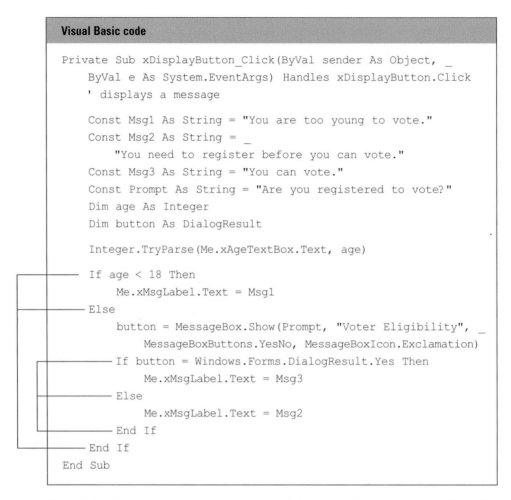

Visual Basic code

```
Private Sub xDisplayButton_Click(ByVal sender As Object, _
    ByVal e As System.EventArgs) Handles xDisplayButton.Click
    ' displays a message

    Const Msg1 As String = "You are too young to vote."
    Const Msg2 As String = _
        "You need to register before you can vote."
    Const Msg3 As String = "You can vote."
    Const Prompt As String = "Are you registered to vote?"
    Dim age As Integer
    Dim button As DialogResult

    Integer.TryParse(Me.xAgeTextBox.Text, age)

    If age < 18 Then
        Me.xMsgLabel.Text = Msg1
    Else
        button = MessageBox.Show(Prompt, "Voter Eligibility", _
            MessageBoxButtons.YesNo, MessageBoxIcon.Exclamation)
        If button = Windows.Forms.DialogResult.Yes Then
            Me.xMsgLabel.Text = Msg3
        Else
            Me.xMsgLabel.Text = Msg2
        End If
    End If
End Sub
```

Figure 5-8: The xDisplayButton's Click event procedure showing the nested selection structure in the false path

Like the version shown earlier, this version of the xDisplayButton's Click procedure first declares the necessary constants and variables and then converts the contents of the xAgeTextBox to an integer. However, rather than checking whether the integer stored in the age variable is greater than or equal to 18, the outer selection structure in this version checks whether the integer is less than 18. If the condition is true, the instruction in the outer selection structure's true path displays the "You are too young to vote." message. If the condition is false, the outer selection structure's false path first displays a message box that asks the user whether he or she is registered. A nested selection structure then is used to determine which of the message box buttons the user chose. If the user selected the Yes button, the instruction in the nested selection structure's true path displays the "You can vote." message. Alternately, if the user selected the No button, the instruction in the nested selection structure's false path displays the "You need to register before you can vote." message. After the appropriate message is displayed, both selection structures and the procedure end. Unlike in the previous version of the procedure, the nested selection structure in this version is processed only when the outer selection structure's condition is false. Both versions of the xDisplayButton's Click event procedure produce the same results. Neither version is better than the other; each simply represents a different way of solving the same problem.

To code and then test the Voter Eligibility application:

1 Start Visual Studio 2005 or Visual Basic 2005 Express Edition, if necessary, and close the Start Page window.

2 Open the **Voter Solution** (Voter Solution.sln) file, which is contained in the VB2005\Chap05\Voter Solution folder. If necessary, open the designer window.

3 Open the Code Editor window. Replace the `<your name>` and `<current date>` text in the comments with your name and the current date.

4 Open the code template for the xDisplayButton's Click event procedure, then enter the comment and code shown in either Figure 5-5 or Figure 5-8.

5 Close the Code Editor window. Save the solution, then start the application.

6 Enter **16** as the age, then press **Enter** to select the Display Message button, which is the default button on the form. The button's Click event procedure displays the "You are too young to vote." message, as shown in Figure 5-9.

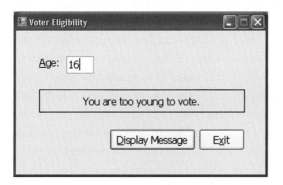

Figure 5-9: Message displayed in the interface

7 Change the age to **25**, then press **Enter**. A message box appears and asks whether you are registered to vote. Press **Enter** to select the Yes button, which is the default button in the message box. The message box closes and the "You can vote." message appears in the interface.

8 Click the **Display Message** button, then click the **No** button in the message box. The message box closes and the "You need to register before you can vote." message appears in the interface.

9 Click the **Exit** button to end the application. You are returned to the designer window. Close the solution.

Next, you will observe some of the common logic errors made when writing selection structures. Being aware of these errors will help to prevent you from making them.

LOGIC ERRORS IN SELECTION STRUCTURES

In most cases, logic errors in selection structures are a result of one of the following three mistakes: using a logical operator rather than a nested selection structure; reversing the primary and secondary decisions; or using an unnecessary nested selection structure. In the next several sections, the XYZ Company's bonus procedure is used to demonstrate each of these logic errors. The company pays its salespeople an 8% bonus on their sales. However, salespeople having a sales code of X receive an additional $150 bonus when their sales are greater than or equal to $10,000; otherwise, they receive an additional $125 bonus. Notice that the salesperson's code is a factor in determining whether the salesperson is eligible for the additional bonus amount. If the salesperson is entitled to the additional bonus, then the amount of his or her sales determines the appropriate additional amount. In this case, the decision regarding the salesperson's code is the primary decision, and the decision regarding the sales amount is the secondary decision, because whether the sales amount decision needs to be made depends on the result of the code decision. The pseudocode shown in Figure 5-10 represents a correct algorithm for the bonus procedure. An **algorithm** is the set of step-by-step instructions that accomplish a task.

Correct algorithm for the bonus procedure

1. calculate the bonus amount by multiplying the sales amount by .08

2. if the code is X

      if the sales are greater than or equal to 10000

           add 150 to the bonus amount

      else

           add 125 to the bonus amount

      end if

   end if

3. display the bonus amount

Figure 5-10: A correct algorithm for the bonus procedure

You will desk-check the algorithm shown in Figure 5-10 to verify that it is correct. **Desk-checking**, also called **hand-tracing**, means that you use sample data to walk through each of the steps in the algorithm manually, just as though you were the computer. Programmers desk-check an algorithm to verify that it will work as intended. If any errors are found in the algorithm, the errors are corrected before the programmer begins coding the algorithm. You will desk-check the algorithm shown in Figure 5-10 three times. For the first desk-check, you will use X as the code and $15,000 as the sales amount. Using this test data, the algorithm should display a bonus amount of $1,350. For the second desk-check, you will use X as the code and $9,000 as the sales amount; in this case, the algorithm should display a bonus amount of $845. For the third desk-check, you will use A as the code and $13,000 as the sales amount. With this set of test data, the algorithm should display a bonus amount of $1,040.

Using the first set of test data (X and 15000), Step 1 in the algorithm multiplies the sales amount by .08, giving 1200. The outer selection structure's condition in Step 2 determines whether the salesperson's code is X; it is, so the nested selection structure's condition checks whether the sales amount is greater than or equal to 10000. The sales amount is greater than 10000, so the nested selection structure's true path adds 150 to the bonus amount, giving 1350, which is correct. After doing this, both selection structures end. Step 3 in the algorithm then displays the bonus amount of 1350.

> **»TIP**
>
> You also could have written the nested selection structure's condition in Figure 5-10 as follows: *if the sales are less than 10000.* The true path then would contain the instruction *add 125 to the bonus amount,* and its false path would contain the instruction *add 150 to the bonus amount.*

Using the second set of test data (X and 9000), Step 1 in the algorithm multiplies the sales amount by .08, giving 720. The outer selection structure's condition in Step 2 determines whether the salesperson's code is X; it is, so the nested selection structure's condition checks whether the sales amount is greater than or equal to 10000. The sales amount is not greater than or equal to 10000, so the nested selection structure's false path adds 125 to the bonus amount, giving 845, which is correct. After doing this, both selection structures end. Step 3 in the algorithm then displays the bonus amount of 845.

Using the third set of test data (A and 13000), Step 1 in the algorithm multiplies the sales amount by .08, giving 1040. The outer selection structure's condition in Step 2 determines whether the salesperson's code is X. The code is not X, so the outer selection structure ends. Notice that the nested selection structure is not processed when the outer selection structure's condition is false. The algorithm then displays the bonus amount of 1040. Figure 5-11 shows the results of desk-checking the correct algorithm shown in Figure 5-10.

Desk-check	Result
First: using X as the code and 15000 as the sales amount	1350
Second: using X as the code and 9000 as the sales amount	845
Third: using A as the code and 13000 as the sales amount	1040

Figure 5-11: Results of desk-checking the correct algorithm shown in Figure 5-10

In the next section, you will view and desk-check another algorithm for the bonus procedure. You will find that the algorithm does not produce the desired results because it contains a logical operator instead of a nested selection structure.

USING A LOGICAL OPERATOR RATHER THAN A NESTED SELECTION STRUCTURE

A common error made when writing selection structures is to use a logical operator in the outer selection structure's condition when a nested selection structure is needed. Figure 5-12 shows an example of this error in the bonus algorithm. The correct algorithm is included in the figure for comparison.

Correct algorithm	Incorrect algorithm
1. calculate the bonus amount by multiplying the sales amount by .08	1. calculate the bonus amount by multiplying the sales amount by .08

2. if the code is X
    if the sales are greater than or equal to 10000
        add 150 to the bonus amount
    else
        add 125 to the bonus amount
    end if
  end if
	2. if the code is X AndAlso the sales are greater than or equal to 10000
	        add 150 to the bonus amount
	  else
	        add 125 to the bonus amount
	  end if

3. display the bonus amount	3. display the bonus amount

logical operator used rather than a nested selection structure

Figure 5-12: Correct algorithm and an incorrect algorithm containing the first logic error

Notice that the incorrect algorithm uses one selection structure rather than two selection structures, and the selection structure's condition contains the AndAlso logical operator. Consider why the selection structure in the incorrect algorithm cannot be used in place of the selection structures in the correct algorithm. In the correct algorithm, the outer and nested selection structures indicate that a hierarchy exists between the code and sales decisions: the code decision is always made first, followed by the sales decision (if necessary). In the incorrect algorithm, on the other hand, the logical operator in the selection structure's condition indicates that no hierarchy exists between the code and sales decisions; each has equal weight and neither is dependent on the other, which is incorrect. To better understand why this algorithm is incorrect, you will desk-check it using the same test data used to desk-check the correct algorithm.

Using the first set of test data (X and 15000), Step 1 in the incorrect algorithm multiplies the sales amount by .08, giving 1200. The selection structure in Step 2 contains a compound condition that determines whether the salesperson's code is X and, at the same time, the sales amount is greater than or equal to 10000. In this case, the compound condition is true. Therefore, the selection structure's true path adds 150 to the bonus amount, giving 1350. Step 3 in the incorrect algorithm then displays the bonus amount of 1350. Even though the algorithm's selection structure is phrased incorrectly, notice that the incorrect algorithm produces the same result as the correct algorithm using the first set of test data.

TIP

As you learned in Chapter 4, when you use the AndAlso logical operator to combine two conditions in a selection structure, both conditions must be true for the compound condition to be true.

Using the second set of test data (X and 9000), Step 1 in the incorrect algorithm multiplies the sales amount by .08, giving 720. The compound condition in Step 2's selection structure determines whether the salesperson's code is X and, at the same time, the sales amount is greater than or equal to 10000. In this case, the compound condition is false, because the sales amount is not greater than or equal to 10000. Therefore, the selection structure's false path adds 125 to the bonus amount, giving 845. Step 3 in the incorrect algorithm then displays the bonus amount of 845. Here again, using the second set of test data, the incorrect algorithm produces the same result as the correct algorithm.

Using the third set of test data (A and 13000), Step 1 in the incorrect algorithm multiplies the sales amount by .08, giving 1040. The compound condition in Step 2's selection structure determines whether the salesperson's code is X and, at the same time, the sales amount is greater than or equal to 10000. In this case, the compound condition is false, because the salesperson's code is not X. As a result, the selection structure's false path adds 125 to the bonus amount, giving 1165. Step 3 in the incorrect algorithm then displays the bonus amount of 1165. Notice that the incorrect algorithm produces erroneous results for the third set of test data; according to Figure 5-11, the algorithm should have displayed 1040 as the bonus amount. It is important to desk-check an algorithm several times using different test data. In this case, if you had used only the first two sets of data to desk-check the incorrect algorithm, you would not have discovered the error. Figure 5-13 shows the results of desk-checking the incorrect algorithm shown in Figure 5-12. As indicated in the figure, the results of the first and second desk-checks are correct, but the result of the third desk-check is not correct.

Desk-check	Result
First: using X as the code and 15000 as the sales amount	1350 ———— correct results
Second: using X as the code and 9000 as the sales amount	845 ————
Third: using A as the code and 13000 as the sales amount	1165 ———— incorrect result

Figure 5-13: Results of desk-checking the incorrect algorithm shown in Figure 5-12

In the next section, you will view and desk-check another incorrect algorithm for the bonus procedure. The algorithm does not produce the desired results, because the primary and secondary decisions are reversed in the selection structures.

REVERSING THE PRIMARY AND SECONDARY DECISIONS

Another common error made when writing a selection structure that contains a nested selection structure is to reverse the primary and secondary decisions—in other words, put the secondary decision in the outer selection structure, and put the primary decision in the nested selection structure. Figure 5-14 shows an example of this error in the bonus algorithm. The correct algorithm is included in the figure for comparison.

Correct algorithm	Incorrect algorithm
1. calculate the bonus amount by multiplying the sales amount by .08	1. calculate the bonus amount by multiplying the sales amount by .08

2. if the code is X
    if the sales are greater than or equal to 10000
        add 150 to the bonus amount
    else
        add 125 to the bonus amount
    end if
end if
	2. if the sales are greater than or equal to 10000
	    if the code is X
	        add 150 to the bonus amount
	    else
	        add 125 to the bonus amount
	    end if
	end if

3. display the bonus amount	3. display the bonus amount

primary and secondary decisions reversed

Figure 5-14: Correct algorithm and an incorrect algorithm containing the second logic error

Unlike the selection structures in the correct algorithm, which determine the code before determining the sales amount, the selection structures in the incorrect algorithm determine the sales amount before determining the code. Consider how this difference changes the algorithm. In the correct algorithm, the selection structures indicate that only salespeople who have a code of X receive an additional bonus amount, which is correct. The selection structures in the incorrect algorithm, on the other hand, indicate that the additional bonus is given to all salespeople whose sales are greater than or equal to 10000, which is not correct. You will desk-check the incorrect algorithm to see the results.

Using the first set of test data (X and 15000), Step 1 in the incorrect algorithm multiplies the sales amount by .08, giving 1200. The condition in the outer selection structure in Step 2 determines whether the sales amount is greater than or equal to 10000; it is, so the nested selection structure's condition determines whether the salesperson's code is X. In this case, the code is X, so the nested selection structure's true path adds 150 to the bonus amount, giving 1350. Step 3 in the algorithm then displays 1350 as the bonus amount, which is correct.

Using the second set of test data (X and 9000), Step 1 in the algorithm multiplies the sales amount by .08, giving 720. The condition in the outer selection structure in Step 2 determines whether the sales amount is greater than or equal to 10000. In this case, the sales amount is not greater than or equal to 10000, so the outer selection structure ends. Step 3 in the algorithm then displays 720 as the bonus amount, which is not correct.

Using the third set of test data (A and 13000), Step 1 in the algorithm multiplies the sales amount by .08, giving 1040. The condition in the outer selection structure in Step 2 determines whether the sales amount is greater than or equal to 10000; it is, so the nested selection structure's condition determines whether the salesperson's code is X. In this case, the code is not X, so the nested selection structure's false path adds 125 to the bonus amount, giving 1165. Step 3 in the algorithm then displays 1165 as the bonus amount, which is not correct. Figure 5-15 shows the results of desk-checking the incorrect algorithm shown in Figure 5-14. As indicated in the figure, only the result of the first desk-check is correct.

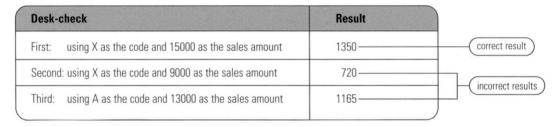

Desk-check	Result
First: using X as the code and 15000 as the sales amount	1350 ——— correct result
Second: using X as the code and 9000 as the sales amount	720 ——— incorrect results
Third: using A as the code and 13000 as the sales amount	1165 ———

Figure 5-15: Results of desk-checking the incorrect algorithm shown in Figure 5-14

Finally, you will view and desk-check another incorrect algorithm for the bonus procedure. The algorithm contains the third logic error: using an unnecessary nested selection structure. Like the correct algorithm, the incorrect algorithm produces the desired results; however, it does so in a less efficient manner than the correct algorithm.

USING AN UNNECESSARY NESTED SELECTION STRUCTURE

Another common error made when writing selection structures is to include an unnecessary nested selection structure. In most cases, a selection structure containing this error still will produce the correct results. The only problem is that it does so less efficiently than selection structures that are properly structured. Figure 5-16 shows an example of this error in the bonus algorithm. The correct algorithm is included in the figure for comparison.

Correct algorithm	Inefficient algorithm

1. calculate the bonus amount by multiplying the sales amount by .08
 	
2. if the code is X
    if the sales are greater than or equal to 10000
        add 150 to the bonus amount
    else
        add 125 to the bonus amount
    end if
end if
 	
3. display the bonus amount
	1. calculate the bonus amount by multiplying the sales amount by .08
	
	2. if the code is X
	    if the sales are greater than or equal to 10000
	        add 150 to the bonus amount
	    else
	        if the sales are less than 10000 — unnecessary nested selection structure
	            add 125 to the bonus amount
	        end if
	    end if
	end if
	3. display the bonus amount

Figure 5-16: Correct algorithm and an inefficient algorithm containing the third logic error

Unlike the correct algorithm, which contains two selection structures, the inefficient algorithm contains three selection structures. Notice that the condition in the third selection structure determines whether the sales are less than 10000 and is processed only when the condition in the second selection structure is false. In other words, it is processed only when the sales are not greater than or equal to 10000. However, if the sales are not greater than or equal to 10000, then they would have to be less than 10000, so the third selection structure is unnecessary. To better understand the error in the inefficient algorithm, you will desk-check it.

Using the first set of test data (X and 15000), Step 1 in the algorithm multiplies the sales amount by .08, giving 1200. The first selection structure's condition in Step 2 determines whether the salesperson's code is X; it is, so the second selection structure's condition checks whether the sales amount is greater than or equal to 10000. The sales amount is greater than 10000, so the second selection structure's true path adds 150 to the bonus amount, giving 1350. Step 3 in the algorithm then displays 1350 as the bonus amount, which is correct.

Using the second set of test data (X and 9000), Step 1 in the algorithm multiplies the sales amount by .08, giving 720. The first selection structure's condition in Step 2 determines whether the salesperson's code is X; it is, so the second selection structure's condition checks whether the sales amount is greater than or equal to 10000. The sales amount is not greater than or equal to 10000, so the third selection structure's condition determines whether the sales amount is less than 10000—an unnecessary decision. In this case, the sales amount is less than 10000, so the third selection structure's true path adds 125 to the bonus amount, giving 845. Step 3 in the algorithm then displays 845 as the bonus amount, which is correct.

Using the third set of test data (A and 13000), Step 1 in the algorithm multiplies the sales amount by .08, giving 1040. The first selection structure's condition in Step 2 determines whether the salesperson's code is X. The code is not X, so the first selection structure ends. Notice that neither of the nested selection structures is processed when the first selection structure's condition is false. The algorithm then displays 1040 as the bonus amount, which is correct. Figure 5-17 shows the results of desk-checking the inefficient algorithm shown in Figure 5-16. As indicated in the figure, although the results of the three desk-checks are correct, the result of the second desk-check is obtained in a less efficient manner.

Desk-check	Result
First: using X as the code and 15000 as the sales amount	1350
Second: using X as the code and 9000 as the sales amount	845
Third: using A as the code and 13000 as the sales amount	1040

correct results, but the second result is obtained in a less efficient manner

Figure 5-17: Results of desk-checking the inefficient algorithm shown in Figure 5-16

As you learned in Chapter 4, Visual Basic provides four forms of the selection structure: If, If/Else, If/ElseIf/Else, and Case. You learned about the If and If/Else forms of the selection structure in Chapter 4. In this chapter, you learn about the If/ElseIf/Else and Case forms, which are commonly referred to as **extended selection structures** or **multiple-path selection structures**.

THE IF/ELSEIF/ELSE SELECTION STRUCTURE

At times, you may need to create a selection structure that can choose from several alternatives. For example, a procedure that displays a message based on a letter grade that the user enters would require such a selection structure. The valid letter grades and their corresponding messages are shown in the following chart.

Letter grade	Message
A	Excellent
B	Above Average
C	Average
D	Below Average
F	Below Average

As the chart indicates, when the letter grade is an A, the procedure should display the message "Excellent." When the letter grade is a B, the procedure should display the message "Above Average," and so on. Figure 5-18 shows two versions of the Visual Basic code for the xDisplayMsgButton's Click event procedure. The first version uses nested If/Else structures to display the appropriate message, while the second version uses the If/ElseIf/Else structure. As you do with the If/Else selection structure, you use the If...Then...Else statement to code the If/ElseIf/Else selection structure.

---

xDisplayMsgButton's Click event procedure

Version 1 – using nested If/Else structures

```
Dim grade As String
grade = Me.xGradeTextBox.Text

If grade = "A" Then
    Me.xMsgLabel.Text = "Excellent"
Else
    If grade = "B" Then
        Me.xMsgLabel.Text = "Above Average"
    Else
        If grade = "C" Then
            Me.xMsgLabel.Text = "Average"
        Else
            If grade = "D" OrElse grade = "F" Then
                Me.xMsgLabel.Text = "Below Average"
            Else
                Me.xMsgLabel.Text = "Incorrect grade"
            End If
        End If
    End If
End If
```

> you need four End If statements to mark the end of the entire If/Else selection structure

Version 2 – using an If/ElseIf/Else structure

```
Dim grade As String
grade = Me.xGradeTextBox.Text

If grade = "A" Then
    Me.xMsgLabel.Text = "Excellent"
ElseIf grade = "B" Then
    Me.xMsgLabel.Text = "Above Average"
ElseIf grade = "C" Then
    Me.xMsgLabel.Text = "Average"
ElseIf grade = "D" OrElse grade = "F" Then
    Me.xMsgLabel.Text = "Below Average"
Else
    Me.xMsgLabel.Text = "Incorrect grade"
End If
```

> you need only one End If statement to mark the end of the entire If/ElseIf/Else selection structure

Figure 5-18: Two versions of the xDisplayMsgButton's Click event procedure

Although you can write the xDisplayMsgButton's Click event procedure using either the nested If/Else selection structures shown in Version 1 or the If/ElseIf/Else structure shown in Version 2, the **If/ElseIf/Else structure** provides a much more convenient way of writing a multiple-path selection structure.

To code and then test the xDisplayMsgButton's Click event procedure:

1 Open the **Grade Solution** (Grade Solution.sln) file, which is contained in the VB2005\Chap05\Grade Solution folder. If necessary, open the designer window.

2 Open the Code Editor window. Replace the <your name> and <current date> text in the comments with your name and the current date.

3 In the xDisplayMsgButton's Click event procedure, enter the code shown in Version 2 in Figure 5-18.

4 Close the Code Editor window. Save the solution, then start the application.

5 Enter **a** as the grade, then click the **Display** button. The button's Click event procedure displays the "Excellent" message, as shown in Figure 5-19.

Figure 5-19: Message displayed in the interface

6 On your own, test the application using grades of **b**, **c**, **d**, **f**, and **x**.

7 When you are finished testing, click the **Exit** button to end the application. You are returned to the designer window. Close the solution.

THE CASE SELECTION STRUCTURE

In situations where the selection structure has many paths from which to choose, it is often simpler and clearer to use the Case form of the selection structure rather than the If/ElseIf/Else form. Figures 5-20 and 5-21 show the pseudocode and flowchart, respectively, for the xDisplayMsgButton's Click event procedure, using the Case selection structure.

xDisplayMsgButton's Click event procedure - pseudocode

1. grade value:

A	display "Excellent"
B	display "Above Average"
C	display "Average"
D, F	display "Below Average"
Other	display "Incorrect grade"

Figure 5-20: Pseudocode showing the Case selection structure

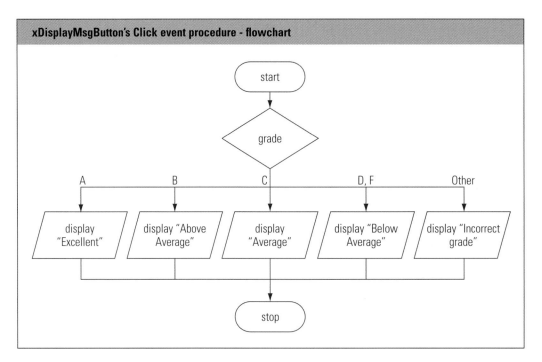

xDisplayMsgButton's Click event procedure - flowchart

Figure 5-21: Flowchart showing the Case selection structure

The flowchart symbol for the Case form of the selection structure is the same as the flowchart symbol for the If, If/Else, and If/ElseIf/Else forms: a diamond. However, unlike the diamonds used in the other selection structures, the Case diamond does not contain a condition requiring a true or false answer. Instead, the Case diamond contains an expression whose value determines which path is chosen. In Figure 5-21, the expression is *grade*.

Like the If, If/Else, and If/ElseIf/Else diamond, the Case diamond has one flowline leading into the symbol. Unlike the other diamonds, however, the Case diamond has many flowlines leading out of the symbol. Each flowline represents a possible path for the selection structure. The flowlines must be marked appropriately, indicating which value(s) are necessary for each path to be chosen.

Figure 5-22 shows the syntax of the **Select Case statement**, which is used to code the Case selection structure in Visual Basic. It also shows how to use the Select Case statement to code the xDisplayMsgButton's Click event procedure. It is customary to indent each Case clause, as well as to indent the instructions within each Case clause, as shown in the figure.

Select Case statement

Syntax

Select Case *selectorExpression*

   Case *expressionList1*

     [*instructions for the first Case*]

   [**Case** *expressionList2*

     [*instructions for the second Case*]]

   [**Case** *expressionListn*

     [*instructions for the nth case*]]

   [**Case Else**

     [*instructions for when the selectorExpression does not match any of the expressionLists*]]

End Select

Example

```
Private Sub xDisplayMsgButton_Click(ByVal sender As Object, _
    ByVal e As System.EventArgs) Handles xDisplayMsgButton.Click
    ' displays a message corresponding to a grade

    Dim grade As String
    grade = Me.xGradeTextBox.Text

    Select Case grade
        Case "A"
            Me.xMsgLabel.Text = "Excellent"
        Case "B"
            Me.xMsgLabel.Text = "Above Average"
        Case "C"
            Me.xMsgLabel.Text = "Average"
        Case "D", "F"
            Me.xMsgLabel.Text = "Below Average"
        Case Else
            Me.xMsgLabel.Text = "Incorrect grade"
    End Select
End Sub
```

Figure 5-22: Syntax and an example of the Select Case statement

The Select Case statement begins with the Select Case clause and ends with the End Select clause. Between the Select Case and End Select clauses are the individual Case clauses. Each Case clause represents a different path that the selection structure can follow. You can have as many Case clauses as necessary in a Select Case statement. When the Select Case statement includes a Case Else clause, the Case Else clause must be the last clause in the statement.

Notice that the Select Case clause must include a *selectorExpression*. The *selectorExpression* can contain any combination of variables, constants, functions, methods, operators, and properties. In the example shown in Figure 5-22, the *selectorExpression* is a String variable named `grade`.

Each of the individual Case clauses, except the Case Else clause, must contain an *expressionList*, which can include one or more expressions. To include more than one expression in an *expressionList*, you simply separate each expression with a comma, as in the *expressionList* Case `"D"`, `"F"`. The *selectorExpression* needs to match only one of the expressions listed in an *expressionList*.

The data type of the expressions must be compatible with the data type of the *selectorExpression*. In other words, when the *selectorExpression* is numeric, the expressions in the Case clauses should be numeric. Likewise, when the *selectorExpression* is a string, the expressions should be strings. In the example shown in Figure 5-22, the *selectorExpression* (`grade`) is a string, and so are the expressions—"A", "B", "C", "D", and "F"—as the quotation marks indicate.

When processing the Select Case statement, the computer first compares the value of the *selectorExpression* with the values listed in *expressionList1*. If a match is found, the computer processes the instructions for the first Case, stopping when it reaches either another Case clause (including the Case Else clause) or the End Select clause (which marks the end of the selection structure). It then skips to the instruction following the End Select clause. If a match is not found in *expressionList1*, the computer skips to the second Case clause, where it compares the *selectorExpression* with the values listed in *expressionList2*. If a match is found, the computer processes the instructions for the second Case clause and then skips to the instruction following the End Select clause. If a match is not found, the computer skips to the third Case clause, and so on. If the *selectorExpression* does not match any of the values listed in any of the *expressionLists*, the computer processes the instructions listed in the Case Else clause or, if there is no Case Else clause, it processes the instruction following the End Select clause. Keep in mind that if the *selectorExpression* matches a value in more than one Case clause, only the instructions in the first match are processed. In the next section, you will desk-check the xDisplayMsgButton's Click event procedure, which is shown in Figure 5-22. This will allow you to observe how the Select Case statement is processed.

DESK-CHECKING THE XDISPLAYMSGBUTTON'S CLICK EVENT PROCEDURE

You will desk-check the xDisplayMsgButton's Click event procedure three times, using the letters C, F, and X. If the user enters the letter C in the xGradeTextBox, the xDisplayMsgButton's Click event procedure stores the letter C in the grade variable, which then is used as the *selectorExpression* in the procedure's Select Case statement. The computer compares the value of the *selectorExpression* ("C") with the expression listed in *expressionList1* ("A"). "C" does not match "A", so the computer compares the value of the *selectorExpression* ("C") with the expression listed in *expressionList2* ("B"). "C" does not match "B", so the computer compares the value of the *selectorExpression* ("C") with the expression listed in *expressionList3* ("C"). Here there is a match, so the computer processes the Me.xMsgLabel.Text = "Average" instruction, which displays the string "Average" in the xMsgLabel. The computer then skips the remaining instructions in the Select Case statement and processes the instruction following the End Select clause; that instruction is the End Sub statement, which ends the procedure.

If the user enters the letter F in the xGradeTextBox, the procedure stores the letter F in the grade variable. The computer compares the "F" with the "A" listed in *expressionList1*. "F" does not match "A", so the computer compares the "F" with the "B" listed in *expressionList2*. "F" does not match "B", so the computer compares the "F" with the "C" listed in *expressionList3*. "F" does not match "C", so the computer compares the "F" with the "D", "F" listed in *expressionList4*. Here the computer finds a match, so it processes the Me.xMsgLabel.Text = "Below Average" instruction, which displays the string "Below Average" in the xMsgLabel. The computer then processes the End Sub instruction that follows the End Select clause.

Finally, if the user enters the letter X in the xGradeTextBox, the computer compares the "X" with the expressions listed in the *expressionLists*. Because the *selectorExpression* ("X") does not match any of the expressions listed in the Case clauses, the computer processes the Me.xMsgLabel.Text = "Incorrect grade" instruction contained in the Case Else clause. It then processes the End Sub instruction that follows the End Select clause. Figure 5-23 shows the results of desk-checking the xDisplayMsgButton's Click event procedure shown in Figure 5-22.

Desk-check	Result
First: using A	"Excellent" displayed
Second: using F	"Below Average" displayed
Third: using X	"Incorrect grade" displayed

Figure 5-23: Results of desk-checking the xDisplayMsgButton's Click event procedure shown in Figure 5-22

To code and then test the xDisplayMsgButton's Click event procedure:

1 Use Windows to make a copy of the Grade Solution folder, which is contained in the VB2005\Chap05 folder. Rename the folder **Grade Solution-Case**.

2 Open the **Grade Solution** (Grade Solution.sln) file contained in the VB2005\Chap05\Grade Solution-Case folder. Open the designer window.

3 Open the Code Editor window. If necessary, replace the <your name> and <current date> text in the comments with your name and the current date.

4 Modify the xDisplayMsgButton's Click event procedure so that it uses the code shown in Figure 5-22.

5 Close the Code Editor window. Save the solution, then start the application.

6 Enter **a** as the grade, then click the **Display** button. The button's Click event procedure displays the "Excellent" message, as shown earlier in Figure 5-19.

7 On your own, test the application using grades of **b**, **c**, **d**, **f**, and **x**.

8 When you are finished testing, click the **Exit** button to end the application. You are returned to the designer window. Close the solution.

SPECIFYING A RANGE OF VALUES IN AN EXPRESSIONLIST

You also can specify a range of values in an *expressionList*, such as the values 1 through 4 and values greater than 10. You do so using either the keyword To or the keyword Is. You use the To keyword when you know both the upper and lower bounds of the range, and you use the Is keyword when you know only one end of the range (either the upper or lower end). For example, the price of an item sold by ABC Corporation depends on the number of items ordered, as shown in the following chart:

Number of items ordered	Price per item
1–5	$25
6–10	$23
More than 10	$20

Figure 5-24 shows the Visual Basic code for the xDisplayPriceButton's Click event procedure, which displays the appropriate price per item.

Visual Basic code

```
Private Sub xDisplayPriceButton_Click(ByVal sender As Object, _
    ByVal e As System.EventArgs) Handles xDisplayPriceButton.Click
    ' displays the price per item

    Dim numOrdered As Integer
    Dim itemPrice As Integer
    Dim isConverted As Boolean

    ' assign the appropriate price per item
    ' to the itemPrice variable
    isConverted = _
        Integer.TryParse(Me.xNumTextBox.Text, numOrdered)
    Select Case numOrdered
        Case 1 To 5
            itemPrice = 25
        Case 6 To 10
            itemPrice = 23
        Case Is > 10
            itemPrice = 20
        Case Else
            itemPrice = 0
    End Select

    ' display the price per item
    Me.xPriceLabel.Text = itemPrice.ToString("C2")
End Sub
```

Figure 5-24: Example of using the `To` and `Is` keywords in a Select Case statement

According to the ABC Corporation's price chart, the price for one to five items is $25 each. Therefore, you could have written the first Case clause in Figure 5-24 as `Case 1, 2, 3, 4, 5`. However, a more convenient way of writing that range of numbers is to use the `To` keyword in the Case clause, but you must follow this syntax to do so: **Case** *smallest value in the range* **To** *largest value in the range*. The expression `1 To 5` in the first Case clause, for example, specifies the range of numbers from one to five, inclusive. The expression `6 To 10` in the second Case clause specifies the range of numbers from six to 10, inclusive. Notice that both Case clauses state both the lower (1 and 6) and upper (5 and 10) ends of each range.

When you use the To keyword, the value preceding the To always must be less than the value following the To; in other words, 10 To 6 is not a correct expression. The computer will not display an error message when the value preceding the To is greater than the value following the To. Instead, the Select Case statement simply will not give the correct results. This is another example of the importance of testing your code thoroughly.

The third Case clause in Figure 5-24, Case Is > 10, contains the Is keyword rather than the To keyword. Recall that you use the Is keyword when you know only one end of the range of values—either the upper end or the lower end. In this case, for example, you know only the lower end of the range, 10. You always use the Is keyword in combination with one of the following comparison (relational) operators: =, <, <=, >, >=, <>. The Case Is > 10 clause, for example, specifies all numbers that are greater than the number 10. If you neglect to type the Is keyword in an expression, the Code Editor types it in for you. In other words, if you enter Case > 10, the Code Editor changes the clause to Case Is > 10.

The Case Else clause shown in Figure 5-24 is processed only when the numOrdered variable contains a value that is not included in any of the previous Case clauses—more specifically, a zero or a negative number.

To code and then test the xDisplayPriceButton's Click event procedure:

1 Open the **ABC Solution** (ABC Solution.sln) file, which is contained in the VB2005\Chap05\ABC Solution folder. If necessary, open the designer window.

2 Open the Code Editor window. Replace the <your name> and <current date> text in the comments with your name and the current date.

3 Open the xDisplayPriceButton's Click event procedure, then enter the comments and code shown in Figure 5-24.

4 Close the Code Editor window. Save the solution, then start the application.

5 Enter **3** as the number ordered, then click the **Display** button. The button's Click event procedure displays $25.00 as the price per item, as shown in Figure 5-25.

Figure 5-25: Price per item shown in the interface

6 On your own, test the application using **6**, **11**, and **X** as the number ordered.

7 When you are finished testing, click the **Exit** button to end the application. You are returned to the designer window. Close the solution.

In Chapter 4's Lesson A, you learned how to use six of the nine comparison operators available in Visual Basic. You learn how to use the remaining three comparison operators in this lesson. You often will find these operators used in selection structures.

THE IS, TYPEOF...IS, AND LIKE COMPARISON OPERATORS

In addition to the =, <>, <, <=, >, >= comparison operators, which you learned about in Chapter 4, Visual Basic also provides the Is, TypeOf...Is, and Like comparison operators. Figure 5-26 briefly describes these three comparison operators.

Operator	Operation
Is	determine whether two object references refer to the same object
TypeOf...Is	determine whether an object is a specified type
Like	use pattern matching to determine whether one string is equal to another string

Figure 5-26: Is, TypeOf...Is, and Like comparison operators

THE IS COMPARISON OPERATOR

You use the **Is operator** to determine whether two object references refer to the same object. An **object reference** is a memory address within the computer's internal memory, and it indicates where in memory the object is stored. When both object references refer to the same object, the Is operator evaluates to True; otherwise, it evaluates to False. Figure 5-27 shows the syntax of the Is operator. It also shows the CalcCommission procedure, which uses the Is operator in a selection structure to determine the button selected by the user.

> **» TIP**
>
> The Is operator is not the same as the Is keyword used in the Select Case statement. Recall that the Is keyword is used in combination with one of the following comparison operators: =, <, <=, >, >=, <>.

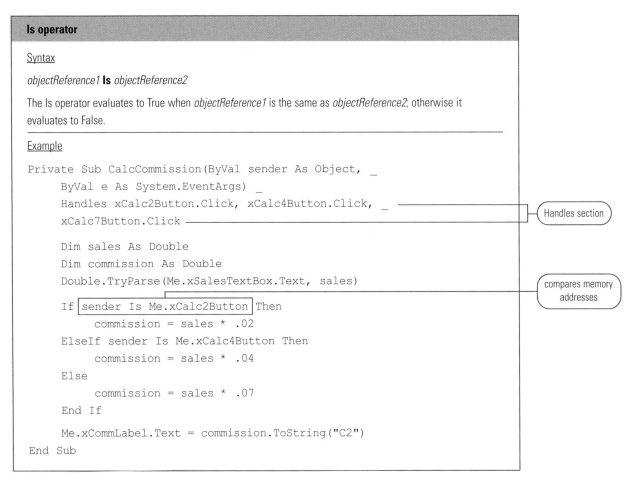

Figure 5-27: Syntax and an example of the Is operator

The CalcCommission procedure shown in Figure 5-27 calculates and displays a commission amount. As the Handles section in the procedure header indicates, the procedure is processed when the user selects the xCalc2Button, xCalc4Button, or xCalc7Button. When one of these buttons is selected, its memory address is sent to the CalcCommission procedure's `sender` parameter. In this case, for example, the memory address of the xCalc2Button is sent to the `sender` parameter when the user selects the xCalc2Button. Likewise, when the user selects the xCalc4Button, the xCalc4Button's memory address is sent to the `sender` parameter. The xCalc7Button's memory address is sent to the `sender` parameter when the user selects the xCalc7Button.

Before the commission amount can be calculated, the procedure first must determine which button the user selected, because each button is associated with a different commission rate. The `sender Is Me.xCalc2Button` condition in the If...Then...Else statement compares the memory address stored in the `sender` parameter with the memory address of the xCalc2Button. If both memory addresses are the same, the condition evaluates to True and the commission amount is calculated by multiplying the sales amount by .02.

If the `sender` parameter does not contain the address of the xCalc2Button, the `sender Is Me.xCalc4Button` condition in the ElseIf clause compares the memory address stored in the `sender` parameter with the memory address of the xCalc4Button. If both memory addresses are the same, the condition evaluates to True and the commission amount is calculated by multiplying the sales amount by .04. If both memory addresses are not the same, the user must have selected the xCalc7Button; in that case, the commission amount is calculated by multiplying the sales amount by .07.

To code and then test the CalcCommission procedure:

1 Open the **Is Operator Solution** (Is Operator Solution.sln) file, which is contained in the VB2005\Chap05\Is Operator Solution folder. If necessary, open the designer window.

2 Open the Code Editor window. Replace the <your name> and <current date> text in the comments with your name and the current date.

3 In the CalcCommission procedure, enter the code shown in Figure 5-27.

4 Close the Code Editor window. Save the solution, then start the application.

5 Enter **1000** as the sales amount, then click the **2% Commission** button. Clicking the button invokes its Click event, which is associated with the CalcCommission procedure. The procedure displays $20.00 as the commission amount, as shown in Figure 5-28.

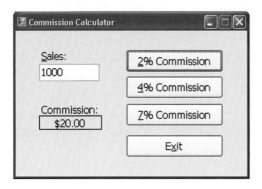

Figure 5-28: Commission amount shown in the interface

6 Click the **4% Commission** button. Clicking the button invokes its Click event, which is associated with the CalcCommission procedure. The procedure displays $40.00 as the commission amount.

7 Click the **7% Commission** button. Clicking the button invokes its Click event, which is associated with the CalcCommission procedure. The procedure displays $70.00 as the commission amount.

8 Click the **Exit** button to end the application. You are returned to the designer window. Close the solution.

THE TYPEOF...IS COMPARISON OPERATOR

You use the TypeOf...Is operator to determine whether an object is a specified type. For example, you can use the operator to determine whether an object is a TextBox or a Button. If the object's type matches the specified type, the TypeOf...Is operator evaluates to True; otherwise, it evaluates to False. Figure 5-29 shows the syntax of the TypeOf...Is operator. It also shows the DisplayMessage procedure, which uses the TypeOf...Is operator in a selection structure to determine the type of control that invoked the procedure.

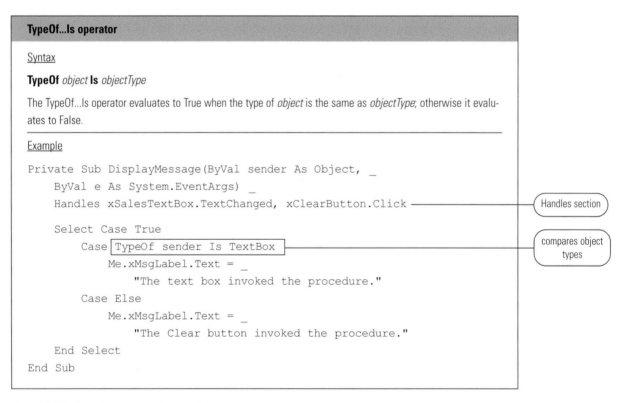

Figure 5-29: Syntax and an example of the TypeOf...Is operator

- Create an animation applet where the object or objects you move wrap around the edges of the applet window, coming back through the opposite side.

To see Java programs that implement these activities, visit the book's Web site at `http://www.prefect.com/java24`.